formal

ACKNOWLEDGMENTS

are made on the page
indicated before each
author's name

337 John C. Bennett
323 Maurice Blondel
319 Enrico Cantore, sj
329 Jean Cardinal Danielou, sj
324 Henri de Lubac, sj
336 Louis Dupré
318 Robert L. Faricy, sj
332 John J. Harmon
333 Paul M. Harrison
339 Richard A. McCormick, sj
322 Wm. Oliver Martin
328 John Courtney Murray, sj

321 Anton C. Pegis
342 Paul R. Ramsey
335 John J. Reed, sj
330 Klaus Riesenhuber, sj
331 John A. Rohr, sj &
    David Luecke
344 Joseph Schiebel
334 Bruno Schüller, sj
315 Piet Smulders, sj
343 Frans van Raalten
317 Norbert M. Wildiers, ofm cap
338 Donald Atwell Zoll

Cover photograph,
"Lake Shore Drive,
Chicago, Illinois"

from
Photographs / Algimantas Kezys, S.J.
©1966 Loyola University Press

Christian Witness in the Secular City

Compiled and edited by
Everett J. Morgan, S.J.

LOYOLA UNIVERSITY PRESS
Chicago 60657

© 1970 Loyola University Press

Library of Congress Catalog Card Number: 75-133951
ISBN 0-8294-0198-9

PART ONE

The Secular City Needs Insights of Christianity

Teilhard and the Future of Faith
1 Piet Smulders, S.J.

The New Christian of Teilhard de Chardin
19 Norbert M. Wildiers, O.F.M. Cap.

Individual, Societal, and Cosmic Dimensions of Salvation
33 Robert L. Faricy, S.J.

Scientific Humanism and the University
43 Enrico Cantore, S.J.

"Who Reads Aquinas?"
60 Anton C. Pegis

The Institutional Effects of Anti-Philosophy
76 Wm. Oliver Martin

Philosophy Fulfilled in Christianity
89 Maurice Blondel

PART TWO

Faith in Christ and Institutional Religion

The Church in Crisis
100 Henri de Lubac, S.J.

Freedom, Authority, Community
118 John Courtney Murray, S.J.

What Good Is Institutional Christianity?
131 Jean Cardinal Danielou, S.J.

Rahner's "Anonymous Christian"
142 Klaus Riesenhuber, S.J.

The Church's Proper Task and Competence
155 John A. Rohr, S.J., and David Luecke

Toward a Theology of the City Church
164 John J. Harmon

Religious Pluralism and Social Welfare
180 Paul M. Harrison

PART THREE

Man Needs Moral Norms for Ethical Conduct

Can Moral Theology Ignore Natural Law?
192 Bruno Schüller, S.J.

Natural Law, Theology, and the Church
201 John J. Reed, S.J.

Situation Ethics and Objective Morality
220 Louis Dupré

Capitalism and Ethics
233 John C. Bennett

PART FOUR

Ethics of Revolution, War, and Pacifism

The Right of Revolution Reconsidered
246 Donald Atwell Zoll

The Theology of Revolution
263 Richard A. McCormick, S.J.

Christianity and Modern War
275 Paul R. Ramsey

Pacifism and Ethics
286 Frans van Raalten

The Future of U.S.-Soviet Relations:
Convergence or Confrontation?
293 Joseph Schiebel

[9] Preface

315-44 Acknowledgments
       & Notes

345 Index

Laboure nat so sore to lerne to be a fole:

That cometh by it selfe without any other scole!

(from Alexander Barclay's English translation,
of 1509, of Sebastian Brant's Das Narrenschiff,
first published in 1494 at Basel)

EVERETT J. MORGAN, S.J.
Associate Professor of Philosophy
Marquette University, Milwaukee

August 15, 1970

Preface

The theme that is developed in the essays of this book might
well be stated in these memorable words from the novel of Boris
Pasternak, Doctor Zhivago:

> Now what is history? It is the centuries of systematic ex-
> plorations of the riddle of death. That's why people discover
> mathematical infinity and electromagnetic waves, that's
> why they write symphonies. Now you can't advance in this
> way without a certain faith. You can't make such discoveries
> without spiritual equipment. And the basic elements of this
> equipment are in the Gospels. What are they? To begin with,
> love of one's neighbor, which is the supreme form of vital
> energy. Once it fills the heart of man it has to overflow
> and spend itself. And then, the two basic ideals of modern
> man--without them he is unthinkable--the idea of free per-
> sonality and the idea of life as sacrifice. Mind you, all

this is still extraordinarily new. There was no history in this sense among the ancients. They had blood and beast-liness and cruelty and pockmarked Caligulas who do not suspect how untalented every enslaver is. They had the boastful dead eternity of bronze monuments and marble columns. It was not until after the coming of Christ that time and man could breathe freely. It was not until after Him that men began to live toward the future. Man does not die like a dog in a ditch--but at home in history, while the work toward the conquest of death is in full swing. . . .

Another "Doctor," professor Eric Voegelin of the University of Munich, has devoted his scholarly work and research to the development of this same thesis, that while man's knowledge of his existence is limited, fragmentary, uncertain, and difficult to grasp, at least he can have some knowledge of his existence in history under God. If this is not true, then human existence would be darkness, and life a complete absurdity, for without the knowledge of some cause or ground of man's and the uni-verse's being or existence then life and the universe remain unintelligible.

It is from this awareness of his utter contingency under God that man develops culture, a viable anthropocentric and theo-centric humanism; man is now seen as a "theomorph" as Romano Guardini describes him. He is not the measure of all things, but God is the final measure of all that is. While it is true that God has given the universe to man in a somewhat unfinished way and expects man to help in the completion of this work, still it remains true that the work must go on under God. Man can be, to some extent, the measure if he takes God as his final measure.

From both theology and philosophy, if they are clearly rooted in the foregoing knowledge, man will possess a norm by which he can make a practical moral judgment as to just what it means to be an authentic human being, and then go on to fashion a sound, just social and political order. For, as Plato has wisely indicated, society is man writ large. Therefore, the character of a given society is the reflection of the psyches of its citizens; the best society will reflect in all of its laws and institutions the pattern of the truth of man's existence in history under God; it will, as it were, write in large letters the kind of social consciences, the understanding of justice and charity found in the intellects and wills of the best men in society. In short, the best, most mature and authentic men will be those who measure themselves and their society by the correct understanding of what is the highest ideal of human conduct and strive mightily to incorporate it in their personal and social conduct.

The essays compiled in each of the four parts of this book were selected to develop and give deeper understanding to these important truths. Some of them are very controversial. I ask of the reader only this: carefully to ponder the content of each article before he condemns it, or takes the opposite position. To do otherwise would seem to indicate a closed mind or a substitution of will for intellect. To act thus is to remove oneself from the region of rational dialogue and debate to a land of ideology, gnosticism, or maybe to that never-never-land of positive secular humanism. May I be permitted to explain the latter in some detail for it is a very evident factor in our milieu in secular city today. That it offers some viable insights for a better world I do not deny, yet it has some built-in shortcomings which I wish to consider briefly here.

Positive, secularistic humanism long ago, even before it began its journey down the centuries, staked out the path or orbit it would follow. Its aim is not to attend to all the relationships we have already spoken of, but only to some of them. So, either militantly and noisily, or quietly and covertly, it eliminates, liquidates, or "drops through a hole in history," any area of reality, of study, research, academic pursuit, or human knowledge that would enable man to see the whole of reality as a "holy" reality.

As a result of this first presupposition, secularism's so-called "progress" meanders down a kind of narrow corridor--outside of which theological, metaphysical and transcendent truth simply does not exist. And, although this corridor, with its deliberately limited horizon may, in the course of time, become a little broader and wider, it must always be kept enclosed, for this is one of the "dogmas" of this kind of ersatz religion, and today millions of the human race believe in it. This is the religion of Bolshevik Communism, but many who would drop dead at being called communists, also do actually profess this religion.

This secularist mentality is, however, basically narrowing, monistic, stultifying, inhuman, and with a built-in logic and dynamism that tends toward atheism. Yet it does have a perennial appeal for man; it is a continuing temptation for man--ancient, modern, or postmodern. There is something mysterious about it that attracts man; something that lurks, as it were, unidentified on the dark side of the moon in man's nature; a perverseness in

[11]

man that seeps upward from a source deeply hidden in his nature that traditionally is designated as original sin.

This hard, confining shell of secularism, in which each age of man tends to surround itself, can be shattered and broken through. The task is difficult, but the opportunity today to ac - complish a part of this work is most evident. For man is in search of values today, and he is more aware than in prior periods of history that to understand man, albeit superficially, is to recognize that the desire which turns the soul toward God, and the appetite which too often succumbs to the fascination of evil are intimately associated; that the deterioration of the well-ordered person leads, not to disorder or confusion alone, but to a perverted type of moral conduct. Blatant disorder could sound an alarm; disguised per - version may go unchallenged. We touch here, perhaps, upon a most critical and vulnerable weakness in man's nature, the always present temptation to stray from what Boris Pasternak refers to in the passage we quoted from Doctor Zhivago: the idea of life as sacrifice; the always present temptation to fall away from the dif - ficult path of the spirit and of falling into the abyss of pride; of sloshing about in this quagmire, and to be content to "die like a dog in a ditch." It is the grace of God alone that can prevent this kind of disaster for humanity.

The Second Vatican Council has given us a compass, and pointed the direction for mankind away from this kind of error. As com - mitted Christians, each of us has a special vocation to be a witness to the truth of Christ in the secular city.

> It is the task of the whole Church to enable mankind to har - monize the entire order of secular realities and direct it toward God through Christ. It is our duty as Christians to explain clearly the principles concerning the purposes of creation, and the use of secular things, and to offer the spiritual and moral supports needed to renew the secular order in Christ. (Pastoral Constitution on the Church in the Modern World)

It is my pleasure to express sincere thanks to several of my Jesuit colleagues at Marquette University for many of the thoughts expressed in this preface, Father John F. Abbick, S.J., associate professor of English, and Father John R. Sheets, S.J., professor of theology. My gratitude also to those scholars who have authored the essays in this book, and who have, together with the editors and publishers, given me the permission to reprint them here.

PART ONE

The Secular City
Needs Insights of Christianity

Teilhard and the Future of Faith

Piet Smulders, S.J.

The subject matter of this lecture is singularly apt for a com-
memoration of Father Wade; for he saw his vocation in preparing
Catholics for the great challenge which the future of society poses
to our Christian faith.

Among Catholics Teilhard was the most articulate and influential of the prophets of this future. He made Catholics aware of
the profound transformation provoked in modern mankind by the
generalization of the category of development in all departments
of thought. He showed in what ways the old faith could be highly
relevant for the future of human experience. Of such importance
is Teilhard's message that some of the major documents of
Vatican II would be inconceivable had he not opened the eyes
of Christians throughout the world to some of the great signs
of our times.

Although first a scientist, Teilhard was always a priest, conscious of his vocation to build up the faith. And although a geol-

ogist and paleontologist whose science studied the past of the earth, of life, and of humanity, his deepest interest turned ever more vividly to the future of mankind. He wrote: "What more can be demanded by these inanimate remains than their testimony about the opportunities still open for the advance of life?"[1] Therefore the future, especially the future of the Christian faith, is always at the very heart of Teilhard's thought.

The central position of our theme imposes several limitations. We will not try to sketch the whole of Teilhard's thought, although almost every chapter of his essays is in some way linked to our question. But we will try to expose his more important reflections in such a way that they may be understood even by those who are not familiar with Teilhard's thought. Nor will we enter into the theological discussions occasioned by that thought. We will give a simple description.

A second limitation stems from the twofold meaning of the word faith. By Catholic faith, one may understand the various teachings contained in the catechism and in the pronouncements of the church's doctrinal authority. Our lecture will not be directly concerned with faith in this sense. Faith may also be understood as an act and an attitude of mind by which, as the last Council says, men freely commit themselves to God who in Christ has revealed himself as our savior. This lecture will take faith primarily in this last sense. Has faith, as a fundamental attitude of mind, a future? Can it be relevant in the new world of science and technology and in that new and dawning world in which man is ever more taking charge and transforming the earth and his own existence?

Certainly those two aspects of faith are complementary. In order to be relevant as an attitude of mind, some of the fundamental teachings of the old faith must, according to Teilhard, be developed in a hitherto neglected direction. For example, he states that in the future man will not be fully able to adore God from on high, unless God is at the same time before us.[2] That is to say, God must not be static, but dynamic and living, engaging himself in the history of the world. Or another example: the Christ of the gospel must assume more cosmic dimensions in order to command our faith in the future.[3] More explicitly than hitherto he must be seen as the head and the heart of the universe. Considerations like these play a major part in Teilhard's reflections on the future of faith. Yet we will not directly touch on them.

We prefer to adhere more strictly to Teilhard's more man-centered approach, by which he tried to convince believers and unbelievers of the value, even the urgency, of Christian faith as an attitude of mind. The renewal of faith as a teaching doctrine then appears as a necessary condition for fulfilling this function. This man-centered approach might be résuméd in the following statements which at the same time will constitute the three chapters of this lecture:
1) History makes sense.
2) Man makes history.
3) In order to achieve a meaningful history, mankind has to choose faith--moreover, the Christian faith.

I History Makes Sense

This statement may seem a truism. If being is meaningful, and if historicity is an essential dimension of all existence on earth, the conclusion seems obvious. But in order to grasp the importance of this statement, one should realize that it has been and is even now widely denied either in theory or for all practical purposes.

Ancient Greek philosophy considered the world as involved in an eternal circular movement. The symbol of time was the snake devouring its own tail or in a more positive way the phoenix reborn periodically out of its own ashes. Stripped of its own mythological imagery, this conception reflects a very real experience.[4] Cultures are born, flower and die. Every new turn fatally evokes the same expectations, commits the same mistakes, and flounders on the same rocks. Is it unjust to recognize the same pessimistic conviction in many forms of modern existentialism? For the existentialist, the only possible sense of being is the personal, individual realization of one's own existence. Every man, in creating a meaningful life, has to start from scratch.

In such worldviews, history as such does not really make sense. Nothing is built up. Nothing really new is born from the labor of past centuries.

The Bible rejects such a conception. It does not conceive historical existence as a circle, but as a road which leads to a promised land. But for all practical purposes, Christians not infrequently fall back on the hellenistic viewpoint. This happens in three ways: when history is conceived as the laborious return to a paradise lost; when the world is merely considered as the place where souls mature; and when the transformations of this world's history are ordained towards the multiplying of souls and towards

3

the fulfilment of the number of the elect established by divine decree.[5] In views like these, history does not really make sense. For its consummation would be merely determined by a divine decree, not by a real fulness of time.

Any such conception of historical existence runs counter to Teilhard's deepest convictions. From the various considerations on which he builds we select two of the more important ones: the one dictated to him as a scientist, the other as a Christian.

1) As a geologist and paleontologist, he is impressed by the fact that in the past the ancient evolution of earth and life has made sense. And the history of mankind in a real sense continues and prolongates this evolution, although on a human level. Therefore he feels justified in assuming that human history makes sense--an assumption which is corroborated by the facts, if we regard them from the right angle. Let us elaborate these reflections.

As seen by biology and genetics, which study the details of evolution, the process of life may look like a chaotic interweaving of chance steps. But seen from very high up and from a vantage point at which the disorders of detail blur into insignificance,[6] evolution reveals a clear and meaningful trend. A man rowing on an inundated area may not see anything but a confused mass of waters, but from the plane flying over it main currents may be clearly distinguished. In a similar way, a bird's-eye view of evolution reveals that it has always moved toward more complex and at the same time more conscious forms of existence and life.

This law of complexification and of the corresponding higher consciousness was one of the major discoveries of Teilhard. It must constantly be kept in mind, for it commands the whole of his further development. If we suppose this law is proven, and if we assume that consciousness represents a fuller form of existence than unconscious life, then the conclusion imposes itself: evolution has made sense because it has produced forms of life of an ever growing value.

Mankind being born

The next step in Teilhard's reasoning says: the history of humanity is the continuation and prolongation, on a higher level, of this same evolution. As a matter of fact, human history reveals, under the chaotic pattern of currents and countercurrents, the same general trend. From the fairly simple sociological forms of primitive families and clans, it has developed according to the law of complexification into the highly sophisticated social structures of modern nations and international organizations. And notwithstanding the evident drawbacks of this process of socialization, it has resulted in an undeniable increase of consciousness. It has made man ever more aware of himself as a person with his own irreducible value. And in our own times it awakens a new consciousness of mankind as such. As a result of the development of the patterns of human life, after the birth of the human person, mankind is now being born.[7] Therefore from a scientific point of view the conclusion is justified: history makes sense.

2) The same conclusion is borne out by Teilhard's Christian belief. Here, two articles of faith come into play: that of creation and that of salvation-history.

Creation and history

Creation, according to the Bible, is not just a past event. God does not only create at the beginning. He creates toward an end and a fulfilment. His creative activity embraces the whole road of the evolution of the cosmos and mankind, from the beginning to its goal, just as it embraces and supports the whole existence and activity of every individual creature. Here one may recall the most classical doctrine of creation, which has always taught that creation is not really distinct from conservation. But this old doctrine acquires new import in view of modern evolutionism. The old doctrine taught that our whole being is God's gift, and that he alone maintains and supports its continuation. Now it appears that the being of the cosmos is not a static, but a fundamentally dynamic reality. Everything not only is as it was, but it develops and builds itself up. In the face of this modern view of the world, faith in God's creation implies not only that God maintains creatures in their primitive state, but that from his gift as from its continual source flows the active development which makes up our existence. Therefore history, which is the dimension of this development, belongs to God's creative gift. It can only be meaningful.

"Salvation history"--a misleading phrase

The same conviction may be expressed in the word: history of salvation. This word calls for a remark. Here for once, the English language is less rich than Dutch or German. Salvation evokes the idea of saving from peril or salvaging from a wreck.

In English, therefore, it is hard to distinguish between the history of salvation and the history of redemption. The Dutch word heil, on the contrary, pertains to the same root which appears in English words like healthy and whole. Therefore Heilsgeschichte means more than the history of redemption: it expresses a history of health and wholeness, even if, in sinful mankind, this implies repairing, healing, and redemption. Is this a mere subtlety of language? I do not think so. By history of salvation and redemption the idea of repairing is evoked and so too the idea of a return to a previous state. In Heilsgeschichte, this idea ranks second; the foremost is history of health and of wholeness and therefore the idea of maturing and growth.

Those are precisely the words which Teilhard prefers in this context. The Old Testament for him is the history of the maturing of the elect people toward such a degree of human and religious maturity that in its womb the Man-God could be conceived. Toward that goal the whole of human history as seen by Scripture tended. In a similar way, after Christ's death and resurrection, the course of history is the laborious process by which mankind acquires a degree of maturity and in which mankind may be achieved as the adult Body of the Universal Christ. To cite only one of Teilhard's formulations: "From the very beginning of the world, everything was moving toward the Infant born of the Woman. And since Jesus' birth, his coming to man's estate, his dying and rising again, everything has continued to move, because Christ has not finished forming himself. . . ."[8] Words like these, taken from one of Teilhard's very first essays, reveal the mainspring of his convictions. He tries to establish and to express them in the cool context of scientific research, but their original source is to be found in his piety.

This then is the last sense of history: the maturing of mankind as a whole, which at the same time is its incorporation in Christ.

II Man Makes History

This statement must be taken in its strongest sense. It is man who, by his activity, builds up that history by which humanity matures toward its final coronation in the all-embracing Christ.

In order to prevent misunderstandings, a preliminary remark is necessary. Teilhard does not deny that the building up of the Body of Christ, and for all that of mankind itself, is a work of divine grace. What he wants to stress is that in this work of grace

6

man is fully active and responsible. As the ancient axiom says: God created you without yourself; he does not save you without yourself. Divine grace does not supplant or suppress man's free activity, but enhances and heightens it.

Now for the main thesis. By the awakening of human conscious - ness, evolution enters into a new phase and state. It becomes gradually aware of itself and takes itself in charge. This process unrolls itself in three phases. From the very beginning, man is to a certain degree aware of the historical dimension of his being. It is proper to man never to live in the stark actuality of the present moment. His every experience is fraught with memories of the past and with expectations for the future. In a second phase, which has extended for several thousand years, man begins to reflect on his own past. He studies history and searches the origins and developments of his own and of other nations. This study of history is not just the fruit of curiosity. Because man is aware of the fact that the structures of his community and even of his own being are to a certain extent the product of the past, he studies history in order better to understand his present existence. It is not by chance that several of the greatest politi - cians of our times, Churchill and John F. Kennedy for example, were serious students of history. Great leaders of nations feel the need to know the forces which have shaped them, the values they embody and the dangers which might threaten them. In men like these one already distinguishes the third phase of the aware - ness of history. Churchill, and more so Kennedy, were conscious of shaping the future.

A new dimension for man

In our times historical consciousness acquires a new dimen - sion. The study of past history is prolonged into what may be called futurology. For an understanding of Teilhard, this is of utmost importance. Until recent times man underwent the changes of his world in a fundamentally passive way. He did not consciously plan the transformations of society nor industrious - ly prepare and realize them. No doubt in times of crisis there always were utopians. But utopia was just an ideal dream, not a planned design which might command present deeds. As the Greek gives us to understand, utopia was essentially ou topos, out of any place and time. It had no link with present reality and activity.

In this respect the founding fathers of the United States and the leaders of the French Revolution marked a turning point. They consciously tried to shape a political structure which avoided the deficiencies of previous forms of government and corresponded to the new conception of generalized personal responsibility. Only with Marx did this planning of the future acquire universal dimensions and scientific foundations of a kind. But for a long time Christians in general remained aloof. Within the Catholic church only the message of Teilhard awakened large numbers of the faithful to the new task.

In the meantime, a number of sciences began to enable man to foresee and to influence future developments. Evolutionism and history showed that society is not a static entity but subject to continuous transformations. History begins to distinguish some of the laws which govern the birth, the flowering, and the decline of past social structures. Sociology, economics, psychology, preventive medicine, and other sciences allow us to analyze the present state of affairs and the distinguishing of its possibilities, deficiencies, and exigencies. At the same time they promise to enable man to transform society into a better, that is, a more fully human one. Utopia has ceased to be a mere dream. It has become the object of reasonable planning and of responsible activity. Mankind is developing a new mastery of its own history. Everything points to the fact that it is tending more and more strongly to take in charge its future.

Teilhard is convinced that Christians should wholeheartedly take part in this new responsibility. They should even be present in the vanguard of this development. For this deep conviction of Teilhard several reasons may be given:

The first, on which he himself does not touch, is that Christians should be more critical than others toward the established order and more sensitive in facing its inhuman aspects.

The second is that the collaboration for development in the eyes of Christians is not a merely human affair but a divine task. Man has been established God's steward in this world. By fully developing the world's potentials and by subjugating its forces to human life, man collaborates in the achievement of creation.

In the third place, Christians should have a clearer view of the goal and the general direction toward which future development must and can be steered.

Finally, Christians should have more courage and confidence in undertaking the seemingly impossible and certainly risky tasks which the future of mankind imposes on the human family.

More than all others Christians should be oriented toward the
future. For their God is not a God of the past, but a God who is
always coming and beckoning to his encounter. Or, in the words
of our first statement, the Christian believes that history makes
sense. Therefore, now that man begins in a conscious way to
shape history, he should in virtue of his faith strain all his forces
to make history meaningful.

III The Future of Faith

As a motto of one of his most important essays, Teilhard wrote
down the following profession of faith:
I believe that the Universe is an Evolution.
I believe that the Evolution proceeds toward Spirit.
I believe that Spirit is consummated in the Personal.
I believe that the supremely Personal is the Christ-Universal.[9]
In this short summary his scientific convictions and his Christian
faith flow together. The foregoing parts of this lecture might be
considered as a commentary on the two first verses of this
profession of faith. In this last part of the lecture the last verses
provide us with a pattern.
We saw how, according to Teilhard, the history of our planet,
if regarded from the right angle, shows that man and his spirit
are not just a chance product of evolution. Evolution, by its law
of growing complexity and consciousness, has resulted in the
spiritual consciousness of man. In a real sense, man crowns the
history of being and life. But at the same time he introduces an
extremely critical phase of that history. For he is taking charge
of his own future. From now on the success or failure of the world
depends on the capability and willingness of man to achieve the
work of creation. This is the tremendous challenge which begins
to face the human family. And it is precisely here that, in Teilhard's
opinion, Christian faith acquires a new urgency.

Faith concerns entire human family

Because of Teilhard's context, the future of faith is not primarily concerned with faith as the means of individual salvation,
but with faith as a condition of the achievement of the human
family as a whole.[10] Once more Teilhard was ahead of his time.
He anticipated what now bursts out everywhere. The realization
of a true human community forces on modern man a fascinating
and anguishing task--to justify religious faith by showing how it

9

sheds light on this road and how it sets men free to follow it with total dedication. To modern man the church proves its own value and truth insofar as it appears to be, in Teilhard's words, "the central axis of universal convergence";[11] that is, insofar as its life foreshadows and prepares that all-embracing communion of personal love which is the only possible fulfilment of human history. This is a change of perspective of the utmost importance for understanding the actual crisis of church and Christianity. For several centuries apologetics showed the legitimacy of the church by turning to its past; now it is demanded that the church open up a future. Here, Teilhard's apologetics set in. He tried to show that the gospel message is fruitful and even indispensable for the future of the family of man.[12]

The main steps of his reflections are summarized in the last two verses of the text cited above: I believe that Spirit is consummated in the Personal and that the supremely Personal is the Christ-Universal. In other, less enigmatic, words we might state that the viability of any further evolution depends on two conditions: 1) It must not destroy but enhance the value of the individual person. 2) It must unify the entire human family in an all-embracing communion of love. Teilhard then proceeds to show that these two conditions belong to the innermost core of the Christian message and promise.

Faith--an inescapable option

In other words--which will provide the pattern of the following exposition--man is, by the logic of his development, definitely engaged on a road of ever-growing togetherness, and he must forthwith further this process of unification with all his forces of insight and freedom. But this effort is possible only if the final achievement of human unity promises at the same time the highest fulfilment of every single person. Therefore the ultimate goal of humanity must consist in an all-embracing community of personal love. And this precisely is the vocation to which the gospel calls: all men of good will united in a mutual charity in the Holy Spirit and in the one Body of Christ, as children of the one Father. Faith is necessary in order clearly to distinguish this goal and courageously to engage on the road leading to it. Therefore, the more the ultimate unification of mankind imposes itself as the only issue of humanity, the more the Christian faith will impose itself as the inescapable option.

These reflections may be elaborated by the following four points:

1) Mankind is definitely engaged on a road of ever-growing togetherness. This is first of all borne out by the signs of our times, which manifestly show that no one man nor any single nation may hope to live in peace and in full human dignity unless it be in a harmony of mutual dependence on and respect for all men and nations. It is further borne out by the logic of evolution and history, which continually tends to the building up of greater and more-embracing complexes. Finally, it is borne out by the nature of mankind; for mankind is a family, and it is his proper greatness that he consciously and with free will realize what he is. So unless man wishes to forsake his human dignity, he must freely engage in this task of unification. As Teilhard has previously been quoted as saying: After man, mankind is being born.

2) But this effort toward unification is possible only if the achievement of unity promises at the same time the fulfilment of the single person. As a matter of fact, how must this future collectivity of mankind be conceived? The more obvious way is that followed by the totalitarian systems of old and modern times which tend to suppress individual consciousness and responsibility and so to suppress the sense of personal identity. The result would be the unity of the ant-hill. Such a perspective is unacceptable. If the process of evolution would finally result in the suppression of personal consciousness, it would destroy its supreme achievement and at the same time its own mainspring. As we saw before, evolution has been a continuous process of higher and more intimate consciousness and, in its human phase, it is driven on by the conscious and free effort of man. But man will refuse freely to go on toward a goal which would destroy his personal self. If there is no other possible issue for mankind than impersonal collectivity, the movement of development would come fatally to a halt. In the end history, which up to now has made sense, would appear contradictory, self-destroying, and therefore senseless.[13]

3) So it is Teilhard's conviction that, in order to inspire and guide mankind on its road into the future, another perspective must be opened up: a final achievement which promises to be the complete fulfilment both of unification and of personal consciousness. But here we stumble on the hard facts of human experience: Apparently these two requirements exclude one another. Unification seems to suppress each person's identity, and the cult of the individual seems to disrupt a person's unity with his fellows. Can there be a third road which over-arches both collectivism and individualism?

11

The gospel's challenge to love

Such a paradoxical final achievement of mankind constitutes the promise and the calling of the gospel. The progression of the unity of mankind is the first reason why the gospel-message will acquire a new urgency. As a matter of fact, our experience knows one type of union between persons in which the deeper the union, the more the partners are personally enriched. This is the union of love. Love, in uniting different persons, does not suppress their unique personalities, but exalts their proper value, for love unites from heart to heart. The gospel invites men to love one another without excluding anyone. That is, the gospel proclaims the possibility and feasibility of all-embracing love. Christ, by his message and his example, has inaugurated a new and only viable pathway for mankind toward a perfectly human unity. The more man becomes aware of the unavoidable future of unification, the more he will perceive the urgency of the fundamental option: either he chooses the unification by force, which is death, or he chooses the way of Christ, the road of life. Tomorrow, which is already clearly dawning, the convincing force and the authenticity of the Christian community will depend on the measure in which it has the courage to proclaim and even more to live the undiluted message of love and deepest respect for every person and every group. It is this example which mankind often unwittingly hopes to find in the church.

4) The fourth step of Teilhard's reflection then says: the key to such an all-embracing love of mankind is to be sought in the love of the personal God. Teilhard would certainly not deny that some people could foster a real charity for one another without explicitly knowing God. As a matter of fact he is convinced that a full dedication to the hopes of mankind is an implicit profession of faith. As he once said: "God is a very simple option, the option between a Yes and a No, between a plus sign and a minus sign."[14] But he would insist that such an implicit acknowledgment of God does not attain its full development unless it flowers in an explicit faith in our God and Father and in his incarnate Son.

Implications of the incarnation

To Teilhard, love is always directed not to abstracts but to concrete persons. The world and even humanity as abstract universal entities are essentially incapable of being loved.[15] Therefore we can dedicate ourselves wholeheartedly to the program of universal justice, mutual respect, and the common well-being of mankind only insofar as we recognize in one another the presence of God and his image. Once again, this is the very marrow of the gospel. It not only teaches that love of God and love of fellow man are inseparable and indeed one, but moreover that the man Jesus Christ is the true God. Because of the incarnation, the affair of humanity is forthwith a really divine affair. By building up the true community of men, we collaborate in the building up of the Body of Christ. Faith has a future in that it reveals to mankind the deepest reality of its longing and activity.

Faith's contribution

We now sum up the main points in which, according to Teilhard, the contribution of faith to the future development of mankind consists; then we will indicate various secondary aspects of this contribution. The main points are these:

1) Revelation assures man that his real destiny is to establish a universal community of peace. Humanity evidently longs for such an achievement but hardly dares to hope for it. The gospel gives him this hope as a divine calling and promise. And by giving hope, it sheds a clearer light to distinguish this goal and the means which might serve it, and it inspires a new courage to enter wholeheartedly on this road.

2) Revelation teaches that the whole of creation is ordered toward this achievement of humanity. Therefore, it assures us that all powers and potentialities of the world can and must be subservient to this goal. Because they can be made subservient, mankind should not be afraid to develop fully such potentialities. In face of the anxiety which may overtake man faced with the evident risks this development entails, Teilhard's motto is: "We must try everything for Christ."[16] These powers must be made subservient: the Bible provides man with a touchstone to distinguish abuse from right use. The right use unites man with his fellows; abuse isolates him.

3) The gospel teaches that this final achievement of human community is an encounter with God. Thereby it not only reveals how deeply personalistic is man's calling: it also inspires the high-spiritedness, which alone undertakes very great tasks, and the humility which is indispensable to pursue them in the face of shortcomings and disappointments.

Among the secondary aspects of the contribution of faith to future development, one might recall the following:

13

1) The mysterious meaning of sacrifice and suffering. On the one hand Teilhard stresses that everybody should build himself up as a fully personal center and that mankind must build itself up as a concentration of such centers. This looks like a fairly self-centered perspective. But on the other hand he emphasizes that this personal and social concentration implies the eccentration of love.[17] He would apply, not only to individual persons but also to societies and to the whole of mankind, the paradox of the gospel, that in order to find one's self, one has to lose one's self. Suffering and death, if accepted, are the means by which this concentrating eccentration is achieved.

2) The promise of forgiveness. With Teilhard, this aspect remains largely implicit. What does forgiveness really mean? Not just an arbitrary eradication of past guilt, but a new opening for those who have closed it on themselves. This new opportunity given is of the utmost importance on the road of progress. We saw that this progress demands a free-willed effort of persons and communities. But because human freedom implies the possibility of faults, man and mankind on their road can hardly escape fatal missteps. This would be a discouraging, even paralyzing prospect. The lifegiving death of our Lord reveals that in this life no fault has to be truly fatal.

3) A divine guarantee of success. Because the progress of mankind is ever more dependent on human insight and endeavor, it is exposed to ever heavier risks. But by his Son's incarnation, death, and resurrection, God has definitely engaged himself in our history. Regarded as an achievement of mankind, the road of development might lead to disaster; but as a divine calling, it cannot but be crowned with perfect result. In Teilhard's words: ". . . the final success of hominization . . . is positively guaranteed by the 'redeeming virtue' of the God incarnate in his creation."[18] Thus the promise of the gospel gives an unshakable hope and therefore an invincible courage to the human endeavor.

4) On the other hand, the gospel warns that one should never be content with the results achieved. As long as time will run, every fulfilment will remain unfulfilled. The horizon mankind longs for will never be attained. This aspect deserves special attention, because it implies a delicate theological problem and because, as we will see, it commands the fundamental attitude of Christians in this world.

Progress and the kingdom

The first problem is in what way human progress is connected with the second coming of the Lord as the final consummation of history.

Vatican II admits they are connected, when it says that, although human progress is to be distinguished from the reign of Christ, this progress is of the highest value for his reign.[19] But the Council's theological advisers did not dare to elaborate further. Teilhard uses a felicitous image. The progress of mankind would charge the earthly pole with such a tension that the spark of the heavenly advent may jump.[20] But one might ask if even this image does not reflect an unwarranted opposition between human nature and divine grace. We cannot now enter into this difficult question on which the best theologians are as yet uncertain.

The problem of the connection between the Lord's second coming and the world's final consummation commands the fundamental attitude of Christians in the face of the changes of this world and all its institutions. Thereby it may decide the future of faith. If no achievement is final, every value is open to development and every establishment is subject to a critical reappraisal. Of this Teilhard is deeply convinced.[21] To him, the whole existence of humanity is a constant movement. Therefore, by definition nothing can be expected from this law. Stagnation means death.

I submit that here lies the real demarcation-line between conservatives and progressives. A good number of people consider themselves as moderate progressives because they do not oppose every change. That is to say, they are not reactionaries. But even so they may be conservatives. For the conservative is he who clings to the status quo and who therefore does not accept the necessity of submitting the established order to fundamental criticism. He may accept new developments, but only if forced to do so by the force of events or after those developments have demonstrated their value. On the other hand the real progressive is not necessarily a revolutionary who denies and destroys the past. The true progressive may remain faithful to the past, but he admits the necessity of being critical in the face of its establishment. His faith in the values of the past consists not in an effort to cling to them, but in his willingness to criticize, develop, and surpass them. Insofar as they are real values, he trusts that they can stand this purgatory.

Teilhard deeply laments the fact that for the last few centuries Christians and especially the leaders of the Catholic church generally took a conservative stand.[22] They were suspicious of new developments in science and philosophy, in social and political order. By an exaggerated cult of tradition, they continually chose the side of the establishment. These Christians did not accept the transformations of society until the new forms had become firmly established. By adopting this attitude, Christians betrayed two of the fundamental tasks which the gospel imposes on them.

They did not protest the indignities which characterize every new order once it has established itself. Christians failed to be the untiring champions of the value of the human person, of his freedom, of his coming of age. Their charity, however sincere, was slow in recognizing the new demands of social justice and political responsibility which now appear as the substructures of the love of one's neighbor. Even now, for fear of upsetting the uneasy balance of cold war, they are not generally among the real advocates of peace. In questions as fundamental as these on the future of mankind, they have failed to be the leaven of the earth and the heralds of God's kingdom.

Because of this absenteeism, they were hardly positive in their contribution to steering the course of mankind. In their mouths, the gospel often became a message more of caution than of courage and hope. With few exceptions they failed to show that the message of Christ opens up a road toward the future of humanity, that it sheds light on the decisions to be made and inspires a generous force to pursue the end of real humanization. Of all religions and worldviews, according to Teilhard's conviction, the faith of the Bible is most capable by its very nature of assuming the future of mankind.[23] But Christians in general for the last few centuries, by being too cautious, created grounds for the opinion that religion is no longer relevant.

Teilhard saw in this attitude of Christians a major obstacle to the church's apostolic mission. As for himself, he tried to be present as a Christian and a priest in the vanguard of science and research. In his own life he sought to reconcile the total dedication to the future of the earth with the love of God.[24] That such a reconciliation is not only possible, but deeply enriches those two poles of human life was the very marrow of his message.

In sum, we may conclude that for Teilhard Christian faith, notwithstanding actual appearances, has a future. This confidence rests on his conviction that the affair of humanity is the affair of God and of his Son in whom the Father has engaged himself in the history of mankind.

But Teilhard tries to reason and to analyze this confidence and, by doing so, to distinguish the requirements which our faith must

16

meet now and in the future. His thought may be résuméd in the following statements:

1) History makes sense: the evolution of our world is not running in cycles, but is a road to an end. This end of all evolution is the full and final realization of mankind as an all-embracing personal community.

2) Because of its very nature, this goal of all history cannot be obtained without the conscious, reasoned, and free-willed effort of the human family. Man has to make true his own history and its fulfilment. For it is the very kernel of human existence consciously to catch up with man's own destiny. More than in the past, the human family is growing aware of this inescapable duty to shape itself. Thus mankind will ever more have to live in a future-oriented way. And this destiny will ever more impose itself, not as a mere individual salvation, but as a fulfilled wholeness of the human family.

3) It is to be foreseen that the Christian message will appear more relevant, the more man grows aware of his vocation. For Christian faith provides a valid description of the goal of man's quest. It calls to a community which is at the same time fully personal and fully collective in a common encounter with the personal God. It sees history as the road to this consummation, and therefore it takes history seriously as the ways of God with man.

By doing so, Christian faith stresses at the same time the gift of divine grace and the responsibility of man.

Faith in man's future

Humanly speaking, faith has a future only insofar as it orients itself toward the future. More than they did in the past, Christians should look forward. This is nothing new. The Christian faith always was a calling out from the home of one's fathers and a "going toward the incarnate God who is coming."[25] But now that mankind becomes ever more aware of its future and dedicates its forces to shaping it, this orientation imposes itself on Christians with a new urgency. They have to engage wholeheartedly on the ways of justice, peace, personal responsibility. For as Teilhard once wrote--and this quotation may serve as an epilogue to this lecture: "One converts only what one loves. Unless the Christian is in full sympathy with the world which is being born . . ., he will never realize the liberating synthesis of Earth and Heaven, out of which may come the parousia of the Christ Universal.
. . . I believe that the World will not convert itself to the heav-

17

enly hopes of Christianity, if Christianity does not first convert itself to the hopes of the Earth in order to divinize them."26

Notes begin on page 315.

The New Christian of Teilhard de Chardin

Norbert M. Wildiers, O.F.M.Cap.

From the very first page, Teilhard de Chardin warns that his book The Divine Milieu is not destined for just anyone, but that it is addressed to a special type of men and a well-defined category of Christians. He does not write, he says, for "Christians who are firmly established in their faith and have nothing more to learn about its beliefs."[1] He does not write, either, for those who find themselves entirely at home in another religion or in another philosophy of life. Between these two extremes there is an interspace where one can meet "the waverers, both inside and outside."[2] We find there Christians living on the periphery of Christianity, feeling unsatisfied with the traditional forms in which Christianity presents itself, and we find there non-Christians who have, it is true, certain sympathies for the evangelical message, but who turn away, disillusioned, as soon as they are

19

confronted with the sociological reality of contemporary Christianity. These two groups have this in common, that they consist of men who have lived the great spiritual revolution of our time, and under the influence of modern natural sciences have discovered a total new vision of the world and of human existence--a vision about which they wonder whether or not it is still compatible with the traditional presentation of Christianity. How can man today be at peace with a Christianity that often veils its doctrine in language and images derived from an obsolete and outmoded world view, which teaches us "to despise the earthly," and which sees the earth as a kind of waiting room for eternity, wherein it is important to practice patience and resignation? What can such a religion still offer men who have learned to see the grandeur of the cosmos, who have discovered its vast dimensions in space and time, and who have heard the great inspired message coming forth from the cosmos: the message that we men are called to conquer this cosmos, that we are called to perfect it gradually through our work, through our many-sided action and effort, to cooperate in a conscious way with its further evolution and to bring it closer and closer to its final completion?

Is there not an irreconcilable contradiction between our vocation as man and our vocation as Christian? Must one who wants to be fully man and to obey his human vocation be forced to renounce Christianity and even any religion? And vice versa: Must one who wants to be a Christian really in the full sense of the word take leave of his human vocation or at least fulfill it in an inferior and hesitating way? This is the dilemma with which many people, consciously or unconsciously, have to cope in our days. The person who does not sense this problem or who considers it of little importance or solved from the beginning--such a person does better to leave the writings of Teilhard unread, for their very core will entirely escape him. But the one who is aware of the dialectic tension between "the human religious ideal" and "the Christian religious ideal," to him Teilhard de Chardin has perhaps something to say, something which will be searched for in vain in other religious thinkers and writers of our time. For these people the book, The Divine Milieu, was written.

The importance of this question cannot be sufficiently underscored. The point here is not one or another academic problem which one can go on discussing for a number of years. Neither is there question of one or another psychological difficulty which can be settled with the help of pedagogical advice or pious devices. The point in question is a fundamental problem which

touches the very essence of Christianity and which consequently
can be solved only from the kernel of the evangelical message.
It is in addition a problem with which many Christians today
are concerned in the measure that they are tormented by the
ambiguity and division they experience within themselves and
through which their consciousness presents a tragical dimension. It is a problem whereby our human and Christian existence
is at stake.

What is the relation between Christianity and earthly culture,
between Christ and the world of science, of art, of politics, and
of economy? Must the Christian consider this earthly culture with
all its content as something worthless, with which the religious
man has nothing to do? Can he quietly abandon this earthly culture
to its own fate, or can he on the contrary cooperate with all his
forces in its edification without being in the least unfaithful to
his supernatural vocation? Has this earthly culture a place and a
function in the divine plan of salvation or does it belong on the
contrary to those things which, from a religious viewpoint, are
without any value? Does this culture pertain to a world of which
Scripture says that "God loves it" (John 3:16), or to this world
for which Christ refused to pray and with which His followers
may have nothing in common (John 17:9)?

The contemporary Christian is in need of a clear answer to
these questions. Ambiguous and evasive words are of no avail.
Now the praises of science, of technique, of social, economical
and political activity have been sounded; now their practices have
been received with excommunication, distrust and disapproval. It
is a demand of our conscience to pose clearly the problem of the
relation between our earthly and our heavenly vocation.

I Historical and Psychological Background of the Problem

If we wish to understand well the seriousness and extent of this
problem, then we should consider for a moment the historical
and psychological backgrounds and antecedents which gave rise
to it.

In the Middle Ages, a problem such as this would not have been
understandable. Religion and culture formed a close unit and were
connected in one great synthesis. The cultural life was permeated
by Christian principles, although they were not always put into
practice. Inversely, theological thinking and ecclesiastical life
appealed to all that science and art had to offer. There could be
no question of a real tension between religion and culture in such

21

a climate. Medieval man had obtained in this regard a high degree of inner unity.

In this situation a radical change occurs at the breakthrough of the Renaissance. From that time on Christianity and culture begin to estrange themselves from each other and the rupture, the consequences of which we perceive now, comes into existence. The condemnation of Galileo gave a mortal blow to a harmonious collaboration between faith and science. More and more, science walked its own ways, free from any link with religion. More and more, too, theology disengaged itself from scientific thinking. Initially such a course of events did not seem dangerous. On the contrary, the separation of the sciences from theology yielded the great advantage that science and theology as well were able to delineate better their own method and task, to confirm their autonomy and to free themselves from any undesired interferences. But seen from a distance this evolution also had great disadvantages. It caused religion to become more and more alienated from Western culture and the latter in turn to begin to lose all religious inspiration. From the eighteenth century on these consequences became more and more visible and the myth of contradiction between faith and science was born. Western culture became a completely in-world culture and the anxiety for earthly progress became the only and exclusive concern of all who received this culture in a significant way.

The result of all this is that the believing scholar is often pushed into a difficult and ambiguous position. He is mistrusted by his unbelieving colleagues because they suspect him of letting himself be influenced in his scientific work by religious or theological prejudices. But also from the ecclesial side he often has to reckon with insinuations because some people have the impression that his work may be harmful to the faith and undermine existing theological ideas. In their encyclicals and addresses the popes spoke in terms of praise about the greatness of science, but in numerous churches priests from the pulpit attacked the "proud science" which would conduce man to his downfall. Better a humble peasant than a proud scholar, was the proclamation, but one forgot to add that humble scholars and proud peasants might exist as well.

In the past those who have attempted to establish a reconciliation between modern thinking and faith have had an especially difficult time. The many ecclesiastical sanctions against authors whose scientific competence and excellent intentions could not be doubted in any way resulted in many people receiving the impression that such an endeavor was little appreciated, and that the Church preferred living in a kind of cultural isolation.

However we look at things, from the eighteenth century on a deep chasm between Church and modern culture came into being. Those of other beliefs received the impression more and more that the Church was an institution alien to life and to the world, which constituted a hindrance to the development of Western culture and no longer contributed a positive value to the progress of humanity. The old criticism of Julian the Apostate, that Christianity constituted a danger for human culture, thus came again to life. When, then, besides the scientific factor the social one also became involved and on this level, too, the majority of Catholics assumed a conservative position, there was an even stronger impression that Christianity signified a brake for human progress. Indeed, neither did the great ideals of freedom and social justice find the hearing to which they were entitled.

In this way the chasm between the Church and the modern world grew wider and deeper. Catholics more or less gave the impression of being outsiders to the cultural life of their time or of participating in it in a hesitant and reluctant way, without enthusiasm, without any inner conviction. They behaved as people of the past, at times even as anachronisms, tortured by nostalgia for bygone days. The dream of a better world, often enveloped in the myth of progress, aroused their resentment and aversion. They endeavored with special zeal to point out the gaps and shortcomings of contemporary culture and to unmask the myth of progress. For the great passion which inspired humanity toward more knowledge and technique, toward world conquest and renewal of life, toward more justice and beauty, they had but a compassionate contempt, as if there were question only of a useless and dangerous venture, bound to fail from the beginning. Should we, then, be surprised to learn that outside the Church the conviction gained ground that Christianity was obsolete and no longer represented any value for the modern world? From Hegel to Merleau-Ponty, with Marx and Comte between, the Church was seen as a power hostile to culture, hampering the emancipation of man, and therefore to be combated with all force. "The Christian," wrote Hegel, "is passive toward his God and indifferent toward the things of this world."[3] In previous centuries, Christianity was indeed a revolutionary force, wrote Ernest Renan, but now it has become "a tranquilizer, a system which is essentially conservative."[4] For

23

Merleau-Ponty, too, Christianity is a religion "from which result, at the same time, generous feelings and a conservative behavior,"[5] which renders people unfit for creative work and pioneering enterprises. It would not be difficult to amplify these few examples with others, and it would be too easy an answer to pretend that all these assertions are inspired only by hatred against Christianity.

We must dare to face the truth: from the Renaissance on, a deep split gradually arose between the Church and modern culture, and often we are not even aware of the width and depth of this gap.

How clearly Teilhard de Chardin realized this problem appears even in his first writings. It is not exaggerated to claim that this contradiction between modern culture and Christianity occupied his mind from his youth and formed the major theme of his meditations. The spiritual climate in which he grew up at the beginning of this century must have filled him with discontent and dissatisfaction; it could not be otherwise. The separation between earth and heaven, between science and faith, between the modern world and Christianity, put him in an untenable situation.

His whole life as a matter of fact derives its deepest meaning from the striving toward unity between these two worlds. He cannot be at peace with a human culture which lacks every religious consecration, and cannot acquiesce in a Christianity which underestimates the greatness of human labor and effort. How can we justify the world in the eye of faith and faith in the eye of science? How can we be fully Christian, without falling short to both? These questions do not leave him for an instant.

Even during the years of his novitiate he is tormented by the question whether he would not do better to forego the religious life in order to follow more closely his scientific vocation. Was there no conflict in wanting to consecrate himself at one and the same time to God and to the study of this world? A wise counselor told him then that God wills both our natural and supernatural perfectioning, and that the one is thus not in the way of the other. This answer was for him a reassurance,[6] but with it, however, the problem was not solved. The very question was how this unity in our thinking and our acting would be realized.[7] It is also striking how this question continues to obsess him and to dominate his inner life, even into the trenches during the turbulent times of war. From his first writings: Ecrits du temps de la guerre (Grasset, 1965) it clearly appears how his thinking in those years was entirely focused on the building-up of a Christ-centered philosophy of life, which would fully do justice to the terrestrial vocation of man. Even with the beginning of his first essay "La vie cosmique," written in Nieuwpoort in 1916, we can read these remarkable lines: "I write these lines . . . in order to express an ardent view of the Earth, and in order to seek a solution to the doubts of my actions; because I love the Universe, its energies, its secrets, its hopes, and because, at the same time, I am dedicated to God, the single Beginning, the single Solution, the single End."[8] The same problem is found again in most of the essays dating from this period. They let us see clearly how this problem is really at the center of his meditation and the ways along which he searches for the solution.[9]

From all this it is evident how a work such as The Divine Milieu is to be viewed against the background of a historical and psychological context. Teilhard de Chardin fully sensed the inner discord which characterized the Christian consciousness at the beginning of our century. From this personal experience this book derives its meaning and authenticity.

II The Teilhardian Synthesis

Let us now turn our attention to the results Teilhard arrived at after many years of search and reflection. In what does the terrestrial vocation of man consist? In what does his heavenly vocation consist? How can this double vocation be lived as a single task, so that both missions reciprocally complement and complete each other? By means of these three questions the teaching of Teilhard will become clear for us.

1 In what does the terrestrial mission of man consist?

Summarized in a concise way we could answer this question as follows: Man is called to carry on evolution and, through his work and effort, to bring the world to completion. In order to understand this answer well, we must recall the whole Teilhardian anthropology. Man, we learn there, is no heterogenous being who, so to say, has been brought from outside into the world. We are not, as Plato thought, descended from another and totally different world, only accidentally connected with this material world. No; man is linked with this earth with his whole being, he is an incarnated-consciousness-in-the-world, and this bond with the world is not merely external and accidental. He has risen from the earth, "the flower on the stem of the world" as Julian Huxley put it, and he is in the continuation of matter, of plant and animal. Even more:

in man the deepest reality of the cosmos reveals itself as bifacial reality. This vision of man flows from the evolutionary world-image. The cosmos appears to us as a great historical process, as an evolving happening, as a world-in-the-making, and this evolving process in its great lines is characterized by a growth in the direction of an ever-increasing complexity and an ever-increasing consciousness. Along intricate and inscrutable ways matter gradually built itself up; atoms, molecules, stars, planets arose. On the outskirts of one of these planets the first forms of living matter arose, and these first forms of life gradually developed further in great variety and increasing wealth of life. As life arose in the bosom of matter, so finally man arose in the bosom of life. He is not loose from the world: he has risen from it and is in his existence continually dependent on the material and living beings which surround him.

But if man is in the continuation of all that has preceded him in time, he also radically differs from all this. Man is a discontinuity in the continuity. He is according to Herder "the first freedman of nature." In him the whole world receives a new dimension, the dimension of self-consciousness and freedom. Seen in the whole of the cosmic history, it is the mission of man to contribute in a conscious and deliberate way to the progress and the completion of the cosmos. In him the cosmos awoke, in him the cosmos came to consciousness, in him the cosmos conquered its freedom, in him it will continue its way--consciously and deliberately--unto its final destination.

It is a grandiose and enormous mission which is destined for man. Where are the limits of the crescite et multiplicamini, replete terram et subjicite eam (Gen. 1:28) of the creation narrative? When we look around us and follow the momentous improvement on the level of natural science and technique, then we perhaps begin to become aware of the possibilities which are enclosed in man. Man is a restless being. No sooner has he brought a task to a conclusion than he already begins to look for new possibilities. No sooner has he realized a plan than in his mind new projects are already taking shape, asking for execution and realization. Never can he acquiesce in what has once been achieved. He is continually expelled from his paradise of rest and safety to go to meet new ventures. At the expense of immense sacrifice and endless effort he has to continue on his way. "An honest workman not only surrenders his calm and peace once and for all, but must learn continually to jettison the form which his labor or art or thought first took, and go in search of new forms. To pause, so as to bask in or possess results, would be a betrayal of action. Over and over again he must go beyond himself, tear himself away from himself, leaving behind him his most cherished beginnings."[10] This is thus the earthly task of man in all its grandeur and many-sidedness: to bring the world to its highest possible perfection through his uninterrupted labor and effort on all levels, and in this way finally to realize himself.

2 According to the Christian conception, in what does the supernatural vocation of man consist?

This question, too, needs reflection. The true vocation of the Christian is not merely to attain his personal salvation in the other life. The true vocation of the Christian is to cooperate in the building-up of the total Christ; he is called to cooperate in the building-up of the Church--aedificatio ecclesiae--of the Corpus Mysticum, and to attain in this way his ultimate salvation as a natural consequence of his striving toward the completion of Christ.

Whoever sees Christianity only as a way toward a more or less egoistically conceived happiness in the hereafter has but a very poor and shortsighted view of Christianity. The integral goal toward which Christianity orientates us lies endlessly farther. "The essence of Christianity," Teilhard de Chardin writes, "is nothing else than the unification of the world in God through the Incarnation."[11] It is the new heaven and the new earth about which Scripture speaks to us. It is the Kingdom of God, whose advent we daily implore in the Our Father. It is necessary to revive in us this great vision of Christianity. All too often we have been satisfied with a narrow, restricted and provincial conception of Christianity. Christianity has been misused to keep people good, submissive. It has been reduced to a set of puerile and pious practices, to a form of external good manners and social conformism, not to mention the many forms of sentimentality, of bigotry, of bad taste, and even of superstition with which it has been draped. In its external appearance Christianity has been counterfeited unto the unrecognizable.

We are to free our faith from these wrong and narrow presentations. Christianity is endlessly much more than just leading a good and virtuous life in this world and then attaining eternal happiness in the hereafter. Christianity has a world-encompassing significance. It is focused on the completion of the cosmos in Christ. Christ is the meaning, the end of the whole creation: in Him everything exists. Through Him and in Him everything has to receive its completion.

27

The vocation of the Christian is, then, also endlessly greater and farther reaching than the personal happiness of the individual in the hereafter. All of us are called to cooperate in the building-up of the world in Christ and to complement what according to St. Paul's word is lacking to Christ's work. We are called to cooperate in the building-up of the total Christ, who according to St. Augustine consists of head and members. We are to be aware again of the greatness and the true content of Christianity.

3 Our integral vocation as man is thus the building-up and completion of creation. Our integral vocation as Christians is the building-up and completion of the Corpus Mysticum. The question which arises now for us is: Is there any connection between the building-up of the world and the building-up of the Corpus Mysticum? Are both realms and missions entirely apart from each other, without having the least in common, or are they related in one way or another, so that they can be lived, to a certain extent, as a unity? This is the central question with which Teilhard is concerned.

The answer he proposes can be summarized as follows: There is to be a certain relation between the completion of the world and the building-up of the Corpus Mysticum, as creation and in-carnation are also related, as nature and grace, too, are in harmony with each other. It is after all unthinkable that there would not be any relation between God's self-revelation in cre-ation and God's self-revelation in incarnation. Is it not rather that the second is to be seen as the continuation of the first? The world is created in Christ and has in Him its existence: both the natural and supernatural order have their existence in Christ.[12] If man's vocation is to bring to completion both the creation and the redemption of the world, through his cooperation, then there must exist a deep inner connection between this double mission.

To bring to light this inner connection constitutes the great theme of Teilhard's theological reflection and especially of his work The Divine Milieu. In a highly nuanced way he shows us how through our work and our suffering, through our total living out of our being man, we really can approach God and contribute to the redemption of the world in Christ. Since it is the same God who reveals Himself in the creation and in the incarnation, so man must realize himself in his double mission: to complete the world and to build up the Corpus Mysticum.

How this is possible will become clear when we ask ourselves of what the completion of the world and the building-up of the

28

Corpus Mysticum concrétely consist. By means of a scientific phenomenology Teilhard de Chardin demonstrates (in his The Human Phenomenon) that the completion of the world ultimately consists of a process of unification and spiritualization which reaches its climax in the point omega. The building-up of the Corpus Mysticum, however, consists of the unification of the world in Christ: the recapitulare omnia in Christo, of which St. Paul tells us.[13] If we now accept the idea that there exists a harmonious relation between the order of nature and the order of supernature, and that nature is destined to be sanctified and completed by grace, is it then not obvious to conclude that every-thing which contributes to the unification of the world possesses an intrinsic orientation to Christ and that the sanctification of our profane activities must thus consist in becoming conscious of this deeper dimension of all human labor?

"In the eyes of such a believer," Teilhard de Chardin writes, "the history of the world takes the shape of a vast cosmogenesis, during which all the lines of the Real converge, without confu-sion, in a Christ, who is, at the same time, personal and universal. Strictly speaking and without metaphor, the Christian who under-stands, at the same time, the essence of his Credo and the space-time connections of nature, finds himself in the happy situation of being able to express himself by the whole variety of his activities in union with the whole of humanity in one great gesture of com-munion. He may live or die; by his life and by his death he realizes in a certain way his God, and, at the same time, he is dominated by Him. In short, in perfect harmony with the omega-point forecast by our theory, Christ--taken in the full realism of his Incarnation --is exactly realizing that spiritual totalization we are expecting."[14]

That is the reason why Teilhard thinks he may conclude: "With each one of our works, we labor--in individual separation, but no less really--to build the Pleroma; that is to say, we bring to Christ a little fulfillment. Each one of our works, by its more or less remote or direct effect upon the spiritual world, helps to make perfect Christ in his mystical totality."[15]

III Significance of This Doctrine

What value and what importance can we attach to this doctrine? With regard to theology, it seems to us that nothing is to be brought against it. The doctrine of the Corpus Mysticum, which in recent times has been brought forth again especially by the magisterial studies of E. Mersch and other theologians, belongs to the very essence of Christianity and Teilhard is right when he thereby makes an appeal to the doctrine of Paul, John and the great fathers of the Church.

Certainly, the Teilhardian synthesis is also in part indebted to anthropology and cosmology as conceived by the author. Here we are no longer in the terrain of theology, but of natural sciences and of natural philosophy. Insofar as the real theological aspect of the synthesis is concerned, his doctrine is fully defensible and cannot give rise to any serious difficulty.

Where to find, then, the originality and the importance of his work? It seems to me that if we are to understand the significance of this work, we must not only situate it on the theological level, but even more so on the historical and the sociological plane. What Teilhard de Chardin was pursuing most of all was to bring about a change, a conversion in the concrete attitude of the Catholic milieus vs. modern culture. If one asserts that his work does not offer anything new in doctrinal respect and is in keeping with traditional doctrine, he still must add that this doctrine was often forgotten and denied in practice.

From the French Revolution on--and in fact even earlier-- one can discern in Catholic circles two attitudes concerning modern culture. On the one side stood those who realized the importance and also recognized the value of the scientific and social trends characterizing their times. They exerted themselves to awaken their fellow believers to the values of this double evolution and invited them to integrate these new values in the Christian conception of life through sustained efforts. It is a pity that their voices were too often suppressed and their insights misunderstood. Neither a Lamennais, nor a Newman, nor a Rosmini, nor a Teilhard found during their life the audience they deserved. The majority of Catholics cut themselves off from their appeal and contented themselves in expressing their aversion to modern culture and to any attempt at realizing a rapprochement between the Church and the contemporary world. Their attitude received a semblance of approval through the syllabus of Pius IX--a semblance of justification, for what Pius IX condemned was not modern culture in its positive and valuable elements, but only what it presented of errors and shortcomings. This sociological situation of Catholicism in the nineteenth century and at the beginning of the twentieth resulted in an ever-widening gap between the Church and the modern world and caused non-Christians to consider the Church more and more as an outdated institution and a reactionary force.

Against this course of events, Teilhard wanted to react. It is our mission, he argued, to recognize first of all what is great and valuable in modern culture before concerning ourselves with its shortcomings and mistakes. It is our very mission to correct and complement these faults and mistakes.

A new type of Christian--this is what Teilhard de Chardin was dreaming of. Against the "bourgeois" Christianity he saw arising a new Christianity as demanded by modern times. In our days we are living the end of a phase in the Church's history and at the same time the beginning of another period. The preceding phase was greatly dominated by the bourgeois climate of the eighteenth and nineteenth centuries, an influence Catholics could not always escape. This bourgeois climate was characterized by individualism and by an exclusive concern for personal well-being. For the Christian.of this period there existed apparently no higher ideal than to attain his personal salvation in the next life. This more or less egoistically conceived blessedness could, however, not be reached without the practice of charity, but this concern was often considered as but a means to make this personal salvation possible in the next life. In this perspective ethics acquired a principally negative character. It was supposed to help us first of all to avoid all that somehow could jeopardize our personal happiness. Hence ethics was often reduced to a kind of nomenclature of sins and a catalog of prohibited things.

This individualistic conception further augmented Christians' disinterest in public and cultural life, and their enclosing themselves in a world of their own. They exerted themselves to establish their own organizations on all levels of life, so as to have as little contact as possible with those who thought otherwise and to feel safe behind the protecting walls of their own ghetto. They had the reputation of always joining the camp of conservatism. Each innovation was met with distrust; whereas the existing institutions, even the most antiquated, were maintained with force, even when their insufficiency had become evident to everyone. The total effect of this attitude was a general immobilism of the Church's life on the level of thought and of action as well.

Apparently this bourgeois form of Christianity is definitively drawing to an end in order to make place for a totally new type of Christian. The highest ideal of the modern Christian consists in cooperating with his whole being in the building-up of the world, in the completion of the Mystical Body. It is not his personal salvation only, but at the same time the realization of the "total" Christ which assumes a place in his thoughts and concern. It is

31

his conviction that he can reach his personal destination only in renouncing himself and devoting himself entirely to the grandiose task which is his in this world.

In this perspective ethics assumes another appearance, wholly orientated to positive deeds. What is of primary importance is not so much the avoidance of sins and imperfections, as that we exert ourselves to realize as much good as possible on all levels. The most valuable Christian is not he who constantly torments his mind with his imperfections, but the one who does his utmost to accomplish his task in this world in the most perfect manner. He does not feel the need to withdraw and to keep away scrupulously from all who hold an opinion different from his. On the contrary, he will strive toward cooperation with all who want on one or another level to realize something good and beautiful. His attention will go by preference to the good he discovers in others and with which he is willing to cooperate in the spirit set forth by Pope John XXIII in his encyclical Pacem in terris.

What matters in the first place for this Christian is the future. The past can never be the main point. He knows too well how the ruins of earlier times, though poetical and picturesque, were all too often a ballast and hindrance for the further development of mankind. He is prepared to try everything, to risk everything in order to bring the ultimate goal nearer. He feels only aversion for the lack of courage and the cowardice of those who neglect the good for fear of danger and risk. He is prompted and driven by the indestructible trust in the triumph of truth and life, in the ultimate glorification and transformation of the world in the light of the parousia. To the rise and flowering of this renewed Christianity, Teilhard consecrates the best of his energies.

Great changes are occurring in the Church's life today. Thanks to the initiative of the great Pope John XXIII Christians question themselves concerning their mission in this world. Through the voice of the Council the Church invites us to assume a new attitude toward modern culture, to develop ourselves in a spirit of openness and readiness to cooperation. In the measure that Christians answer this call and become aware of the new situation they are living in, they will realize both the greatness and importance of the work accomplished by Teilhard de Chardin.

Notes begin on page 317.

Individual, Societal, and Cosmic Dimensions of Salvation

Robert L. Faricy, S.J.

A central problem for Christianity today is this: What are the relations between the individual, the societal, and the cosmic dimensions of salvation? What is the relation between personal salvation and the salvation of the community, of society as a whole, of all mankind? And what is the relation between the salvation of man and the salvation of the cosmos? Further, what is the importance of the societal and the cosmic aspects of personal salvation? Is the universe, the cosmos, properly speaking an object of salvation? If it somehow is, what does this mean for me, for the individual Christian? Admitting the societal or communal nature of salvation, what does this communal aspect of salvation mean in terms of my Christian life? The whole question is complex. It involves the effort to understand, in terms of salvation, the relations between person and society, and between man and cosmos. Moreover, it involves the effort to determine what these relations mean in everyday Christian life, in prayer, in action, in evangelism, in all forms of Christian worship, witness, and service. How do we answer these questions?

One may distinguish two general answers, two overlapping positions held by contemporary Christians. On the one hand, there is a view that sees Christ working in all of history, bringing forth the final transformation's first fruits in man's personal life but--inseparably--in man's life in society and in the world. Christ renews us not only in ourselves but in our relation to other men and in our relation to the world. This view stresses the intrinsic inseparability of the personal, social, and cosmic aspects of Christ's work.

On the other hand, there is a view that sees Christ's work as taking place primarily through His Word to persons. There will be certainly a final transformation of all things in Christ; but, until the end, Christ's work is primarily the work of the renewing Word of God addressed in forgivingness to the sinner. The work of the Church, therefore, is the work of addressing the transforming power of the Word, the work of bringing the Word to persons. There should be, of course, a real spill-over into the social, secular order; but that spill-over, while good and the work of God, is not the chief concern of the Church. The main task of the Church is conversion.

We have, then, in contemporary Christianity two basic viewpoints. The first is that the redemptive work of Christ, carried on in time by the Church, is the renewal of persons and of society and of the world, a renewal aimed at, and to be consummated in, the final transformation at the end of time. The second is that Christ's work of salvation and the salvific work, therefore, of the Church is to address the saving Word of God to the hearts of men; the Church's work is conversion to Christ. These two viewpoints seem to be at bottom irreconcilable and in many ways opposed. It is clear that they result in differing approaches to Christian living, to different kinds of Church activity and of missionary action. They are not viewpoints that are strictly confessional; they are both found in almost all Christian denominations.

There are many ways of approaching the problem. It could be considered in terms of the distinction and relation between the sacred order and the secular order. It could be discussed in terms of faith and action. My intention is to treat this whole matter in terms of the Christian person and his relation to the person of Christ. The question is: What is the societal dimension of this interpersonal relationship between Christ and the Christian, and what is the cosmic dimension of this relationship?

34

My method is to form a tentative theological hypothesis that takes into account the relevant scriptural data as well as contemporary man's understanding of what it means to be a person. I am aiming at a theological hypothesis that makes as much sense as possible and that is productive of reflection, discussion, and, ultimately, better understanding of Christianity so that it may be better practiced.

I

What is a person? A person is, by his very nature, relational, open to relation with other persons and, ultimately, with a personal God. Because a person is essentially relational, the idea of person cannot be understood apart from the idea of person-in-relation-to-other-person, apart from the idea of society. A more productive question than "What is a person?" is "What is the relation between person and society?"

In the domain of life, whenever we find a true union we find that the union differentiates the elements that are united. Whether we speak of cells united to form a living body of the members of a society, or of the elements that make up any synthesis, true union never confuses the elements united, it differentiates them.[1] On a baseball team, for example, the players are differentiated according to function, according to the positions they occupy on the team. Union differentiates. At a deeper level, in the union of persons that we call friendship, there is again a differentiating union. Persons who are friends become, through the friendship, more themselves, more person. Union differentiates, and union of persons personalizes the persons united. This is above all true of marriage. To the extent that the marriage is a happy and successful union, the husband and wife grow as persons. They do not merge into one amorphous mass; on the contrary, each achieves his or her own personhood precisely through the union with the other person. When a union is truly human, a union of persons that is a union from the interior, from the heart, that union further personalizes the persons united.

Society is a union of persons. And to the degree that societal union is really a human union, it is a union that personalizes. We grow as persons to the degree to which we enter into society, to the degree to which we go out of ourselves to be united with other persons. It is simply in accord with the essentially social structure of human nature that persons grow and develop as persons to the extent that they go out of themselves and unite with other persons.

For the Christian, there is one personal center for all mankind. This is the meaning of the incarnation, death, and resurrection of Christ; God has sent His only Son for man's salvation, and He has raised up that Son so that, risen, He may be the personal center for the unity of all men. Personal union with Christ is, obviously, the most personalizing union possible; it is more than personalizing, since it is a saving union, a union of grace and justification. Since Christ is the saving personal center of mankind, of human society, when the Christian is most united to Christ he is most involved in society. Conversely, to be united with Christ, he must be united with his fellow men. "If any man says he loves God and does not love his neighbor, that man is a liar." We grow as persons, then, to the degree that we go out of ourselves in Christian love to other persons, and, above all, to the extent that we go out of ourselves to Christ, the saving personal center for all men.

A first conclusion is this: person and society are not opposed. On the contrary, person and society are correlative. To the degree that I help to build up society by helping others, I myself grow as a person. We do have a more or less engrained prejudice that inclines us to think that the notion of the individual person and the notion of the collectivity are opposed notions. Often we tend to consider person and society as opposed, as though personal freedom and growth varied inversely to the degree of the development and organization of society. This prejudice probably has as part of its root the unpleasant sense of constraint and of loss of freedom that the individual sometimes experiences when he finds himself involved in a group. It is simply the prejudice of human selfishness and egotism. Our human selfishness inclines us to adopt an isolationist attitude with respect to other persons in the illusion that personal fulfilment lies in getting what is ours, in building bigger barns and filling them with grain. But this is an illusion; personal fulfilment and personal involvement in society are not opposed, they are correlative.

A second conclusion is this: personal involvement with Christ and personal involvement in the needs of other persons are inseparable; for Christ is not only Saviour of the individual person, He is the unifier who has come that all may be one in Him. Christ unites us to one another by drawing us to Himself. Love of Christ and love of neighbor are two sides of one coin. In Christ's words, "Whatever you have done to the least of these, my brothers, you have done to me."

36

The relation between the personal and the societal aspects of salvation is that they are inseparable and correlative. Personal salvation is essentially societal salvation. Personal fulfilment does not lie in trying selfishly to become fulfilled but in going out of ourselves in Christian love to Christ and to others for His sake. This means dying to our own selfishness: "Unless the grain of wheat fall to the ground and die, it cannot bear fruit." And, "if any man try to save his life in this world, he will lose it; but if he loses his life for my sake and the sake of the gospel, he will find it."

II

What is there to say about the cosmic dimension of salvation? What is the relation between the personal aspect of salvation and the cosmic aspect? Is the cosmos relevant to an understanding of salvation, or is salvation a matter of personal conversion, of existential decision? How we answer these questions depends on how we understand the place and function of Christ's saving power in the cosmos. Christ is Saviour of the person and Lord of the cosmos; but what does Christ's lordship over the universe have to do with His saving the individual person? Is it simply that He who is my Saviour is also Lord, and His lordship of the cosmos has nothing directly to do with my personal salvation? Or is my salvation bound up intrinsically not only with the salvation of other persons but with the salvation of the cosmos? In an effort to investigate the New Testament teaching on the cosmic dimension of salvation, I would like to outline briefly some of the main elements to consider in such an investigation, as these elements are found in John's Gospel and in Paul's epistles. Exegetes differ in their understanding of the relevant Johannine and Pauline texts, and my own outline here will necessarily contain several personal theological options and interpretations.

The first part of the Prologue of John's Gospel identifies Christ with the Old Testament wisdom through whom God creates and with God's creative word. The idea is also present of a creative word, a logos, who is the ordering principle of the universe, the principle of the organization and harmony of the cosmos. The Prologue pivots on the central verses which concern personal salvation: "But to all who did receive Him, to those who have given Him their allegiance, He gave the right to become children of God. . . ." In the second half of the Prologue the creative Word of God is identified with Jesus and as the Son of the eternal Father.

37

Christ is, then, God's creative Word, the principle of the existence and the order of the cosmos. "Through Him all things came to be; not one thing had its being but through Him." Christ is, moreover, God's Word of revelation and self-communication to man. "The Word was with God and the Word was God. . . . The Word was made flesh, He lived among us, and we saw His glory, the glory that is His as the only Son of the Father, full of grace and truth." Finally, Christ is God's Word of promise and salvation. To all accept Him, who believe in Him, "He gave power to become children of God."

The fundamental idea of the Prologue is that Christ brings the word because He is the Word. This is worked out in the body of John's Gospel in terms of the light, life, and truth that Christ brings because He is the light, the life, and the truth. The import and purpose of the Gospel is that we believe in the word that Christ preaches and, particularly, that we believe in the Word that He is, that we adhere to His person, that we enter into loving interpersonal relationship with Him.

For John's Gospel, creation, the work begun "in the beginning," is fulfilled through the response of men to God that is faith in Christ, adherence to Christ, being joined to Christ. Creation and salvation are intimately connected. God's work of creation is completed and brought back to Him through the faith response of men to God-present-as-Saviour in Christ. It is through Christ working in history through His Church that men are brought to salvation; but not only men are brought to salvation. What is brought to completion and fulfilment in Christ is the work begun "in the beginning." It is the entire cosmos that, through men in Christ, is brought back to the Father.

John and Paul have the same basic doctrine regarding the cosmic aspect of salvation, but they have two different theological approaches John's theology of creation and salvation is expressed in terms of interpersonal encounter. John's central basic metaphor is human discourse: Christ is the creative Word spoken by God who returns to God in the response of men. Paul expresses the relation between creation and salvation in more organic terms; it could be said that his central basic concept is that of the body.

For Paul, as for John, all that exists comes from God, but all things come to be through Christ and remain in existence through Christ (1 Cor 8:6). The doctrine of the first three chapters of Ephesians is that God's whole creation-salvation plan has from the beginning been centered on Christ. That plan is "to bring everything together under Christ as head" (Eph 1:10), for Christ is the

38

ruler of everything and He "fills the whole creation" (1:23). God's
plan of creation and salvation is in process now, and the Church
has a central place in that plan. Christ is the ruler of everything
and He is the head of the Church. It is in the Church that Christ
is present in His fulness (1:23), and it is through the Church that
God's plan in Christ is made manifest (3:10-11). Creation has
not been finished; it still goes on in the working out of God's over-
all plan; and the central axis of the working out of God's plan in
Christ is the Church.

Much the same teaching, though fuller and in some ways more
polished, is found in the first two chapters of Colossians, especially in the hymn in the first chapter (Col 1:15-20). All things
have been created in Christ, and through Him and for Him, and
"He holds all things in unity" (1:17). Christ is the head of the
Church, His body (1:18); and He is, moreover, the head of the
cosmos, which is also called by Paul Christ's body (2:10).[2] That
is, Christ is the head of the cosmos and the head of the Church.
The cosmos is His body, and also the Church is His body. The
Church, then, has a certain cosmic character, and it has a central place in the cosmos. It is clear that, although Christ is the
head of the cosmos, it is not yet that all things are reconciled
in Christ. All things are reconciled in principle by Christ's
redemptive death on the cross. But the working out of that reconciliation takes place in time. In the light of this, creation and
redemption can be seen to be two aspects of one great mystery:
the reconciliation of all things in Christ. For God's plan is that
"all plenitude be found in Him and that all things be reconciled
through Him and for Him" (1:19). In the plenitude of His cosmic
supremacy, Christ embraces all things: God who saves, men
who are saved, the universe, all visible and invisible powers.
All things are created in Him, are reconciled in Him, find their
fulfilment and salvation in Him. In Paul's vision, everything is
somehow suspended from the risen Christ, and finds its meaning
and value and even its existence in Christ risen. "In Him all things
hold together," and "In Him all things and He in all" (1:17; 2:10;
3:11). The Christ of Paul is the Christ in whom all creation is
recapitulated.

If all things are in some way to be reconciled in Christ, then
the cosmos itself must be somehow an object of salvation. The
cosmic text of Rom 8:18-25 has been much discussed, and some
points seem clear. It is the totality of creation that shares in
God's plan. The hope of mankind is also the hope of all creation.
Creation and salvation are inseparably connected. Whatever has

39

been created has been created to be saved, is object of salvation, and this includes the whole cosmos. The salvation of the cosmos is situated by Paul in the context of man's salvation. More precisely, Paul situates the salvation of the cosmos in the context of the Resurrection, in the context of the salvation of man's body. The salvation of the cosmos is a consequence of man's salvation, especially of the salvation of man's body through resurrection. The cosmos is not just an instrument of man's salvation; it is itself object of salvation.[3]

At this point I would like to draw some conclusions about the cosmic aspect of salvation. To begin with, for both John and Paul there is a necessary intrinsic connection between creation and salvation. Creation and salvation are not so much two Christian mysteries as they are two facets of the one great mystery of God's total plan to bring all things to fulfilment in Christ. Creation is not thinkable apart from salvation. A cosmos that is not ordered to salvation would be, in the vision of John or Paul, inconceivable. This does not mean that salvation is not grace. The salvation of the whole cosmos, as well as the salvation of any person, is grace. But we know that salvation is grace not because we can conceive that God could create something that would not be ordered to salvation. We know that salvation is grace because it is offered freely by God; and we know that God offers it freely because it is accompanied by the sure sign of freedom: it is offered out of love.

Creation and salvation are indissociable, and so too are the cosmos and Christ. For John and Paul, the cosmos exists in, through, and for Christ. For Christian theology, the question "What would the world be like without the Incarnation?" makes little or no sense. The world is inconceivable without the Incarnation; for Christian theology, the cosmos is unthinkable apart from Christ. A first conclusion, then, is that salvation and creation, Christ and cosmos, are intrinsically related and necessarily connected.

A second conclusion is this: for the Christian, the cosmos is personal because it is grounded in the person of Christ. Christ is the personal center of the cosmos. "Besides those attributes that are strictly divine and human (those attributes to which theologians have paid the most attention up to now), Christ possesses -- in virtue of the working out of the implications of His incarnation -- attributes that are universal, cosmic, attributes which show Him to be the world's personal center."[4] The common center of things, "Christ can be loved as a person, and He presents Himself as a world."[5] "To the eyes of the Christian . . . Christ invests Him-

self with the whole reality of the universe; and at the same time
the universe is illumined with all the warmth and immortality
of Christ."[6]

III

The risen Christ is, then, the personal center of society and
the personal center of the cosmos. I would like to include "society"
and "cosmos" in one concept, that of "world." I do not intend to
use the term "world" in the sense of that part of the world that
Christ advises us to have no part of, that part of the world that
moves away from God. Nor do I want to use the word "world" in a
neutral sense. By "world" I mean here the world that God so loves
that He sent His only Son to save it. The question now is the question of the meaning of the world--human society and the entire
universe of which society is a part--for the salvation of the individual person. From the point of view of salvation, what should
be the relation of the Christian to the world?

For the Christian, the world is not hostile, nor is it indifferent.
The Christian can have a positive, personal relation to the world,
a certain interpersonal mutuality with the world. For the Christian,
the world has a friendly and even loving face because it is rooted
in the person of the risen Christ. The Christian, more than others,
can and should have faith in the world, faith in man, faith in human progress and in man's efforts to build up the world. And the
Christian, more than other men, can and should have hope in the
future of man, hope in the world's future. "For the Christian, the
eventual success of man on earth is not merely a probability but
a certainty, since Christ is already risen--and in Him, by anticipation, the world is already risen."[7] The world moving into the
future can be believed in, hoped in, loved, because it is grounded
in Christ risen, the guarantor of its ultimately successful outcome.
What is more, because true union of persons is personalizing,
union with Christ through involvement in the world is personalizing, makes for personal and Christian growth and development.

In the light of all this, there is surely a specifically Christian
responsibility for the world. In a world that is moving toward an
ultimate synthesis of all things in Christ, in a world that is in
the process of a painful and gradual unification in the direction
of its final transformation, the Christian, precisely as Christian,
has a heavy responsibility to contribute whatever he can to the
forward progress of society and of the world as a whole. The
Christian, as Christian, should take with the greatest serious-

ness his political obligations, his social obligations, his obligations to contribute as much as he can to the work and the research that are in the direction of the world's forward progress toward Christ. The Christian should advance God's kingdom in every domain; his faith imposes on him the right and the obligation to throw himself into the things of the earth.

Christian morality has too long been a naturalistic and static morality of equilibrium, a morality that exists to protect the individual and to protect society. In the past, morality has been understood as a fixed system of rights and duties aimed at maintaining a static equilibrium among individuals. But this is not really Christian morality, because it is not aimed at the reconciliation of all things in Christ. A truly Christian ethic is an ethic that is aimed at the highest development of the person, of society, of the world. The primary purpose of a Christian ethic should not be to protect but to develop, to unify, to move forward.

The task of the Church, then, is much broader than conversion, much more than simply bringing persons to a change of heart and a personal, existential decision for Christ. The work of the Church is transformation: transformation of persons, of society, of the world. This is not to say that we should look for a new Christendom, for an updated version of thirteenth-century Europe. It is to say that the world, as world and in keeping its own very worldliness, is to be transformed and brought closer to Christ. This is, in my opinion, the Christian task: to build up the world in every way in the direction of the final fulfilment when God will intervene, the world will be transformed, Christ will definitively weld the world to Himself and hand over the kingdom to the Father, and God will be all in all. And it is only in participating fully in the social and cosmic aspects of salvation that the Christian can respond to the gift of salvation that is offered to him in Christ. This is central to Christianity and therefore central to Christian life and to Christian evangelization.

Notes begin on page 318.

42

Scientific Humanism and the University

Enrico Cantore, S.J.

Thoughtful men are increasingly concerned with the rift between the so-called two cultures. Debates and discussions, however, seem to have failed so far to bring about the desired mutual understanding. Probably one basic reason for such an unsatisfactory outcome is a certain too narrow way of conceiving science and the scientific culture. Accordingly, the aim of this article is, first of all, to discuss science in its cultural totality as a humanistic experience; secondly, to examine in what way the university can contribute toward a new, unified humanism.

I Science as a Humanistic Experience

Formally, science will be taken here in the usually accepted sense as a cognitive approach characterized by a specific aim and method. The aim is the realization of the intelligibility present in observable reality; the method is observation of whatever type whose results can be tested on an interpersonal basis.

Yet the contention of this essay is that science cannot be properly understood in its cultural implications unless realized as an experience involving the whole man. Consequently, after a few preliminary considerations, I shall examine in what sense science can be called a humanistic experience involving both objective and subjective aspects.

1 Preliminaries: Some Common Misconceptions of Science

Science is such a massive phenomenon that it can hardly avoid being misunderstood in one way or another. For if it is difficult not to have any idea of science, it is more difficult to form an adequate conception of it. Thus we have to begin our study by examining some widespread misconceptions which threaten to falsify the whole problem under investigation.

(a) A caricature of science. A certain popular idea of science is no less than a caricature. Science is seen as a hybrid mixture of practical recipes and mystical cult. The scientist is conceived as a combination of magician and charlatan, inebriated by his own success, cocksure in his approach to all kinds of problems. Science is then interpreted as a wishful self-projection of homo faber, a popular myth upheld by the evangelical fervor of its devotees and the material advantages it ensures. Naturally enough, this view does not entirely lack foundation. Some scientists do indeed act like, and also think of themselves as, infallible priests of an almighty goddess--but it goes without saying that science, as a creative undertaking, has no use for such myopic conformists. Nor is there any need to insist that the scientific myth, once exposed, clamors for its own debunking. Intelligent man, including the scientist, enjoys a good chuckle at his own expense.[1]

(b) Scientism. A more sophisticated opinion sees science as a perfectly justified intellectual venture, but constitutionally bent on overstepping its natural limitations. The view is that, although science for itself would be acceptable, it must actually be held down because of its inborn tendency to exaggeration. In other words, science is interpreted as scientism. Now, here again, evidence for such a view is not totally lacking. Critics, particularly when dealing with sociology and psychology, have an easy time in pointing out the exaggerations which have marred these types of science.[2] Yet it would be easy to retort that a philosophical interpretation of science (whether uttered by Comte or the Vienna Circle) is no justification for mistaking it for science itself. At any rate, suffice it here to note that no exaggeration can be invoked to belittle the achievement. Without the achievements of science, how could its allegedly exaggerated public image have arisen and become so influential?

(c) Objectivism. A third misconception of science, a philosophical one, must still be mentioned. Science is seen as an undertaking which consists exclusively in giving a mathematical description of the objects that can be perceived through the senses. Measurement is interpreted as contributing continually increasing approximations toward the ideal scientific representations which constitute a kind of mathematical limit for such approximations. The procedure of science is viewed as geometrization, that is, description of reality in a hypothetico-deductive way, essentially abstract and world-foreign. Furthermore, since science aims at objectivity, namely, at representing reality as this can be perceived by any subject whatsoever, science is seen as essentially objectivistic. "It is typical of objectivism to restrict itself to observable reality and take it for granted. Such an attitude aims at the 'objective truth' of this reality, that is, at what has an absolute validity for reality itself and every rational being, namely at what this reality is in itself."[3] As a general consequence, science and its methodology are compared to a very useful and reliable machine which anyone can learn to operate without understanding the reason for its success.[4] The result is that science is taken to be absolutely impersonal: as though the scientific aim were that man, the maker of science, should be excluded from his own creation.[5] Now, no creatively thinking scientist would be able to recognize science in this description. For to him science is a total human experience, involving both a growing realization of reality and a growing participation of the subject himself.

2 Science as an Experience of Objective Intelligibility

Trying to systematically outline the nature of science as a lived reality, we have to dwell first on science as an experience of objective reality. For science, while not objectivist, is indeed objective. It consists in the realization of a man-independent order, power, and directed dynamism.

(a) The experience of order. Science begins with a personal experience of objective order. That is to say, science is born when the human person, by entering into direct contact with existing reality, perceives an intimation of objective regularities. This is

45

the moment when knowledge presents itself as a problem calling for solution. It is a personal call to investigate: if man generously responds, he becomes a scientist. For then, and only then, what is usually called science can develop: systematic observations are undertaken, measuring devices are thought out, hypotheses and theories propounded.

The evidence for such a personal nature of science is plentiful. To begin from the beginning, it is no wonder that astronomical discussions paved the way to the development of modern science: the heavenly order is easily observable by everybody. However, scientific astronomy did not start until Kepler had the insight and unconquerable enthusiasm to seek for a precise formulation of the objective order he was convinced was present in Tycho's empirical data. The same personal conviction has animated the other trailblazers throughout the centuries: Galileo studying the regularities of earthly motions, Dalton pointing out the stoichiometric regularities in chemical reactions as an intimation for the existence of atoms, Mendel investigating the statistical regularities recurring in hereditary transmission, Einstein wondering at the anomalies in the electro-dynamics of moving media as accepted at his time. What is significant here is the nature of the scientific experience. Real science is not an empiricist collection of sense impressions, but an intellectual realization of objective order to be disentangled from the overwhelming complex and confusing data of observation. The experience of order is absolutely fundamental for science; so much so that it alone accounts for the so-called accidental discoveries. In such cases, in fact, the genius of the discoverer consists in realizing the presence of a regularity to be investigated where other observers see only a meaningless multiplicity.[6] In short, order as a personally experienced reality lies at the roots of and constitutes the most prized achievement for creative scientists. "Pure science untiringly pursues the search for this hidden order, these ultimate realities . . . the search for truth is the real reason that justifies the efforts of pure science and constitutes its nobility."[7]

(b) The experience of ordered power. Science, which begins as an experience of order, comes to maturity when man realizes that matter, counter to a widespread opinion, is essentially active. Matter, being able to interact in a regular way, has the source of order in itself. To be sure, the idea that matter is active in some way is as old as mankind: it is enough to think of chemical reactions which can be traced back to prehistory. Yet, the discovery of intelligible ordered power is one of the greatest achievements

46

of modern science. The tale of Newton and the apple may well be a fable, but it contains a profound truth. For it is the parable of the immanent orderliness in material reality which for the first time was so strikingly experienced and expressed in precise language. The Newtonian synthesis served as an example; the whole of subsequent science patterned itself after it. For the realization of ordered power is the ultimate step in the scientific quest for intelligibility of material reality. Man has then achieved understanding. In fact, matter, being powerful, supplies an internal explanation for its own observable regularities of motion, association, and structure. These are but the necessary outcome of the interactivities taking place between the various bodies engaged. On the other hand, this understanding constitutes the final stage in the scientific endeavor. In fact, the ultimate court of appeal for science is recourse to observation. So, once the scientist has realized the observable power of matter, nothing remains for him to do but willingly submit himself to this fundamental fact.

(c) The experience of oriented dynamism. A third aspect characterizes the scientific experience of order. The ordered power of matter experienced by the scientist is not the source of an immutable sameness. On the contrary, it gives origin to an all-encompassing, oriented dynamism. The idea of evolution has been introduced into science by biological observation, but it actually embraces matter as a whole. Matter is essentially changeable. According to experimental discoveries, in fact, it is not possible to think of some fundamental particles which can be conceived as the unchangeable building blocks of the universe. However, universal change is itself subject to order. Actually, regularity of interaction accounts for repetitive orderliness, while the ability of matter to associate in increasingly complex structures accounts for the observable universal dynamism. It is the triumph of quantum mechanics to have provided the key for understanding the general evolutive trend. We know now in principle how nonliving matter evolves, from the so-called plasma state to solid structures.[8] Also concerning the evolution of life, current experimental and theoretical research seems to be on the brink of presenting a satisfactory explanation. In summary, the power of matter revealed by science is not a crushingly blind might but an essentially intelligible becoming. This is perhaps the most striking achievement of science as an objective experience, the fact that matter is intelligible in an unforeseeably rich way. Static and dynamic order, unity and multiplicity appear

47

no longer as contradictory, but rather as complementary aspects of the same reality.

3 Science as Experience of Creative and Dependent Knowledge

A second characteristic of science as a humanistic experience which has to be considered concerns the knowing subject. While science is a realization of the object, it is also a self-realization of the subject as a creative, and dependently creative being.

(a) The experience of creativity. As already mentioned above when dealing with science as an experience of order, the scientific endeavor is far from being a passive reading of data. It is a boldly creative activity.

The first creative intervention of the scientist concerns the attitude that he has to take toward reality as an objective observer. He must be able to divest himself of the instinct according to which man is at the center of the observable reality, that is, he must overcome the instinctive phenomenism which make sense observations appear to have an absolute value. It is no paradox to say that the very objectivity of science is only arrived at through the creativity of the scientist. Galileo used to marvel at Copernicus' "sublime intellect" because this astronomer "with reason as his guide resolutely continued to affirm what sensible experience seemed to contradict."[9] In fact, one of the main features of the progress of science consists in overcoming more and more the subjectivity inherent in human sense observation. This is obtained by devising increasingly sensitive and precise instruments, and also through elaboration of mathematical theories which take increasingly into account the subjective intervention of the observer. Another aspect of scientific creativity consists in the process of idealization and description. Concretely existing objects are extremely complex; direct observation provides a mass of data in which no over-all order seems to be detectable. The ability of the scientist consists in idealizing the object under investigation by reducing it to its essentials (for example, Galileo studying the motion of falling bodies as the motion of pointlike masses moving in a vacuum), then disentangling a precise mathematical regularity for such idealized objects from the mass of observational measurements. Finally, the greatest achievement of scientific creativity consists in explanation. Even at the level of scientific description by means of mathematical laws, man is confronted with an infinity of observable phenomena which, to be completely understood, have to be reduced to an objective unity. The clas-

48

sical example is presented by the situation of mechanics after the works of Galileo and Kepler. Numerous mathematical laws were available describing the motions of earthly and heavenly bodies. Did these various kinds of motion form an unrelated multiplicity or were they the expression of an intrinsic unity due to an objective interactive power of matter? The genius of Newton provided the answer through the law of universal gravitation.

The experience of creativity is essential to the understanding of science as a self-realization of the subject. Science is essentially creative: there is much truth in the frequently drawn comparison between the activity of a scientist formulating a new theory and that of the originally productive artist. The originally thinking scientist is aware of the tremendous intellectual power of man which comes to bear fruit in his work. Hence, the scientist rejoices and is enthusiastic over this realization. Yet, it is a quiet joy, conscious of the limitations of the achieved success (Newton used to compare himself to a child playing with pebbles on the shores of the unexplored ocean of learning). For scientific creativity is essentially dependent.

(b) The experience of dependency. The scientist employs his creativity to attain objectivity; hence it can be said that he is creative in order to be dependently faithful toward reality. The realization of dependency of human knowledge is one of the most typical components of the scientific experience. Actually, the frequently immense labors of the discoverer are sustained only by the desire to know and make known something which is already there. This should not, of course, be taken in the sense of belittling creativity, yet the fact remains and this is what the scientist is proud of. He does not want to read anything into reality, but just to manifest what is present in reality itself. Dependency on reality is so clear a factor that even the scientist acting as an inventor feels himself bound by it. In fact, he aims at producing something which, truly, does not yet exist as such in reality, but whose objective possibility he has seen embodied in the materials presented to him.

To understand scientific objectivity it is therefore necessary to take into account this experience of dependency. Checks and counterchecks of scientific results are not due to any mania for precision nor to any exaggeration of objectivity. Scientific objectivity is a very demanding methodological rule to exclude any form of subjectivism or subjective arbitrariness. It can be called a form of asceticism to which scientists willingly submit in order to honestly serve the human community. As a consequence there seems to be no more successful way of misrepresenting the scientific endeavor than to brand it as objectivism.

(c) <u>The</u> experience <u>of</u> inexhaustible <u>progressivity</u>. A third aspect which marks out science as a subjective experience is its realization of the inexhaustible progressivity of knowledge. Knowledge reveals itself to the scientist as neither pure passivity nor pure activity. Science is neither a mere collection of facts nor an intuition of essences. Rather it is a complex, never-ending interactivity between man--both as individual and social being-- and matter. In fact, science is first established when man is able to describe in idealized mathematical form the observable regularities of matter. Then science reaches maturity when man is able to explain, that is, he succeeds in deducing the multiplicity of observable regularities from the observable interactive properties of the intervening bodies. But the process of description and explanation is a never-ending one. Fresh observations will manifest hitherto unsuspected features of matter, hence call for a renewed effort of description and explanation. All of science develops in this way. A clear example is provided by the transition between classical and quantum mechanics.

Realization of knowledge as inexhaustibly progressive is one of the chief features of the scientific experience. Scientific knowledge is progressive in the strict sense of the term. New observations never contradict the positive information of the past but add new data which lead to a deeper understanding of the already existing information. So science develops by retaining the provedly true knowledge of the past while shedding its unilateral and exaggerated interpretations. Progress of scientific knowledge, however, cannot be seen as an asymptotic tendency toward a mathematical limit. For new observations present really new information, namely, strikingly unexpected features of matter. In other words, matter reveals itself as literally inexhaustibly intelligible to the mind of the investigating scientist.

4 <u>Awareness</u> <u>and</u> <u>Awe:</u> <u>The</u> <u>Humanistic</u> <u>Challenge</u> <u>of</u> <u>Science</u>

It is obvious from the preceding that it is not possible to properly understand science by reducing it to a narrowly specialized type of research nor by identifying scientific experience with sense observation. Concrete contact with observable reality and constant reflection upon it affect man as a whole. Thus science entails a new way of perceiving reality and man himself.[10] In this sense it is possible to speak of science as a humanistic experience. The consequence

is that science calls for a systematic rethinking of man's relations
to reality: in short, for a new humanism. What remains to be done
in this section is to summarize the humanistic implications of science and the conditions the scientific mentality deems essential
for the formulation of a satisfactory humanism.

(a) <u>Awareness</u>. The first humanistic implication of science is
man's new awareness of himself and of the world. Scientific man
is very much aware of his own personality, first and foremost as
a creative thinker. He knows how to mold new intellectual tools of
knowledge when necessity arises. He feels confident of possessing
the key to knowledge of material reality. Hence scientific man is
aware of reality as open to his own personality. Matter stands
before him in its objectivity: gone are magic and any form of
anthropocentric phenomenism. Scientific man knows his own
limitations, being himself a part of the observable reality. But
he has also learned how to fashion matter according to his will.
Knowledge is power. Scientific man is man who has come of age,
and is capable of taking his destiny into his own hands.

(b) <u>Awe</u>. What is frequently called the scientific optimism, however, is not disjoined from a deep awareness of unanticipated
problems. Scientific man has acquired a new sense of respect for
reality, combined with reverence, puzzlement, and often dread.
It follows that awe is the second most prominent humanistic implication of modern science. Man is now confronted with a new
reality. Nature manifests itself as a powerfully self-constructive
order but such that it can never be grasped by the human mind
because it is inexhaustible in its intelligibility and subjected to un-
ceasing dynamism. As a consequence man, while rejoicing in his
success, cannot help seeing that this very success breeds awesome
problems.

Science raises disturbing questions because of what it says.
There is first of all the problem of knowledge itself. How can man
get to know reality by means of abstract conceptions, fixed and
rigid and perfectly perspicuous in their mathematical formulation,
while reality is supple and changing and inexhaustible, and never
to be anticipated with certainty in the concrete behavior of individual cases? These are questions which, to use Einstein's words,
must "burningly interest" the reflective scientist.[11] Then there
is the problem of objective order. Why does an objective order
actually occur, an order expressible by means of general mathematical propositions, while the world itself is made up of individuals,
continually subjected to change and chance? "One may say 'the eter-

nal mystery of the world is its comprehensibility.'"[12] Still, the problems raised by science do not only concern what science actually says. Scientific success presents problems also because of what it leaves unsaid. Indeed, if science is knowledge, why is science itself unable to account for its own ability to know, as shown by the fact that the most contradictory interpretations of science have been offered by the various schools of thought? Moreover, if science is knowledge, why does it not answer the most significant questions pertaining to the meaning of human life and the existence of the universe? If, on the other hand, there are other forms of knowledge besides science, what are the mutual relationships among these different cognitive approaches? Finally, there is still another class of worrisome problems raised by scientific success. They regard the enormous power with which science entrusts man. If science is knowledge capable of making man dreadfully powerful, why does it not supply also guidance to man in the use of this power? To sum up, science has contributed mightily to make the world a source of astonishment and even fear to man. As a consequence, modern man has become more of a problem to himself.

(c) The humanistic challenge of science. In the light of the foregoing the reason of the cleavage between the two cultures now appears clear. Science is a new, all-encompassing experience for man which defies any labeling in terms of hitherto current philosophical categories. Science is neither an empiricist recording of sense information nor an aprioristic formulation of universal and necessary laws, but rather a continually developing dialectical exchange between man and matter. Science entails a new over-all conception of man and reality: hence scientific man is a new man. It follows that he cannot be satisfied with any ascientific form of humanism, precisely because it is based on an ascientific vision of reality. The intercultural cleavage, therefore, manifests the inadequacy of traditional humanism. In the light of the new facts, this humanism must appear meaningless to scientific man. Even worse, it must appear harmful to him when it claims to be the only acceptable form of humanism. Polemics, however, are fruitless. Only when we try to go beyond them do we see that scientific man is not against humanistic values. He merely wants the new problematic to be taken seriously. In other words, the profound dissatisfaction of the scientific man with the other culture has to be viewed for what it really is, a challenge rather than a rejection. Here I shall try to outline the principal requirements for the elaboration of a scientifically acceptable

humanism. (i) Humanism has to be objective. There is no question of objectivism here. This requirement is simply that no proposition be admitted as true unless it has been submitted to an
interpersonal test, which ultimately consists in a direct experi-
ential contact with reality itself. Scientific man is convinced that
he achieves his highest perfection as a person when submitting
himself to the actually existing reality. Hence he is against any
form of subjectivism and apriorism. That is to say, he cannot
accept any assertion when forced on him from the outside, on
philosophical or political or religious grounds. He wants to test
truth on its own merits, on the basis of its openness to the total
experience of man. (ii) Humanism has to be concrete. Man has
to be helped to find his place squarely in the midst of matter.
Man is indeed matter: there is a continuity between man and the
remainder of material reality. But man is also the summit of
evolution, for he is matter which has come to consciousness of
itself. Hence scientific man experiences both a partnership and
a struggle between himself and matter, a special relationship in
which he himself must always emerge as the chiefly responsible
partner. It follows that scientific man is not against spirit. Rather,
if the spirit has anything to mean to him, it must manifest itself
through matter and prove its worth in matter. For the same reason it cannot be said that scientific man is against God. He is not
antitheistic, but he is certainly disgusted with any religious conception founded on a self-satisfied prescientific world view.
Rather, we can say that scientific man is open to the divinity,
provided this can prove its presence and communicate itself
through matter. Therefore, here again, more than ever, the
position of scientific man has to be seen for what it really is:
not a denial, but a challenge. In fact the new man feels confident
that a personal God can well stand the test of manifesting Himself
through concrete personal experience. Moreover, only such a
God can be acceptable, because He alone can leave operating room
for the creativity of man. (iii) Humanism has to be dynamical. If
personal experience is the ultimate source of knowledge, and man
has been born for knowledge, he must be continually open to experience. This has to be so, despite all the insecurity and the
changeability involved in such a continual opening. Such an openness to progress is, for the scientific mentality, an absolute requirement precisely because the conquest of truth is a never fully
accomplished undertaking, given the inexhaustible intelligibility
of reality. Accordingly, what scientific man objects to in philosophy
is mainly the closedness of its systems which makes them incapable

of assimilating unanticipated new pieces of information. The dynamism, however, required by the new humanism cannot be limited to the cognitive field, but must extend to the ethical realm. That is to say, it must leave room, and provide inspiration, for human creativity. Scientific man is essentially creative: hence a satisfactory humanism must help him to better understand and more fruitfully develop this creativity. Indeed, only under this condition can humanism appear worthy of its name to scientific man, namely, as the bearer of a significant message and the instrument of man's greatness.

II The University and the Crisis of Modern Man

When seeking for an answer to the problems affecting modern man, it is natural to turn to the university. For this is the place where thinkers congregate and the man of the future is formed. However, at first sight it seems difficult to speak even of a specific nature of today's university, let alone of a humanistic role of it. Indeed, the university appears to be merely a manifold fact, often the product of chance development. Normally, it consists in a collection of departments whose sole aim seems to be growth: increase in number to cover more and more branches of knowledge, increase in specialization of research. As a consequence, man appears to be smothered rather than helped by the diversity and the multiplicity of the university activities. The question remains: Is there still place for humanism at the university, that is, for man's reflexive cognition of himself and of his place in the world? Despite the outlined difficulties, the answer should leave no doubt, if only the university wants to keep faith with its living tradition.

1 The Humanistic Nature of the University

What makes the university unique among the institutions of learning is its aim to educate instead of instructing. In fact, the university does not intend, properly and centrally, to supply information or to pass on a specialized skill, but to help young men and women to develop their personalities. Now a young human being cannot grow to be a person unless by realizing his proper place in the world and by training himself to meet the continually arising challenges with a conscious and purposeful responsibility. Hence it is possible to speak of a specifically humanistic aim of the university, both as a place of universal learning and as a center of research, precisely because the nature of the university is to educate man to maturity.

54

The first contribution of the university to humanism flows from its multiple unity. In fact, universality of outlook, actively developed into a unified personal standpoint, is central to the educative purpose. A little knowledge can be a dangerous thing indeed. According to the much-quoted dictum, those who consider only a few things have no difficulty in deciding. So it is clear why universality of outlook is so important for a sound humanism. Overspecialization engenders the obstinacy of the bigot; truth is transformed into error by lack of perspective. This obvious psychological fact has a profound reason: the idea of man is necessarily falsified by any one-sidedness. As a consequence, there should be no tight compartments of knowledge since reality forms but one whole. Compartmentalization of knowledge is but a methodological necessity, the result of mental abstraction. Thus, if man has to be understood and be led to self-understanding, all forms of knowledge have to be taken into consideration, lest any omission prejudice the accuracy and reliability of knowledge altogether. The second humanistic contribution of the university originates from its being a center of research. Man cannot come to maturity unless he comes to realize both the value and limitations of knowledge. Now the nature of knowledge cannot be understood except through actual practice of knowledge itself, and a continual reflection on it. To conclude, it seems necessary to assert that, at the present time no less than in the past, the university can successfully achieve its aim only by being humanistic.[13] Practical problems, however, remain plentiful. To find an indication toward a solution we have now to consider briefly the origin of the modern crisis of man.

2 Man and Science: The Anthropological Crisis

The crisis of modern man, his sense of insecurity and problematicity, is a theme frequently discussed by contemporary philosophers. "We are the first epoch in which man . . . no longer knows what he essentially is, but at the same time also knows that he does not know."[14] However, it seems that usually the problem is not seen in the right perspective. For the anthropological crisis is generally blamed on science in a way that does not take into proper account the positive contribution of science itself to the development of man and his self-understanding. In fact, it is not right to criticize science as a cause of problems to man because of its technological and sociological applications. The humanistic problems of science, as we have seen, are mainly theoretical,

the result of a new world view. Furthermore, it is wrong to blame
science, as though the problems raised by it were due to a lack
of self-control and exaggeration on the part of science itself. The
fact is that science is the source of crisis because it raises objective questions which cannot be ignored by the progressing man.

The factors which led man to self-questioning at the beginning
of the modern era are varied. The critical spirit of the Renaissance, fueled by the literary discovery of ancient skepticism,
was an important element. Another source of questioning was the
realization, due to geographical discoveries, that the Western
standards of man were by no means so absolute as they had hitherto been thought to be. However, the influence of science on the
anthropological problem seems to have surpassed all other factors both in profundity and lasting effect. Beginning with Copernicus modern man lost his bearings in the face of the scientifically
known reality. This, of course, was not due to the fact that the
earth was demoted from its central position in the universe, but
rather to the challenging spirit of science. The Copernican hypothesis seemed to call in doubt whatever had been considered un-
assailable up to that date: testimony of the senses, harmony of
the universe, religious interpretation.[15] The instinctive cosmo-
logical representation of the man-in-the-street was blown to
pieces, to be replaced by an endless succession of less and less
familiar conceptions. The success of Newtonian mechanics
seemed to leave man adrift in the infinity of space and time, at
the mercy of deterministic, purely mechanical laws. Man was
rightly frightened when facing the apparently meaningless certainty offered by science.[16] Yet the comparative security of the
Newtonian world was itself shattered by further developments.
Space and time proved to be not absolutes, but functions of the
state of the observer: as a consequence, the universe ceased to
be imaginable at all. As for the certainty of determinism, it was
gradually realized that this was itself no more than a rough generalization, resting on the observational fact that all physical
laws are statistical. In addition, the unchangeability embodied
in static conception of reality was brushed aside by the discovery
of the dynamical nature of reality. Finally, the very possibility
of an absolute certainty was called into question. This was the
case when it became clear that even what was considered the
paragon of indubitability, Euclidean geometry, was no more than
one among many possibilities. As a final result, there should be
no wonder that the anthropological crisis was and is on with all
its weighty impact.[17] And yet, it is important to point out, the

crisis of modern man due to science cannot be seen as a setback, but rather as a sign of progress. For this crisis originates from the realization of objective problems which cannot be ignored. Prescientific man was content with a phenomenistic conception of reality as possessed by the man-in-the-street. Hence, the grandiose humanistic syntheses based on it, despite their notable value, were only too liable to the charges of superficiality and anthropomorphism. The first contribution of science to the creation of a new humanism, therefore, was no less significant for its being largely negative. It consisted in doing away with what was actually pseudo-information, because not based on any precise observation. It was necessary to destroy man's rationalistic bent, prone to identify reality with his own conception of it. Man had to learn that knowledge is an extremely complex interactivity, and that reality is inexhaustibly intelligible. Then, chastened and better aware of himself and of reality, man is finally in a better position to build up a new humanism. For science, as discussed above, clamors for a new humanism.

3 Methodological Indications for a Humanistic Role of the University

In the light of the past developments it is now possible to speedily disengage some methodological indications for a humanistic role of the university. These can be reduced to two fundamental ideas. Man is essentially a whole; hence the university must provide the setting for studying him as such. The anthropological problem has reached its present complexity as the result of a long historical development; hence the method for attempting a solution has to be the genetical one.

(a) Wholeness of man. The aim has to be the understanding of man as a whole. For man's problem is the problem of a unique totality, embracing whatever man is and can become in body and mind, as an individual person and as a social being. Now here precisely the role of the university becomes vital. In fact, this knowledge of man cannot be obtained without science, since man is quite clearly also an observable being. To quote one of the leading anthropological philosophers of our time: ". . . the depth of the anthropological question is first touched when we also recognize as specifically human that which is not reason."[18] Science alone, however, is obviously not enough. For the investigating man cannot content himself with considering man as an object, while ignoring that he himself is a man having a per-

57

sonal experience of man. Hence philosophy is needed, as a systematic self-reflection. "He can know the wholeness of the person and through it the wholeness of man only when he does not leave his subjectivity out and does not remain an untouched observer."[19] From this, practical consequences for cooperation at the interior of the university follow naturally. What is needed is an earnest interest in man to be seriously studied from all relevant points of view. Hence it will be comparatively easy to overcome the shortcomings of departmentalization. Discussions of concrete aspects of the anthropological problem can form the object of interdepartmental seminars and symposia. Deeper investigation of the same questions can constitute the object of systematic research in interdepartmental institutes leading to academic degrees.

(b) Genetical approach. The issues concerning man, however, remain extremely complex. A complementary methodological indication, therefore, must point out the way of facing their complexity without prejudging the issue. Now it is clear that man is essentially a becoming being who has come to be a problem to himself through his development in time. It follows that we can best hope to understand him by following the same development, both of man as an individual and as a social being. Thus the genetical approach constitutes the second guideline for the university as a humanistic institution.

Here again the contributions of the university as a center for both science and philosophy are essential. Science is invaluable, because all positive information concerning man and reality is supplied by science, and science has a characteristically developmental nature. Philosophy is indispensable because, as already mentioned, man cannot come to understand himself without self-reflection. In particular, the present-day situation appears promising for a systematic interdepartmental academic research. In fact, modern scholarship has been amassing a great wealth of genetical information and reflection touching upon all fields (history of science and philosophy, scientific study of man's phylogenesis and ontogenesis, philosophy of history).[20] As a consequence, it does not appear too daring to think that man has finally all the tools for elaborating a satisfactory humanism, an open synthesis not plagued by the traditional inadequacies overemphasizing either the subject or the object, either science or philosophy.

Conclusion

The condition of man in the scientific-technological era is undoubtedly one of crisis. But according to all indications this is a crisis of growth. In fact, modern man is puzzled and deeply dissatisfied not because of a wanton rebellion against the past, but because of the emergence of new, unexpected problems. The crisis consists in the fact that man has not yet been able to find his suitable place in the midst of the enormously rich and powerful world he has discovered. Now it is fascinating to think that this crisis, if properly resolved, can mightily contribute to bring man closer to the realization of his ideal. Man has always felt attracted by the ideal of wisdom. Prescientific man dreamed of an all-encompassing conception of reality by means of which he, both spectator and actor, could walk on the way toward continual progress. Now, what had been a mere dream in the past can become a fact in our days. The telling factor is science, if properly understood in the full human sense of the term. Science, in fact, has provided man with reliable information covering precisely the whole of reality accessible to man's positive investigation. Science has also shown to man concretely that he can continually progress. So modern man is faced with the exalting task of attaining the sapiential ideal in a measure unthinkable in the past. To be sure, the task remains difficult: a satisfactory scientific humanism is still to be born. However, it is encouraging to realize that modern man, come of age, possesses all the prerequisites for attaining the desired aim. Information is plentifully at his disposal in the universities. Historical reflection has helped him shed past prejudices and limitations. So let us confidently hope that modern man will be able to genuinely recapture his living tradition of complete growth and creatively bring it to fulfillment.

Notes begin on page 318.

"Who Reads Aquinas?"

Anton C. Pegis

I

The title of this essay is not original. It was used some months ago as a caption over a book review in the London Times Literary Supplement. The anonymous reviewer had before him two volumes of the new translation of St. Thomas' Summa Theologiae now appearing in England and the United States. In order to thread his way through some of the intricacies of St. Thomas' exposition, the technical questions involved and their technical subdivisions, the reviewer had to be more than casually interested in the Thomistic way of doing things. As it turned out, he was not, he lost courage very early and appealed to the mood of the day as a defense. Who reads Aquinas? he asked, as though to say, Why bother with St. Thomas' Aristotelian distinctions in this day and age? And indeed, who does read Aquinas today? This question needs to be asked, even if it has no answer. In our day Thomism is experiencing an unprecedented decline in popular favor. Worse still, the decline is visible in Catholic departments of philosophy across the United States and Canada and not only in non-Catholic quarters. What is the meaning of this state of affairs, how did it come about, and what, if anything, can be done about it at the present time? These are the questions to which, in a general way but from the point of view of a single observer, I should like to propose an answer in the following pages.

The outstanding facts in the case are well known. During the last decade the teaching of St. Thomas Aquinas--of what is commonly called his philosophy--has suffered an extraordinary eclipse. Now, that any thinker of the past should experience a decline in influence or popularity at any moment in history is not particularly surprising. Plato has had his ups and downs across the centuries, and so has Aristotle. At the moment, St. Anselm of Canterbury and St. Bonaventure, who have been in relative obscurity in recent years, seem to be entering a new and more favorable climate in human thought. As for St. Augustine, he has never been far away from the living centers of human intellectual interest at any moment in history. But what is happening to St. Thomas Aquinas is, if not unique, at least unusual. I am thinking of the rapidity, the vigor and even the violence with which he has been--and is now being--deserted. The question, therefore, is to know why such a large-scale reversal has so quickly been effected by Catholic teachers of philosophy in the United States and Canada, not to refer directly to any other country.

A first explanation may be that, in spite of appearances, there has never been any deep philosophical attachment to St. Thomas in our Catholic colleges and universities. Otherwise, how explain the sudden and startling discovery that he is outdated in his teaching, narrow in his perspective as a Christian thinker, rigid and static in his philosophical outlook, indeed an antiquated intellectual guide speaking always of being whereas we are today living in a world of evolutionary becoming? The London Times caption may amuse or possibly even irritate us if we happen to be in any way attached to the thought of St. Thomas Aquinas; but we are dealing with a much more serious problem when we ask how it is that St. Thomas' presumed followers have had such a relatively sudden and easy change of heart--or head.

An observer who pretends to a little more than a casual knowledge of the situation can be excused if he does not accept such a superficial reading of the current difficulties of Thomism. But how is the situation to be read? In the first place, it is not possible to question the devotion with which Thomism has been taught in Catholic colleges and universities. The writings of St. Thomas have been studied for years in those very areas in which the opposition to Thomism is today most critical, namely, metaphysics and the philosophy of man, not to ignore the whole realm of ethics and the problem of natural law. Why have St. Thomas' notions become so rapidly outdated and repudiated?

Every philosophy teacher in a Catholic institution, whether he be a convinced or a disenchanted Thomist, must answer such a question for himself. My own remarks apply only to myself and simply reflect the experiences I have had as a teacher of philosophy in Catholic institutions for over thirty years. Many judgments, by many students, both favorable and unfavorable, will be needed before anything like an adequate assessment of the fortunes of contemporary Thomism can be reached. And such judgments will be useful, since we are today witnessing what is surely the ending of that very reality which, back in the thirties and even the twenties, we were calling the Thomistic philosophical renaissance. How is it that a philosophical movement that began with such vitality and high hopes, and had such an optimistic and urgent sense of its new birth in the modern world, should now be a weary and confused reality among so many modern Thomists?

Any present-day answer to the question has all the benefits of hindsight and all of its dangers. Hindsight, certainly, is a great teacher, but like the epilogue of a play it comes at a moment when the main action is past and you find yourself walking out of the theater either nodding in assent or shaking your head in puzzlement or dissent. I can wish that, some thirty years ago, we all saw what we see--or think we see--today. But, granted all its wisdom, the one thing that hindsight cannot do is to undo the past. What I say, then, has all the limitations of a backward glance at history, but what I say is unprejudiced--that is, if it be allowed that a person who still remains a Thomist can be unprejudiced. In any case, my criticisms are intended as interpretations of what has happened and not as judgment in favor of what might have happened. I say all this because the position of a Thomist today is very different from what it was when I began as a teacher. A popular movement, by its very popularity, does not need to explain itself; when that movement comes upon difficult times, at the very least it must try to understand and judge itself in order to continue to exist. Where does a Thomist stand today?

II

Speaking as one who chooses to remain a Thomist, I would like to propose, first of all, that the chief cause of the eclipse of modern

62

Thomism lies within Thomism itself. No doubt, many Thomists will be annoyed to read that Thomism is in serious trouble today as a consequence of the manner in which it has been held and presented as a philosophy by the majority of modern Thomists both here and in Europe. Nevertheless, looking back on modern Thomism as a philosophical movement in the twentieth century, I see it in the main as a rootless abstraction, an easily pieced-together fabric of Thomistic texts, drawn from St. Thomas himself and his commentators. Such a Thomism really reflected no one's philosophy; on the contrary, it acted as the chart of a master philosophy that Catholic teachers have in fact used as a yardstick with which to measure the intellectual health of other philosophers. Thus erected into a sort of ageless IBM philosophical computer, it would seem that St. Thomas has not even needed to be studied for himself or for the sake of the student; his teaching merely needed to be applied to the modern world in order to supply answers to questions, solve problems, and bring truth to a truthless society. I would be less than honest if I did not say that this aspect of philosophical Thomism has been a noticeably widespread phenomenon in its modern diffusion. Many Thomists did think of Thomism in this way and there is no point in denying the fact. Rather than deny it, it seems better to reflect on the fact itself, to wonder about its meaning, and to consider its role in the development of Thomism in the twentieth century.

As soon as one is willing to look at Thomism objectively as a modern philosophical movement, going back (let us say) to the time when in 1882 Cardinal Mercier inaugurated the chair of Thomistic philosophy at the University of Louvain, it becomes clear that there have been two Thomistic movements in the modern world, each with its own character, intellectual texture and philosophical purpose. There has been what may be called a purely philosophical Thomistic movement, carried on by those whose primary aim was and has continued to be to create a Thomistic philosophy in the modern world, autonomous as a philosophy, perfectly distinct from the theology of St. Thomas Aquinas, and open--indeed, anxiously open--to the modern sciences and generally to the world of modern knowledge. Cardinal Mercier was himself a strong and zealous proponent of such a Thomism, conceived in modern terms in the modern world and with modern interests.

But there was also a second kind of Thomism that grew up alongside this philosophical movement. It developed as part of the general study of medieval philosophy, and it was interested in the examination of medieval scholasticism. As far as St. Thomas himself was concerned, it aimed to formulate a precise and accurate account of his life and writings, of his doctrinal career in Paris and in the several cities of Italy where he was active and, in larger terms, of the Christian synthesis that he created within the world of the thirteenth century and in answer to its needs and conditions. Many historians of the thought of St. Thomas come to mind when we look at him from this point of view. There are such illustrious names as Maurice de Wulf, Martin Grabmann, Pierre Mandonnet, M.-D. Chenu, and Etienne Gilson. This historically minded Thomism has sought to return to St. Thomas Aquinas himself, to his intellectual world, to his personal interests and problems, to his actual writings and all the technical and exegetical questions that they pose; more generally, it has wished to discover the very person whom we call St. Thomas such as he was in the concrete conditions of the career that he marked out for himself, the life of a Christian theologian.

These two Thomisms, the one philosophical and the other historical, were not opposed movements, and very often they even blended together. But, looking at them with the exasperating clarity of hindsight, we can recognize that they were distinct movements, and that each had its own dominant interests and direction. I am speaking here of a difference in movements and not necessarily a division among persons. All of us, I think, were in varying degrees touched by both directions in the Thomistic movement. Nevertheless, what was visibly dominant in some Thomists was a desire to become as Thomists modern philosophers, and they did think that they could create a modern philosophy, called Thomism, out of the writings of St. Thomas Aquinas; on the other hand, other Thomists, though they aimed to be students and even followers of St. Thomas as well as philosophers in their own right, were slow to identify these two aims: professing fully their indebtedness and allegiance to St. Thomas, they yet thought that their own philosophy (whatever it was or would be) could owe its light to St. Thomas but not its substance--this was theirs. Between the philosophical Thomists and the historical Thomists there remained an unexpressed difference of opinion on the proper way to apply the adjective "Thomistic" to themselves and their work. In calling themselves Thomists, did they mean that they were transmitting someone else's philosophy to the modern world, namely, St. Thomas' philosophy, or did they mean that they had a philosophy of their own and were calling it Thomism? The first alternative was and is untenable; the second confronts the Thomist with the necessity of deciding how, if he calls himself a Thomist, he can

properly speak another man's philosophy in the process of
creating or professing his own.

There will naturally be disagreement on this conclusion. On
the further premise that disagreement is not particularly useful
if it rests on any ambiguity, let me try to be as clear as possible
in what I am saying. Of the two Thomisms that I have mentioned,
I believe that one is on the way to dying and the other will live. I
believe that the so-called modern Thomistic philosophical synthesis of so many manuals in Latin and other languages, the
synthesis that has been built into a modern philosophy out of St.
Thomas' writings, is bound to die and indeed is now dying. It
is dying from what seems to be, at first glance, its virtue. As
a modern philosophy, Thomism has aimed to present itself as
the common philosophy of the human intellect, and even as a
philosophy that can call itself universal and perennial. And this
has been its challenge and difficulty. For, as between being
Thomistic and being modern, it has not clearly determined whose
philosophy it is; and, aiming to be a universal philosophy, and
therefore everyone's philosophy, it has become by default an
impersonal philosophy, impersonal and, what is much worse,
depersonalized. In other words, the process of becoming a
modern philosophy has both impersonalized and depersonalized
Thomism. This is the historical fact. As a modern synthesis,
Thomism is no one's philosophy, and it is dying for that reason.

Everyone knows that St. Thomas was a medieval theologian
whom the Church continues to honor not only as her Common
Doctor but also as the best spokesman of her theology. But, on
the whole, we have been slow to appreciate many things about
St. Thomas, no doubt because of our own occupations. We have
been slow to appreciate that he was a theologian, the nature of
his theology, and the concrete dimensions of its thirteenth-century involvement; we have been especially slow to understand the
consequences of saying with Maritain that St. Thomas' philosophy
is a theologized philosophy. Rather, we have traditionally followed
another course. Since St. Thomas was a theologian who also had
and used a philosophy in his theology, Thomists since at least the
sixteenth century have thought that they could separate the philosophy from the theology and present it as Thomistic philosophy,
removed from any influence from the Thomistic theology and
hence fully autonomous in its rational unfolding and general organization. Naturally, such an autonomous Thomistic philosophy has
had to be drawn from many parts of the Thomistic theology in
order to be a complete or, at least, a reasonably adequate human

synthesis, just as, for this same purpose, it had to be given several structural props from St. Thomas' commentators, and especially Cajetan and John of St. Thomas.

Now there is no doubt that St. Thomas wrote most of the things that have gone into the making of the modern philosophical synthesis created by his disciples and manualists. But there are some things that St. Thomas did not do and for which he cannot be made responsible in modern Thomism even when it bears his name. The two summae, from which the Thomistic philosophical synthesis is chiefly drawn, are both theologies, everything in them St. Thomas specifically wrote as a theologian (sub ratione Dei, as he said), and the only synthesis for which he is personally responsible is a theological one. We know from what he has written how and on what grounds St. Thomas has distinguished between theology and philosophy, and we can see how he has respected his own distinction between these two orders in building his theology. But we do not know how he built his philosophy since this is precisely what he did not do: he never created a philosophy as such. True, we can see many ways in which he might have done it, and we can even visualize the general order and spirit of his philosophy if he had had one. But, in fact, he did not create a philosophical synthesis as such for himself. If we judge by what he said and did, he decided that as a Christian thinker, face to face with Aristotelian philosophy in the Latin world of the thirteenth century, his job was to create a Christian religious synthesis in answer to Aristotle, that is, a theology in answer to a philosophy. This is what he did. Who, then, is the author of "modern Thomistic philosophy"? Not St. Thomas, since the modern philosophical synthesis does not as such belong to him. St. Thomas did not piece together his own texts into a continuous and autonomous philosophical structure. Apparently, the modern Thomist is not the author either, since the philosophy in this structure is supposed to be that of St. Thomas, or at least to stem from St. Thomas. And yet, it cannot be his. Once more, who is the author of modern Thomistic philosophy if St. Thomas has contributed the materials for it from his theology but not the philosophical synthesis, and if the modern Thomist has contributed a synthesis for materials that are not his own? It looks very much as though neither St. Thomas nor the modern Thomist can lay claim to authorship in this situation; which is another way of saying that no one can. But what is a philosophy without an author?

This conclusion directs our attention to what is in reality a long-standing difficulty within modern philosophical Thomism.

66

A "philosophical" Thomism is a synthesis that St. Thomas might have, but in fact never, created. St. Thomas' philosophy spent its life serving a theology, not serving its own ends. As a man, St. Thomas was personally present in his philosophy as a theologian, with a theologian's vision, commitment and engagement. To repeat, his philosophy was a theologized reality. Now the starting point of any philosophy--from that of Plato to that of Heidegger--is the personal decision of some man to be a philosopher, the decision and the concrete involvement. This is what gives to a philosophy its character, its movement and its historical life. A philosophy is as concrete as a philosopher--as concrete and personal--since his life is both its vehicle and its substance. There was, certainly, a Thomistic philosophy in St. Thomas if we are referring to the philosophical notions and principles that he formulated for use in and by his theology. But there was no Thomistic philosophy in the sense in which, for example, St. Thomas himself knew that Plato and Aristotle were philosophers or in the sense in which we know that Kant and Bergson are philosophers in the modern world. To put the point in thirteenth-century language, in the presence of the philosophers St. Thomas was, not a philosophus, but a theologus philosophans, a philosophizing theologian, a man who worked as a theologian in his own philosophy.

It will not be easy to accept such a result, but there is no escape from it. All genuine philosophies are personal, however much they aim to be universal and objective in their vision. What is personal to St. Thomas is his theology, in which philosophy lived as an instrument, much as the brush in his hand is the instrument of the eye of the painter and words are the instrument of the mind of the poet. In this concrete sense, modern philosophical Thomism is suffering from the want of an author and in such a Thomism there lies a still unresolved dilemma. How can there be a modern Thomistic philosophy if, in the sense of being an autonomous reality, there was not a medieval Thomistic philosophy?

III

To understand both the full force and the present relevance of this question let us here consider the direction taken by the historical Thomists, and especially that taken by Gilson, on the whole subject of St. Thomas' philosophy. In 1944, toward the end of the second world war, Gilson published two classic books in Paris. One was the second edition of his La philosophie au moyen âge, which has never been translated into English; the other was the

67

fifth edition of his Thomisme, later (1956) translated into English under the title The Christian Philosophy of St. Thomas Aquinas. Invited to review these first postwar books, I had no choice but to call special attention to Gilson's continued and impenitent insistence on presenting the philosophy of St. Thomas within its theological setting and according to its theological order--that is, from God, across creation, to the return of creation, and especially man, to God. Now according to St. Thomas himself, God is the last subject of philosophy, the last, the most difficult and the most exalted. Yet here was Gilson continuing to set forth Thomistic philosophy, not according to the order that St. Thomas himself had considered to be philosophical, but according to the order of the Thomistic theology, that is, the order that St. Thomas had in fact followed. Gilson has done few things to irritate the modern Thomistic philosophical world more than this total resistance to their demand that he recast the philosophy of St. Thomas into a philosophical mold and give to it a philosophical order. Why this refusal, indeed this adamant refusal, destined to be repeated in a work published in 1960, The Elements of Christian Philosophy, drawn almost exclusively from the writings of St. Thomas Aquinas?

The reason falls into two parts, both decisive for the notion of Thomism in the modern world. From the side of St. Thomas, the reason is that, having created no philosophical synthesis of his own by the fact of doing the work of a theologian even within the use he made of his own philosophical tools, St. Thomas cannot be endowed with such a synthesis by any modern interpreter, not even for historical purposes. From the side of the modern interpreter, engaged in the study of St. Thomas Aquinas for whatever purpose, including the desire to become himself in some recognizable sense a Thomist, the reason is that no one can philosophize in another man's name. The modern Thomist can philosophize in his own name, and then his philosophy bears the name that he has, however great his debt to St. Thomas may be. As a student of St. Thomas, limiting himself to what St. Thomas thought and even to the philosophy that he had within his theology, the modern student can give an account of that philosophy as a historian and with historical faithfulness. If he does so, he is bound to present the philosophy of St. Thomas such as it was in its own world, in its own time and circumstances, and with its author's overriding theological engagement. In this sense, the Thomism of St. Thomas himself must be, even for the modern Thomist, the philosophy of a thirteenth-century theologian, engaged as a theologian in the intellectual world and the concrete problems of his day. In this same sense, there is no other Thomism and, strictly speaking, none is possible.

The dialogue between St. Thomas and the modern Thomist, therefore, turns out to be more complex and more sophisticated than most Thomists have generally recognized. It contains certain historical ground rules that need to be respected if the dialogue is to exist at all. A modern Thomist may not wish to become a historian of the personal thought of St. Thomas Aquinas, but he must become historian enough in order to read the writings of St. Thomas with adequacy and fidelity within the framework of the world in which their author worked. Otherwise, what guarantee does he have that he will not misread and misuse these same writings within the vastly different framework of the twentieth century? There is no doubt that the deepest ambition of the modern Thomist has been to live intellectually in communion with the world of the twentieth century, and especially with the science that is such a gigantic foundation for the ways in which we think today. There is as little doubt, however, that St. Thomas has himself lived as a sort of prisoner within the otherwise legitimate ambitions of modern Thomists. He has been pilfered and misread for the sake of modern purposes, he has been "modernized" for the sake of these same purposes, he has been bent and stretched and variously modified to fit the intellectual vision of the modern Thomist. But all this otherwise understandable Thomistic activity, whatever its merits, has not rested on a proper appreciation of St. Thomas as a theologian in his own world. His religious aims and his intellectual occupation with what were the modern problems of his day have been almost totally ignored. This is why we are now on the threshold of a new age in our dialogue with St. Thomas Aquinas. At least, we can see today that these questions need to be raised, and especially we can see the necessity of taking the proper measure of the man with whom we are undertaking to engage in dialogue.

Those who have been occupied with the historical study of St. Thomas, consequently, have not felt that they have buried themselves in another world or another time. Today is the time for them to say so. They have felt that the dialogue with St. Thomas requires two things, both of them equally important for the very success of the undertaking. In the first place, St. Thomas has to be understood such as he was in his own day. In the second place, we who are modern, or at least say and think that we are modern, must then undertake to measure the distance between St. Thomas and ourselves and to establish the ground of our own modernity. The historians of St. Thomas have revolutionized our knowledge of St. Thomas the thirteenth-century man, the theologian, the writer, the thinker, the Aristotelian. We have learned how much and how intimately St. Thomas belongs to the thirteenth century and to none other, as well as how much his Christian vocation was to engage in the conflicts of his own age and to bring intellectual order to them. But we have also learned from these same historians what ultimate and permanent truths St. Thomas himself intended to teach even within the concrete conditions of his world. We have learned what notions St. Thomas meant to use as enduring theological and philosophical principles and how he threw light on the issues of his world by the play of these principles on the problems confronting his contemporaries. We have learned to understand St. Thomas as a Christian theologian aiming to see all reality and all knowledge within the perspective of the purpose of the Christian revelation, namely, the salvation of man. We have learned that to introduce the world of the philosophers, and especially of Aristotle, into the living framework of the historical world of human salvation was one of his most cherished aims as a Christian theologian. Trying as such a theologian to make room for philosophy within the Christian city, that is to say, within the developing kingdom of God in history, St. Thomas was everywhere conscious of doing a religious work in assimilating and using Aristotelianism within his theology. Let us add that, as a religious work, it could succeed in the face of philosophy only if he used philosophical principles according to their proper meaning and scope, even when he transcended their purpose as a theologian in doing so.

The question is to know what the modern Thomist, having himself modern aims, is called upon to do in the presence of this growing historical picture of St. Thomas Aquinas. The trouble has been that, very often, the modern Thomist has not thought it necessary to learn these historical lessons and perspectives about St. Thomas Aquinas. As a result, not knowing how to read or to study St. Thomas in his thirteenth-century world, the modern Thomist has not known how to make him part of the twentieth century or how to be himself what he says he is, namely, a modern Thomist, which is to say, someone who is recognizably modern in his intellectual engagement and recognizably Thomistic in the signature of that engagement. Here is the most decisive aspect of the question with which we began. After the misadventures and the failures of the last hundred years, how does one genuinely and successfully become a modern Thomist, and is the venture possible and tenable?

May I state as candidly as I can what a present-day Thomist should answer? It is unavoidable that not all will share in the answer, but, then, that is the normal fate of all philosophical options. The answer that I wish to propose can be summarized, at least in its premises, under three headings.

First, St. Thomas was a theologian who framed a Christian theological synthesis in the thirteenth century that is still visible, but in different ways, in the <u>Summa Contra Gentiles</u> and the <u>Summa Theologiae</u>. The point of this synthesis was to present, at that moment in history, the Christian revelation in terms of its own historical mission, the salvation of man, and, in the process, both to save and to use all human knowledge (including philosophy) as part of a sacred view of all reality. Such was the theology of St. Thomas, a religious effort to expound the origin and the end of all things within God's dialogue with man in the formation of the kingdom of God. The formation of the kingdom of God was the root source of St. Thomas' theological synthesis, even as it had been, under different historical conditions, the source of St. Augustine's synthesis in the <u>City of God</u>.

Second, within this religious and theological perspective, St. Thomas used philosophy, and eminently that part of philosophy called metaphysics, in order to achieve his theological synthesis. Externally, at least, we can explain this fact by the metaphysical character of the age--I mean, the pressure of the newly arrived Aristotelian philosophy in the Latin university world of the thirteenth century. In any case, the fact is there. Aristotelian philosophy, speaking its newly acquired Latin language, and what is called scholastic theology are contemporaneous phenomena in the thirteenth century, contemporaneous and interrelated. There really was no scholastic theology before the thirteenth century. St. Thomas' own scholastic theology had as one of its main historical objectives the assimilation of Aristotle's philosophy, and especially his metaphysics, physics, ethics and psychology. But to achieve this immense intellectual objective St. Thomas had to create many philosophical notions and principles of his own either as catalytic agents of the assimilative process or as its Christian foundation. In other words, St. Thomas had to create the Christian basis on which--and on which alone--the assimilation of Aristotle within Christian theology was possible. Thomistic philosophy as such, as distinguished from the Aristotelian philosophy that St. Thomas both assimilated and in the process transformed, consists almost

71

entirely of this Christian basis that made the historical entry of
Aristotle into the Latin world possible.

Third, the Christian philosophical foundation created by St.
Thomas for a thirteenth-century historical purpose was more than
anything else a metaphysical doctrine of being, but it included not
only the nature, principles and basic notions of such a doctrine,
but also its visible influence on philosophy as a whole. The Thomistic metaphysical notions and principles, both in themselves
and in their presence in the rest of philosophy, are that part of
St. Thomas' philosophy that time has not aged, even when it is a
fact that many present-day philosophers (including Catholic philosophers) have no taste for metaphysics or, at least, for St.
Thomas' metaphysics. In any case, though St. Thomas has no
philosophical synthesis of his own, he does have a metaphysical
outlook, expressed in metaphysical principles and notions that
can serve as the permanent ground of a philosophy, provided only
that one is willing to create a philosophy on the basis of such a
foundation. Now the only point that I wish to make in this conclusion is that, though St. Thomas might, and indeed can, contribute the metaphysical light by which a modern philosopher can
create a modern philosophy, that modern philosophy does indeed
have to be created as the work of a modern thinker, himself involved in a living and personal way in the modern world. What is
no less important, that modern philosophy must bear the signature
of its modern author, his signature and, above all, his responsibility. We are now in the presence of the fundamental decision that
I wish to propose concerning the current situation--not to say mis-
fortune--of Thomism as a philosophy.

It cannot be too often repeated that philosophical notions always
grow out of their world, serve it and then, like man himself and to
the same extent, grow old along with it. In this sense, philosophy
is as perishable as man is, as perishable and also as permanent.
Whether a philosophy exists as an autonomous synthesis or as the
instrument of a theology, it has the same chances of dying and not
dying that man himself does. Let me insist, first of all, on the
perishable side of philosophy. This consists in its general knowledge, its science and its engagement. Bergson's philosophy is today dated, and, without a single doubt, the time will come when
Heidegger's philosophical speculations will likewise be dated--
perhaps after the turn of the next century. The science of Kant is
the science of Newton, and that is certainly dated. Moreover,
what is the historical purpose of Bergson's philosophy if not to
refute the mechanism and the materialism of the late nineteenth

century? The spirit of Bergsonianism has clearly survived that historical purpose, but one can scarcely understand it as a living philosophy, or as a whole, apart from the historical engagement that it had. Similarly, can one really understand Plato apart from what has been called the "flowing philosophy" of Heraclitus, the relativistic theory of knowledge that the sophist Protagoras built on it, or the corruption of a Periclean Athens to which (at least in Plato's eyes) such a relativism in philosophy, education and politics inevitably led? Historical examples are endless, but they point to one lesson. Every genuine philosophy has been engaged in its own world and in the problems of that world; indeed, that is why it has existed. But, for this very reason, an important part of every philosophy dies with and in its world, namely, the part that is serving its age and is involved in it. It is, in a real sense, that part of his philosophy that a man spends among his contemporaries, in the belief, sometimes only obscurely per-ceived, that what will grow old in him and pass away with the pass-ing of his world is the servant of that which will survive.

A part of the philosophy of Plato has survived, but can we see that philosophy as a whole across twenty-three centuries and more? Can we see what was in Plato's mind when he looked at an Athens that had committed political murder in 399 B.C. by putting Soc-rates to death? Certainly we can see the historical event itself, we can see how Plato looked at it, but the anguished vision of the young Plato, followed by his blazing decision to become a philo-sophical reformer, this we cannot see in its concreteness, any more than we can see Plato himself. This is part of the perish-able dust of history, which we can visualize and respect from a distance because we can see from Plato himself how he looked at his age, how he was involved in it, and what principles guided his uncompromising search for truth and justice in a turbulent and dying Athens. But Plato is dead, his personal historical en-gagement died with him; so, too, St. Thomas is dead in his own world and for the same reason. Only, this is not the whole story, nor is it the whole lesson of history. The human intellect does not die in history, even when a man and his historical engagement live and die; the human intellect lives in history engaged but not dying, present and engaged in an absolute and undying way within the world of time.

This conclusion marks the true parting of the ways between a Thomism that has simply repeated a past philosophy and, at the very least, the possibility of a Thomism that owes to St. Thomas his metaphysical principles but not his philosophy and that is willing to take from him these principles and build on them the personal philosophy of a living thinker. Such a thinker deserves to be called a "Thomist" because his philosophy, far from being a repetition of St. Thomas' philosophy, is rather a new creation guided by those metaphysical principles of St. Thomas that were as free of time and age in the thirteenth century as they are today.

Does a philosophy such as I have described, it will be asked, really deserve to be called Thomistic? I can only say that it is Thomistic by virtue of its metaphysical grounding, and especially its notion of being. That metaphysics of being is in the end the only genuinely philosophical reason that anyone can have for being a Thomist or for thinking of himself as one. If he is a Thomist in this sense, the rest will follow from him. In any case, I am saying that metaphysics is that part of any philosophy that neither ages nor dies in history; it is therefore that part which not only raises the vision of a philosopher above the world of nature and the per-spective of the sciences of nature, but also gives to his philosophy its absolute anchorage as a work of the human mind.

The present misfortunes of philosophical Thomism are a fact, but no more than a fact. There is no danger that the metaphysics of St. Thomas will pass away as a result of these misfortunes. It is a permanently available reality in the writings of St. Thomas the theologian, which modern Thomists must learn to read with more historical concern than they have done in the past, and especially with more awareness of the theological state of phi-losophy in the Thomistic writings. The metaphysics of St. Thomas can guide and establish a modern philosophy, provided (to say it again) a living philosopher undertakes to create it and to live it in his world. St. Thomas cannot himself be the author of any modern philosophy, and it has been a costly experiment to think that he can. But those who are living can frame a philosophy in their own names and under their personal responsibility. That is the only way in which a true philosophy can exist, that is to say, by the engagement of the mind of a living philosopher, rooted in the soil of his own time. Hence, if the so-called Thomistic philosophy of the recent past is passing away, let us at least not allow it to disappear without learning a lesson from the event. What is pass-ing is an illusion, not a philosophy. It was an illusion not to rec-ognize that St. Thomas had the philosophy of a theologian, that is to say, a philosophy that his occupation made into a theology. It was no less an illusion to think that such a theologized reality, without an autonomy of existence or purpose of its own, could be pieced together as a living philosophy by others when it did not

74

begin as an autonomous philosophy in St. Thomas himself. We cannot, for whatever purposes, give to St. Thomas a philosophy that he did not have, and he cannot give us the philosophy that we can acquire only for ourselves. Let us recognize an important if harsh lesson. What is passing from history is not any teaching that St. Thomas himself created; what is passing is the philosophical Thomism that has had no author in the modern world. That passing has nothing to do with St. Thomas himself or with the intellectual edifice he erected in the thirteenth century. But that historical passing has a great deal to do with our appreciation of St. Thomas himself, his theology and his philosophy; it has also a great deal to do with ourselves. Let the impersonal Thomism of the last hundred years pass. But let us, who continue to read and follow St. Thomas, contribute our personal philosophical engagement at the moment of taking his principles from him. The result will be a new reality, and even a new Thomism, risking its life, like any other philosophy, in the human community.

Notes begin on page 321.

The Institutional Effects
of Anti-Philosophy

Wm. Oliver Martin

Colleges and universities are faced with a problem of curricular
chaos, and most of them are being forced, for various reasons, to
do something about it. This is especially true in matters concerned
with what is called "general" or "liberal" education. One basic
question: What kinds of knowledge should students have in order
to be "generally" or "liberally" educated? Yet without clarity
about the "order of knowledge" this question is unanswerable.
The "order of knowledge" is concerned with the discovery of
characteristics and structures that define different kinds of knowledge, together with that of the relationship of each kind of knowledge with other kinds in terms of relevant evidence. If this is
lacking, then one may expect a crisis in higher education.

In this essay we shall be concerned primarily with the status
of philosophy in the curriculum of the college and university.
This is not an arbitrary choice, nor does it reflect merely the
subjective interest of the writer. Any problem concerned with
the crisis of the university is one dealing primarily with the
purpose of a university, and that is fundamentally a problem

of the philosophy of education. For the problem of the "philosophical foundation of the university" is a fundamental one. There
is no such thing as the physical, chemical, biological, geological,
poetical, or bacteriological foundation of the university. Even to
deal with the "sociological foundation" is, in part, very much a
philosophical enterprise. Hence, if one suspects chaos in the
university, one may reasonably look to the philosophy department
and what it stands for.

Let us sharpen the issue. If there is philosophical truth, then
the university should conform to it. If it so conforms, then it
must insist that the students and the "public" know the truth,
for this is one of the most important of all human concerns. On
the other hand, if there is no truth, or if philosophical "statements" do not offer insights into truth, then no university should
pretend to have a philosophy department.

We shall be concerned primarily with the logic of a thesis,
and not with a degree of consistency manifested by any university.
For our present purpose, we shall refer to colleges and universities
in the United States, public and private, which have become separated from any religious heritage.

An order of knowledge is possible only if it is admitted (a) that there
is such a "thing" as truth and that truth is discovered, not created by
man; (b) that it is not a function of the man's interests, but rather
that truth is that by which man's interests are appraised; (c) that truth
is manifested in different kinds and modes according to the aspects
of Being studied; (d) that therefore there are different kinds of
knowledge because there are different kinds of evidence; (e) that the
fact that there are many kinds of knowledge does not preclude the
possibility that they all refer to aspects of Being and hence are
"one;" (f) that different kinds of knowledge may be related, one
way being that of "presupposition," as when we say that a knowledge of physics presupposes a knowledge of mathematics; (g) that
the integration of knowledge is a philosophical problem, one about
which there can also be truth.

Because of the peculiar relation of the order of knowledge to
institutions of higher education, disorder in knowledge will cause
disorder in the ends and purposes of the institution. The meaning,
the nature, and the structure of a university cannot be determined
apart from presuppositions about the order and kinds of knowledge. If those responsible for the forming of curricular programs
do not have such knowledge, they will simply "create" it. That
is, instead of being creative in the discovery of truth, they will
attempt to create "truth." Since knowledge can only be discovered,

77

not created, what will be created is opinion serving some practical interest--an interest that perhaps reflects a personal and/or institutional purpose, not an interest in the cooperative search for truth.

Generally speaking, a relatively intelligible order of knowledge is to be found in institutions concerned with technology and the theoretical physical sciences. For civil engineering a knowledge of physics is necessary, and for the physician a knowledge of anatomy is necessary. These truths about knowledge are so absolute that, if questioned, charity would demand the ascription of a sense of humor to the critic, for he could not be serious. By way of illustration, let us suppose that a first-year medical student informed the Dean that he did not like anatomy, and requested that he be allowed to drop the course and substitute one in Surgery. The humor of such a request would perhaps relieve the daily ennui. However, if the student were really serious and insistent he would be expelled.

Or, again, let us suppose that in this medical school there were a professor of anatomy who spent his time attempting to prove to the student that there is really no kind of knowledge that is anatomy, that there is only function, not structure. He explains that the course will be based on the history of "anatomical ideas." Furthermore, the students will be free to believe the ideas they wish. Otherwise, they would be indoctrinated with a given view, and that would imply that anatomical science is a closed system. It would also be denying the existential freedom of the student. Now, in this case the Dean would quickly dismiss the professor, despite the claims to the right of academic freedom. Even the A.A.U.P. would defend the Dean.

If we go to the liberal arts division of the college, we often find that the relationship of sanity to insanity is reversed. A student may not like philosophy because he finds it difficult. He discovers that he need not take a philosophy course; all that is required is that he take something in the "humanities." According to the catalogues, this requirement is necessary in order that he may become "cultured." He quickly changes his course, substituting Public Speaking for Philosophy. He might have taken anything from Arabic to Zoology. His choice was dictated by his desire to be "effective" in human relations. Perhaps his advisor assured him that such a course is more practical than philosophy because "the big problem today is the breakdown of human communications."

In fact--though for wrong reasons--the student was fortunate, for had he taken philosophy he might have found that what are grounds for firing an anatomy professor become a criterion for promoting a philosophy professor.

The logic teacher leads the student to believe that logic is really mathematics, or the converse. There is a course called "Metaphysics," but the student learns that there really is no metaphysical truth. In fact, metaphysical "propositions" are supposed to be cognitively meaningless. "God exists" really means "some people believe in God." The professor of "ethics" tells the student the course is passed around among the faculty, that it is his turn, but that there really is no such subject; or that there are as many "ethics" as there are people (or peoples) and there is no evidence for one rather than another. When we say that someone is good or just, we are not really talking about a person or his acts, but rather about ourselves, our feelings. The students are told that all this will be better understood when they take a course in "Analysis."

In short, a philosophy department is the only one in the university that insists that it has nothing to teach. The majority of faculties find this situation quite congenial. The scientists like it because they can now construct any "world view" that they wish, based upon the "unity of science." This is justified because the "philosophers" have told them that the only kind of knowledge is "science." The rest of the faculty likes it (with exceptions, of course) because they are free to be as "creative" as they wish. The administrators like it (pragmatists as they probably are) because there are no "first principles" to embarrass them in their "creatively" remolding the university to the "needs of the people" in this great era of "dynamic change." The Board of Trustees neither likes nor dislikes it, precisely because it has not the slightest idea of what is really going on. The chances are that it would be only by accident, or by mistaken appointment, that a member of the Board attained his status because he was philosophically qualified in matters having to do with the philosophy of education, in particular, because of his knowledge and wisdom concerning the purpose of a university.

One might wonder why, in this case, the philosophy department does not voluntarily abolish itself in accordance with its own "principles." This would be to mistake the motivations of the "philosopher." Without the department, he lacks an audience, status, and income. Since all definitions are nominal anyway,

the trick is to define "philosophy" to mean the negation of philosophy, i.e., "anti-philosophy." This can be and has been done
in various ways. It is the characterization of much, if not all,
of ideology--methodical materialism or "scientism" and certain
forms of existentialism.

Understandably some may consider this descriptive tour of a
university to be an uncharitable caricature, a gross oversimpli-
fication, and with respect to educators, a dastardly canard. On
the contrary, I suggest that thus far what has been said is actually
a disciplined and understatement. One might object that the leaders
of (state) higher education really intend the true, the good, the
beautiful; that they are human; that for many reasons a university's curricular and organizational setup is not as perfect and
reasonable as one might wish. And, one might ask, is it not a
lack of charity to evaluate and condemn the very intentions of
many professors and leaders in educational charge? Cannot
philosophers and scientists differ among themselves without
being accused of an evil conspiracy?

At this point we must pause to make a distinction, one which,
if not understood, makes criticism unintelligible and communication impossible. There is a difference between an evaluation
per se, and a description made because of a valuational concern.
An example will illustrate.

Suppose I say that Communism, based upon Marxism-Lenin-
ism, is atheistic; that Communists intend to control the world
and abolish religion; that this is an evil conspiracy. Am I evaluating or describing? With but one exception I am describing,
merely reporting. What I am saying is: this is in fact what the
Communists believe and what they intend. Is it, or is it not,
true? The question of values is irrelevant to the answer. The
dialectical materialist and the theist may agree each with the
other. They agree on what in fact each intends, to the degree
that each is consistent. There is disagreement, at least on the
part of an authentic theist, not on the intentions of Communists,
but on the truth of their beliefs.

I made only one evaluation: namely, that the conspiracy is evil.
There is agreement on the fact of the conspiracy. No Communist
would seriously deny it, for he points with pride to the Party's
own history of it. Now, in that the anti-Communist must appeal
to evidence when he condemns Communism, the knowledgeable
Communist might well respect him for his understanding of what
in fact Communism really is. Nevertheless, it is only because
the anti-Communist believes that Communism is essentially

evil that he calls attention to what Communism is, and warns against it.

The example is similar to our discussion of what goes on in many universities. That there are "philosophy-teachers" who (and philosophy departments that) deny even the possibility of philosophical truth is a statement of fact, although calling attention to such a fact undoubtedly reflects an evaluation to the effect that "something is wrong" in such a situation. When we report an intention we are not judging the intention. Now, to the question: Are there "philosophy-teachers" who teach that there is no philosophical truth, who teach, under the guise of philosophy, that there is no such knowledge as philosophy; in short, are there anti-philosophers who pretend to be philosophers and who pretend to teach "philosophy"?

To the naive, a full answer in terms of evidence requires volumes. In the space we have, we may give two examples in illustration--one that is theoretical, the other a mixture of theory and practice. Let us first consider the view of Professor Rudolf Carnap, one of the leaders of the Viennese Circle of some thirty-five or forty years ago.

In common with other members of the Viennese Circle, Carnap accepts as a "posit" the "verifiability criterion" of factual meaning, which states that the factual meaning of a sentence is the method of its verification. This was linked with the notion of sense experience as found in the empiricist tradition. Carnap tries to show that the only language possible is physical language, a universal language in terms of which all facts can be expressed. The only facts are those of the physical sciences, or those that can be reduced to them. "Our approach," he says, "has often been termed 'positivist'; it might equally well be termed 'materialist.'"[1] In fact, "the thesis that the physical language is the universal language might be denoted as methodical materialism" (p. 420). Carnap would prefer the term "physicalism." At any rate, if it is deduced that "If we have a single language for the whole of science the cleavage between different departments disappears. Hence the thesis of physicalism leads to the thesis of the unity of science" (p. 421).

Now in terms of this "philosophy," what happens to philosophy? It is simply reduced to nonsense. Language has two functions, expressive and cognitive. Scientific statements are cognitive, and hence truth and falsehood are relevant. All philosophical statements, other than those dealing with "logical syntax," are nonsensical so far as knowledge and truth and falsity are concerned. "So-called statements of metaphysics . . . can be only the subject matter of syntactical statements, e.g., of a statement which asserts their syntactical illegitimacy, i.e., which asserts that they are nonsense" (p. 399).

Ethics, as knowledge, vanishes. Empirical ethics is psychology, and not ethics at all. Normative ethics is "a pretended investigation of what is good and what is evil, what it is right to do and what it is wrong to do" (p. 430). Actually, "it does not assert anything and can neither be proved nor disproved" (p. 430). Hence, there can be no ethical knowledge. Ethical statements are meaningful, however, as emotive expressions.

Epistemology (the theory of knowledge), in any sense other than logical analysis, is likewise disposed of (cf. pp. 394, 453). The same befalls the "philosophy of nature."

> As there is no philosophy of nature, but only a philosophy of natural science, so there is no special philosophy of life or philosophy of the organic world, but only a philosophy of biology; no philosophy of mind or philosophy of history or philosophy of society, but only a philosophy of historical and social sciences; always remembering that the philosophy of a science is the syntactical analysis of the language of that science. (p. 455)

Traditionally there has been "philosophical psychology," as well as "empirical" or "experimental" psychology, but Professor Carnap leaves nothing untouched. He says:

> When we have eliminated metaphysical problems and doctrines from the region of knowledge or theory, there still remains two kinds of philosophical questions: psychological and logical. Now we shall eliminate the psychological questions . . . from philosophy. Then, finally, philosophy will be reduced to logic alone . . . (p. 433)

Carnap has thus disposed of the whole of philosophy. And what about logic? That has vanished, too. For logic simply is not "the syntactical analysis of the language of science." Only the word is preserved.

It would seem a fair judgment to say that Carnap together with other members of the Viennese Circle wish to abolish philosophy. Further, they would have to deny that their own position is a philosophical one. Such a judgment is hardly necessary, how-

82

ever, in that we may take Carnap's word for it. In the introduction to a paper "The Physical Language as the Universal Language of Science, " Carnap says:

The reader may find it easier to understand the main article if I preface it by some remarks on the general nature of the views held by the Viennese Circle to which I and my friends belong. In the first place I want to emphasize that we are not a philosophical school and that we put forward no philosophical thesis whatsoever (p. 394).

A stronger declaration of war could not be made in the intellectual realm. The position taken is that of anti-philosophy. It is a misuse of language to use the term "philosophy" to stand both for what is denied and for denial itself.[2]

Thus far we have examined the war only in abstract. Let us now consider its institutionalization when an anti-philosopher became a member of a philosophy department. One's immediate reaction might be that such a state of affairs could not happen. But it did.

Although Carnap put the stamp on his own positivism upon the recognized image of the movement [the Viennese Circle], Schlick was its catalyst. In 1922 Schlick was appointed Professor of Philosophy in Vienna University. The appointment was initiated by a group of scientists led by Hans Hahn. Schlick had been trained in physics . . . [3]

Of course, once an anti-philosopher has been brought into a philosophy department by scientists, it becomes easier to bring in another anti-philosopher, and so on. This has occurred in recent decades, especially in public institutions. Hence, these institutions find both philosophy and authentic religion rather embarrassing.

At this point let us be clear as to what we are saying. We have reported a state of affairs, what Carnap and the Viennese Circle stood for, namely, the destruction of philosophy. Whether Carnap and others of similar persuasion are correct is not at the moment the issue. Rather, the issue is a logical one. Either there is or there is not philosophical knowledge. A university simply cannot have it both ways. If there is to be philosophy, then there is no room for anti-philosophers and, logically, the converse is also the case. If the university tries to have it both ways, then it institutionalizes an absolute contradiction. A contemporary tragedy is that this is not more often seen for what it is: institutionalized schizophrenia.

Any one of a number of universities could be cited, but let us choose what in the public mind is considered one of the greatest of them all--Harvard. During World War II a committee of Harvard professors was appointed to consider the problem of "general education," and a report was written and published.[4] In making a brief examination of the Report, the particular problem we shall be concerned with is the place to be given the philosophical and scientific (experimental or natural) disciplines. This problem is important, for the Report itself is a major manifestation of the modern "Philosophy of Education."

Much of the first part of the Report is philosophical in nature, which is what one would expect in a discussion on general education. We are told that such education must be moral, productive of wisdom; it should enable students "to think effectively, to communicate thought, to make relevant judgments, to discriminate among values" (p. 65); "all modes of inquiry must be adapted to the material under consideration" (p. 154); not all subjects are of equal value (pp. 38, 57); "the object of philosophy would appear to be the bringing together of both facts and values" (p. 62). There is the implication that philosophy is not only a valuable but a necessary part of general education.

Science is defined in terms of subject matter and the kind of proposition sought. The scientific method alone is not sufficient for all knowledge (p. 154). Science is "restricted" (p. 150), describes only a certain aspect of things and events (p. 152), is not normative but merely describes "things as they are" (p. 151), is concerned with repeatable phenomena, not the uniqueness of events (pp. 60, 151), and is concerned only with a special kind of evidence (p. 152). "Science is prepared to deal only with those aspects of reality which lend themselves to its methods of appraisal. Great confusion in the public mind has resulted from the failure to appreciate this fundamental and self-imposed limitation" (p. 152). There is no confusion of subject matter or of types of probanda in defining the nature of philosophy and science. Philosophy is admitted to have content, to be based on types of propositions different from the scientific, and to be valuable and necessary in general education.

However, when in Chapter 5 they apply the theory to Harvard, we find that the analysis is entirely forgotten. What is the place of

84

philosophy in general education? It is really difficult to say. "One of the obstacles in the way of an agreement is uncertainty about the role of philosophy" (p. 209). No analysis is made of the nature of philosophy. After mentioning that since the 18th century the natural and social sciences have apparently taken over its function, and that "it would be serving no good purpose to require every student to take a course in philosophy" (p. 209), suggestion is made that it might be helpful to those to whom it might be helpful, but not "for those to whom the methods of philosophy appear abstract and unreal" (p. 209). Philosophy is no longer something to be defined in terms of subject matter. Just what it is, is rather mysterious. It seems to be concerned with what some other disciplines are, but by the use of some peculiar "methods" which apparently have no logical justification in terms of the subject matter studied, and which can be accepted or rejected at the student's caprice according to the psychological criterion of whether or not they "appear unreal."

We find the same gulf between theory and practice when dealing with the question of science courses. Apparently, it is right in theory to speak of types of probanda, kinds of subject matter, the meaning of general education, the nature and structure of knowledge, but these things should not be taken seriously in practice. Science is no longer restricted, descriptive of the general aspect of repeatable spatio-temporal phenomena. Nor is the body of science obtained by the use of special methods. "The body of science includes not only special knowledge and skills but conceptual inter-relations, a world-view, and a view of the nature of man and knowledge . . ." (p. 222). "The claim of general education is that the history of science is a part of science. So are its philosophy, its great literature, and its social and intellectual context." (p. 222).

Our present interest is not the psychological and institutional causes which, 1) confuse the two quite contradictory views of philosophy and science, 2) hide under "the claim of general education" an irresponsible use of the term "science" (by the committee's own admission, p. 152), and 3) produce blindness to the fact that a discipline that is related to science is not the same thing as that to which it is related. We would merely point out the consequences. There will be no dearth of "philosophical ideas" as a result of the practical program; students will receive such ideas from every teacher.

Lacking will be responsible philosophical reasoning and analysis. This describes much of higher education; it hardly

85

need be dignified by a committee report. In the earlier part of the Report, where some analysis is made and differences in subject matter are perceived, the function of philosophy as an integrating subject is admitted. However, in constructing the practical program no one seems to know what philosophy is, and subject matters are confused. Under the guise of something called "science" a student is handed a philosophy; it is a "scientific world-view" (p. 221). But the educational wells have been poisoned. How can the student ever question such a position when the tools of rational criticism are taken away? If there is only science, and not philosophy, how can one possibly learn any other than a "scientific world-view?" If the philosopher doesn't agree, then he has "only a remote appreciation of the nature of science" (p. 222).

It is easy for philosophers to blame scientists for a situation of this kind. But, however responsible the latter may be, the guilt of philosophers is even greater. They have reaped the consequences of philosophical nihilism they have sown in the past. Having themselves broken down the order of knowledge through various anti-metaphysical tendencies, they should not be surprised if others are "uncertain" about the nature of philosophy. The scientist, in turn, may be reminded that responsible philosophy is not obtained by verbal magic, namely, the equivocal use of the term "science." The propositions of science constitute one kind of subject matter; the propositions about science as a kind of knowledge constitute a quite different kind of subject matter. One may be an authority in the former, and be quite ignorant about the latter. The latter problem is that of the order of knowledge, something quite different from the order of atoms or other material things.

We have called attention to the growing interest of specialists in their own field of knowledge qua knowledge. In itself this is potentially good. But "interest" is not the same thing as "knowledge." The historian may ask: What is history? The scientist may ask: What is science? Both may attempt to answer their respective questions. But unless they know what they are doing, they may only increase existing confusion by rationalizing the fragmentation and disorder of knowledge.

Understand that when the historian considers the nature of "history" he is engaged in an enterprise that is outside of history qua history. When the scientist considers the nature of "science" (experimental) he must understand that the problem he is dealing with is not itself a problem of experimental science. These are philosophical problems, each requiring a different method of approach, and, in particular, evidence of a different order. In short, if the scientist is to consider the nature of his science as such, then he must bring philosophical knowledge to bear on the philosophical problem. And when he does so he is functioning as a philosopher, for better or for worse. It will be for the better if he has disciplined himself first in philosophical studies, and then attempts to see his special subject in the light of other kinds of knowledge, in terms of a whole pattern of relationships. It will be for the worse if he magnifies his own small part and attempts to interpret the whole in terms of it. It should be noted that in both cases the scientist is "broadening out beyond his speciality."

Volumes could be filled illustrating how scholars identified professionally with special fields of knowledge have become very much "interested" in general or liberal education, have "broadened out" beyond their own fields simply by encroaching upon others in the most irresponsible fashion, and in the name of "coordination" or "integration."

We have dealt with the crisis in the university only with reference to the nature of philosophy and its negation. Of importance is the understanding of the meaning of anti-philosophy, and not merely the particular illustrations of it; for philosophy by its very nature is such that its perversion will affect almost everything else.

With the withering away of political philosophy negated by positivism, political science is reduced to behavioristic "social science." Social science, in turn, may have little to do with the truly "social," just as, under the same influence, natural science may have nothing to do with the "nature of things." A serious student who finds the philosophy department denying philosophy in the name of "language analysis" may go over to the English department, only to hear "philosophizing" done ideologically by English teachers who may care little for English. Along with this the student may become acquainted with the theater of the absurd, the anti-novel, the anti-hero. The tragedy is that, although he will hear much about "values," he may forever--and without knowing it--be separated from wisdom about the nature of virtue. Theology may be taught by an anti-theologian, and, through the "cult of sincerity," anti-love may be presented as love. Morality will be denied in the name of morality by what, I am sure, is a new "linguistic transformation rule," i.e., the "old" immorality will be defined as the "new morality."

87

We have analyzed only and offered no solutions. Solutions will come gradually with increased concern on the part of students, teachers, and boards of trustees. In a sense it is always later than we think. But it is not too late. The seriousness of the crisis has penetrated even to Time magazine. In an essay titled "What (If Anything) to Expect from Today's Philosophers, "[5] the editors recognize in a general way what we have tried to spell out in particular. They point to the fact that "philosophy today is bitterly segregated." After pointing out why, they offer some hope in suggesting that "the philosophers are beginning to re-invent philosophy." But the hope is a cautious one, for the last sentence warns: "But the shadows are deep and the time for an awakening is at hand."[6]

If this is true, and I believe it is, then two suggestions would be in order. First, that philosophy departments have teachers who differ because they believe in truth, not because they do not. Second, that philosophy departments be made as respectable on the campus as, say, the physical education department. This is asking a lot, I suppose, especially on the part of state universities whose certainty that man has a body is in startling contrast to its certainty that man has a soul.

In summary, however, may I be so presumptuous as to utter a warning? Moral and intellectual nihilism develops not in the minds of workers and peasants, but in the ideological interests of "intellectuals" (not scholars), in institutions of "higher learning" which have become separated from the moral and religious tradition which gave birth to them. Man is conceived to be essentially a biosocial organism. Knowledge is reduced to the formal and (empirically) factual, and the practical is reduced to the "expedient." The ethical, metaphysical, and theological subjects are thought rationalizations of timid, uncourageous, anti-progressive men who lack the skill to manipulate material reality. Generations of students emerge from such chaos unable to distinguish wisdom from sophistry. There is a gradual dulling of the moral consciousness and the ability to distinguish between responsible differences of opinion based on knowledge, and the incredible differences of irresponsible opinion that can arise precisely because no one understands exactly what he is talking about, since words and concepts have been reduced to ideological weapons.

The honest and concerned student is correct when he senses that something is wrong.

Notes begin on page 321.

Philosophy Fulfilled in Christianity

Maurice Blondel

Catholicism is nothing if it is not everything. Its very name would be a lie if anything at all escaped its design, the only one intended by God's providence. This means that we must reject absolutely the widespread notion of a religion that would have its moments of glory or its restricted domain but would not permeate the whole atmosphere we breathe and all the forms of our activity. Without fully noticing it, many people live and argue as if nature, science, and public life lay outside the concern of Christ. For them the only genuine Catholics are "religious professionals."

We seek to justify a different attitude. Philosophy, in our opinion, is the fullest expression of accumulated research into nature, life, and the meaning of reality. By its witness it should show that thought and action finally testify in favor of the responses that Christianity brings to the anxieties of consciousness. . . .

On the one hand, we will have to show that the interior preparations necessary for Christianity do not appear in our midst as a kind of growth foreign to human nature as such. On the other

hand, we will be all the more bound to preserve its irreducible
originality by making it perfectly clear that, however much individuals prepare for its reception, Christianity comes into their
lives as something absolutely novel. Though it imposes an absolute
obligation on man, who cannot with impunity sidestep his one supernatural calling and destiny, Christianity remains, even so, an ut-
terly gratuitous gift of God.

Man's restlessness

Our effort to insert Christian thought into the stream of human
thought begins by recapturing, as best we can, the history of
mental activity in its furthest origins, "the birth of intelligence."
An inquiry into that birth-process reveals not only a succession
of progresses and partial successes but also setbacks, which can
be accounted for only by that mind-set which has rightly been
called "religious expectation." If human thought is honest and
consistent about its strong and weak points and is on guard not to
sin against the light by either downgrading or overrating itself,
then it normally passes beyond the visible world, the realm of
science, metaphysical speculation, and pleasures of the spirit--
only to find awaiting it at the end as at the beginning that restlessness for which nature holds no remedy.

The typical state of humanity is found realized in two historically circumscribed facts. First, there is the original promise and
messianic hope, entrusted classically to the Jewish people but
found in different degrees of intensity in all ages. This unrest,
despite many disappointments, is ever born anew in unshakable
confidence. Only by being untrue to oneself can this experience
be ignored or shrugged off. What drives this restlessness forward? How explain the fact that human thought is always in dis-
equilibrium, somehow constantly getting ahead of itself?

But history presents human thought to us in another state, that
of Catholic security, in which alone thought seems finally to
have found the solution to its riddle, the secret of its destiny, its
true place. These two thought-states correspond. Outside this
call and perfectly adapted response, all is difficulty and incom-
prehensibility. Outside this correlation, thought stands in the
anguish of those voyagers Plotinus depicts for us, on the shore of
the sea in starless darkness.

Limits of intelligence

We wish to set forth the conditions necessary for the emergence of consciousness and mental activity as well as the limits inevitably imposed on every finite intelligence. Fundamentally, thought yearns for the perfect unity of itself with what is, in imitation of the perfect union of the Father with his Word. But so divine a union is inexorably reserved to God. However strongly illumined by uncreated light it be, human thought must fall short of the perfection of God's thought.

Revelation does, however, offer us through grace the possibility of overcoming this disproportion between human and divine thought. We can become, as St. John says, "children of God" and sharers in the divine light even to the point of one day beholding It as it is, face to face. Christianity, then, despite its unforeseeable and gratuitous character, appears no longer as something foreign to us, an intrusion, an enslavement or degradation of man. No, it bursts upon our vision as something longingly half-awaited in that it crowns the whole edifice of nature and thought.

We now understand better why Christianity is rightly called Good News. It is indeed a remarkably new thing, yet at the same time as ancient as the upward surge of creation from the beginning. Thus are reconciled two characteristics of Christianity which at first seemed incompatible: its absolute transcendence and its inmost preparation at the very core of the universe.

Looking deeper into what thought is, the better to grasp the Christ-plan, we see how "God owed us nothing, yet more he could not do for us." God's creating and uplifting man are both pure liberality. Yet he could have done nothing more grand for us than what he actually did.

Meditating on what thought is in itself and on the immense difficulty involved in elevating created entities to the capacity for thinking, one stands astonished at this marvel of creaturely elevation. Absolutely speaking, the act of thought is the inmost life of the Holy Trinity itself, where unity is consummated in the light reflected from the Father to his Son in the reciprocity of the Spirit's love. Outside this trinitarian realm there is nothing but darkness. How possibly conceive a light kindled outside this fire? Let us not imagine a brightness other than the divine light of God. Nothingness does not exist. Better to imagine that to produce creatures, especially spiritual beings capable of knowing and loving, God, according to the expression of St. Paul (Phlp 2:7), had made room in himself to allow creatures to establish their own life and thought

91

in him. But they remain themselves while enjoying this share in divinity. Intelligent beings cannot by some absorption be confounded with God, like sparks that fall back into and are lost in the fire from which they come. Thus the divine love and power are one in simultaneously producing and limiting thinking beings which, while sharing in the divine light, are distinguished from it by the limitations that are the very condition of a personal life, proper beatitude, a new extension of the reign and glory of God.

Similar conclusions

The problem of thought, studied as freely and deeply as possible by a philosophy bent on rendering intelligible the genesis of mental activity, comes to conclusions conformed to the demands of Catholic theology. These demands can be summarized from a rational standpoint in three propositions: (1) There is no other light but that of God and his Word; this light enlightens and vivifies every man who comes into this world. (2) But no creature can naturally and completely participate in the divine thought-life. Only by highly deficient analogy can created intelligence be said to strive for, without attaining, this unity of being and truth, like a sun which cannot be gazed upon directly. (3) Nonetheless, if to think in its fulness is proper to God alone, whom the ancients already spoke of as Pure Act and Thought of Thought, it is possible to attain by grace an infusion of that light, a participation in the divine spirit.

So Christianity does not blacken the darkness of our natural faculties. If we want to embrace it, it affords us the power to become children of God and to communicate with the eternal Word incarnate in our nature. This Word dwells in each of the faithful and mysteriously occupies the center of the soul, which otherwise remains dark and empty. Still, the soul is destined for him, and by him and with him becomes the principle of illumination for even the divine life in us. All creaturely thought is really oriented towards the desire of such a solution, but its terminus remains naturally inaccessible and, therefore, gratuitous on God's part.

Two characteristics of Christianity are hereby recognized and reconciled. Conforming to the essential drive of the intelligence invincibly yet fruitlessly aspiring to see and possess God, Christianity can be refused to intelligence without injustice. No necessity makes God the debtor of his creature; and the supernatural gift that establishes our thought in intimate union with the Word remains purely liberality, sublime discovery, charitable initiative.

Problem of action

Like the problem of thought, the problem of action leads us to conclusions that ought to be made clear in order to show us still better the secret grandeur of the divine plan as we find it set forth in Catholicism. The problem of action is: How can there be a truly active secondary cause? Most of our actions are really reactions to influences we undergo. Is absolute initiative, then, possible for created entities?

Malebranche, Leibnitz, and certainly Spinoza held that we are moved even when we believe we do the moving. The post-Kantian metaphysicians and the immanentist philosophers of recent times erred in the opposite direction. So convincingly did action seem to imply an absolute commencement that they concluded by suppressing the Pure Act of God to make room for becoming, and especially for the obscure though sovereign élan of man. How can philosophy from a Christian point of view do justice to imperative and well-founded demands such as these?

We take as point of departure for our inquiry the invincible impression we have of being genuine causes. Yet unmistakable analyses reveal that in most of our actions we undergo a variety of influences. We are torn between the evidence of our constant passivity and the conviction that we nonetheless possess a genuine initiative without which we would not be conscious of being active, nor for that matter, of being passive, nor even of being conscious beings. Any profound study of action runs up against this passivity-activity dilemma.

Liberty involves destiny

So formidable a problem is this that thinkers have often disguised it or limited themselves to enunciating the terms necessary for a solution without making distinctly conceivable the relation between these terms. Doubtless, to formulate the problem is no mean accomplishment. It is indeed the merit of the Thomistic doctrine to have fearlessly affirmed simultaneously with the divine pre-motion the liberty of the rational creature. Admittedly in this view it is hard to grasp how God wills our volitions to be free while he alone establishes their possibility and realization. In a marvelous formulation of descriptive exactitude St. Bernard determined that each of the agents, God and man, was the author of the whole act. But does his description resolve the problem? A methodical and complete study of human action should at least strive to resolve it.

Liberty does not consist in partial choices independent of one another. All fragmentary decisions only set in motion or heighten life's major decision and partake of liberty only insofar as they are somehow related to that supreme alternative in which our very destiny is involved. True, presented in apparently trivial circumstances, lesser objects sometimes become vehicles for total option, but only insofar as they put at stake our fundamental attitude toward the good, duty, fidelity to the light and to our calling.

Therefore, rather than consider liberty and action in their occasional manifestations, we ought to pose the problem where it truly exists. The question of liberty of action forces us into a dilemma: whether to participate in the divine initiative by identifying our will with the very will of the First Cause, or through a selfish autonomy to say, "I will not serve." Thus philosophy poses the same problem from below that Christianity poses from above, and in practically identical terms. At what depths rational inquiry and religious demands meet! This convergence, neither arbitrary nor avoidable, manifests the fundamentally realistic character of Christianity; for all the avenues of philosophy, painstakingly traveled to their limit, converge toward this central intersection where we seek to establish our lookout point.

Still we have not yet arrived there. Though seeing more clearly than heretofore the terms that must be joined, we do not yet see why this cooperation of two so disproportionate activities, God's and man's, is demanded. Nor do we see how this union will be achieved, which will leave man the dignity of being a cause and the possibility of a quasi-divine action ultimately meriting beatitude. Rather than press this problem, we wish now to travel another road and show how the problem of being, like that of thought and action, leads philosophy by a process intrinsic to herself to the same solutions that adumbrate what Christianity offers us as a fulness filling and infinitely surpassing the aspirations, premonitions, and entreaties of every rational and religious expectation.

Problem of being

The problem of being, first broached by ancient philosophy, has come to appear so profound that modern philosophers often skirt it and betake themselves to the problem of knowledge, as if the critique of our faculties could exhaust philosophy and cause ontological curiosity to disappear. Many maintain that our intelligence reaches only phenomena, relations, becoming, subjective states, and immanent activity. Hence, Being-in-itself and even being-in-us is no longer studied as a mysterious reality but is relegated to the history of positive science and to the progress of the spirit in constructing an edifice of universal relativity.

Difficulty remains

To juggle a problem, however, is not to solve it. From diverse quarters a neo-realism is arising, and the obscure but no less insuppressible problem of God is being forced on the attention of the most liberal and critical minds. So the ancient difficulty reappears: Is there an absolute being? And if there is, how conceive other beings alongside or in it? Must we with Spinoza absorb into the Unique Substance all that exists? Or, if there are other beings that truly deserve the name, how find room for them in the fulness of Being-in-and-by-itself?

If beings really are, the problems of their reality is as difficult and necessary to solve as is the problem of the reality of the divine Absolute. Philosophy continues its search for the key to this double enigma. Here again, bold investigation should prepare us for the reception of Christian revelation. Being-in-itself, this revelation tells us, is no crude, unthinking substance, nor pure thought without reliance and love, but a very trinity of persons in one indivisible nature. Though completely sufficient in its perfect, ever active life, Providence has out of sheer liberality called created entities to a participation in its infinite beatitude. Assuredly, being in such finite entities is not immediately equal to the thought of and familiarity with an end only glimpsed and desired. Yet this congenital disproportion, absolutely necessary for distinguishing the Creator from every conceivable creature, does not impede a progressive assimilation, a meritorious cooperation, and a union which, with no confusion of natures, can become filial adoption and ultimately, in theological language, a joyous fruition of the divine happiness itself. This manner of being, then, has at once a subsistence proper to itself and an inalienable dependence on its unique and sovereign cause. It owes nothing to any being but God who, in a sense, is all in each. This being of creatures is so real that spirits endowed with liberty can separate themselves from the divine life to the extent that it were better had they not been born. Yet this separation is their own doing and is possible only because the union, to be good, supposes voluntary option and the free use of divine grace.

Unique problem

We see, then, to what lengths we must go to give the problem of being an irreducible significance. This problem must not be confounded with the problems of thought and action. Precisely because our thoughts do not fully comprehend their object and our actions never attain their total end, being in us cannot be reduced to its idealistic or pragmatic aspects. Between the consciousness we have of ourselves and the term of our aspirations, yawns, so to speak, a naturally unbridgeable gulf. The problem of being remains unique because being in us is never only what we know or what we accomplish but resides in that mysterious center in us which no natural good nor light of reason can at bottom fully satisfy or illumine. It should not then surprise us that philosophy, unable to solve this problem, often turns away from it. Nevertheless, to put us in the presence of what the Areopagite called the abysmal profundities of every created being remains its strict duty.

Thus by all the avenues a bold philosophy ought to follow, we come to unveil certain real profundities of being whose existence we cannot deny and whose depths we cannot plumb. In so doing we understand the philosophical sense of the following assertion by which some wish to summarize the Thomistic doctrine of finite being: If the mind recapitulates in itself the whole of nature, this is because it itself is essentially capable of God and because our reason is made for being in all its variety and plenitude.

But in thus describing philosophical demands in their fulness, are we not secretly inspired by Christian revelation? Yes, in a sense. However, as Fénelon wisely observed, a philosophy which without deviating, erring, or stopping short runs the full course of its development to its legitimate goal is really a "romanticizing of philosophy." Why not, then, turn on more brightly the dim light already available to us? Why not distinguish between what can and ought to be accessible to well-ordered reason and what can be accessible only to revelation? A comparison may help us understand this often misunderstood procedure. We listen to an opera. But, though hearing voices singing, we do not catch the singers' words. Put, however, before our eyes a libretto and we immediately understand the entire text being sung. Will we say that libretto alone causes us to hear the words? No, because we already perceived the opera's melody, and without this perception the written text would not have instilled in us the musical and literary joy derived from it. In somewhat the same

way revelation confirms, makes precise, purifies, and universal-
izes many truths themselves not beyond all rational capacity.

Do we hereby risk presenting Christianity as the simple complement of a philosophy that would by its demands pre-establish
the foundation and even the framework of the supernatural order?
This most welcome question really leads us to the problem of the
specifically Christian, which no amount of human speculation can
possibly anticipate. Christianity has rightly been called the Gospel
or Good News, for it is a novelty so grand that its riches remain
unknown to people apparently very familiar with it. "He is among
you and you do not know Him" is as true today as it was in the days
of the Baptist. We will, then, escape the criticism that our entire
prior effort may have suggested. Either, our objectors say, we
seek by an immanent study of human nature to prove the conformity of reason and grace, or we so suspend nature on the supernatural that it now seems impossible to remain on the purely
natural level. In a word, we oscillate between the abuse of im-
manence and the abuse of transcendence, each equally ruinous
for the equilibrium of Catholicism.

Two conclusions

At the end, therefore, of this essay devoted to the philosophical
preparation for Christianity, we must insist on these two conclusions: (1) The solutions that philosophy can and ought to propose in answer to the problems of thought, action, and being not
only leave the field open for Christian doctrine but show in this
doctrine an unhoped for answer; a marvelous correspondence to
our longings, to be sure, but in such a way that no presumptuous
demand on our part can result from this correspondence. Human
speculation, far from itself pretending to supply the answers,
spontaneously recognizes its impotence and indigence. (2) Imperfect as its deficiencies make it, the natural order could remain
viable in itself and be squared with the divine justice and goodness. Let no one accuse us, then, of falling from Charybdis into
Scylla. The role of philosophy is here doubtless delicate and even
perilous; all the more reason for not shrinking from a task that is
only formidable because it ought to be very profitable.

Notes begin on page 323.

PART TWO

Faith in Christ and Institutional Religion

The Church in Crisis

Henri de Lubac, S.J.

For some time now it has become commonplace to point out that we are witnessing a crisis of civilization. In making such an observation we have no need of Teilhard de Chardin's quasi-prophetic intuition of nearly half a century ago which anticipated and predicted this crisis. It is evident to all of us that the crisis we are now witnessing is more acute and more accelerated than those of other periods of history. Until only recently we spoke of it as a "mutation." Today, when describing a new phase of this crisis, another word is fast becoming prevalent: the word "destruction." In a recent paper on the subject of violence in the fine arts presented to the Académie des Sciences Morales in Paris, Monsieur André Chastel expressed himself in these words: "Our age will most probably be characterized by the rapidity of development which has led to what may be called, by anticipation, an irresistible and mysterious autodestruction."[1]

Monsieur Chastel is an historian of art, and art frequently exercises--in its extreme inventive forms and pursuits which may at times appear scandalous to us--an anticipatory role.[2] But we need not turn to art to know where we stand. The frenzy of violence which is exploding or is latent in different areas of our planet, whether it is feared as a wild force or seen as giving rise to the hope of another society--of another humanity--both new and wonderful, is not something accidental and short-lived. A shrewd observer of the contemporary scene, Monsieur Erik Weil, predicted it some fifteen years ago:

> Today, the contradiction between private life and society is a fact, and one which poses a problem to our way of thinking. . . . It is true that most men in modern society do not express an awareness of their problematic situation in so many words; it is even possible that they have no such awareness, at least consciously. But whether it is registered or not, it exists and it acts; the proof is to be found in the number of those who are unbalanced (those who classify themselves as being unbalanced) in the most advanced of societies: the suicidal, the neurotic, those converts to false religions . . . , alcoholics, drug addicts, criminals "for no reason," and those who chase impressions and distractions. The same feeling of dissatisfaction explains the movements of protest against the reality of society, the harangues and sermons of those who rebel against everything and rise up in protest not against this or that feature of the social organization, but against organization insofar as it is characterized by calculating rationality and who set up, as an alternative to the unpleasant reality of dehumanization and reification the abstract dream of pure unregulated existence.[3]

Just two years ago Erik Weil was able to make the same diagnosis with even more assurance, and the facts would seem to bear him out quite emphatically:

> The working society has domesticated the animal let loose by the struggle between individuals and groups. Society has emptied man. . . . It has done away with exterior pressure and the pressure brought by arbitrary masters, but it has not freed man, if every liberation of man is a liberation for a meaningful life. . . . Society has universalized man by rationality but without allowing him to state what his undertaking means. It provides time for the individual to

enjoy himself; it does nothing, it can do nothing, to enable him to think, to give meaning to the world, his world, and to himself in his world. The result is the boredom which comes from infinite and senseless progress, boredom from which only disinterested violence offers escape.[4]

Partners in crisis

Paul Ricoeur, in an independent way, makes the very same diagnosis when speaking of a world, our own, which he sees as more and more rational and at the same time more and more meaningless. "It is not surprising," he says, "that, in this age of planning, the activity of intelligence, having been reduced to the laws of computer-thinking, must be paired with nothing else than the radical protest of the beatnik or the absurdity of a purposeless crime."[5] I would add that it is no less surprising that the crisis has affected especially the young, and that throughout the world it has taken the form of a university crisis, and that it has resulted in a universal confrontation.

Confrontation

Nor should we be surprised if, in principle if not in all its manifestations and in its nihilist issues, this violent crisis gave rise to an echo of sympathy, at times ardent, in many Christian consciences. How, after all, could the Christian not be expected to react against a system which misunderstands and misinterprets the dignity of man, which smothers his soul, and which shuts him off from hope? How could he avoid seizing this opportunity to show his troubled brother the meaning which, from the first preaching of the gospel of Christ, illuminated the life of his community? This is exactly what did result in more than one instance. There was no lack of young Christians in particular, strong in their faith, who carried to others the light which was within them. On the other hand--and this may seem surprising--this same crisis resounded with great force both within and against the church, because this very same spirit of confrontation, once it had taken hold of so many believers, turned them against the community to which they belong: and at one and the same time, as they continued to be fascinated by this modern world, they were confronted, challenged by others. Of course, the present situation within the Catholic church cannot be reduced to such a paradox. Yet this paradox is one of its most visible characteristics, and it is this

102

very paradox that we must sketch, at least in its broad outlines.

The generalized confrontation of today is two-fold; it attacks the structures of established society as well as the intellectual patrimony which this society hands on to us; and it does so right at its very roots. And in both of these areas we see it at work at the very heart of Catholicism. [6]

We are not speaking here, needless to say, of serious criticisms, limited in objective, which come from competent and responsible men, men concerned with just reforms or adaptations which have become necessary--although the most decisive renewals stem less from the plans of reformers than from the creations of saints. Nor am I talking about those criticisms-- even those which are excessive and exaggerated--which are inspired by love. I do not want to give the impression that all the questions being raised today are to be looked upon as subversive attacks on the church. Quite the contrary. The last word has yet to be written; "everything has not been set down for us and handed to us. We still have much to accomplish, much ground to cover, much searching to do."[7] But I feel obliged to point out--and each day brings us new examples--a bitter and vindictive disposition, which has decided ahead of time to spare nothing; a will to run down, to speak ill of, a sort of aggressiveness directed equally against the church's past and its present-day existence, against all forms of its authority, against all its structures, at times not even bothering to distinguish between what stems from historical contingency and what is essential to it--i.e. what is of divine institution.

There is a straining, a sifting at work in certain minds, which tends to push into the shadows all that the church has accomplished over the centuries, all that it has brought to fruition in the human personality, what it has discovered, what it has constantly renewed through charity, and what it has drawn from the Scriptures and continues to sustain in the souls of its children. In innumerable writings, whose arbitrariness exceeds that of works quite justly denounced as being deformed by apologetic objectives, its history is misrepresented in a detestable way.

Tradition misunderstood

It is, of course, quite easy, faced with an infinite number of facts and considering human misery, to find things to poke fun at or to be indignant about. Its tradition, which is so frequently ignored, is felt only as a weight to be carried, whereas it is before all else a living, actualizing force. Because we do not make the effort to attach ourselves to this tradition we look upon it as something of a past long since dead.

In addition, the authority of the church is seen as a mere exterior power, and a hostile one at that; and when it is exercised it is looked upon as tyrannical. Its magisterium is only endured with impatience; its declarations are considered abusive, bitterly debated, and at times rejected entirely. There are even those who do not hesitate to stir up public opinion against it. It would seem that some have lost even the slightest inkling of the very nature of and requirements for Christian freedom.

I stand in amazement at the good conscience of so many sons of the church who, never having accomplished anything exceptional in their own right, who have neither taken time to think nor ever really suffered, who do not even take time to reflect, and yet who, each day, urged on by an unknown and unknowing crowd, become the accusers of their mother and their brothers. How frequently, when listening to them, I have thought how much more the church, the whole church, would be within its rights to complain about them!

Word of caution

Two years ago one of the most noble and most learned men of our generation made reference to this situation. The very moderation of his words makes them all the more urgent. I am speaking of an Anglican convert to Catholicism, Bishop Christopher Butler, formerly the abbot of the Benedictine community at Downside, an influential member of the recent Council, and today auxiliary bishop of London. "You will allow me, " he said near the end of 1967, "after having been a part of the Council and having been delighted with its work, to make this observation: certain phenomena in the life of the church today urge me to call to the attention of all that in the course of time the charismatic life can destroy itself if the divine rights of the magisterium are not sincerely recognized and loyally respected."[8] More than a century earlier, while considering the critical phase through which the church in England was passing, the great Newman expressed himself in words which seem to predict what is unfolding before our very eyes:

The present open resistance to constituted power, and [what is more to the purpose] the indulgent toleration of it, the irreverence towards Antiquity, the unscrupulous

104

and wanton violation of the commands and usages of our
forefathers, the undoing of their benefactions, the prof-
anation of the Church, the bold transgression of Ecclesiastical Unity, the avowed disdain of what is called party
religion [today we would speak of sociological religion]
. . . the growing indifference to the Catholic Creed . . .
the arguings and discussings and comparings and correct-
ings and rejectings, and all the train of presumptuous
exercises, to which its sacred articles are subjected.
The numberless discordant criticisms on the Liturgy,
which have shot up on all sides of us; the general irritable
state of mind, which is everywhere to be witnessed, and
craving for change in all things; what do all these symptoms
show, but that the spirit of Saul still lives?--that wilful-
ness, which is the antagonist principle to the zeal of David
--the principle of cleaving and breaking down all divine
ordinances instead of building up?[9]

Newman goes on to evoke the punishment which is in store
for such an attitude.[10] I will not continue the quotation. His remarks have already introduced us to another sphere, the intellectual sphere of confrontation.

Principle of oppression

It has been rightly remarked that, when intelligence is reduced
to computer-thinking, it becomes a principle of oppression for
man. This is what we learn from the analyses of an Erik Weil and
a Paul Ricoeur. What follows is a violent revolt, one which expresses
itself by an exaltation of the irrational and which criticizes the alien-
ating results of rationalized society. However, as is so often the
case, this revolt remains the prisoner of the presupposition which
provoked it. Thus the two opposites which confront one another
remain united in the same genre. The calculating and constructive
function on the one hand and the critical and destructive function
on the other are the two opposite orientations of the same understanding; whereas what is needed if we are to reach a positive
solution to the crisis is the opening up of an entirely new dimension. This would be the reinstating of the mind in all its integrity
by having recourse to its contemplative function (and I use "contemplative" in its widest sense).[11] But this is exactly what is
usually missing; and it is what is also lacking when the actual

crisis of intelligence reaches even those who believe, at which time it finds its way inside the faith so as to undermine it.

Actually, when the critical function alone is active, it succeeds rather quickly in pulverizing everything. It makes it impossible to see what is invariable in the mind of man and in doctrinal tradition. It clouds over the continuity and the unity of revealed truth as seen in diverse cultural expressions which coincide with and follow one from another. As a result, divine revelation, inasmuch as it does not reach man except through signs, finds itself reduced to a series of thoughts and interpretations which are entirely human. Christian faith, in its first authenticity, becomes no more than a fact of culture, important surely, but, as such, out-dated.

Impact on theology

Theology, then, or what we still refer to as theology, should give an immediate answer to the questions of man here and now without in any way being concerned with mankind in general; and the theologian, instead of deepening his understanding of Christ's message, should have no other concern than that of being "current" so as always to be more "up-to-date."

Consequently, disdaining all real critical spirit, the spirit of criticism prevails. It has a field day, naturally, in sacred literature, whose final objective is reached only through images and symbols. The Christian thinkers of centuries past are looked down upon as if they no longer had anything to say; the traditional formulations of faith are stated in such a way as to appear ridiculous, so as to hasten their replacement. And under the pretext of merely changing this or that word or phrase, it is the very essence of our faith which runs the risk of being sifted away. The idea of a deeper understanding of mystery is replaced by the elaboration of a philosophy which sees itself as far superior, and then it is no longer the object of faith which changes; the specificity of faith disappears as well.

We borrow from anywhere those elements which can be exploited in a negative sense. Who among us is not familiar with the use made of the works of Bultmann--by men who are incapable of a critical study of his works!--or with the constant repetition of one or two phrases of Bonhoeffer? Whatever is recriminatory, whatever excites, is declared prophetic, even if it is evident that it stems from ignorance or from a biased opinion, or from concessions made to what is currently in vogue--and this

106

is the exact opposite of what we mean by prophetic! A literature then develops which is superficial. It is crammed full of slogans borrowed from the advertising world. It fills shelf after shelf in our bookstores and spreads all the more quickly because it is not addressed to the critical intelligence and because it favors all sorts of confusion.

We must not be afraid to say so: there is nothing in all of this that is promising. A faith which dissolves itself is unable to engender anything whatever. A community which breaks up is incapable of radiating or of attracting others. Agitation is not synonymous with life. The last hatched slogan is not necessarily a new thought. The noisiest critics are frequently the most sterile. True daring is something else again, as a Protestant theologian recently remarked, and many attitudes which pretend to be daring are no more than "a sort of escape into confrontation."[12] The power to create is not always given to those who pride themselves on being creative--and this applies even more to what concerns our faith and our life as Christians.

Faith revival

Such remarks, I know, run the risk of classifying their author as "conservative," "reactionary," or simply "out-dated." It is, however, no less clear that the entire future of the church, all the fruitfulness of its mission, all that it should and must bring to the world, depends today on an energetic revival of faith. To liberate the Christian conscience from a morbid negativism which is eroding it, from an inferiority complex which is paralyzing it, from a web of ambiguity which is smothering it--this is the very first condition for renewal in the church.

The program for this renewal was traced by the last Council. Everyone uses it as a reference (or used it as such), but in a hundred different ways. Actually, the Council is little known and followed even less. Many of those who pretend to be the only ones to have taken the Council seriously sneer at it today. Almost the very day the Council ended a deformed and deforming interpretation began to spread. Those who worked at the Council are the first to recognize this.[13] Let me give you some examples.

Due regard for tradition

The constitution Dei verbum centers the regard of the believer on the person of Jesus Christ, the substantial Word of God, "the

mediator and at the same time the fulness of revelation." It shows
Scripture as testifying in his behalf. It articulates the two Testa-
ments one in relation to the other. And at the same time as it
encourages the critical work of exegetes, it recalls very force-
fully the need to read Scripture in faith and to interpret it according to tradition. And yet many interpretations of this very
constitution cloud over the person of Christ; the Old Testament,
itself deformed, is held up as being opposed to the New; the
result is a narrow biblicism which disregards any and all tradition and in the process manages to swallow itself up; and from this
stems the notion of a "faith-in-the-future" in which it is hard to
see what, if anything, is left of the gospel of Jesus Christ. We
would do well to listen to a warning from the pen of a Protestant:

> There should be no question in the church, wrote Karl Barth,
> of jumping over the centuries, so as to link ourselves direct-
> ly and immediately to the Bible. . . . This is what biblicism
> has done, loudly rejecting the symbol of Nicaea, orthodoxy,
> scholasticism, the fathers of the church, the confessions of
> faith, so as to be rooted, as they say, only in the Bible. And
> yet, curious as it sounds, this procedure has always resulted
> in a very 'modern' theology. These biblicists share the phi-
> losophy of their times; they find their own ideas in the Bible;
> they free themselves from the dogmas of the church but not
> from their own dogmas or their own conceptions.[14]

The constitution Lumen gentium speaks first of the church as
a mystery, a gift of God. Those who belong to this church make up
the people of God, those who are tending toward the eternal city.
All are called, within the church, to holiness. To lead them on
their way to God, our Lord gave the church a hierarchical constitution, the episcopal college, whose head is the pope and whose
mission is three-fold: to teach, to sanctify, and to govern. Yet,
from many sides, it would seem that the only part of this doctrine
that some would wish to retain is the idea--or rather the expres-
sion--"people of God, " so as to transform the church into a vast
democracy.[15] By means of an analogous misinterpretation they
corrupt the very idea of episcopal collegiality, wanting to stretch
it to include all orders and mixing it up with that of a government
by assembly. This interpretation is exploited in an absurd way against
the person of the pope. They criticize what they call the "institutional church" in the name of an ideal of Christianity that is the very
opposite of the Catholic faith and the history of its beginnings. In

this way they have not only encouraged abuses and disorders in the practical order; the divine constitution of the church in its very essence is affected.

Gaudium et spes on openness

With regard to the constitution Gaudium et spes--which certain people would like to retain as the only constitution--if it recommends an "openness to the world, " it does so in specifying how this openness is to be understood; it does so in the name of a dynamism of our faith, in opposition to a fearful or egotistical closing in upon ourselves which was the sign of a loss of vitality; it does so to fulfil in the world the role that the soul plays in the body, following the celebrated expression of the Letter to Diognetus mentioned by the Council; finally, it does so to penetrate the world with the spirit of the gospel of Christ and to announce to the world the salvation that comes from Christ. But is it not just the opposite for some? Does not such an "openness" become a forgetfulness of salvation and of the gospel, a tending toward secularism, a loosening of faith and morals? Finally, this "openness" becomes for others a loss of identity, in a word, the betrayal of our obligation toward the world.

Because the Council, following the desire of John XXIII, did not wish either to define new dogmas or to pronounce anathemas, many conclude that the church no longer has the right to judge anything or anyone; they recommend a "pluralism" which is not the pluralism of the theological schools but that of entirely different beliefs from those of the normative faith. We know, too, how the decree on religious liberty is falsified when, contrary to its most explicit teaching, some conclude that there is no longer any need to preach the gospel, whereas it stresses the urgent need of this very preaching (whatever the delays might be in the practical order and whatever form this preaching might take due to circumstances). How many more analogous observations might be made concerning the constitution on the liturgy, which some have turned into a mockery, as well as the decrees on ecumenism, the religious life, and others! The word "renewal" can cover a multitude of abuses![16]

Whither goest thou?

A caricature which appeared in an American weekly seems to me to translate the feeling of confusion of an ever-growing number of observers as they look at what is taking place in the Catholic church today. It shows an ecclesiastic getting into a taxi. The driver turns around in his seat and asks--not in the usual way: "Where to, Father?"--but in biblical terminology: "Whither goest thou?" Where is the church going? That is the question that is on everybody's lips. Is the church going to decompose or is it going to renew itself according to the letter and the spirit of the Council to better fulfil her mission in the world?

Everything I have said so far should not be interpreted as a sign of pessimism on my part. The promise of Christ cannot fail. The Spirit of Christ will not abandon his church. Even today this Spirit breathes; it inspires wonder--hidden for the most part. Today we have a better knowledge of those wonders called forth by the Spirit in previous generations; wonders so frequently minimized. Tomorrow we will know of the wonders of our own generation. What I have sketched in a few words is a noisy ideology; despite the waste--all too real--that it has already caused, it does not yet affect life in its depth. It is not a serious theological reflection, nor a methodical pastoral plan, nor the flowering of new forms of apostolate, of self-giving, of service; nor is it the silence, the sacrifice of so many humble Christians whose fidelity is well beyond all crises and who are known to God alone.

Not new but renewed

If we notice the facts of common, everyday worldly-mindedness which pretend to be so many improvements tracing the path of the future (whereas they actually accentuate the failings of a not too distant past), we are also witnessing, as a result of the prompting of the Council, an extraordinary fermentation which allows us to speak not of a new church certainly, but of a church of renewal. There are many whose prayer and reflection are not troubled by ideology and talk and who are no less actively charitable, more ready than ever before to accept any transformation which charity might require. Even among those who instinctively stiffen in a defensive way and who are fearful of even desirable change, many would have accepted what their spiritual leaders asked of them if they had not been deceived by so many false renewals.

If the present generation is not as rich in great names as was France in the first half of this century, there are nonetheless real prophets among us who shake up our consciences by pointing out the important social works of today; who remind us that an interior conversion is required without which whatever we might accomplish

110

will not be lasting; and, as always, they will not be recognized as prophets until much later; they will be vilified because they do not flatter opinion and because their message seems a hard one. And yet, aided by the work of the Spirit, they help to maintain the church in the right direction by clearing new ways which will allow it to go forward.

We would do well to look at the freshness of the Christian life that is so visible in the young churches of countries such as Africa and that one day will give a new impetus to all of us. And think of those persecuted Christians in certain countries who have remained heroically faithful, whose faith has been strengthened and purified by a long period of trial, and who know from experience the price of their faith. When one day we will be able to share their experiences with them, the communio sanctorum which never ceases to exist between the different members of the church will enable us to go forward, and, if we want to make use of it, a new opportunity to humanize our world will be ours because of them.

Critics blind to signs of hope

These signs of hope are present in the church today. When I spoke earlier of those who seem to make a speciality out of criticism, I was anxious to make one point: precisely their refusal or inability to recognize these signs. Their outlook is so clouded that they are blind to the most profound reality, today as well as yesterday, either because they are dreaming of a perfect church which, we know only too well, they will never find, or because, soured by the gospels, they imagine that they have outgrown them and can no longer appreciate what these very gospels have accomplished in the past. Their aggiornamento of the church is a desire for complete change, and they attack what for a faithful Christian is and always will be most precious in the church. They have something in common with Hymenaeus and Philetus whom St. Paul mentions to Timothy, who felt that they were already resurrected and whose superiority and illusion of spirituality turned them away from the living God to the adoration of the idols of their hearts.[17]

And yet these signs which I pointed out above do exist today, despite their criticism; and they are capable, despite so many causes of affliction, of keeping us hopeful. Still another sign is to be seen in those men--and they are many--who, though outside the church, seek God without always realizing that they are seeking him. But even if these signs were not as evident as they are,

111

our hope would still be strong; for it is in times of obscurity that hope is most beautiful. But we have these signs! At the very center of our history the gospel of Christ was inserted; that gospel which is Jesus himself.[18] And it remains inserted in our history as an ever-living source.

The church, which was entrusted with the gospel of Christ, draws from it both nova et vetera in each generation. This is exactly what the church did once again at the recent Council, and it did not appeal in vain to the initiative and freedom of all. There was a risk there, certainly, the risk of misunderstandings, of abuses of all sorts; and the church foresaw them. It was a foregone conclusion that the application of the Council would result in a certain number of mistakes. Yet frequently these errors are no more than accidental, and even in the cases where they are more serious they are not all beyond repair.[19] The Council foresaw the risk[20] and took it because it was confident in the Spirit, and what we see today will not keep us from rejoicing.

There are conditions, nevertheless, which seem to me to be essential if--overcoming the present crisis much like an airplane which struggles for a time against the storm before attaining a higher altitude--we wish to stop spinning in a circle of vain activity so as to be able to go forward. In conclusion I will indicate two conditions which seem to me to be absolutely essential in this regard.

The first is the love of Christ Jesus. It is this love which makes a Christian a Christian; this is one thing that will never change.[21] From century to century and individual to individual it takes on different forms, different nuances, but it can never be lacking.

Love of Christ passé

Today this love of Christ Jesus is under attack. It is looked upon as out-of-date, an illusion, or it is ridiculed. The arguments are many and found everywhere by those who are anxious to drive it from the Christian heart. There are those who tell us that when we speak with the Jesus of history--the only real Jesus--we are speaking to a phantom because he is inaccessible to us. For others the succession of cultures, foreign one to another, pushes Christ further away from us each day so that we can no longer accept as our own the dogmatic definitions of the early church. Still others convince themselves and attempt to explain to us in the name of progress--progress in psychology and more especially in psychoanalysis--that such a love binds us up in a "religion" which is sentimental, unworthy of an adult, and one we must courageously abandon to enter into "real" faith. Or they tell us this love of Jesus Christ puts us back in history or up in the clouds and that if we are to be faithful to the zeal which has its source in Christ we must look for this love not in the person of Christ but in the men of today and tomorrow. Others, finally--those who look upon themselves as philosophers, and perhaps they are--invite us to a higher level of reflection. They go out of their way to make us see that real Christianity can no longer be what it was in the past and what it has been up to recent times. They can no longer find the church in the narrow personalism of an Origen, a Bernard, an Augustine, a Thomas Aquinas, a Möhler or a Newman. Nor are they able to recognize it as it was lived by the first apostles and especially by St. Paul and by so many count-less saints who had no time for pretentious theories.

Human spirit diverted

It would seem that from all horizons of knowledge, starting with hermeneutic and stretching to the highest level of specula-tion, the progress made by the human spirit in recent years has been funneled together so as to turn us away from this love of Christ Jesus, this love from which St. Paul declared that nothing, absolutely nothing could ever separate him.[22] How foreign this would be to Teilhard de Chardin who just yesterday cried out in a paraphrase of the Apostle: "I know that nothing in the world, no matter how superb or how vast it might be, can overshadow or separate us from him. Neither the angels, nor life itself, nor death, no height, no depth, no past, no future, is capable of separating us from the love of Christ."[23]

If exegesis is true, if it is faithful, the figure of Jesus will always shine forth, stripped of mediocre interpretations. He will be more enigmatic for some, more mysterious for others. And if we look closely enough we will see that negations or limi-tations proposed by certain exegetes are the result of what I would refer to as a "philological massacre."[24] Only recently someone was able to write that if we are to consider the central problem raised by the hermeneutic of the preaching of Jesus in a way which, rather than doing violence to the texts actually unites them, thereby making the different series of affirmations intelligible, we will discover that the best possible foundation to build upon is the Christological dogma of the church.[25] Like-wise, without in any way minimizing what the human sciences

113

have to contribute, we are forced to admit that in the absolute
statements and totalitarian pretensions of a certain number of
the representatives of these sciences they go far beyond the
limits of their competence and give an additional proof of a dogma-
tism which is both foreign and contrary to the scientific spirit.[26]
Those who confuse the love of Christ Jesus with some blind sentimentality run the risk of opening roads which will lead us to what
St. Paul characterized as "sine affectione."[27] As for opposing
the love of neighbor and the love of Christ which is its source,
this seems to me to be purely arbitrary. Those who have drunk
at this source for the past twenty centuries make this all too evident. We have only to think of Charles de Foucauld, the "universal brother," or of Jules Monchanin, and of how many others![28]
If I am to decide what is true Christianity I always prefer to find
it in the saints who live it, today as in the past, and who do not
try to leave it, rather than in the philosophers who pretend to
look down upon it from above. And this preference, I assure you,
is not and should not be taken as a criticism or a minimizing of
the role of philosophy.

The above reflections have been sketched rapidly; they are not
a refusal on my part to consider the objections raised by others.
Quite the contrary. I see these reflections as a pressing invitation
to carry through a vast program of research which, despite an
incredible mass of work too little known and poorly popularized
among the faithful, has not yet attained all the fulness or the
hardiness desired. The alliance between the critical and the religious spirit is always a means of measuring Christian renewal.
And yet if we still have a long way to go in this regard, nothing
should stop us from repeating with assurance what was said earlier
by the eminent scholar John Ladrière:

> Our works disappear in the dust of centuries, in the uni-
> versal hemorrhage which leads everything in the world to
> death. But a day dawned which will never end. It came to
> us from the obscurity of Nazareth and reaches down to us
> through the centuries; it leads us beyond time, beyond all
> births and all deaths to the moment of judgment and comple-
> tion, into the life to come, into the very depths of eternity,
> to the very center of truth. Hope has already begun; it can
> never end.[29]

Indiscriminate criticism

The second fundamental condition is the love and concern for Catholic unity. It is closely linked to the love of Christ. The shop-worn contrast which some still delight in making even to-day between the church and the gospel of Christ is an easily ex-ploitable theme because it is all too evident that the church seen in her members is never completely faithful. Sin, which is to be found everywhere, does not spare the church--neither sin nor all the other marks of human frailty. It is no less true, however, that it is still the church which brings us the gospel of Christ; and, still more important, it is more true today than ever be-fore that the generalized criticism of the church is linked to a movement which draws away from the gospels. The stubborn-ness with which some refuse the teachings of their spiritual leaders so as to follow world opinion is but one more sign of this separation from the message of Christ.

I would not be so concerned if this were something from out-side the church. But when each one takes as his mission to criti-cize everything, when each one thinks of himself before all else, when each one sets out to rewrite dogma and morality according to his own wishes, the church disintegrates. When the center of unity becomes the target of the most impassioned attacks, each one feeling that he has the right to criticize the successor of Peter before the whole world on any point whatever, the church itself is thereby wounded. Those who take this liberty do not fully realize what they are doing. Regardless of what pretext they may invoke, however, they are turning their backs on the gospel of Christ, and they scandalize, in the fullest sense of the word, many of their brothers. Whether they wish to or not, they encourage the formation of small groups whose sectarian pre-tensions are equaled only by the poverty of their spirituality. The weakening of faith is coupled with the decomposition of the Christian community. They insult all those who hold on to what their faith requires of them as Christians. Inasmuch as it de-pends on them, they ruin the church. A church in which this form of disorder exists and where such morals are accepted is doomed, for it cannot be efficacious; it will have no missionary zeal, no ecumenical force.

Cohesive power of witness

In conclusion I would like to refute these excesses--excesses
disguised under impressive titles--with a very simple witness,
the witness of an exceptionally intelligent woman who spent her
life helping the poor in a hostile and atheistic milieu. Since her
death in 1964, some of the notes and letters of Madeleine Delbrêl
have been published. Whoever reads them will be able to recognize and learn what an authentic Christian spirituality is and be
able to compare it with the refined purity of certain cerebral
spiritualities in whose name "ordinary" Christianity--the only
one familiar to the saints and to the ordinary Christians for the
past twenty centuries--is criticized. This is what Madeleine
Delbrêl wrote in 1952:

> Inasmuch as I have, for the past eighteen years, shared
> the life of a people not only without my faith but with no
> memory whatever of Christianity; inasmuch as I feel in-
> timately connected to what the church in France brings to
> me both nova et vetera; and inasmuch as I am convinced
> that our fidelity requires an ever more ardent mission-
> ary zeal as well as a stronger rooting in obedience, I
> decided to go to Rome in the name of all . . . , and so
> that this would be an act of faith and nothing else, I ar-
> rived in Rome in the morning. I went directly to the tomb
> of Saint Peter. . . . I spent the entire day there and I
> left for Paris in the evening.[30]

There is nothing grand about so simple a gesture. Yet it will
do more to maintain the cohesion of the church than so many opposite gestures which merely dig away at this very cohesion.
Such a sense of the necessity of Catholic unity is prior to and
subsequent to all legitimate discussion--within the limits of
divine institution and without unduly forcing the church's hand--
of the best means of governing the church at a given time and
in given circumstances.[31] On this point I am in no way attempting
to limit or disrupt research. Rather, I wish only to create a
climate which will permit this research to be carried out.

Speaking before this noble assembly in this great University
of Saint Louis, I am conscious of not having spoken--as some
of you may have expected me to do--as a learned man. Perhaps
I should ask your forgiveness. I do feel, however, that I have
spoken as a theologian. And is it not necessary, when the seri-

ousness of the hour requires it, that the theologian know how to suspend for a moment his historical studies or his personal con- structions--to which he would be wrong to attach an exaggerated importance--to recall that his entire existence as a theologian and all the authority that his profession gives him are rooted in the task that he has received: the defense and the explanation of the faith of the church? 32

Notes begin on page 324.

Freedom, Authority, Community

John Courtney Murray, S.J.

Some people today speak of a "crisis of authority" in the Church; others speak of a "crisis of freedom." For my own part, I should prefer to speak of a "crisis of community." The reasons for this description of the situation will appear, I hope, in what follows.

Vatican Council II did not create the crisis; its roots are deep in the past. But the Council brought the crisis into the open. In the first place, the Declaration on Religious Freedom said, in effect, that in political society the human person is to live his relation with God, or even with his private idol, in freedom -- within a zone of freedom juridically guaranteed against invasion by any form of coercion. This proposition, the Council added, is the product of a biblical insight, though centuries of secular and religious experience were needed in order to bring it to explicit conceptualization.

In the second place, the Constitution on the Church in the Modern World affirmed, in effect, that the relation of the Church to the world and of the world to the Church is to be lived in freedom. Freedom, Paul VI said in his momentous address to statesmen on Dec. 8, 1965, is all that the Church asks of the political world--freedom for its apostolic ministry, freedom for the Christian life, freedom for spiritual and peaceful entrance into the political world, there to make moral judgments when political affairs raise moral issues. In turn, the constitution generously acknowledged that the world too has its rightful freedom to live its own life--or rather, its many lives: political, economic, social, cultural, scientific--in accordance with autonomous dynamisms and structures. These respective claims of freedom, the Council implied, are likewise rooted in a biblical insight--that the Church is of God, and so too, though in a different way, is the world.

Having laid down these propositions bearing on freedom, the Council inevitably raised the next question, concerning freedom in the Church. Is not the Christian life within the Christian community to be lived in freedom? Even the essential Christian experience of obedience to the authority of the Church--is it not somehow to be an experience of Christian freedom in the evangelical sense? This is the question, not directly touched by the Council, which now commands serious theological consideration in the light of the doctrine of the Council and of its spirit--indeed, in the light of the Council itself as a splendid "event of freedom" in the ongoing life of the Church.

From a historical point of view, the need for new reflection on the relation between authority and freedom in the Church derives from the fact that presently this relation exhibits an imbalance. In order to grasp this fact, it will be sufficient for the moment to go back only as far as Leo XIII and to consider three aspects of his thought.

First, there is his retrospective reading of history, visible, for instance, in the famous "Once upon a time" paragraph in Immortale Dei. Once upon a time there was a Golden Age, the medieval period. It was the age of Christian unity, of the alliance of the Two Powers, of the obedience both of princes and of peoples to the authority of the Church. Then came the Reformation. Essentially it was a revolt against the authority of the Church, and in reaction to it the Church laid heavy, almost exclusive, emphasis on its own authority. Later, by a sequence that was not only historical but also logical, there came the Revolution. It was essentially a revolt against the authority of God Himself, launched by the revolutionary slogan: "No one stands above man" (homini antistare neminem). Again in polemic re-

119

action, the Church rallied to the defense of the sovereignty of God, of the "rights of God, " of the doctrine that there is no true freedom except under the law of God.

Both of these reactions were historically inevitable and doctrinally justifiable. The Church fashions its doctrine under the signs of the times, and the Reformation and the Revolution were then the signs of the times. But the doctrine formed under them could not but exhibit a certain hypertrophy of the principle of authority, and a corresponding atrophy of the principle of freedom.

In the second place, there is Leo XIII's conception of the political relationship between ruler and ruled in civil society. It is a simple vertical relationship within which the ruled are merely subjects, whose single duty is obedience to authority. Only in the most inchoative fashion does one find in Leo the notion of the "citizen, " who is equipped with political and civil rights and protected in their exercise. His emphasis falls on political authority, which is invested with a certain majesty as being from God, and which is to be exercised in paternal fashion in imitation of the divine sovereignty. In turn, the submission of the subject is to exhibit a certain filial quality. Moreover, society itself is to be built, as it were, from the top down. The "prince" is the primary bearer and agent of the social process. Qualis rex, talis grex. The ruler is to be the tutor and guardian of virtue in the body politic; the whole of the common good is committed to his charge. The people are simply the object of rule. Leo XIII's political doctrine was plainly authoritarian. It was fashioned under the political signs of the times--the laicist conception of the state and the Jacobin conception of the sovereignty of the people. In that moment in the history of continental Europe, Leo could not assume the patronage of political freedom.

In the third place, there is Leo XIII's ecclesiology, as summed up, for instance, in the encyclical Satis Cognitum (1896), in which he says: "We have faithfully depicted the image and figure (imaginem atque formam) of the Church as divinely established." The encyclical is, in effect, a lengthy, profound, magisterial commentary on the Vatican I constitution Pastor Aeternus, which was the splendid sign of the theological times. The portrait of the Church that emerges is really a portrait of the role of the apostolic office, and in particular the Petrine office, in the Church. In consequence, the ecclesial relationship--to call it such, on the analogy of the political relationship--is the simple vertical relationship between ruler and ruled. The function of the faithful

120

appears simply as obedience to the doctrinal and jurisdictional authority of the Church.

It was within these perspectives that the classical doctrine on the relation of freedom and authority in the Church was fashioned. Those who hold office make the decisions, doctrinal and pastoral. The faithful in the ranks submit to the decisions and execute the orders. The concept of obedience is likewise simple. To obey is to do the will of the superior; that is the essence of obedience. And the perfection of obedience is to make the will of the superior one's own will. In both instances the motive is the vision of God in the superior, who is the mediator of the divine will and the agent of divine providence in regard of his subjects, in such wise that union with his will means union with the will of God. The further motive, to be adduced when obedience means self-sacrifice, is the vision of Christ, who made Himself obedient even unto death.

The trouble is that this classical concept of the ecclesial relationship is today experienced as being true indeed, but not the whole truth--as being good indeed, but not good enough to meet the needs of the moment. The signs of the times are new. The age of anti-Reform polemic has gone over into the age of ecumenism. The will of the Church to break with the world of the Revolution has given way to a new will to effect that "compenetration" between the Church of today and the world of today of which Gaudium et Spes has spoken. The perspectives in which history is now viewed open out not from a supposed Golden Age in the past (whose luster is now seen to be dulled with the tarnish of much immaturity), but from the present moment. They are set not by nostalgia for the past, visible even in Leo XIII's Satis Cognitum, but by the solid doctrine of the eschatological character of the Christian existence, which requires it to look resolutely to the future--to the coming-to-be of the Kingdom.

New signs of the times have become visible and were fully recognized at Vatican Council II. The first is man's growing consciousness of his dignity as a person, which requires that he act on his own responsibility and therefore in freedom. The second is man's growing consciousness of community, of that being with the others and for the others which is revealed, for instance, in the phenomenon of "socialization" in the sense of Mater et Magistra. The Church in Council assembled clearly assumed the patronage--though in no patronizing sense--of these two related ongoing movements in the growth of human consciousness. The Council further undertook the renewal and reform of Christian doctrine and life in the light of these new signs of the times. In particular, the times demand a reconsideration of the classical concept of the ecclesial relationship--a new development, doctrinal and practical, in the relations between authority and freedom in the Church.

The difficulty with the classical conception, as experienced at the moment, is clear enough. It is sometimes stated by saying that obedience is a bar to the self-fulfillment of the individual. The statement may conceal a fallacy--an individualistic concept of self-fulfillment, and a failure to realize that self-fulfillment is not simply an affair of freedom but also an affair of community. Briefly, self-fulfillment is the achievement of freedom for communion with the others. Therefore it is also somehow an affair of obedience to authority; for in every kind of community there is always some kind of authority.

The fallacy aside, it must be said that the contemporary difficulty with the classical conception is rooted in a truth--in an experience of the truth that the signs of the times reveal. What is really being said is that sheer submission to the will of the superior and mere execution of his orders do not satisfy the exigencies of the dignity of the person. They do not call into play the freedom of the person at its deepest point, where freedom appears as love. Still less do they exhaust the responsibilities of the person, which are to participate fully in community and to contribute actively to community. Thus stated, the contemporary difficulty is seen to be entirely valid. It is not to be solved by methods of repression. Nor will it yield to mere reiteration of the principle of authority: that authority is to be obeyed simply because it is authority.

There is need, therefore, to view the issue of freedom and authority in the new perspectives created by the signs of the times--that is, to view the issue within the context of community, which is the milieu wherein the dignity of the person is realized. Community is the context both of command and of obedience. Community is also the finality both of command and obedience. Authority is indeed from God, but it is exercised in community over human persons. The freedom of the human person is also from God, and it is to be used in community for the benefit of the others. Moreover, since both authority and freedom stand in the service of the community, they must be related not only vertically but also horizontally, as we shall see.

It may be well to remark here that there is no univocal definition of the ruler-ruled relationship, because there is no univocal definition of community. This latter term is analogous. The realities it designates--the family, political society, voluntary associations, the Church--are somewhat the same and entirely different, one from another. In the case of the Church, which is at once a family and a society and a form of voluntary association, the essential thing is to attend to the uniqueness. Within the uniqueness of the Church as a community, the uniqueness of the relation of Christian freedom to ecclesiastical authority comes to view. Happily, Vatican Council II, which raised the issue of freedom and authority in the Church, also created the perspectives within which its resolution becomes newly possible. Four aspects of conciliar ecclesiology are pertinent here.

In the first place, the Constitution on the Church (Lumen Gentium) presents the Church in the first instance as the People of God. The first characteristic of the People is that it "has for its condition the dignity and the freedom of the children of God, in whose hearts the Holy Spirit dwells as in a temple" (9). The basic condition of the People is therefore one of equality in dignity and freedom, established by the common possession of the Spirit. A consequent characteristic of the People is its charismatic quality as a prophetic, royal and priestly People. The Spirit "distributes special graces among the faithful of every rank, and by these gifts he makes them able and ready to undertake the various tasks and offices useful for the renewal and upbuilding of the Church, according to the Apostle: 'To each is given the manifestation of the Spirit for the common good' (1 Cor. 12:7)." In particular, as the Constitution on Divine Revelation (Dei Verbum) says, God through the Spirit "uninterruptibly converses with the Bride of his beloved Son," and the Spirit continually "leads unto all truth those who believe and makes the word of Christ dwell abundantly in them" (8). The dignity of the People and its common endowment of Christian freedom importantly consists in the charismatic quality of its members.

In the second place, the Council presents the Church as a communion (koinonia). Its infinite inner form is the Holy Spirit Himself, the subsistent love of Father and Son, therefore the gift of Father and Son, who is the presence of God in the midst of His People. In consequence, the Church is in the first instance an interpersonal community, whose members are united in love of the Father through Christ and in the Spirit, and also united with one another by the Spirit of Christ, through whom they have access not only to the Father but to one another. The consequence here is one of immense importance, namely, that as an

123

interpersonal community the Church is an end in itself, an ultimate reality, as eschatological reality in a temporal realization thereof. As a communion sui generis, the Church has for its primary purpose simply to be a communion. As such it will endure beyond time, forever, in what is called the communion of saints.

In the third place, precisely as an interpersonal communion of love, the Church has a service (diakonia) to perform toward all humanity. That is to say, the divine love that is the form of the People reaches out through the People, in witness (martyrion), to draw all men into the communion of love, so that they may participate in the response of faith and love to the love whereby the Father loves His own People, purchased by the blood of His Son. In other words, precisely as an interpersonal community sui generis, the Church is also a functional community, that is, a community with a work to do, an action to perform--the action of God in history, which is to "gather into one the children of God who are scattered abroad" (John 11:52). Moreover, the work of the community, which is a work of love, is not extrinsic to the thematic of the community; it is woven, as it were, into this thematic as an essential element of it. That is to say, the interpersonal community, united in love, is also united by the missionary work of love to which it is called by its very nature.

Regarded as a functional community, however, the Church is not an end in itself but a means to a higher end--its own growing self-realization and perfection as an interpersonal community. There will come a day when the Messianic function of the Church will have been finished--the Day of the Lord, when the gathering of the People will be complete and the reign of Christ definitively established: "Then comes the end, when he delivers the kingdom to God the Father" (1 Cor. 15:24).

In the fourth place, the Church is not only a community of faith and love but also a visible society; it therefore exhibits a structure of authority and a juridical order. Moreover, the Church is an organized society precisely as a community of faith and love with a function to perform in history. The societal aspect of the Church is not alien or extrinsic to its communal and functional aspects, but essential to both of them and inherent in each of them. That is to say, the organization of the society is required by the purposes of the community, both for the sake of its own unity as an interpersonal communion and also for the sake of its action in history. The hierarchically ordered society--its structure of authority and its juridical order--stands in the service of the community, to assist in perfecting its unity and in performing its function.

The structure of authority in the Church is unique, as the community it structures is likewise unique. It is both doctrinal and jurisdictional--a power of authoritative teaching and of imperative rule. Moreover, the structure is not merely a matter of political and sociological necessity, as in the case of the civil community. This latter is simply a functional community, which is therefore organized only in order to get its work done-- its work being what is called the common good. Here the unique difference appears. The Church is organized as a society sui generis in order that it may be what it is--a community sui generis, an interpersonal, eschatological communion of faith and love and a historical, missionary community whose work in history expresses its own inner reality.

These four themes in the ecclesiology of Vatican II are, of course, entirely traditional. The order of their arrangement, however, is distinctive; so too is the weight of emphasis distributed among them. For Leo XIII, for instance, the Church was both community and society, indissolubly; so it is presented in Satis Cognitum. But the weight of his emphasis falls heavily on the societal aspect and on the structure of authority in the Church. It may be fairly, if rather broadly, said that Leo XIII comes to the notion of the Church as community through the notion of the Church as society. And in his construction, the functions of Christian freedom are not readily apparent; they are, in fact, obscured. Authority seems, as it were, to stand over the community as a power to decide and command. In contrast, Vatican II comes to the notion of the Church as society through the notion of the Church as community. Authority therefore stands, as it were, within the community, as a ministry to be performed in the service of the community. Within the perspectives created by this newly accented construction of traditional doctrine, the ecclesial relationship can be more adequately understood and therefore stated with a new nicety of balance. In particular, the functions of Christian freedom emerge into new clarity, in themselves and in their relation to the correspondent functions of authority. The new clarity radiates from the notion of the Church as community, now made newly luminous.

The functions of authority appear to be three, in hierarchical order. And each of them is a function of service to the community.

The first function is unitive. Authority is to be and do what God Himself, through Christ and in the Spirit, is and does. He

125

gathers, unites, establishes communion. This too is the primary function of authority. Moreover, God gathers His Church by initiating and sustaining with men the "dialogue of salvation," brilliantly described by Paul VI in Ecclesiam Suam. God communicates with His People, eliciting from them the response of faith and love. His call to them is an imperative laid upon them, but it is an imperative because it is, in the words of Paul VI, a "demand of love" (domanda di amore), to which the response must be free. So, too, authority performs its unitive function through dialogue with the charismatic body of the faithful. The purpose of the ecclesiastical dialogue, as of the divine dialogue, is to build and strengthen the community: to guide it, under the guidance of the Spirit, toward the full truth. About what? About itself, in the first instance. The dialogue is to deepen that "self-awareness" on the part of the community which was a major theme, and also a major achievement, of Vatican II.

Authority therefore elicits from the charismatic community of Christian faith the insights of each into the faith, for the enlightenment of all. . . . Moreover, authority stirs the love of the charismatic members of the community for the community, to be shown in service of the community. Finally, authority solicits the informed concern of the community for the work of the community-- its relations with the world, its mission of salvation and its spiritual mission in the temporal order. . . .

The primacy of this unitive function of authority, to be discharged through dialogue, results from the primacy of the notion of the Church as an interpersonal community whose conscious unity is an end in itself. This primary dialogic function also depends for its performance on the reality of the People of God as a charismatic body, whose basic condition is one of equality in Christian dignity and freedom. It follows therefore that the unitive function of authority is to be carried out under respect for this basic condition. Lumen Gentium is careful to provide room in the Church for all manner of legitimate diversities and pluralisms --in rites, theologies, spiritualities, apostolates, etc.--which, so far from damaging the unity of the community, constitute an enrichment of it. The principle of the Declaration on Religious Freedom--that there should be in society as much freedom as possible and only as much restriction as necessary--applies analogously in the Church. Only "in necessary things" is unity itself necessary.

It may be remarked here that the modes and manners in which authority is to perform its unitive function through dialogue are still problematical today, in this era of assestamento (adjustment).

New structures of communication need to be created [for instance, the Synod that will meet in 1967]. Older structures need reformation, as in the case of the Roman dicasteries. Experiments are called for that will yield the necessary experience. The problem is not simply to conceptualize in theological terms the relation between authority and freedom in the Christian community, as it appears in new perspectives; this relation must be lived, in all concreteness and practicality. Thus the experience of life will give vitality to the theology.

The second function of authority may be called decisive or directive. It hardly needs lengthy description, since it already is a familiar thing, prominent perhaps to the point of undue emphasis in the classical conception of an older day. The decisive function is necessary because the Church is a community of faith, and it was to the magistery that the guardianship of the deposit of faith was committed. The directive function is needed because the Church is a functional community organized for action in history. It is to be noted, however, that the necessity of the function is not merely a matter of efficiency, to insure that the work of the Church gets done. The necessity is grounded in the very nature of the community. The point is to insure that the work done is the work of the Church, which it is when it is done under direction. The even more important point is to insure that the Body acts as one in the action of its members, singly and collectively.

Thus the decisive and directive function of authority is in a true sense a modality of its unitive function. Moreover, the performance of this secondary function supposes that the primary function has already been performed; that the dialogue, whether doctrinal or pastoral, has been afoot between the community and its teachers and pastors; that therefore the decisions and directives, without ceasing to derive their force from apostolic authority, are also the decisions and directives of the community, whose common good they serve.

The third function of authority is corrective or punitive. It is an accidental function, in the sense that it is necessary only because the People of God, on its pilgrim way through history, is a sinful People. It is also a function of service to the community, which needs to be protected against the egoisms--whether of thought or of action--that would destroy its unity or damage its work. Again, therefore, this function of correction appears as a modality of the unitive function of authority. What comes to the fore today is the need that the corrective or punitive function of authority should be performed under regard for what is called, in the common-law tradition, "due process." The demand for due process of law is an exigence of Christian dignity and freedom. It is to be satisfied as exactly in the Church as in civil society (one might indeed say, more exactly).

Three functions of Christian freedom in the Church correspond to the three functions of ecclesiastical authority. They are likewise functions of service to the community.

The primary function may be called, for the sake of a name, charismatic. It is the free response of the community and of all its members to the unitive function of authority, whose initial act is the invitation to dialogue (on which the Council more than once laid emphasis). The Spirit is given to the Christian not only for his own sanctification and enjoyment, but also for the growth of the community in conscious self-awareness and for the fuller deployment of its action in history. Concretely, the community uses the gift of the Spirit by sustaining its part in the dialogue with authority, in that confidence of utterance that reveals--in our times, as in those of the Acts of the Apostles--the presence of the Spirit.

This primary function of Christian freedom corresponds therefore to the nature of freedom in its most profound sense--to the nature of freedom as love, as the capacity for self-communication, as the spontaneous impulse to minister and not be ministered to, as the outgoing will to communion with the others. "For you were called to freedom, brethren," St. Paul proclaims (Gal. 5:13). Whatever else the call may imply, it is a call to love: ". . . through love be servants of one another" (loc. cit.). The forms of service within the community are manifold, but the primary service to the community is to participate in the dialogue of salvation that is continually going on in the community. This participation is the first exercise of Christian freedom. It is also an exercise in obedience, in the horizontal dimension that obedience assumes when it is situated, with authority, within community, and therefore in dialogic relation to authority, united to authority in a ministry of love toward the community.

The second function of Christian freedom may be called, again for the sake of a name, executive. It corresponds to the decisive and directive functions of authority. It also corresponds to the formal moral notion of freedom as duty--the freedom whereby one does what one ought to do. Here, of course, obedience may occasionally appear as self-sacrifice. The act of obedience is not, of course, per se an act of sacrifice; it is simply an act of Christian freedom. Obedience assumes a sacrificial quality only when

128

Christian freedom meets the resistance of what Paul calls "the flesh." And the premise of obedience as sacrifice is always the profound nature of freedom as love--the love whereby one freely engages oneself in the paschal mystery. Hence obedience, as an act of Christian freedom, even when it is sacrificial--especially when it is sacrificial--is always the way to self-fulfillment. It is the expression of one's self-awareness that one is called to be in the image of the Son Incarnate, who freely gave His life for the many and thus "went His way" to the self-fulfillment that was His resurrection. Finally, whether sacrificial or not, the executive function of Christian freedom, which consists in acceptance of the decisions and directives of authority, is always performed within the community, in and for which He works. Therefore this secondary function of freedom is related to the primary function, the charismatic function of love whereby I contribute in dialogue to the unity of the communion that is the Church. The dialogue is not an end in itself; it looks toward decisions and directives. In their issuance and acceptance, the community comes together in a new way.

The third function of Christian freedom may have to go without a name, unless one calls it self-corrective, in order to mark its correspondence to the corrective function of authority. It is the free act of Christian refusal to "submit again to a yoke of slavery" (Gal. 5:1). More broadly, it is the Christian rejection of the temptation, inherent in the psychological notion of freedom as choice, to "use your freedom as an opportunity for the flesh" (Gal. 5:13). One might call it the "mortifying" act of Christian freedom; the word may not be popular today, but the notion is still Pauline (cf. Rom. 8:13). In any event, it is the act whereby Christian freedom stands forth in all its evangelical newness, unique among all the modalities of freedom that men have claimed or hoped for or dreamed of. "It was that we might be free" in this new way, says St. Paul, "that Christ has freed us" (Gal. 5:1).

The aim of this brief essay has been simply to suggest how the rather fleshless skeleton of the classical conception of the ecclesial relation may be clothed with flesh and animated with blood. The skeleton remains; the classical conception of the vertical relationship of authority and freedom. But it needs to assume a more Christian and therefore more human form by standing forth in the living flesh and blood that is the Christian community. More abstractly, the vertical relationship of command-obedience needs to be completed by the horizontal relationship of dialogue between authority and the free Christian community. The two relationships do not cancel, but reciprocally support, each other.

This more adequate understanding of the ecclesial relation-ship does not indeed dissolve the inevitable tension between freedom and authority. But by situating this perennial polarity within the living context of community, it can serve to make the tension healthy and creative, releasing the energies radiant from both poles for their one common task, which is to build the beloved community.

Notes begin on page 328.

What Good Is
Institutional Christianity?

Jean Cardinal Danielou, S.J.

The problem of the institutional aspect of Christianity is the subject of lively controversy these days, and there are some who
challenge the whole idea. The first thing we must do is define our
terms precisely and thus avoid false problems. On the one hand,
everyone agrees that it is necessary to have a dialogue between
the Church and civilization. Likewise, everyone rejects the
dualistic view which would treat faith and civilization as if they
were two entirely separate worlds. On the other hand, no one
dreams of maintaining purely and simply the medieval idea of
a state religion. It is not a question of holding on to Constantinian
Christianity but rather of doing for our age what Constantine did
for his. But this is precisely the problem: What place must the
institutional aspect have in our modern notion of the relationship
between the Church and civil society? It is this institutional aspect which seems to me to be essential if we are to have a Christian people.

We must admit first of all that the Church is an institution by its very nature. In fact Christianity has two basic aspects, of equal importance: On the one hand it is the gospel, the message of salvation which we must constantly present to mankind. This prophetic aspect is of the very essence of Christianity. It challenges every man in the name of God's word. But Bergson is mistaken when, in contrasting open and closed religion, he places the institutional aspect wholly on the side of closed religion. It is perfectly clear that there is an institutional aspect which in no way depends on closed religion, but is just as essential to Christianity as the gospel. Christianity is also the Church, and this necessarily goes back to the state of things as instituted by Jesus Christ. If there is one thing about which we can be absolutely certain, it is that Jesus Christ intended to found a Church. He devoted a great part of his public life to the formation of a group of apostles, and entrusted this institution with the task of transmitting his message. Consequently, anyone who overemphasizes the prophetic aspect of Christianity in relation to the institutional aspect is attacking the very essence of what Jesus Christ intended. There is no more mistaken view of Christianity than that held by Harnack, who said that Christ was a prophet of love and that it was the Christians who, after some time, made an institution of Christianity--and this in keeping with a basic law governing every human community which says that, once a group of men come together, they must be given a certain number of institutions. This is simply a caricature of the origins of Christianity.

On the other hand, Christianity, especially in the Western world, did not serve simply to transmit to us the salvation which comes from Christ. It also served as the form by which religion itself was made present at the moment in our civilization. Here, it seems to me, we must take into account the difference between revelation and religion. For its part, revelation is based on an event; it comes from another world and directs us toward another world. Religion, on the contrary, is something that belongs to human nature as such and therefore is essential to civilization as such, inasmuch as civilization comprises all the best elements of a people. Here the problem of institution is the problem of the place of religion in human society. In its statement on non-Christian religions, Vatican II acknowledged the value of religion qua religion. In its document on religious liberty, which is so important in the present controversy, the Council insisted on religious liberty as a fundamental human right, basing its stand on the right of religion to be expressed socially. The Council did not concern itself directly with the gospel at this level, but restricted itself to arguments based on the natural law.

In fact, a civilization in which worship, in which the religious dimension of man is not expressed socially, is a civilization which, as civilization, is imperfect from a human point of view. This brings up the whole problem of "religion and civilization" in a way completely different from the ordinary, which sees civilization existing at a purely secular level, to be covered over by a veneer of faith. There is an intermediary sphere which needs to be considered. Civilization contains a religious element, and I submit that a civilization in which the religious element is not presented is not a true civilization. Therefore we must do away with the false contrast between "religious" and "temporal," as if religion itself were not a part of temporal civilization as such.

Christianity destroyed the traditional religions of the West. But in destroying them, it served not only to transcend them but to replace them. Religion is not a luxury for a certain number of privileged people. It is something essentially human and therefore for everyone. The problem, then, is to make it present institutionally in society, from its most basic forms to its highest forms. The Christian priesthood must correspond to these different aspects. In normal circumstances, most people have to deal with the priesthood only when it is a matter of sanctifying the essential acts of human existence--birth, marriage and death. It would be a crime to turn Christians of this kind away from the Church and hand them over to atheism. Certainly most of them would be taken in hand by the new paganisms which would develop (we agree, of course, that a pagan is just the opposite of an atheist). The problem is not to turn away these Christians, but to enable them to rise progressively to a higher level. In caring for the elite, we must not forget the masses. . . .

The real tragedy of modern Christianity lies less in the lack of gospel spirit among Christians (on this point there has been some progress in comparison with other centuries) than in the lack of visible presence of Christianity in society and in the city. The modern city is tragically secular. Nothing there reminds one of God. How can man be expected to meet God there under these conditions? Of course, this situation is not something inherent in the modern city as such but rather in a disincarnation of Christianity which takes refuge in the purely internal domain and no longer shows itself outwardly. Such conditions lead irrevocably to a suffocation of the Christian life of the people. The real tragedy is that many Christians and priests are accomplices in this act. They seem to have just one idea, to align themselves with the secular world. They complain loudly about triumphalism whenever religious acts are performed in public. . . .

If by Christianity is meant a certain historical order which existed in the Middle Ages, a certain type of relationship between the Church and civil society, I have no desire at all to restore such an order. I love my own age too much for that. But if by Christianity is meant an order of things in which Christendom forms part of civilization, in which children are as a rule baptized and people are married in church, in which not only individuals but (as Peguy says) the race itself is evangelized, then I believe sincerely in the permanent truth of Christianity. This seems to me to be the normal result of preaching the gospel. I do not think that Constantine represented the end of authentic Christianity. Rather, he signified its full flowering. Obviously, then, in Christianity there are Christians at every level. But, for me, that is the way things should be. Christianity must be on the scene, present through its churches, its sacraments, its priests, in order to be accessible to all. Naturally, not all will make use of these things to the same extent.

The problem before us is twofold. First of all, we must fight step by step to defend the Christian people where they exist. I have a very brotherly feeling for those engaged in this struggle, whether Polish or Spanish, Bretons or Basques. Certainly there is no question of keeping things the way they are, but neither does it make sense to squander what we have. When we realize the great amount of work involved in the evangelization not of individuals, but of whole peoples, we would be insane to lose the gains we have made. But it is also clear that the problem before us is one of evangelizing a modern society, an urban civilization, a scientific culture--and this in such a way as to make present a dimension of worship without suffocating it. Only to the extent that Christianity is made present as an institution can there be a Christian people. Of course, the Church cannot neglect the masses without ceasing to be the Church of the poor, that is, without ceasing to be the Church of Jesus Christ.

What I have said thus far may seem paradoxical in the light of the present situation in which religion itself seems to be challenged by some people. However, it is certain that the social reality of religion corresponds, on the one hand, to the past history of mankind taken as a whole and, on the other hand, to its future; that is, I do not believe that modern civilization has necessarily been desacralized by science. On this point we have the following words of Paul VI:

We have become accustomed to putting religion on the margin
of sense experience and of scientific reason, confining it to
the areas beyond our own information about the immense
sphere of nature's mystery, as if religion were based on
ignorance of the possible solutions of obscure problems that
science may one day succeed in solving.

Now religion is returning as something urgent--not just
coming back from the outer boundaries of sciences to which
it had been relegated, but going above and beyond the scientific field to penetrate to its very heart. Drawing upon
all that is and all that bespeaks order, law, purpose and
beauty . . . religion is providing . . . a youthful capacity
to pick up the hymn of creation once again and to enlighten
and bless everything. A natural religion . . . is reborn;
even the great scientists of our time not only do not disdain
to perceive it at the heart of their research, but they even
expect to find and recognize it there. (Discourse on January
26, 1966. English text from The Pope Speaks, v. XI [1966].)

There are many today, of course, who are scandalized by such
words. But for me this idea of "a natural religion being reborn"
contains a profound truth: We do not yet face a renewal of Christianity, but rather a prior act, namely, the birth of a new paganism
of the future. Teilhard and Tillich both bear witness to this fact--
that a new type of religious man exists--when they show that there
is in modern man a certain religious dimension which does not
coincide with traditional ideas about religion but is no less real.
The tragedy today is the dissension between the religious soul of
modern man and the whole body of religious forms with which he
feels himself "out of step." This is different from saying that
modern man lacks a religious dimension (the religious phenomenon as such will be an essential element of technological civilization just as much as it was of past civilization). This is a line of
thought with which I am in total disagreement; it speaks of civilization as being desacralized. Along this line, even Maritain holds
some positions which will, it seems to me, ultimately lead to re-
grettable consequences, to the extent that he has set up much too
simplistic a contrast between sacred and secular civilization. To
admit such a separation between civilization and religion is something which can only bring extremely serious consequences.

This presence of Christianity in civilization is essential if we
believe in the future of a great Christian people--that is, if we
refuse to accept the idea that the Church will become simply a

small elite group. Obviously, nothing in the world will stop people from having metaphysical and religious crises. No one questions this, and therefore it does not concern us here. But it is clear that there is one thing which the world of tomorrow can stop and that is that there will still be Christian peoples--in other words that Christianity will be accessible to the poor. The poor means all comers. It means a capitalist just as much as a common laborer. It means a man of the street, any one at all.

Obviously, the possibility of mankind as a whole becoming Christian is conditioned by environment. Some say that this means a "sociological" and thus formalistic Christianity. This is exactly what I refuse to accept. Just because religious practice is conditioned sociologically, does not mean that this Christianity is purely formalistic. Naturally most people living in a situation which is opposed to what they believe in do not have sufficient strength from their own personal life to react against such a situation. The tragedy right now occurs if we admit that we are interested only in the avant-garde communities in Christianity, and then sacrifice that tremendous reality, the mass of Christian people. At the same time, I am perfectly aware that this mass of Christian people is a dead weight, and very often a scandal to the unbeliever. But I also think that the fact that religion remains accessible to such an immense number of people is something pertaining to the very essence of both religion and the Christian message, and that a Church which became a Church of the elite would be simply a caricature of what Jesus Christ intended.

Here I return to the question of freedom. Certainly there is only one thing that God is interested in, a love freely given. But to speak of freedom without considering the conditions for freedom is to speak in empty abstractions, to be completely unrealistic. Our freedom is conditioned by our temperament, by our education, by our environment. Many times we have to create the conditions which make it possible for freedom to be itself. St. Augustine teaches that freedom is not a point of departure but rather a goal, and that one must create the conditions which make it possible for man to be himself. But it is perfectly normal for men to be incapable of being themselves at the outset. And this is where the conditions for freedom play an important role. It is strange that, in an age in which the sociology of religion is so well developed as a science, there exists such a lack of appreciation of the importance of the sociological factor in sincere religious practice.

On the contrary, we should be extremely sympathetic with the normal state of affairs in which the sociological factor is an im-

portant element in the religion of the masses, in the formation
of a Christian people. Our mission should aim at these goals:
(1) proclaiming the gospel: the prophetic element; (2) establishing
the Church: the ecclesiastical institution; and (3) Christianizing
civilization: Christianity. In a country where the culture is not
imbued with Christianity, Christianity continues to appear as a
peripheral phenomenon. This is precisely the problem faced today
by the missions in Africa and Asia: The Christians there have
suffered greatly in being uprooted from their cultural traditions.
We say that there should be an African Christianity, an Indian
Christianity; that is, a Christianity which becomes incarnate in
the very core of a civilization and permeates it fully. Otherwise
it will seem to be something foreign. Now it has been our good
fortune that, at the cost of tremendous difficulties, all this has
taken place in Western countries. The fact that our civilization
is still imbued with Christianity means that, whether we want it
or not, there exists a Christian element which makes Christianity
present in every aspect of life. Christianity can form a part of
the culture, and it is through this Christianized culture that all
can encounter it; that is what the word "Christianity" means.

By Christianity we do not mean certain historical structures,
certain compromises between churches and great powers, certain types of institutions. We do not want simply to preserve in
the future the same forms of Christianity that we had in the past.
But the problem posed by Christianity is a problem for the future,
and the opinion that this is a problem concerning only the past is
highly debatable. The process which resulted in Constantine was
completely beneficial--despite the drawbacks of his regime--be-
cause it made possible the conversion of the masses. I feel strongly
compelled to wish that Christianity be shared by the greatest possible number of people, with all the risks that are involved; for it
is clear that, when Christianity is presented to the masses, it
takes in people of every kind. But it is God and the angels who
will separate people one from the other on the last day, not us.
Furthermore, there may well be more religious experience and
authentic Christianity reflected in the life of this or that person
whom we reject from our little militant communities than exists
among the actual members of these same communities. We must
not raise up a new generation of Pharisees.

I have said that a Christian people is possible only in an environment which supports it. The ideal, of course, is that the
entire environment promote and make possible a Christian people. This ideal of Christian institution is precisely what Chris-

137

tianity is, a world in which the whole body of institutions, the whole general rhythm of life really allows people to be Christians. But sometimes the environment is an obstacle which prevents the poor from being Christians. In that case it is a matter of setting up-- not simply by way of defending and preserving the past, but by reflecting attempts and initiatives of a truly prophetic character-- great movements of Christian activity which would be a kind of anticipation of the future and which hopefully would spread. This is where the dimension of the Christian family comes in. It is first of all through the Christian family that Christianity appears as a tradition and not simply as a personal choice. The creation of a certain environment is clearly what makes the faith possible.

There is another aspect of Christian institutions to be considered: the influence of the spirit of the gospel on civilization through institutions which are specifically Christian. The Church must become involved in the problems of modern civilization. Vatican II found it impossible to set aside the problems of our technological civilization and concern itself only with the heavenly Jerusalem. There are simple matters of material aid in problems which have nothing specifically Christian about them. When we begin to tackle much more difficult problems, we find a certain Christian spirit diffused throughout civilization. For human values, science, civilization itself, all have a certain autonomy which remains whole and entire in relation to the Church. And, along this line, everything which smacks of domination by the Church in fields which do not properly belong to it must be more and more eliminated. But Gaudium et Spes adds that "if autonomy means that things do not depend on God and thus must not be referred to him, no one who knows God can fail to see that such statements are absolutely false." Civilization must be directed to a certain order--that which best fulfills the meaning of human destiny in the plan of God.

If this be true, we cannot agree to a dichotomy between the sphere of civilization and the sphere of religion under a new aspect. We have said that religion as religion is an element of the city. But it is also true that temporal activities are not something that can be considered secularized in the sense that they have absolutely nothing to do with God and the divine destiny of man. The real problem facing civilization today is not so much technological progress in itself as the directing of technology to man's final end. Now here, though the Church may have nothing to impose and nothing to say in an authoritarian way (as it does when proclaiming the message of Jesus Christ), nevertheless it has to serve and in fact cannot fail to serve; that is, it cannot fail to work to direct this civilization toward true human goals. There is no dichotomy between sacred history and human history.

I wish to conclude by examining the reasons underlying the position taken by those who defend Christian institutions. As a matter of fact, just as we refuse to admit any opposition between sociological Christianity and personal Christianity, so it would seem equally reasonable to admit that the witness of the gospel on the one hand, and the cultural and institutional apparatus on the other, are perfectly complementary. I believe that the proclamation of the gospel and the practice of the beatitudes are essential to Christianity. But, at the same time, I hold that any failure to grasp the importance of institutions is opposed both to the divine structure of the Church and to practical common sense.

Forming part of the background of this debate is a common tendency of some theologians today to overemphasize the Word at the expense of the institution, the faith at the expense of the sacraments. But here we are faced with another aspect of the same school of thought: the tendency to play down the institution as the means by which the Church becomes incorporated into civilization and to prefer the animating spirit to the institution itself. What, then, do we have to fear from the institution? We can approach it from different aspects. The first concerns the relationship between Church and State. One great fear that many contemporary Christians have--doubtless because of certain unfortunate occurrences in the past--is the close affiliation of Church and State. It is true that there is a real danger here. But I am afraid that it is more a matter of personal reaction to the past than a realistic view of the future. Obviously the separation of Church and State is a luxury which can be permitted in a capitalist regime, where private capital can provide for the needs of the churches--with the disadvantage of another type of affiliation coming from another quarter. But considering the fact that we are tending towards an ever greater socialization, it is obvious that no important organism can continue to exist without the support of the State. And as for the myth of a Church that is poor but free, it may not be difficult for the theologians ensconced in their ivory towers to sing its praises; but those responsible for the welfare of the Church know that nothing worthwhile can be accomplished without an economic substructure.

On the other hand, what the Church is asking for here is not a privileged position, but a simple acknowledgment of the natural right of religious communities to enjoy the ordinary conditions of existence in the city. This is the teaching developed in Vatican II's

139

declaration on religious liberty. And here I go back to what I said in the previous paragraph in order to draw some logical conclusions. For a Christian people to exist, it is not enough for them to have the support of the Christian community or even for society to live according to the moral teachings of the gospel. The particular society must also acknowledge that the religious dimension in all its various forms is an essential aspect of the common good of the city. Otherwise, as I have said, that laicist and secularistic society will not be in accord with the moral teachings of the gospel, nor even with morality based on the natural law, which admits that the Church has the right to be acknowledged by the city. It is on these grounds that the priest is not the pariah in society that he is often treated as, but has his place--and does not have to rely on his own resources for his support in society.

The Church demands this right to exist in the city first of all on the purely cultural level. In what concerns houses of worship and their place in the new urban civilization, it is necessarily dependent on public powers. But, in addition to the needs of worship proper, the Church obviously needs certain facilities to fulfill its mission. And this brings us to the subject of temporal institutions. The proclaiming of the gospel message demands publishing houses and the media of press, radio and films. The formation of Christians demands schools, youth movements, adult groups. Maintaining a place in the world of ideas demands centers of research and universities. A Church deprived of these means of action would be unable to maintain its presence in the very bosom of society and thus to reach mankind as a whole. And, on this point, we should realize that its leaders have not ceased to carry on their courageous struggle wherever totalitarian governments wish to confine Christians to the sacristies.

But, some will ask, is that any reason why the Church needs its own institutions? Could it not exercise its influence through faith and love in the very heart of institutions other than its own? And, as Father C. J. Geffre recently argued, if it has its own schools and movements, is there not the danger that, contrary to what it intends, it will "build for itself a Christian world alongside of the 'world,' instead of Christianizing the world as it grows" ("Desacralization and the Spiritual Life," in Concilium v. 19)?

I agree wholeheartedly that the ideal would be a society in which the Christian spirit would so permeate the secular institutions that the Church would not need its own institutions. That is precisely what Christianity is. In some countries there are still some worthwhile traces of this Christianity. The names are still the names of the apostles and the feasts are Christian feasts. I agree that it is precisely this new Christianity which must be established.

But we must be realistic. If the Church is within its rights in demanding of the public powers the concrete freedom proper to every religion, then it follows that the pluralism which exists as a fact in so many countries today obliges the state institutions to observe a neutral position. This is to say that the synthesis of Christian values and human values, which we said was so necessary for the existence of a Christian people, will not take place there. The fact of Christianity having its own institutions in the field of education and research is not at all a means of conserving or preserving the past, though it can be that at times. It is first of all a means of looking forward to the future wherein the rough outlines of a new style of Christianity can be filled in. From another point of view, these institutions render service to the secular city to the extent that they take on the task of working out a synthesis of spiritual values and technological progress--a task which is so important today and which the state itself cannot accomplish.

Notes begin on page 329.

Rahner's "Anonymous Christian"

Klaus Riesenhuber, S.J.

There has been a recent opening out of official Catholicism toward dialogue with other Christians and solidarity with men not
professedly Christian. These contacts have lent urgency to the
question of precisely how an enlightened Catholic ought to regard
the personal worth of these individuals so shadowed up till now
by stress on their engulfment in error. Such a shadow foredooms
our friendliness to disappointment or superficial compromise.
Only as somehow sharing in the salvation brought by Christ can
anyone be welcomed to our dialogue. . . .

The anonymous Christian is the person who has in fact a positive relation to Christ's redemptive act and to his Church, but
not as a member of the visible Church which officially represents
Christianity. He belongs to that part of the "people of God" that
has actually been touched by the reality of the redemption without being members of the visible Church. Such a classification
is not readily accessible to our human thought-patterns, partly
because it has no directly perceptible structure. Partly too it

is a merely transitional state whose meaning and definition can be seen only in the light of the finished product, namely the member of the Church in the fullest sense. The goal of being "a perfect Christian" thus enters into the dynamic definition of each existing man, no less than of us declared Christians who also realize that goal so imperfectly. The phenomenon from which we start our inquiry is not dogma as formulated, but the developed Christian consciousness. This is an outlook on the significance of being a man and Christian which is of much greater fulness and depth than we can formulate in any proposition.

The Christian is aware of himself as the object of God's free and grace-filled appeal in history, an appeal which is the summoning word of God's own self-revelation given just as truly to all other men. God discloses himself to men in his Son's Incarnation, whose meaning and goal are thus the self-communication of God to the whole of humanity. This favor of God made available in the Incarnation is actually received by men in groups and individually through a historically conditioned process. Man's bodily and social structure on the one hand, and on the other God's free decision to give this grace by an embodied sacramental-ecclesial channel, account for membership in a visible Church as the earth-bound goal of God's saving work.

Membership admits degrees

The Church is neither in its membership nor in its definition identical with the totality of mankind invited to salvation. Rather it is a "sign lifted up for the Gentiles" (Is 11:12, DS 3014) and thus set apart from the rest of men. Membership in the Church requires not only the fulfilment of conditions additional to the possession of our common humanity, but also differentiation and gradation in proportion as these conditions are divergently fulfilled. On this point Rahner's Lexikon article (6, 223) represents a shift from his earlier defense of a yes-no membership not admitting variations of degree. He now sees the notion of "membership" as having various degrees, at some point of which the Church itself has the right to draw a recognizable line juridically distinguishing members from non-members. She may even deliberately push this line more to the right or more to the left corresponding to the better realization of God's salvation-plan at successive stages of her time-bound existence. She may recognize the simple rite of valid baptism as conferring a certain submission to her visible structure. Full juridical membership requires

143

further the public acknowledgment of her doctrines and unity with her authorities. Yet mere fulfilment of such juridical require-ments cannot constitute the fullest degree of membership in a body whose true character is interior justification or the state of grace.

Thus on the one hand by even the mildest norm the largest section of mankind is perforce left outside Church membership; on the other hand, only in and from the Church can the whole of humanity attain its one and only existential goal. So the question of Church-membership acquires an existential relevance far beyond the juridical.

We may begin from the axiom "No salvation outside the Church," which rightly expresses the dogma that membership in the Church is not merely a prescription but is in the nature of things and indispensably a condition of salvation. But along with this we must keep in view God's will that all men should be saved, a really much more universal and operative norm.

Real, non-juridical members

Since God wills the salvation of all men, a necessary condition of salvation cannot be a juridical Church-membership beyond the scope of the majority of mankind. So there must be either "a kind of Church-membership which is genuine without being ju-ridical"--or we might prefer to say "a way of belonging to the Church other than by membership." What can we lay down about the nature and requirements of this "state of being saved" apart from full official membership in the visible Church?

Man's salvation-goal is attained not by the grace of God as such, but only by the grace of Christ. Since every being is char-acterized by its final aim whether he recognizes it as such or not, it is just as highly probable that there should be "Christians without knowing it" as that there should be "theists without know-ing it." The phenomenon of the anonymous Christian presupposes and includes a belonging to the Church at least in the sense of an ordering towards her. Moreover this belonging must be some-thing visible, since it is a visible Church; a purely interior im-plicit acceptance of the Church (votum Ecclesiae) corresponds inadequately to the necessity of the visible Church for salvation.

144

Goal of saving intervention

From this dilemma we derive the proximate focus of our inquiry: "How can men who have never heard of salvation in Christ
or of his Church believe in him and be visibly in relation to his
Church?" An answer can be found by putting straight first some
presuppositions which the goal established by God's saving intervention has implanted in both nature and supernature. Then we
can show how a man by his compliance with these presuppositions,
transcendentally underlying the level of his free decision, makes
a personal decision for Christ and thereby orders himself even
visibly toward the Church.

The Christian sees himself as addressee of a revelation made
freely by God without any inner necessity. This means not merely
that man's creation was optional on God's part and that man's sin
thereupon suspended what claims he might have had. It moreover
presents revelation as an I-Thou relation or dialogue between God
and men, in such a way that the addressee possesses an enduring
"structure" (Verfasstheit) independent of the revelation. This enduring structure must be conceived as continuing independently of
whether or not God either makes his revelation or finds man
receptive to it. In short, there is a "nature" of man distinct from
his supernatural condition. Moreover, it follows that the supernatural and the revelation do not share that peculiar quality of
man's "nature," whereby it is transcendentally affirmed even in
the very act of trying to negate or refuse it.

It further follows that there is something in the empirical
structure of mere man enabling him to receive and express God's
self-communication. This is only a way of saying that man's
nature must be spirit, in the sense of unlimited transcendental
openness to unrestricted being. What is called man's "obediential
potency" to receive revelation is not some competence coordi-
nated with various others, but is his spiritual nature itself. Our
every earthly encounter of knowing and willing is made possible by
the unfenced horizon of our spirit, which clutches for the infinity
of God in and through every particular object.

Expectancy of unexpected

For human intelligence abstracts form from the particular
given in sensible imagination. Abstraction occurs in that the
particular is seen against the background of being itself, which
background is grasped in intellect's clutching towards it. Being

itself, as a condition of the possibility of the knowledge of limitation itself, must be of itself pure, unlimited positiveness, thus
ultimately God himself. But God is grasped here not as object
(for the clutching towards him is a condition of the possibility of
the grasp of any object) but precisely as objective. This grasp
on the part of finite spirit puts man in a sort of expectation of
revelation which is an expectancy of the unexpected; a sort of
ontological alert for God's self-communication. This amounts
to a positive though conditional ordering to supernatural communication of grace. To this extent the Maréchal school has been
right in its insistence on the Thomist "natural desire of the beatific vision" as central to any metaphysic of spiritual nature.

So far we have attained only the possibility of being an anonymous theist: the man who possesses an inner ordering toward
God and his revelation. Next we must inquire whether this natural ordering is toward Christ too. It seems unlikely since Christ
is the freest and in this sense the "most unpredictable" occur-
rence in the whole of reality, and so not deducible from the nature
of man. But he is also the most decisive and important, and even
in a way the most evidently related to mankind: He became man
"for us men." His knowableness cannot be just tacitly tucked in
under a general metaphysics of knowledge; he is unique, too mysterious, and existentially meaningful.

God's own self-expression

By "the Word was made flesh" is ordinarily understood merely that the Word took on one among many realities alien to itself.
But Christ's human nature is to be regarded preferably as precisely that which comes to be (both with respect to essence and existence), when the Word realizes himself outside the sphere of the
divine. After all, we say the Word became man, and not merely
that a human nature began to subsist in him. The man Jesus is
really the visible form that God takes on when he empties himself.
So the humanity of Christ is not something planned independently,
prior to the plan of the Incarnation, but is the ontological and
existential result of the Word's emptying itself. This man is
precisely as man God's self-utterance (Äusserung) in his self-
emptying (Entäusserung), because God expresses himself in
somehow pressing himself out. But our human nature is identical
with that of Christ, and is therefore equally the potential expression of the self-emptying God.

146

Thus we might give this most radical definition of man: "The potential otherness of God's self-emptying and the potential brother of Christ." The obediential potency, respectively for hypostatic union and for (Christ's!) grace, is not just a potency among others, but is human nature itself. Since human nature is not understood immediately in itself (selbstverständlich), but is known from its act, it must be known most clearly and stripped most definitely of its mysteriousness by means of its highest possible act, that of being God's own other.

No adequate speculative analysis of man (Anthropologie) is thus possible without Christology. And Christology itself unless treated as part of the dogmatic theology of man risks verging on the mythical.

What is thus grasped "from above" in the fact of God's self-expression should be able to be shown somehow also "from below," from the uniqueness and dynamic finality of human nature, even though such a demonstration is possible only because we possess knowledge of the Incarnation as a fact. It is man's very being to be pointed beyond himself toward the mystery of God, not to grasp it but to be grasped and disposed by it. It is of his nature to be taken over, for he loves, and to step out into the unknown, for he trusts. And only in giving himself in love and trust does he come to his own. In this transcendence of human nature itself is already sketched the outline and idea of a way in which it can be taken over root and branch by God himself: the idea of a God-Man. The Incarnation is the eventual supreme fulfilment of human nature even considered in itself, since human nature really "is" in the extent to which it gives itself away.

Condition of self-giving

The ultimate and remotely discernible goal of human nature is thus its fulfilment as the otherness-in-being of God himself. This capacity and orientation of human nature is not just a coincidental suitableness to God's supernatural salvation-plan. Nature itself must rather be understood as that which God posits as a condition of communicating himself to it most intimately in an act of self-emptying. God's first and basic decree is thus the communication of himself; second, as indispensable means for this, man in his nature; third, as condition of man's possibility, the whole material creation.

Not only is God's act of creating an instrument of his self-communication. Even the possibility of creating is so grounded

in God's self-communicating capacity that God's creative power
must be seen as a secondary derivative of his primary arch-
capacity of communicating himself to the other. Creature may
be defined "the grammar of God's potential self-utterance."

Unforeseeable endangered?

But do not these insights into natural design and orientation
of the creature toward God's self-communication destroy the
strictly supernatural, undue, and unforeseeable character of God's
revelation? Do they not also compromise our own earlier contention that revelation must of its nature be dialogue, free of
debt or compulsion? If the possibility of Incarnation can be deduced from human nature itself, is not God's infinity restricted?
No, because the very possibility of Incarnation is seen only
in the existential situation of its revelation as a fact. Moreover,
although obediential potency is in nature not a mere nominalist
"absence of contradiction," but a real something, yet it does not
destroy the free unindebtedness of the supernatural. For even without the implementation of that free decision, creation would not be
meaningless. What we call the obediential potency is concretely
nothing other than human nature itself, and the perfectioning of
person by the encounter of spirit with world is already itself an
absolute value. Even beyond that, the potency would have a value
as making it possible to hear not merely God's utterance but also
his eloquent silence in case he should choose not to utter himself.
Summarizing: Man is by his very nature conditionally ordered
to God's revelation and self-communication in the God-Man. The
transfer of this conditioned to an unconditioned goal of man is God's
free decision. Nevertheless, this decision cannot remain an internal intention of God available to man only by revelation in (the)
Word. Rather the divine will disposing of the creature must necessarily attain form within this creature, as a real determination of
its being (but not its nature!).
What God wants as the unconditioned goal-directedness of the
world is a real determination inside it. Being ordered toward a
supernatural goal is not just a juridical new name for something
whose reality is not affected. It is a real element within the being
of man prior to freedom and justification, and this reality may be
called "the supernatural existential." It is supernatural and undue,
since it is not yet given in the gift of "nature itself," (nature in
sense antithetical to supernature, grace), but freely donated
(eingestiftet) by God into nature. But once given, the supernatural

existential must not be conceived as lying on the fringes of man's being; for what is most superior is also most deeply interior. The whole dynamic finality of the remainder of creation is also gathered up and bound into the supernatural destiny of man, directed out of himself, in such a way that he can find no harmonious completion within his own natural sphere. Thus, strange as it seems, the conditioned realities of grace and incarnation become the unconditioned meaning and goal of man's being, insofar as their communication becomes the principle of harmonious unity of the whole natural creation.

The supernatural existential is given to man irrefutably and independently of his acceptance or rejection of grace. Man's refusal of what penetrates and orients his whole nature can only be regarded as a disease, not a private safekeeping of some portion of his being untarnished by such refusal. This is the reason why turning away from Christ means complete damnation.

If this grace to which man is finally ordered is to be essentially supernatural (and consequently not naturally attainable), it must consist in uncreated grace, God's communication of himself. This communication as supernatural can be received by man only if the "receiving" itself is supernatural, due to the aid of created grace. Otherwise God's own self-giving would be made finite, earthly, and powerless by being received according to the capacity of the receiver.

Not intermittent, capricious

The universal salvific will of God suggests that this created grace be available to all men at all times, and thus be not an intermittent and capricious intervention on God's part but an enduring preconditioning offer (Angebot). Thus for every man, surrounded as he is by God's saving will concretized in the existential offer of grace, there opens out constantly a transcendent supernatural horizon toward the God of grace. This concretized offer of grace, rendering man capable of adequately receiving God's communication in word and deed, contains already a sort of (inner, not public) revelation. Thus every man lives within the pale of a salvific will of God revealing itself in the enduring offer of grace.

Our theological anthropology has up to this point treated only man's individual and transcendental aspect, not the embodiment of these traits of his being in the categories of the perceptible and social. We must decline this further inquiry, because it adds

149

no decisive evidences for our chosen theme of what it means to be an anonymous Christian.

We must note finally that the "supernaturally salvific will of God revealing itself in the existential offer of grace" pertains to man's very nature, not in the sense that word had in Christian asceticism as antithesis to grace, but in the modern sense of nature as antithesis to person, i.e. those determinations of man prior to his free decision. How far it pertains also to "person" we must next inquire. Röper extends the term "anonymous Christian" to all men irrespective of their acceptance of the supernatural call, whereas Rahner more correctly requires for it a kind of implicit personal acceptance.

Man's predetermined nature is intended to be freely accepted and thus imprinted with the stamp of his personality. Man's spirit never comes in contact with a given object without turning in upon itself and "realizing" (perceiving/fulfilling) itself the more by that very act. In free decision man determines not merely an external object, but also the innermost core of his own being, in relating himself to that object.

Affirms whole given nature

To this extent any decision of freedom involves a measure of disposing of the totality of the acting subject. Hence, whoever by free decision says yes to himself and thus accepts himself, affirms thereby (in varying degree) his whole antecedently given nature with all its structures, not prescinding from its only partially conscious predeterminations. This transcendental function of freedom comes into play only by conflict with environment, but in any element whatsoever of that environment.

What actual realities are touched by the transcendental freedom of a subject's self-acceptance? The object of the choice must be somehow known. Purely juridical situations are not attested in consciousness, but realities of nature are, and the more in proportion to their nobility. Therefore the reality of the supernatural existential offer of grace in man must somehow dawn upon his consciousness in order to be the inescapable object of free choice.

This a priori norm can be further established a posteriori by the experience of individual men. In that experience, admittedly, no sharp line of demarcation is perceptible between nature-spirit and the transfusing supernatural call of grace. The respective products of the two planes are mingled in all our experiences,

150

but in such a way as to make perceptible a different emphasis or degree. The a priori norm must be applied in order to distinguish the realities which coalesce in the genuine datum of experience.

Such supernaturally transfused experience is found in the experience of the heart's unlimited yearning, of radical optimism, of unquietable discontent, of anguish at the insufficiency of all we can reach, of radical protest against death, of being face to face with absolute love, precisely there, where it cannot be grasped and seems to be enveloped in silence, in the experience of guilt which still leaves hope. All these are only concrete poignant expressions of man's basic experience that life is lived from out of Mystery, is grounded and enveloped in It, that he lives in Its shadow and harkens to Its voice.

This awareness of mystery is itself already a directedness toward God-as-father serenely but inexorably recognized as making possible every earthly knowledge and love. Every awareness of absolute obligation also includes God as supreme worth and essential will, even in the act of questioning his existence. Any self-styled atheist who has learned to accept the fact of his transcendent nature with its mystery and its moral compulsion has thereby accepted God. So far he is only "a theist without knowing it."

He becomes, further, "a Christian without knowing it," insofar as the only goal which his nature now has owing to his "supernatural existential" must somehow be reflected in consciousness. This is true first because of its ontological nobility and secondly because of its inwardness to his spirit. A third reason is that the grace offered to man is divinizing and is already a sort of beginning of the beatific vision.

Here is even a fourth reason: Nature's own awareness of transcendence is based upon the natural formal object of spirit, included as horizon in every act of knowing and willing; but since no natural intensifying of a purely natural potency will render possible a supernatural act, the formal object of spirit in this order must be supernatural and must be as such "included in consciousness" though not as an object known, nor even experientially distinguished from simultaneous data of consciousness (e.g. the natural formal object). Thus concupiscence is experienced in man as something alien and out of place, precisely insofar as it is compared with the grace which is simultaneously being experienced, since concupiscence in fact conflicts with grace but not with nature.

Grace filled with word

Grace as offered and experienced as offered cannot be regarded as a "thing" antithetically corresponding to some revelational content of God's word. Rather, just as God's word itself is full of grace, so his grace is full of word, revelatory.
Communication of grace is thus always fundamentally a revelation of dogma to the individual. The supernatural existential
is the ground of an inner existentiell experience of what is
historically and officially proclaimed as revealed. The total
content of revelation is nothing other than the Trinity's divinizing
self-communication to man in uncreated grace. Yet the existential offer of this communication is precisely what man experiences! Thus the content of revelation is already "given" within
him before the word of revelation is spoken. The grace prerequisite for receiving a revelation already virtually contains
that revelation. The verbal revelation makes explicit and reflex
in consciousness what was somehow there already. Christianity
(inclusive of grace, Incarnation and Trinity) is the clear articu-
lation of what man experiences obscurely in concrete existence.

If then offered grace and revelation are a reality present in
every man, then he can personally say yes to them. Since they
are "contained in consciousness" as its un-objective horizon and
its inner dynamism, a man's very encounter with the world includes already occasion for rejection or acceptance of what he
himself is. But in accepting himself as he is, the man accepts
God's grace and revelation within him, and thus makes a supernatural meritorious act of (implicit or virtual) faith, though he
know it not. Whoever says yes to his own being-a-man, says
yes to the Son of Man, and is thereby a Christian without knowing
it.

Yes to oneself, yes to God

Thus the silent uprightness of patience amid routine duties
is the form under which many a "pagan" says yes to his own being
and thereby to God. This definitive yes is to be divined in man's
continually choosing the good rather than the evil in any particular
matter which may confront him. Death especially affords occasion
for the definitive acceptance of the meaningful, challenging Mystery, in that he gives himself to It in trust.

Every grace of God is a grace of Christ, not merely by some
price-tag fastened onto it externally, but by an inner structure

conformable to its origin in Christ's salvific act. But since the Church is only the prolongation of the mystery of Christ, every grace is a grace of the Church and every acceptance of it is an "existentiell" acceptance of the Church (quite apart from the inexorable social character of all men's actions, or any positive decree of Christ in this matter).

That real directedness toward Church-membership is not something purely internal. Just as man is not "spirit plus body" but spirit insofar as finding expression in body; just as grace too is incarnational and sacramental: so too any man's implicit acceptance of the Church is perforce to some extent embodied in a bodily and perceptible expression. This does not yet mean that anybody, nor necessarily even the man himself, can understand the expression.

Perceptible, not perceived

At root and in their fulness there is perfect unity between the two realities of "justification" and "historicosocial perceptibleness of salvation by visible connection with the Church." Yet the two are not simply identical, and their corresponding phases can be quite unconnected, except at their inexorable outset-point in the nature of man as "Christian-without-knowing-it." Outside the Church there is no salvation, as the axiom rightly puts it, insofar as salvation presumes a "perceptible" connection with the Church, which is not the same as a "perceived" membership in it. In default of adequate availability of revelation, sacraments, and the official Church, a man who personally says yes to his own supernaturally preconditioned nature has made himself a Christian without knowing it.

It follows that Christianity is not one religion to vindicate its place among many, but the actuation of and judgment upon what men recognize as religion. The pervasive un-Christianity of the world is not so depressing when we recognize the extent to which people not officially Christian are really Christian after all and share doubtless in the same faith and grace. The visible Church takes on the appearance not of a snobbish salvation-club, but of a shock-troop riding at the head of all the world's Christians. The Church's duty of enrolling all men in her visible ranks is not diminished. She is not just a medium of salvation, but also its symbol which is not complete until the heathens are enrolled; also the grace given to the heathens demands expression in the Church. Moreover, she offers them greater possibilities of salvation than anonymous Christianity; for, the more explicit an existential value is, the more easily and perfectly can it be realized. Her own apostolate is her effort to bring to a fuller unfolding and more reflex awareness the sketched and often actualized Christianity which those outside share already with her own members.

Notes begin on page 330.

The Church's Proper Task
and Competence

John A. Rohr, S.J., and David Luecke

The writers of this article--a Jesuit priest and a Lutheran min-
ister--are both working on secular campuses in doctoral programs
concerned with the administration of the secular affairs of society.
We consider ourselves very sympathetic to the cause of renewal
in the Church and greater involvement of the Church in society.
Yet in discussions between ourselves on the problem of the whole
Church of Christ, we have found we have similar reservations
about the thrust of current tendencies among churchmen. The
present article is our analysis of these tendencies and our response to them. Though critical of certain assumptions and objectives our contemporaries seem to entertain, we consider that
our remarks come from within the current movement in the Church
for greater relevance to modern man.

The first of our reservations stems from an uneasy feeling that
today's impatience with the Church has a frantic character. There
is always need for the kind of wholesome restlessness that is born
of divine discontent; this enriches the Church with an awareness

of being a Church of sinners and therefore an ecclesia semper reformanda. It is praiseworthy to want to see the Church involved in the City of Man. But the impatience we criticize goes beyond that: it seems to demand that the Church not only concern itself about the great problems of the day, but also produce answers.

Too often we are reminded how little the Church has to say to the Negro, to the poor, or to the great ones of this world who decide the issues of war and peace. If "having little to say" means that in recent years the Church has not been concerned with these issues, we can only deny the charge. If it means that the Church has had little success in translating its concern into effective action, we must agree. From our agreement, however, we do not deduce a deficiency in the Church. It is a misunderstanding of the Church's nature to accuse it of infidelity to the gospel because of its failure to easily solve the great issues of our day. Christ did not provide a panacea for the economic and political problems of society. His followers have no special title to the human wisdom necessary to solve the great, complex problems of this world.

We sense that a contrary assumption underlies the endless, wearisome discussions on the "role of the Church" in war and peace, racial harmony and so on. Impatience with the Church in its failure to find answers to such questions seems to rest on the gratuitous assumption that there is a distinctively Christian ethic for every social disorder. We cannot agree. If a Christian were to cease believing in Christ, it is difficult to see how he could reasonably change his views on these questions. To be sure, a Christian's faith should deepen his concern, and it is to be hoped that his concern would stimulate insights into these vexing issues. But to look to one's faith in Christ as affording a head start in the race for substantive solutions to social problems is misguided. Such an assumption defies--to some extent--the principle of the autonomy of the secular, namely, that there are areas of human endeavor in which man is on his own and in which the Church, despite its passionate concern, has no particular professional competence.

The lack of such competence must not, however, be a cloak for a callous indifference to the tragic lot of sinful man. The Church must use what resources it has to reach meaningful answers. When it fails, though, it cannot be cast aside as an unprofitable servant any more than we reject the government, the universities or other human institutions that, like the Church,

156

have failed to solve these problems. The Church enters the arena
of human affairs on an equal footing with its fellow dwellers in
the City of Man. Its divine origin does not guarantee immediate
success.

We see in the impatient demand for visible results another,
and a deeper, problem in the Church. It is a growing embarrassment with the supernatural. This takes the form of increasing reluctance to introduce a supernatural dimension into
discussions of human problems. Such embarrassment comes
from the laudable desire to be heard today. "Relevance" is the
word, and it is a crucial word for the ministry of the Church.
Yet it can cause a dangerous backlash. In the society of today
it is the problems of this world, not those of the next, that are
to be taken seriously. The message of man's broken relationship with God and of the full weight of God's answering judgment
is not so much unwelcome in the modern world as ignored. Proclaiming that message to a hostile world is not half as painful
as being ignored by people who do not care. In such a situation
the road to relevance becomes all too clear. Gloss over what
seems to be of no concern and concentrate on the problems
society does seem to care about. The irony is that this embar-
rassed silence about the supernatural renders the ultimate success of the pursuit of relevance most unlikely.

We do not at all suggest that the prophets of the dead God have
won the day. We doubt if that is the Church's problem today. Rather, this embarrassment with the supernatural takes the form
of speaking for only half a God. The God of love and intimate concern for every human being is very much alive for the young
generation of churchmen. Here is a God that can be made directly
relevant to people concerned with peace movements and civil
rights. The simple fact is, however, that the Christian God is
also a God of judgment and condemnation. His love finds its full
meaning only in the context of eternal judgment and the definitive
word of mercy in Christ. That is what makes His love uniquely
different from human love. To speak of His love outside this context is to add nothing new to the human scene. When the God of
Judgment is shelved, sermons on love are only inspirational poetry.
Those whose goal is to inspire can find an audience without much
difficulty. But in their concern for relevance they run the risk of
tagging along pathetically behind the secular bandwagon of social
concern. . . .

Another criticism of ours comes from the suspicion that churchmen are in danger of succumbing to that peculiarly American dream

of the perfectibility of society. Not a few observers of today's youth have noted its lofty sense of idealism. There are many reasons for this development in our affluent culture; but can the Church abrogate its critical function and accept any cultural idea that seems to be "for a good cause"?

We do not attack idealism, but we think churchmen should temper it with theological realism. It is theologically unsound and irresponsible to accept, consciously or unconsciously, the ideal of a humanly perfectible society. We sense that many of our contemporaries are swept along in a humanist movement that has just this ideal as its goal. A culture that is committed to the Great Society and its war on poverty is to be commended and eagerly supported. There are limits, however, to what political programs can accomplish. Their effectiveness is generally confined to correcting major economic and social injustices. Is it being trite to observe that the problems of society go much deeper? Prejudice, violence, selfishness, fear, ignorance and oppression are all grounded in the basic predicament of man. The cause of that predicament is theological, not sociological. The judgment of God on sinful men and their societies cannot be wished away.

An idealism that would do away with violence, prejudice, fear and oppression without first reconciling men to God is doomed to failure. Churchmen who serve an idealism that discounts this reality are doing a double disservice. The first is to the Church, by diluting its message. The second is to society, by letting it build great expectations it cannot fulfill. Disappointment and increased bitterness must result. Social programs have unavoidable limitations. To let their leaders and the people they serve overlook this fact can lead to disaster--a foretaste of which is offered in the present violent riots. We would not retard the search for social justice, but we think the Church is in danger of forfeiting its unique contribution to this task if it ignores the theological dimension of the problems society encounters.

A further concern we share is the growing fixation on change for the sake of change. To a degree, this sort of fixation is inevitable in a time of renewal and the accompanying unfreezing of the old. The younger generation has always had the role of rocking the boat. . . . But unless a specific resettling of the load is intended, we fear this boat-rocking will become little more than the aimless amusement of children. To be sure, the Church needs new forms and structures for its liturgy, theology and organization, and the appropriate response in times of renewal is to experiment. Indeed, "experimental" ministries and liturgies have become the

158

new frontier in the Church. But it does not follow that anything new and different is always better. The change may be for the worse. The search for what to keep and what to revise is not easy. We look mostly in vain for truly useful experimentation. Where are the controls necessary for any scientifically acceptable experiment? In what form are data being collected? Who is processing the data? When and where are conclusions to be reached? To take the comfortable way out by refusing to look at the new is surely irresponsible, but no more responsible is the gratuitous assumption that the old forms have lost their value and should be cast off forthwith.

In the previous section we have discussed our criticisms of several tendencies among our young fellow clergymen. While we share their desire for a more effective and meaningful ministry, we feel their unrest betrays a misunderstanding of the institutional nature of the Church. In the six points that follow we shall address the difficulties we have mentioned above from the perspective of the nature and limitations of the institutional Church.

We use the term "institutional" in its neutral and objective sense. It is not synonymous with the Establishment. Our intention is not to condemn or to defend the policies and actions of current Church administrations. All too often this could be defending the indefensible. Rather, we propose to look at the work of the Church in the light of how it is organized and how it functions in society. From this perspective, what the Church can and, more important, cannot expect to accomplish becomes more apparent.

One of the difficulties in talking about the institutional Church is the common assumption that this is a purely human enterprise separate from the divine. A "building block" theology that distinguishes between divine acts, such as administration of the sacraments, and human functions, such as social action, does not do justice to the mysterious nature of the Church on earth. The divine and human inseparably permeate each other in the Church, as they do in its Founder. Thus the forms and functions the Church adopts on the organized, institutional level are as much "Church" as any other phase of its existence. Our six points follows:

1. . . . In becoming a Christian a man is not delivered from the responsibilities that are his as a human being. Although his faith may not enhance his insights into human affairs, it surely does not absolve him from concern. The same is true of the Church on the institutional level. Although the power of the Church

159

is frequently overrated, no one can deny that it enjoys abundant resources, which one can reasonably expect to be of considerable help in solving human problems. Among these resources we observe virtuous and learned personnel, supranational organization, wealth, prestige and experience. The fact that the Church has a transtemporal, supernatural mission does not free it from the duty to use the temporal resources it has acquired along the way to help mankind in its needs. The supernatural mission of the Church is no guarantee of special competence in temporal affairs, but neither is it an excuse for inaction.

It may seem we have reneged on our pledge to avoid a "building block" theology by our sharp distinction between the temporal and transtemporal spheres. In reply we insist that it is the same Church--with the mystery of both its human and divine elements-- that operates in both spheres. To put it bluntly, it is the Church of Christ, not just the human aspect of the Church, that lacks special competence in human affairs. We feel this statement can be justified by an appeal to the life of Christ Himself. Is it irreverent to suggest that our Lord enjoyed no special competence in solving complex social problems? We know He was deeply concerned with the injustice He saw, but did He evidence any special skills in formulating administrative techniques that might have ameliorated the inequities of the Roman tax system or put an end to the economic conditions that made slavery necessary?

2. Perhaps it is an erroneous notion of what ministry is that leads to this search for a Christian social ethic. It is only natural to look to the Church for special competence in those areas in which it exercises its ministry. Today, however, we hear of the inner city "ministry," where the Church joins and sometimes leads the secular forces that struggle for social justice. We would suggest that such work, important as it is, is not strictly ministry because it is not an area in which the Church has any special charism. It enters the inner city with the same doubts and misgivings as the mayor, the Board of Education and the police. If we must call this vital work "ministry," we should find another word to describe that activity in which the Church does have special competence--e.g., preaching the gospel, administering the sacraments and broadcasting the good news of our share in Christ's victory over sin and death.

This is not the place for wearisome quibbling over terms, but it is no quibble to insist that the Church is doing two different things when it baptizes an infant on Sunday afternoon and when it lobbies for increased Aid to Dependent Children on Monday morning.

The two activities are not unrelated, but they are surely different. If ministry is associated with special competence, then inner city work must not be called ministry, for this would place impossible demands upon the Church. If ministry is not associated with special competence, then it becomes everything the Church does. Such a definition strips the term of all meaning.

Our insistence that the Church's inner city work is not ministry does not expel the Church from the urban ghettos. It must be there, but not for the same reason that it exercises its ministry within its sphere of special competence. It must be in the inner city because it cannot avoid the responsibilities of citizenship in the City of Man.

3. In the strident tones of the Vietnam debate, and the scandal found in the fact that the churchly nest shelters both hawks and doves, we see a misunderstanding of the institutional unity Christians can legitimately expect. Those who support the war are not spared the charge of making a mockery of the gospel, while critics of the war are berated for denying their faith in refusing to join the crusade against godless communism. Underlying the frantic charges and countercharges is the implicit assumption that all Christians should reach the same conclusion on the war. Such a position would seem to follow from the assumption we have already criticized, namely, that there are no pat answers flowing from a specifically Christian social ethic. If there were such easy answers, it would be reasonable to assume there was one Christian answer to Vietnam, and the righteous fury directed at those Christians who reject it would be justified. In the absence of such a simplistic ethic, we feel the best a Christian can do is to show how the position he defends is not inconsistent with the gospel.

This is a far more measured claim than we are accustomed to hear from those who tell us we need only "read the gospel" to discover what we should think about Vietnam. There is a considerable difference between what is not inconsistent with the gospel and what is demanded by the gospel. An attentive awareness of this difference might remind the religious participants in the Vietnam debate that there is no scandal in Christians disagreeing over the moral implications of American foreign policy.

4. In our critique of this kind of Christian social ethic, we have tried to steer a middle course between those who would relegate the Church to the sacristy and those who demand that it be a social prophet of unfailing wisdom. It is to be hoped that our plea for moderation will put into perspective the significance of any particular commitment the institutional Church might make,

161

for we feel it is important to realize that the whole of Christianity does not stand or fall on the Church's contribution to a particular social problem. The Lord must be worshiped and the gospel preached no matter what happens in Vietnam or in our urban ghettos. The Church cannot become so identified with a particular cause that its success would allow complacency or its failure apostasy. Those who say the Church is useless as long as Negroes are denied justice imply that the Church's worship is merely a means toward building a better world--and if the better world is not forthcoming, the worship was in vain. We suggest the worship of God is an absolute value that needs no further justification.

The purpose of our building the City of Man is to enable us to enhance the worship of God. We do not love God in order that we may love our neighbor; rather, we love our neighbor in order to grow in the love of God. The Church must surely bear a proportionate share of the guilt for the tragedy of our cities, but this guilt must not become a death certificate, for the total life of the Church never was and never could be exhausted in a temporal concern of this nature--even so paramount a concern as the future of our cities.

5. We cannot share the horror of our contemporaries when they first discover the Church's fascination with the status quo. They state quite correctly that the Church has lost much of the revolutionary élan that characterized its Founder, but they forget that Jesus was a person and not a religious organization. The Church cannot be the true Church of Christ without also being a religious organization. In the latter capacity, it is extremely difficult for it to overcome the sociological forces that underscore the conservative tendency of nearly all religious organizations. This tendency is not always bad. Christianity has often made important contributions to the stability of the regimes it has encountered throughout its history. The same is true of the other great religions of the world. The Church's contribution to stability is made not in its capacity as Christianity, but in its capacity as religion. This stabilizing function of the Church is not likely to endear it to angry young men in a revolutionary age, but to wish it away is futile. Rather than fret over the built-in conservatism of the Church, let us rather rejoice in such remarkable persons as Pope John or Dietrich Bonhoeffer or Martin Luther King, whose genius consisted in affirming the revolutionary spirit of Christ within the conservative framework of His Church.

6. Finally, a comment on how the Church can be used by secular forces. This question is as old as the Constantinian Church.

162

From Constantine to Hitler the Church has always been faced with the danger (and all too frequently with the reality) of a sell-out to secular interests. In its involvement in the affairs of men, the Church can never afford to become so identified with a particular position that it cannot stand apart from it and criticize. If, however, the Church becomes too intransigent in its insistence on its own independence, it cannot play an effective role in the political arena.

To play this role effectively, the Church must be willing to be used by secular forces. It cannot have it both ways--hoping to preserve its social effectiveness and its political virginity. The question of the correct sort of involvement is one of degree.

The patriotic preacher who delivers a flag-waving harangue on the Fourth of July must recognize that he is an instrument of government policy. He contributes to the stability of the nation. The inevitable minister, rabbi and priest who decorate most civic functions are surely being used by government. This is not bad; in most cases it is probably quite good. Nevertheless, we must be aware of just what is going on. This is no less true of the religious leaders who lend their services to protest groups or to the "Liberal Establishment." When a university chaplain blesses a draft-card burning session, he is being used by secular forces no less than the minister who prays for the success of the nation in arms. All clergymen who are willing to get involved in the affairs of men must be willing to subject themselves to being used by the forces of the secular city. They must, however, constantly be on their guard lest their service become a sellout.

There is danger of a sellout only when the Church rejects its role as the conscience of those it serves. If it is silent when the world proclaims its own message of salvation through human progress, it betrays Him who alone is the Way. If it encourages men in the belief of a world made perfect through human effort alone, it trades Jerusalem for a tower of Babel. If, in the excitement of helping men live, it forgets to tell them how to die, it abandons Him who is the Resurrection and the Life. Its involvement in the affairs of men can never deliver it from its divine commission to remind men that they stand under God's judgment; that without the grace of Christ they are "senseless, faithless, heartless, ruthless."

These are hard sayings that must be said, and who can say them save the Church of Christ?

Notes begin on page 330.

163

Toward a Theology of
the City Church

John J. Harmon

Jesus Christ. In these two words all of human life is summed
up--the life that the Church lives for the sake of the world, and
the life that the world lives for the sake of the Church.

For our thinking, our acting, our praying--for everything that
is blessedly human--Jesus Christ is the first fact, the absolute
beginning. He is neither derivative nor prospective, the end of
a thought process or the possibility of a future salvation. For
me, for my brother, for believer and unbeliever, for the whole
human race and its history, for every bit of creation, he is now,
at this moment, absolutely and unavoidably determinative.

For every soul, then, the only crucial question is this: what
has happened to me, to us, in Jesus Christ? What exactly is it
that he has done to me and my brother, that he does to me and
my brother?

I believe it is precisely from avoiding this question, or di-
minishing it, that most of the misshapen life in the Church and
in the world originates. Since we fail to realize who we all al-

ready <u>are</u>, we become instead what is momentarily most convenient.
It may seem presumptuous and irrelevant to begin this essay with
words about Christ. Yet I'm not only beginning this way, but will
continue and expand this initial thought, since my experience in
the life of the Church in the city convinces me that the great detriment is theological rather than practical--if we may for the moment incorrectly sever these two. I am absolutely certain that it is
not primarily a new program that we need, new techniques, new
research, new experimentation, new expenditures, even new at-
titudes--but rather a new look at the Gospel, a theological recovery.

There is a story about a minister doing graduate work who was
required to write a paper about the South. This he did, examining
the area in careful detail--historically, geographically, sociologically, and economically. When the paper was returned it bore this
comment from the professor: "This is an excellent paper--for a
Marxist. But does it mean nothing to the South that Christ died and
rose?" I'm certain it's the same question that we must ask about
our present concern: "Does it mean nothing to the city that Jesus
Christ died and rose?"

Let me continue then with this basic question: what has happened in and through Jesus Christ?

I will try to answer in two ways. First, with a preliminary and
very tentative statement of what the risen Christ has done; a statement that admittedly leaves many questions unanswered, but at
least can be used as a starting point. Then I will explore some implications of this statement by using it as a base for criticism of
the way the Church has existed in the city and for possible new
directions. The racial movement will supply the principal illustrations, since this is <u>the</u> mirror in which we must see the
urban church today. However, it should be plain that this movement is merely the sharpest exposé of the malfunctioning of our
life toward <u>all</u> of the issues and people of the city.

> My brothers think what sort of people you are, whom God
> has called. Few of you are men of wisdom, by any human
> standard; few are powerful or highly born. Yet, to shame
> the wise, God has chosen what the world counts folly, and
> to shame what is strong, God has chosen what the world
> counts weakness. He has chosen things low and contemptible,
> mere nothings, to overthrow the existing order. And so
> there is no place for human pride in the presence of God.
> You are in Christ Jesus by God's act, for God has made
> him our wisdom; he is our righteousness; in him we are

165

consecrated and set free. And so (in the words of Scripture), 'If a man is proud, let him be proud of the Lord.'

As for me, brothers, when I came to you, I declared the attested truth of God without display of fine words or wisdom. I resolved that while I was with you I would think of nothing but Jesus Christ--Christ nailed to the cross. I came before you weak, as I was then, nervous and shaking with fear.

Cor. 1:26--2:3, N.E.B.

Jesus Christ has established peace among all men. He is Lord-- not of some future existence or of an earlier apostolic existence-- but of all life, here and now. And as a result, all is well between me and my neighbor. We are brothers. The atonement as ac- complished fact is the theological key for the life of the Church in the city.

This peace is not an idea, an ideal, or a principle; it is the most concrete and real fact of our present existence. When I meet a man for the first time--any man, Christian or not--I meet somebody whom I already know profoundly, because I al- ready know the most important thing about myself and him: the fact that we have been made interlocking human beings by Christ. He may not know this, and I may refuse to honor it by creating urban concentration camps for him; but Christ's unifying Lordship over the two of us remains nonetheless. There is nothing that can destroy it--even though all the visible evidence seems to contradict it.

And so I can embrace this man without fear, because there is nothing special, nothing frightening, we two have to do in order to be human beings together. We only have to recognize, expose, and implement what is already done. And I can listen to him without fear, knowing that even though he may deny Christ, he can still speak a word of life to me since he is Christ's.

The fact that we are able to forgive one another, for example, rests on the fact that we are already ontologically one; that is, we do not create forgiveness, rather we acknowledge and expose the condition of forgiveness that already exists among us. And the fact that we are able to love one another rests on the prior fact that we are ontologically one; that is, we do not create love, but rather we uncover the condition of love that already exists among us. Conversely, the fact that we can really hate and destroy rests on the same foundation; for real evil is only possible when it strikes against real love, when it tries to destroy what is truly-- and not just ideally--at the heart of our existence.

166

Because of this deep, indestructible unity we have been freed from the deadly necessity of becoming imperialists and saving ourselves by achieving an ascendency over our neighbor through violence. Hatred, oppression and social malformation come from a deep desire to be somebody in the eyes of my brother and all of society; they are perverted ways of creating unity. But the Gospel message of peace, charity and forgiveness is the recognition that this desire has been accomplished forever in Christ. We need no longer let our anxiety lead us into violence, but simply accept the mutual life that is already ours. The only life that is life, is a life together, in which we seek to share together the whole spectrum of human experience, from pain to joy.

It is when I deny this unity with my brother that I begin to embrace what the Bible calls sin and death. The origin of sin and death is the denial of Christ's victory. This denial of the unity of life creates an unnatural, inhuman condition which is no longer a life in freedom but a sort of half-life under the dominion of death.

This is why the particular mark of the city today, segregation-- racial, social, economic, ecclesiastical--is so destructive. It imposes a condition of death upon the total community body; it forces all in the social body into a way of existence that is for all unnatural and degrading.

It is to celebrate the peace, joy, love and forgiveness in- destructibly imbedded in the common life of human society that we do the Eucharist, the action that continually reconstitutes us as Christians and is ultimately the most concrete summary of what our life in the city should be. We don't do the Eucharist in order to create a new condition between God and men, or among men, or to remind us of an ideal condition, but simply to lift our hearts in thanksgiving for the condition of organic unity that already exists and rules our lives. God in the Eucharist restates it for us and brings it back into remembrance--in the biblical sense of remem- brance. That is, we are in the Real Presence of the God who saved us in the event of our creation-redemption; and he recalls for us not only what life really is, but also that his presence is real in all of human existence.

And we bring all our pain, pettiness, hatred, and disobedience to the Eucharist, not in order to discard them, but because it is only in the context of real life that sin and death can best be recognized and then become the condition out of which healing emerges. The reason the Church commonly takes so negative a view of the city and its people is that we forget, as the Eucharist doesn't, that new life grows out of sin and deprivation, rather than over against it. Most sharply put, since Jesus is the person in history in whom the effects of sin are most visible, therefore it is by his wounds alone that we are healed.

The life of the Church in the city is at many places a repudiation of this victory of Christ, and a substitution of other, lesser determinants of human life for those of the Gospel. Perhaps this is because it is precisely in the city, with its rich concentration of people and movements, of pain and joy, that our ontological reality is most embarrassingly present--and therefore most apt to be rejected. And when I use the word "Church" I mean all organized Christian bodies, since our juridical separation is in no way so real or significant as the amazing unity we have achieved in our urban deficiencies.

For example, the power and presence of fear in the Church. We do not ever describe our life under this heading--it is not one of the marks of the Church--but it is present in the city Church at every level.

We see it in the way main-line Protestant parishes run away from the inner-city, and, without any sense of the spiritual death created in the act of abandoning brothers, either disband or replant themselves in more racially and economically segregated areas. While a host of prudential reasons have been exploited to rationalize this movement--and a similar retreat of individual Christians--the real and unspoken one is this: a fear of the new people who continually pour into the city.

The architectural evidence of this fear is everywhere. Most of the church buildings occupied by Negro congregations in inner-city ghettoes were abandoned by white Protestant christians. We have been seduced by our fears into thinking of congregational life as a refuge for certain types of people, rather than an affirmation of the marvellously diverse human community that the Lord has established.

And when, as in the case of Catholic parishes, this fear has not led to the actual removal of parishes, it has produced just as effective deterrents--for example, a parish ethos which very effectively rejects the dispossessed and the different, and makes the parish into a safe compound, not unlike the missionary compounds established under white, imperialist powers. Two Negroes went last year to a major Boston Catholic parish; as the procession passed them they heard one acolyte say in surprise to his companion, "Hey, look at the niggers!" And the real tragedy is that the very size and importance of this parish rest precisely

on the success it has had in being un-catholic--preserving itself
as a sanctuary for certain ethnic groups.

This fear is absolutely irrational for Christians, since all we
have to do to involve even the strangest new people in the life of
our congregations is to open our arms. "They" are already a part
of "us" in the most important sense, and our job is merely to
rejoice, and accept and implement this theological fact.

And we make a profound mistake when we explain this whole
frightened retreat under the heading of tactical error or sociological ignorance. It is certainly this; but the fear is far more basic.
And if we never explain how needless and unbelieving the fear is
for those under the Lord, we will perpetuate this disobedience.
The so-called "white backlash" in urban areas, presently being
exploited by a native fascist political movement, arises principally from among Christians who have retreated from their brothers.
And in the degree to which their fear is unexamined, unresolved,
and unexposed to the Word of God by the Church, the Church herself is actively nourishing a foul disease. She even nourishes it
in the uncritical support given the suburban fair housing movement,
which rests on the frightened assumption that while it is good for
Negroes to move into white areas, the reverse is not true, and
no realistic encouragement is given to a flow of whites into Negro
areas. If our goal is a visible expression of the integrated life
given us by Christ, we should properly adopt whichever tactic
is the most expedient.

The class and racial fears that create this compound mentality
are matched by another fear that impedes the Gospel in the city:
ecclesiastical fear. We are frightened of Christians outside our
ecclesiastical limits; we are even frightened of those within our
limits, but in other parishes.

Again, one might assume that the way Christian bodies minis-
tering in the city develop completely isolated, overlapping pro-
grams--apart from uniting in occasional ceremonial incantations
against liquor licenses, crime and poor garbage removal--is the
result of a lack of knowledge of the real needs of the metropolitan
area. It isn't. It comes directly from not believing that the risen
Lord has really given us an inescapable solidarity which far super-
sedes in importance our juridical boundaries. So then the only way
of life open to us is sectarian and competitive, and this gives birth
to fear.

And this fear operates even within church boundaries. Let someone try to list the evidence of real mutual interdependence and concern within denominations. The general rule in the city is compe-

169

tition and indifference: competition for parishioners and for larger slices of monetary help from denominational headquarters, and the indifference of wealthy parishes just a few blocks away from financially shaky ones. I can remember so well how each year I would examine the parochial statistics published by our Epis-copal diocese to see how well "my" parish had done in com-parison to adjoining parishes.

And it does no good to work towards "more cooperation" and "joint action" if we do not first acknowledge why we have been so isolationist and sectarian. Structural realignment and new techni-cal competence are no substitute for theological honesty. The old, unresolved fear will merely reappear in a new guise.

Our fears are so numerous:

We fear pentecostal and evangelical Christians who meet in store-fronts; we talk about them in very condescending terms, as though their way of responding to the Gospel in the city were childish and irrelevant. Perhaps our fear is a confession that they have a quality of obedience that we have largely lost, and that to listen to them as brothers would be too painful.

We have a fear of the freedom God has given us, which re-sults, for example, in parochial schools and Protestant Sunday Schools that make discipline and orderliness the main rule, and therefore expel or rebuff too casually those urban children who, for good reason, do not perceive "law and order" in such positive terms--the very children, incidentally, who are sensitive and honest enough to react against our barren catechetical formulas.

Our fear of freedom also results in an automatic liturgical life (no matter how many ceremonial and ritual anachronisms there are) that places a premium on following exact patterns of worship and resists any free movement of the Spirit or accom-modation to new movements and people within the city. Witness today the great pain it frequently causes to have freedom move-ment rallies, which are an important new para-liturgical expres-sion, occur within city church buildings. We fear, in other words, a liturgical expression which brings together in a sharp way the Gospel and the most pressing issues of the day.

We have a fear of unpopular causes, which has led the city church into the safe function of being an ambulance for the establishment--attempting to pick up the pieces of people being shattered by the system--rather than pressing for social revolu-tion. Again, there is no clearer evidence of this than in the freedom movement, in which the established urban churches, both black and white, have almost without exception not led, but

cautiously waited, and only now begin to authenticate the protest
--like the coward in James Russell Lowell's hymn of protest
against slavery who "stands aside till the multitude make virtue
of the faith they had denied."

We fear for our property, which leads us to limit those we
invite into our buildings to people who will either cause the least
damage, or contribute the most to their upkeep.

We have a fear of young people, especially teen-agers, who
often see more clearly the injustices in urban life because they
have not yet been forced into surrender. And this fear of young
people, whose protest we usually define only in negative terms
("delinquency," "drop-out," "gangs," etc.) results in much
church-sponsored group work being an effort to "help them adjust," rather than train them to be maladjusted to a sick way of
life, and to use their freedom to help transform the situation in
which they live.

It is useless to continue a catalog of our fears, because they
are so numerous and because they intersect with other disloyalties
in our life which we must go on to examine. The main point is to
perceive what it means that we, who know that mankind has been
set free from fear, are in so many ways frightened people; and
that our fears have been fused into our attitudes, our liturgy,
and our corporate structures.

Fear, as the non-violent movement has so clearly shown, often
passes into violence when it confronts its victim at first hand--
when the one who has been barred from the common life finally
presents his grievances in an unavoidable way. We call this
moment today the "crisis in the city"; and I would like to discuss
under the heading of "imperialism" the violence that often emerges
from within the Church when we attempt to reply to this crisis,
rather than merely running from it.

There are two currents of imperialism in the city church today,
indeed, in the Church everywhere. One is what one might call
"pedagogic imperialism," and the other is "programmatic imperialism." The first is the conviction that the Church alone
has or should have the answer to any issues in society; the second
is the conviction that the Church has, as an institution, a programmatic way of responding to issues. Neither view is very confidently held, because there is so much evidence of their failure.
Yet they are not abandoned, because the theological ground of a
new position has not been clarified.

The violence implicit in our imperialism is not quickly apparent, because we have already defined the forms in which

171

violence exists in such a way as to exclude our own. But it is very present--in the way we impose the responsibility for the crisis on other people and other forces; the way we refuse really to share the pain of this crisis by prescribing remedies that skirt the real illness; and the way we close our ears to the word of God about ourselves that comes from other people's pain.

On November 17, 1963, the American Bishops at Vatican II issued a pastoral, "Bonds of Union," which dealt in large part with the racial issue. It is a perfect example of "pedagogic imperialism." Similar documents could be culled from Protestant sources. I use this because of the nature of this occasion, and also because the political structures of many northern urban centers are heavily Catholic--which means that it is often through the Catholic Church that the Church as a whole can best see herself in the city.

The Bishops essentially said two things, one explicitly and one implicitly. Explicitly they condemned materialism and secularism as the source of the racial conflict; implicitly, they excused the Church of any responsibility for the terrible racist disease.

The attack on materialism, a familiar target of religious teaching, can be easily blunted by placing the increasing wealth of urban churches over against the increasing poverty of the urban dispossessed. Surely in each of the See cities represented in the magisterium--cities undoubtedly all having their racial and economic ghettoes--it is the Church as a whole that is materialistic, rich in buildings and capital investment, and especially rich in power. But even more important, its materialism is implicit in its increasing reliance in the city on a programmatic approach rather than on the Gospel as it is exposed in the ordinary human life of the city. I will deal further with this shortly; but it's good to recall now William Stringfellow's frequent observation regarding Protestantism, that it will only be able to really serve in the city when it is willing to become poor, poor in the sense of trusting in God's word as the source of its life.

The Bishops' attack on secularism is even more revealing and embarrassing. It represents the almost endemic inability of Christians to honor the Lordship of Christ over the total saeculum, and to recognize that Christ is present--perhaps in painful incognito-- in all of his world; and that what falls within the category "secular" is not to be feared and attacked, but to be listened to and learned from and loved. It is because of our imperialistic anti-secularism that we so often enter the urban scene thinking we bear great gifts, and therefore totally unprepared for the far greater gifts for us already present among the least, the last, and the lost. For example, the popular and violent myth that the lower class white person is the most anti-Negro is directly due to our unwillingness to accept the world as it really is; for it is precisely this person who does in so many ways live a life in common with Negroes in the mixed urban ghettoes--that is, live as the Lord has made it necessary for all of us to live.

But most glaring is the implicit denial on the part of the Bishops that the Church shares in the blame for the racial illness. The only beginning point we have for any perception of the urban situation, as it really is, is to confess our own participation. And the fact that we don't reflects the same theological poverty that motivates our anti-secularism: our fearful unwillingness to recognize that in Christ we are completely a part of this world, of its pain as well as its joy. To affirm our culpability is not a sign of disgrace or impotence, but a grateful admission that the healing word and presence of Christ for His Church is most powerfully present at the point of our failure. It was in Egypt, in the situation of slavery and degradation, that God approached Israel.

This "pedagogic imperialism" helps shape a similar "programmatic imperialism," under which urban church bodies elaborate ambitious projects on a parochial and city-wide level in order to "help people." This is perhaps more a Protestant expression than a Catholic; and it has a similar anti-secularism--a distrust of the possibility of "secular" agencies doing a sufficient job.

The urban church today supports case work institutions; extensive recreational programs; remedial reading; alcohol, drug and prisoner rehabilitation; urban renewal planning, etc., etc. Nobody can deny that these efforts have had great benefit and deserve great praise.

But two things must be said. First, all of this work exists because urban society as a whole has not accepted its proper responsibility for these needs; and surely it is not right that the Church become the means whereby the community body can escape its obligations. Secondly, an essential mark of so many of these efforts--and this is the imperialistic violence--is the way they implicitly deny the possibility that a new way of life can emerge from within the situation itself. Rather, it is generally assumed that the people are helpless captives of their own inadequacies and that a new form of health has to be superimposed from outside. And the chief sign of this is the way those who design urban church programs often refuse to live themselves at the point of crisis--an implicit confirmation of the impossibility of real and healthy life ever coming out of that situation.

173

Surely the central function of the Church in the city, as everywhere, is non-programmatic; it is to celebrate the Eucharist, to nourish Christians in Scripture and theology, and to provide a constant stream of people who know themselves to be free in the Lord to respond to and bear the pain and joy of urban life--that is, to live within it and not outside of it. And whatever programs do emerge should not be ecclesiastical;--should reflect the fact that it is with and through those who bear the chief burdens of our social sicknesses that we all can see most clearly what and how things should be done. In the same way that our social revolution envisions the end of the absentee landlord, there must be an end of the absentee ecclesiastical planner.

At this historical juncture the decision as to the nature of church programs is extremely important. The present system fulfills an ambulance function, and relieves from the community as a whole the responsibility of meeting some of its problems. And this is one reason so much suburban money is being produced to back these church programs: they ameliorate some of the symptoms without exposing and attacking the deeper issues. We preserve the ambulance system, in other words, not only because it gives us something to do in an age when people are saying that the Church is irrelevant, but also because it gives us something not to do.

But the ambulance period is past, if it ever could be justified. The so-called "riots" in Harlem, Rochester, and elsewhere are essentially healthy cries for revolutionary attack on the real roots of the urban concentration camps. To continue the ambulance mentality into a revolutionary period is to become counter-revolutionary!

Therefore parishes especially need to be freed at this moment from the imperialist burden (the "white man's burden," if you will), and begin to supply people ready to push for an urban revolution, an American revolution. And here we already have a faint model: the way urban Christians have responded to the freedom movement. The pattern has not been for parishes as a whole or city-wide organizations to become involved--except for purely nominal, verbal affirmations. Rather, individual Christians have responded and united themselves with other people of all sorts to form action groups that force the issue right into the "secular" order. It has been essentially a para-parochial, para-ecclesiastical action-- and this is as it should be.

Supporting this pedagogic and programmatic imperialism is a sacramental isolationism.

174

One reason the Church can presume to lecture the world (rather than learn together with the world) and program for it (rather than from within it) is because the most distinctive element of her life, her worship, is so ecclesiocentric that she becomes blind to the deepest issues of society. The Church at worship is the Church learning in each age what it means to serve and be served by humanity. But if the worship becomes introverted, then the only issues clearly perceived will be churchly ones--having to do with the survival and well-being of the Church--while the great human issues will become appendages of the needs of the Church. This explains why we have all been so blind to the racial issue until recently: we could only see it--when we did--in terms of the integration of parish life in changing neighborhoods. But to see only this is to see nothing! The key urban issue of our time had been reduced to an ecclesiastical housekeeping detail!

But the sacraments are not actions and signs relating solely, or even primarily, to the Church. Before they signify anything to or about the Church, they speak about the world which includes the Church. More properly, they cannot say anything substantial to or about the Church unless their primary secular character is carefully guarded.

Baptism, for example, is not merely an entrance into the Body of Christ, an initiatory rite, along with Confirmation, for the Church. Rather, it is the graceful sign of the prior entrance of all humanity into brotherhood in Christ, the Body of the human family which he has established in peace. When the Church baptizes she is saying in effect: what is true of this person is true of all. In fact, it cannot be true of the one baptized unless it be true of all. And if one says, why then baptize, the answer is simple: it makes "all the difference in the world" whether or not you know who you are--witness the life of the Church in the city today!

It follows also that the ecumenical question of the validity of Baptism (and all the sacraments) hinges on a form and intention that are to be far more broadly seen than they are now, when they've degenerated into rudimentary technical requirements. Validity must be restated in terms that include the form and intention with which all those participating in the rite are acknowledging and acting out a prior commitment to a human way of life among all men.

I count it as a sign of particular importance that I first met my most recent Godchild on a picketline downtown, protesting de facto segregation in the schools; and that when she was baptized in a

Boston Episcopal Church on Easter Eve, I was sitting-in and fasting
in an Episcopal Church in North Carolina. And when I sent her a
telegram of congratulations I spoke of her Baptism as a graceful and
effective "demonstration, " and felt that this was good theological
terminology. . . . There is a danger, incidentally, that the present
ecumenical consensus on the validity of the Baptism of separated
brothers has been found at the expense of avoiding this secular
dimension of the sacrament.

If what I'm saying is true, then certain prohibitions clearly
exist that are important for our life in the city. The Church cannot at the same time baptize some people and retreat from others;
this may well be invalid Baptism, as well as certainly being an
invalid mission. Nor can we affirm the Lordship of Christ in and
over all humanity in the baptismal rite, and at the same time refuse to bear the pain of overthrowing the urban death camps; this
also may well be invalid Baptism, as it is certainly an invalid
response to human suffering.

I realize all the problems this view produces. But does it really
produce more problems than to just continue with a sacramental
theology which somehow helps sanctify human misery and alienation?

The same worldly dimension emerges when we consider Holy
Matrimony.

This sacrament speaks of an indissoluble unity between two
people. But this unity is not at its heart something that develops
over the years between the partners, within the fabric of the
home. Marital unity is not something that develops within the marriage, as we generally imply in our teaching. More basically, it
depends upon and flows out of the pre-marital unity that existed
between the partners as a result of the victory of Christ. At every
point in the growth of a marriage, especially the moments of great
pain and hostility, it is this prior ontological fact that makes the
continuance of life together possible.

The implications of this are many. One is of special importance
today, the question of "racial inter-marriage." As the great cities
become more and more the crucial points in the racial revolution,
the significance of this sexual issue heightens.

Almost universally white parents have a deep sexual fear in
their hearts. Unquestionably, for example, in a city like Boston
it is this unspoken fear that stands behind the refusal of the School
Committee to even admit that de facto segregation exists and therefore have to mix children in the schools.

And how has the Church responded to this fear? At worst, the
churches have discouraged such marriages, --which is at least an

176

honest reflection of the basically racist character of white American christianity. It is very rare, for example, that churches in the city, Negro or white, develop programs that place white and black teen-age boys and girls together.

At best, the churches have given prudential approval to such unions, by saying that there is no objection in the Gospel to this, and that it is a purely personal decision in any event--but of course one must recognize that society as a whole still does not approve. The one thing we never say unequivocally is: yes, it is very good for Negro and white to marry--especially today!

In other words, because we have treated Matrimony in an unworldly, private way, and have overlooked in our teaching the implications of the pre-marital ontological union, we can only look at "mixed marriages" as somehow being in a special category and be forced to use a special phrase to describe it. And since marriage has always been an area of human life in which the Church has had the deepest influence, it is probably true to say that the sexual aspect of our urban racial sickness is most due to the churches. Happily there are increasing marriages of this sort in the cities; but most of them, of necessity, occur outside the orbit of the organized church.

Again, the sacrament of Penance or Confession is also largely compressed into too small a focus. For most people it is a matter of individual healing; a few see it as a participation in the healing of the Body of the Church. But how many see it as having any connection with the healing of the community body, which really has to be its initial focus if it is to reflect the life together that God has given us.

The collective conscience of German christians has been examined on the issue of their death camps. But who examines our conscience about our urban death camps? Do any of the issues we currently define as being central to the urban scene ever come within the context of confession? Another way of asking this is: how many of us clergy are ourselves exposed enough to the injustices of the city to make confession, Protestant or Catholic, a place where Christ's world has to be taken seriously? . . .

Finally, a word about our language.

Fear and violence and isolationism create a camouflaging language which not only hides from us the way we really are, but more important, makes it almost impossible to get at the deepest issues. It is significant, for example, that we've invented the term "integrated parishes" to describe those that are only being what the Lord has made it necessary to be; and the fact that

we don't use the term "disintegrated parishes" to describe those
resisting the life given us by Christ means that the significance
of the issue is almost lost. Similarly, the term "racially mixed
marriages," when "racially unmixed" would be far more revealing and instructive.

Furthermore our protective language tends to make it impossible to hear what Christ is saying to us in this urban world. It is
a barricade rather than a means of communion, as I've already
implied regarding our sacramental terminology. We've had a
deluge of language--books, conferences, committees, and re-
search--on the urban question, but substantially our position is
no different from where we began, and this in part is due to the
sickness of our words. One is sometimes led to suspect cynically
that the reason we are so given to talking about this issue is
precisely because we know that little can come of it; that our
language will protect us from the consequences of the Gospel.

Consider just the most basic and necessary word, the word
"Church." It has a terribly divisive quality. While it exists only
because of the Lord who embraces and unifies the whole universe,
almost every time it is used it creates polarizations of hostility
and separation: the Church against the world, the good against
the bad, the spiritual against the materialistic, the Christian
against the Communist. And to use the term uncritically means
to accept and nourish the separations embodied in it. God may
well, in His world, be raising up children of Abraham out of
stones, but we won't recognize them because we've already defined them, and, as it were, excommunicated them. Just think
of the hostile character of the derivative term, "unchurched,"
which is almost universally used when programs of urban missionary strategy are being outlined.

Consider the words we use to describe some people in the city.
There's a whole litany of contemptuous phrases, beginning with
"bums," "delinquents," "winos," "hippies," and ranging to supposedly kinder terms such as "drop-outs," "disadvantaged" and
"culturally deprived." But all of these, especially the kindest,
incorporate meanings which resist the emergence of the word of
God in the situation. All of them reject fearfully the ontological
connection that ties us together and creates a mutual responsibility for whatever form of life exists. None of them signifies the
human equality that exists among God's people--which then makes
imperialism a foregone conclusion. And none of them allows an
exposure of the quality of grace so especially present in the city
situation--so that it becomes quite easy for the average christian

to think that the Church sees escape from the city as the normal course of human life.

Is it any wonder, then, that illiteracy has arisen as a significant urban issue? It is necessary that at some point in the urban body this sick language be resisted!

Clearly we have to guard our language, recognize its ambiguous and transitional character, and renew it. But language grows as a representation of a way of life; and the renewal of language will not come through special conferences or research on "the problem of our language," but through a new form of life--through a process in which words have to become incarnate, and in which the incarnation of men at the heart of our poverty will give birth to renewed words.

And yet this seems almost impossible today when those Christians--who are most concerned and vocal about the urban scene-- those who control urban renewal programs as well as the language structures--almost always choose to live outside the place they're trying to understand and help. It is very significant that many of those employed by churches to minister expressly to the city voluntarily place their own life among those who have abandoned the inner city. This fits the imperialist pattern and the intensity of our fear; but it says even more about the possibility of language renewal. When you make such a free choice of the place and people you will become a part of, you need a divisive, sick language in order to justify your decision. If you can't continually describe inner city people under categories of sickness, how can you support your free decision not to place your life among them?

It is for this reason that we must end at the point where we began. The impoverishment and harshness of our language forces us back to the point where all words have their truest meaning-- the Word of God in Scripture and the Word of God incarnate. Our fears, our violence, our imperialism, and our sacramental isolationism force us back to this point too. And this does not mean that all of the other aspects of urban life examined in this essay are unimportant; but rather that their great importance only begins to be perceived as we begin to understand more completely what it means that all human life exists as life together under the Lordship of Jesus Christ.

Notes begin on page 332.

Religious Pluralism and
Social Welfare

Paul M. Harrison

The traditional alliance between social work and religion in America is broken. Social theory in general, and theories of social work in particular, are developing a philosophy that is totally independent of theological support. Several decades ago, Troeltsch observed that these secular theories have "far out-distanced the social philosophy of the Church." Nevertheless, in many instances the churches still remain preoccupied with an ir-relevant defense of traditional and antiquated social theories.

The Monastic-sectarian, the Medieval, and the Calvinistic models of social welfare served a useful purpose, both as ideal theoretical types and in their actual historical mixtures. These models still survive in the churches, and in modified forms the latter two persist in significant sectors of our secular com-munity as well. In the field of contemporary social theory, how-ever, they are becoming increasingly irrelevant.

We can briefly characterize the familiar assumptions of these models. According to the Medieval philosophy, social order was

ordained by God. Poverty and privilege were also divinely instituted. The individual should thus accept his God-given role;
he should fit in and seek salvation by obedience to the Lord God,
to the lord of his manor, to the priest of the parish, and to the
Natural Law as it was rationally perceived in the given structures
of society. The rich should give alms to the poor, not only to relieve the distress of the unfortunate, but also to store merit in
heaven for their philanthropic acts.

This thought is reflected in a document of our time. Pope Pius
XI, in the encyclical on Christian marriage, comments on the
problem that arises when God gives an over-abundance of children to impoverished parents: ". . . in the [secular] state such
economic and social methods should be adopted as will enable
every head of a family to earn as much as, according to his
station in life, is necessary for himself, his wife, and for the
rearing of his children. . . . " "Christian charity toward our
neighbor absolutely demands that those things which are lacking
to the needy should be provided; hence it is incumbent on the rich
to help the poor. . . . They who give of their substance to Christ
in the person of His poor will receive from the Lord a most
bountiful reward when He shall come to judge the world; they who
act to the contrary will pay the penalty."

The Calvinistic model became a hydra-headed monster. It can
be briefly characterized as the neo-Calvinist, Puritan, "inner-
worldly ascetic," Spencerian, laissez-faire, liberal Protestant
model. According to this theory in its very influential Spencerian
phase, wealth is a certain mark of virtue and merit. It is the inevitable fruit of disciplined labor and frugal abstinence. Poverty
is neither a divine nor social accident but, with few readily-ap-
parent exceptions, occurs solely as a result of willful disregard
for the basic rules of enterprise and integrity. One should relieve
the grossest needs of the poor because--as in the Medieval model--
philanthropy does the soul good and is evidence of one's benevolent
temper. But the rich should not give too much to the poor since it
may lead to their further corruption and will certainly not encourage them to help themselves.

It is well-known that organized social work in America was
predominantly Protestant in orientation, and it is instructive to
observe the development of social work in the twentieth century
as it gradually sought release from its religious associations. In
the early part of the century emphasis was upon case work. The
underlying assumption of the supporting religious ethic was that
the social worker should seek to adjust the unfortunate client

to the laissez-faire environment of disciplined enterprise.

Group work was the next stage in the development of social welfare practice. It certainly evolved in part as an instrument of efficiency in a business environment where efficiency is a sacred by-law. To be sure, greater numbers of clients could be handled by fewer workers, but it was the new philosophy that supported group work that marked the more significant change. Now it was assumed that individuals were not necessarily and solely responsible for their position and behavior. They were deprived because of membership in social groups that were as malformed and ill-adjusted as they, and which contributed to and reinforced their attitudes and actions. To adjust the individual to the whole society was not enough. His family, his peer group, his school, or his place of work must also be evaluated as a source of tension. Many of the ideas in the Social Gospel, of course, parallel this development in social work.

In the present stage of social work, community organization and reorganization are increasingly emphasized. It is not surprising that this marks the sharpest break from the social philosophy of most of the Jewish and Christian religious groups. A recent survey of white Baptist ministers in the northern states indicated that 85% of the respondents considered themselves to be either Conservative or Fundamentalist in theological and social orientation. The percentage would perhaps not be as high in other denominations, but the liberal Baptist ministers were not only dismayed by this figure, they were also surprised.

At the present historical juncture, religion and professional social work are in several important respects moving in opposite directions. As religion is losing its authority and broad moral influence, social work is gaining in economic affluence and institutional power. The disparity can be illustrated by comparative examination of religious and public welfare budgets. In 1930, the total expenditure for private welfare work, including non-religious work, was estimated at 1.3 billion dollars; in 1960, the total expenditure was about 6 billion. By comparison, the increase in public welfare expenditures is astronomical. Federal, state, and local welfare budgets totalled 6.5 billion in 1935 and advanced to 71 billion by 1964.

Religion has moved from its position of social inclusiveness. It is becoming increasingly voluntary and personal in orientation and more and more sensitive to the need for freedom of expression and practice. Liberal Protestants have deplored this tendency for decades, but it is from within the liberal sector of Protestantism that there persists the now-familiar anti-institutional movement which takes one form in a call for "religionless Christianity." Social work is moving in the opposite direction. It started at the point religion is now reaching, with emphasis upon individual charity, voluntary philanthropy, and a personalized approach to the service of the needy. Obviously, public welfare is assuming the social service burdens of the churches, but far more is occurring. It is the social agencies and services that are now becoming inclusive, often impersonal, automatic, and collective in orientation. The average man of the future may not belong to a church or synagogue, but he most certainly will participate in social security, be serviced by a public health agency, and perhaps, if he is unemployed, he will be assured a guaranteed annual income at a level that does not destroy his spirit by automatically condemning his motivations.

As Western man improves his ability to satisfy his material needs, he appears to be less comforted by the orthodox ways of fulfilling his religious needs. Religion and social work are still travelling on the same highway, but in different directions. Fourteenth century man could not effectively meet his material requirements, but he could answer complex spiritual questions. Twentieth century man has reversed these techniques. Possessing the potential power for universal affluence he is spiritually impoverished, and although he knows it, he appears incapable of doing anything about it. However, religion and social work remain interested in fulfilling both the physical and the spiritual needs of man even though the traditional ambivalence of religion toward the material factor is matched by the ambivalence of the humanistic social worker toward the spiritual.

Social workers, perhaps more than any other professional group, seek in their occupation to combine the fruits of scientific, humanistic, technological, and spiritual activities of man. It is for this reason that social workers do not, in an intuitive way, wish to sever their alliance with any of the institutional activities that will contribute to the service of mankind. Both with the increased institutional power and prestige, the inevitable bureaucratization, the need to become more and more technically oriented and trained, and the inclination to develop procedures and language that are increasingly mysterious to the laymen, the alliance between social workers and other professionals is undergoing strain and the distance between social workers and laymen is increasing.

Meanwhile, the tension between the professionals in religion and social work is intensifying. As the priests lose their authority and power, they find it increasingly difficult to recruit young men of quality and ability into their ranks. In contrast to social work, the distance between priest and laity is closing as the liturgies and dogmas are translated into the common idiom, and the church continues to speak of the co-operative priesthood of the laity. As the church lowers its professional criteria, social work raises its qualifying standards. In a word, as the professional social workers gain greater mystery and increase the distance between themselves and their clients, the priests lose their official charisma and traditional mystique and move closer to the people.

There is a crucial factor in this reversal of roles that must not be minimized. The priests may be losing their spiritual relevance, even among those religiously loyal people who admit they have a great need for their intended services, but this is a situation which never threatened the social workers since they were needed in a readily observable and material way even before they existed, and they will be needed until society and man are born again.

American social work, however, has a critical need of its own. Social work is seeking to develop a new model, a new social philosophy and theory of value that will guide its operations as it was once guided by the Calvinistic and Medieval models. This is evident in the published work of many social work theorists.

These theorists have never strived to develop a value-free science The best among them have known that their philosophy and theory of value must, in great part, emerge from and account for the ideals and beliefs of their clients and the more extensive participating public. In this situation social workers are faced with a permanent dilemma. In their field activities, the workers must not assume a judgmental and moral stance in their therapeutic relation to the client public, but at the same time they must encourage a spirit of moral judgment within a society whose structures and values sustain and excuse exploitation and injustice. It is at this point in the development of a new social theory of values, and in the education and evangelizing work that is so necessary, that it remains profitable, even imperative, for social work to maintain its alliance with religion. The fact that religion, at least relatively speaking, is losing its former opulence and influence may be a gain for both religion and social work.

As Troeltsch observed, it is the discontented minorities that produce the creative and critical social protests. Perhaps it paints an incredible portrait to imagine churchmen as the discontented and creative social prophets. But we have already witnessed an unforeseeable and surprising event when the priests, ministers, and rabbis linked arms in the civil rights crusade and risked and gave their lives. I hazard the guess that as social workers increase in affluence and prestige, their prophetic ranks will diminish and their concern for the security of their institutions will rival the present attitude of the priests toward the essential preservation of their sacred communions. If the social workers continue to increase in status and power, another role may be switched between priest and social worker. The social worker may become the high priest of the community, servicing the needs of his clients, seeking to determine their problems, even striving to define their beliefs.

Religion will not give up easily what it believes to be its appointed task in history--to provide the normative philosophy for the whole society and to speak the judgmental and redemptive word to the principalities and powers. John Bennett says that the special contribution religion can make to social work arises "from the very fact that churches are under no local or national authority. They exist in response to a divine revelation which local or national public opinion cannot control." The statement obviously requires qualification but it does point to the religious stance of a significant sector of our national community.

We cannot create a new social philosophy in the isolated quiet of our academic studies, a fact that is known better by social workers and ministers than it is by sociologists and theologians. Without underestimating the contribution that the academic theorists can make, the new philosophical model must emerge out of the flux of the changing social environment. In order to be viable, every sector of the population must contribute to its development. Despite the widespread secularization of our society and the notoriety that the "death of God theologians" received in the popular press, churchmen may still make an important contribution to the development of a new social philosophy, for I suspect that the "death of God" is due primarily to the almost total acculturation of the church, to the compromise that the churches have effected with the most privileged sectors of our society, to the loss of prophetic vitality, and to the widespread disinterest in the cry for social justice that sounds throughout the land.

The voice of the new "secular theologians" is now being heard in their praise of the technical advances of the secular society and the opportunities it promises for all men, low and high. They also applaud the secularization of the church. Now they believe it may be possible for the worshipper to love the neighbor without being distracted by ancient ecclesiastical idolatries as he bends his knee in the awesome liturgical presence of clerical self-adulation. The secular age can be characterized as a time of involuntary clerical humility. If the churches are to maintain their status, the soft robes of the priest will probably be replaced by the heavy mantle of the prophet.

The moving witness of the priests and sisters, the rabbis, and the ministers at Selma was as necessary as it was dramatic, but the national as well as the world community requires more than an occasional act of prophetic courage. Churchmen can also serve the human community by critically exposing the marked in-adequacies of the ancient social philosophies, and by co-operating in the creative development of the new social model. The mini-mum requisites of that model appear to be as follows:

(1) Whenever possible the new social philosophy must be based on principles that are subject to empirical and pragmatic verifica-tion. This is required because diverse groups of churchmen seek to work with each other, but also, with welfare workers and social scientists. We must assume that the cherished truths of the most powerful secular and religious groups are subject to the tests of historical and social and scientific experience. While everyone must be devoted to his beliefs or risk the loss of his integrity, we are compelled to distinguish between the social purpose and the social effect of our ultimate principles. When the effect is destruc-tive we must seek anew for the original intention of the principle.

It is no simple task to seek for a mode of discourse that will satisfy the interests and beliefs of Protestants, Catholics, Jews, social workers, and social scientists. Christians and Jews should give more serious consideration to a theory of ethics that is grounded in the assumption of the social scientists that all man-kind has the same basic needs which must be fulfilled if humanity is "to become and be human." This assumption should not be treated as a stranger in the house of religion. It is supported by biblical revelation and by religious tradition; it has also been af-firmed by rational philosophy, and most recently, it has been reinforced by the systematic investigations of the empirical disciplines.

The universal striving for equity and justice between men is a reflection of man's common needs and inclinations. Reinhold Niebuhr says that there are some general principles of justice that define the right order of life in any community. There appear to be no living communities which do not have some notion of justice that transcends their positive laws and by which they seek to judge their customs and legislation. "Every human society does have something like a natural law concept, " he wrote, "for it assumes that there are more immutable and purer principles of justice than those actually embodied in its obviously relative laws."

(2) The new social model must be based on a morality that synthesizes the knowledge of revelational theology, rational philosophy, and the empirical social sciences. There are ideas --we can call them "corresponding assumptions"--that appear to constitute areas of agreement between the religious ethicists and western social scientists. These corresponding assumptions exist at points where the social scientists and religious ethicists are talking about the same phenomena and developing analogous conceptions to interpret the data. For example, there are three assumptions of correspondence that may be potentially useful and provide a basis for the development of a more systematic relation between religious ethics and social science. On the theological side, these are the conceptions of creation, sin, and redemption. Creation corresponds to the sociologists' assumptions about the nature and function of man and community; sin corresponds to sociological theories of social disorganization, or anomie, or the war of all against all; and redemption is analogous to the sociologists' (at least) implicit hope for an integrated society.

(3) The content of the new social theory must be discovered in the continuing dialogue between diverse interests and powers, with no group, religious or secular, claiming a monopoly over truth. It is this kind of situation of dialogue that Paul Lehmann may have had in mind when he wrote that the rigorous and systematic "clarification of ethical principles and their application to concrete situations is ethically unreal because such clarification is a logical enterprise and there is no way in logic of closing the gap between the abstract and the concrete. Ethics is a matter not of logic but of life. . . ."

If this is true, consensus with respect to fundamental principles, values, and goals must be maintained. Dialogue in diversity, no matter how pluralistic our community may be, does not signify approval or affirmation of consistent moral relativity. Consensus must exist with respect to our basic beliefs about the nature and destiny of man and society. Without this consensus, the political community will experience acute anomie and die out.

187

Fr. John Courtney Murray summarizes these first two points. "The whole premise of the public argument, if it is to be civilized and civilizing, is that the consensus is real, that among the people everything is not in doubt, but that there is a core of agreement. . . . We hold certain truths; therefore, we can argue about them. There can be no argument except . . . within a context of agreement."

(4) Whether we call it sin or self-interest the new philosophy must contain the assumption that every human group seeks to gain a preeminent place in society. This is true not only of the politicians, the businessmen, and the military, but also of the priests, scientists, and the social workers.

The priests of the churches should remain peculiarly sensitive to this issue. The history of the churches bears dramatic witness to the fact that any social group--secular or religious, lay or professional--is subject to corruption when it becomes the prime guardian of social welfare. It is an ironic confirmation of human sin that the churches begin to realize the necessity of becoming consistently critical of secular morality only upon being reduced to the position of the despised and suffering servant.

In the arena of social welfare we run the greater risk today that the former hegemony of church dogmatics will be replaced by the dogmas of social work philosophy. The new priests of the natural and social sciences are no better equipped than the old religious presbyters to avoid advocacy of untested assumptions about the nature of man and society. The secular city is filled with new philosophers whose metaphysical assumptions are all the more dangerous because they deny their existence. Whether they are optimistic about man in accord with neo-Marxian or utopian evolutionary theories, or pessimistic in accord with theories of behaviorism and social determinism, it should be clear that scientists, despite the vaunted disinterest of their method, are forced, willy-nilly, to assume certain things about the nature of man and society that cannot be empirically verified. It is at this juncture of empirical and non-empirical judgments that we possess the opportunity for seeking ways more systematically to relate religious and secular morality.

(5) The social philosophy must reflect the view that human problems are both spiritual and material. Man is not only a biological animal. He will die not only for food, but also for a cause. No less important than the material fruits of justice is the visible concern of the community to achieve that justice.

Bernard Meland seems to be belaboring the obvious when he says "there is human degradation that results from poverty and from the lack of proper and adequate means to heal and nurture the body. There is also human degradation that follows from the pursuit of physical well-being when this is made the chief and all-absorbing end of life." But these words stand as a corrective to the basic credo of the new philosophy for the social and political advocates of the Great Society, and to the credo of the theological advocates of man come of age in the secular city who appear to envisage a date in the not-distant future when the perfect society will be realized in history. In that day, both social worker and priest will be irrelevant, but in the meantime, both priests and social workers should keep before them the reminder that "spiritualism and materialism are polar opposites only in the sense that each has pursued excessive measures in opposite directions. Each of them roots in a one-sided conception, or possibly a misconception, of the nature of man."

(6) If, because of the impact of the new automation, full employment cannot be achieved, an adequate income apparently can be. It is at this point that the most imaginative creativity is required of the churches. Max Weber notwithstanding, it is the Jewish and Catholic as well as the Protestant tradition that contributed to the development of the uncompromising gospel of work, and assisted in the creation of the gospel of unlimited competition. But now perhaps a greater challenge faces the churches. If the fantastic workless society should become a reality, can civilization be maintained? There is no evidence that any man who experienced subjective uselessness ever retained his moral integrity. The new philosophy must teach men that they can serve their community in a fashion that is even more creative than the ways of economic productivity. In this manner only, can workless man avoid degenerating into a worthless creature. We must seek, therefore, not only to maintain political democracy, but to create social and economic democracy as well.

It is Sebastian de Grazia, a philosopher of social science, who wrote: "The theologian is right. Why not admit it? More than anything else the world needs love. . . . Love cannot follow its true course which is Justice unless the competitive directive is removed from barring its path. America, which was among the last to receive the competitive directive, may be the last to let it die. And this truth applies not only to the community of the nation. . . . There can be no single world-embracing political community until the idea of competition as the guiding principle for the relations of man is ruled out."

(7) Finally, the new philosophy must therefore speak of the welfare of the universal nation. It is at this point that the words of the religious prophet should be most clearly enunciated. It is the universal God who speaks through the house of religion. We have been humbly forced to learn in our experience of national pluralism that no group possesses the universal truth in all of its grandeur, and so we must learn that in the situation of international pluralism, the welfare of this and every nation requires the discovery of a consensus between all the nations and a concern for the social welfare of all men if any will survive.

Notes begin on page 333.

PART THREE

Man Needs Moral Norms for Ethical Conduct

Can Moral Theology Ignore Natural Law?

Bruno Schüller, S.J.

The doctrine of natural law has lost considerable ground among Catholic theologians in recent years. Attempts to solve moral questions by appeals to natural law frequently meet with scepticism. The old optimism of quick sure solutions in all matters has turned to disappointment in the face of problems presented by capital punishment, atomic war, and contraception. Many ask if the very process of natural law thinking has not led us to a dead end.

This scepticism is caused by a new awareness of historical development in relation to a natural law which seems to stem from a static conception of man. Philosophy is not so readily admitted to the realm of theology today and natural law seems to be merely the result of philosophical reflection. Men feel that theology should be learned from history and that many distortions of Christian faith were introduced by reliance on philosophical concepts and categories. For the task of theology is to listen to the word of God in Scripture and tradition but not to the word of some philosopher.

Do these men then deny the existence of a _lex naturae_? Hardly, at least no Catholic theologian would. Scripture, tradition and the magisterium all guarantee it. What they do challenge is whether moral theology has to rely so heavily on natural law reasoning as it has till now. Once acknowledged, cannot the _lex naturae_ simply be set aside by the Christian who has a much clearer awareness of God's will in the words and deeds of Christ?

First we will try to answer this last question and then examine how well natural law meets the demand for a historical interpretation of human morality. Finally we will consider some of the difficulties in moral understanding and moral-theological proofs which really seem to be the problem at the root of much of the present scepticism.

Law of nature defined

We will make no distinction between natural right, natural moral code, and _lex naturae_. From the side of the knowing subject natural law can be defined as the complexus of all those moral (and legal) norms of behavior knowable to man by reason independently of God's revelation. For without access to revelation man can only rely on the natural humanity of mankind for the validity and meaning of moral commands. Opposed to this is the _lex gratiae_ or those divine commands which refer to the Christian in so far as he is a "new creation" in Christ. This _lex gratiae_ is only knowable by faith.

The classic NT scripture proof for the _lex naturae_ occurs in the first two chapters of Romans. Why does Paul bother at this point to mention that the pagans know the moral demands of God without the Torah? This simply clarifies his larger theme in the first four chapters of Romans: Justification is not by the power of the law but by faith in Christ Jesus (1:16ff). Although justification is by observance of the law (2:13), since original sin neither Jew nor pagan has observed the law (3:10-12). "All have sinned and fall short of the glory of God;" they can only hope for justification by God's grace through the redemption of Christ (3:23-24).

The gospel of justification by faith can only be understood if we first see the guilt of all mankind. The Jews are guilty by the Torah, which they have not followed; the pagans are guilty by the moral demands of God known as their creator, which they have ignored, "and so they" too "are without excuse" (1:20). This question of the natural moral law arises only in so far as it is

193

provoked by the gospel and helps toward understanding the gospel. Here then is the formula by which alone theology as such can speak of the natural moral law: beginning from the gospel and leading back to it again.

This insight, however, does not tell us whether Christians, to whom the Lord himself revealed God's will, are also directed to natural law to learn God's will at times. Suppose that the primitive Christian community had accepted, directly or indirectly, certain rules of moral behavior from their pagan surroundings. This would be a recognition that norms outside the Judaeo-Christian revelation apply to Christians and also reveal God's will to them.

Why look outside?

But why should the primitive community do this? Because Jesus did not leave a code of prescriptions for every possible situation in life. They always looked first to the words of Jesus, but very soon found situations demanding moral judgment which went beyond Jesus' commands. In 1 Cor 7 Paul rejects divorce saying, "I give charge, not I but the Lord." Then concerning mixed marriage he says, "to the rest I say, not the Lord."

How does Paul try to learn God's will in cases where he knows no express command of the Lord? Paul takes over the norms developed by the Jews of the diaspora. They did not bring their legal disputes before pagan judges; so Paul forbids the Corinthians to do it (1 Cor 6:1-7). They made it a duty to obey pagan authority, and so Paul advocates loyalty. There is nothing specifically Christian about the motivation, even in the famous passage of Rom 13:1-7.

Taken from Hellenism

Significantly, Paul takes over from Hellenistic Jewry catalogues of virtues and vices which show the influence of popular Stoic philosophy outside the sphere of revelation of the word. The moral concepts in Phlp 1:4-8 are characteristic of the moral philosophy of Hellenism. Another example of this influence is the domestic admonitions in Col 3:18-41; Eph 5:22-26; Ti 2: 1-10. They follow the same scheme as those of Stoic moral philosophy: duties of spouses, duties of parents and children, duties of masters and slaves. Of course Paul obtained these admonitions indirectly through Hellenic Jewry. In the NT they

194

have Christian motivation, but only slightly so in Col 3:18-41, though more distinctly in Eph 5:22-23 and 1 Pt 2:13ff. Even Paul's theology of conjugal obedience (Col 3:18) and Christian marriage (Eph 5:22-23) introduces no new duties or moral commands which were not part of the domestic admonitions of the times, namely that husbands love their wives and wives be subject to their husbands.

From the foregoing one point is certain: The apostolic parenesis contains moral directions stemming from the natural moral law as known outside the sphere of the revelation of the word. So moral theology cannot be denied the use of moral insights of philosophical origin. Can moral theology then ignore these insights? The procedure of the primitive community would lead one to suspect that Christians are directed to the lex naturae when the express commands of Christ and the apostles do not suffice for the moral evaluation of a life situation. But this question cannot be answered by Scripture alone; it calls for theological reflection as well.

Perception of moral values is a sort of intuition. Hence the validity of a moral value cannot be strictly proven but only pointed to. Good and evil, merit and guilt, and so on can only be phenomenologically described, not strictly defined. Faith in revelation cannot be the way such values are logically and primarily perceived, since the knowledge attained by faith is not by means of intuition but is transmitted through signs. Christian faith is a knowledge based on God's authority. The encounter between believing man and revealing God takes place by means of language. In God's use of man's language, the moral "vocabulary" extends as far as the natural moral experience of man. If this is so, it seems that God can reveal only those moral insights which man knows or could know through his natural moral experience.

Lex gratiae communicable

Such a conclusion would be hasty. Since men's natural existence images God, his language must be capable of being a sign of a divine reality. The NT moral message (lex gratiae) is new and not deducible from the lex naturae, since it appears to man as a "new creation" in Christ. Christ's grace is task as well as gift. Yet this demand can be communicated to man since grace has its analogous image in nature. The moral conception corresponding to the lex naturae can point to the supernatural reality of the lex gratiae. A believer can only hear and understand the message of Christ because he understands and expresses him-

195

self as a moral being prior to God's words of revelation. The creator first confronts man with his will in the lex naturae, thus making man a possible "hearer of the word." Natural moral law is man's potentia oboedientialis for the lex gratiae.

Is the Christian free to seek God's will either in the message of Christ or in the lex naturae? These are not really alternatives; for whoever earnestly turns to Christ for direction thereby proves (prior to Christ's answer) that he knows he is called as a moral being to direct his life by God's will. When in faith he understands Christ's answer expressed in human speech, Christ's word makes the natural law more accessible to him. Otherwise he could not understand the law of Christ, for man grasps this only insofar as it is mirrored in natural law.

This leads to the much-discussed question: Does the NT contain substantially new commands not belonging to natural law? Historically speaking, have men who had no direct contact with Judeo-Christian revelation come to the insight that morality equals love of God, neighbor, and enemy? Even supposing that history answers affirmatively, there still is no proof that Christ's grace was not responsible. If history's answer is negative, one comes to no information about the true content of natural law since original sin could have caused the failure.

The answer must come from an ethical reflexion on the ontological level. Since without faith man knows nothing of his supernatural vocation, as soon as a moral norm becomes clear without faith as its basis, then its content is part of natural law. The commandments of love of God, neighbor, enemy, of humility and faith and hope, usually called specifically Christian, can all become clear from analysis of human existence. These are precepts enjoined on man because as God's creature he exists with others like himself.

Faith is a good example since it is most easily objected to as a natural precept. According to K. Rahner, man is by nature that being who can be called to believe in God's word and who understands himself most deeply as this possibility. Man would not be able to grasp or relate to himself Christ's call to faith, unless he knew immediately from his natural understanding of existence what faith means as man's answer to God's word.

The newness in the law of Christ is not the content of what is required, but the new kind of love, hope, and humility demanded. Because he is "a new creation in Christ," the gift of supernatural grace transforms all areas of the Christian's life. For Christians the precepts of the lex naturae are also those of the lex gratiae, but not as if they were simply identical, but because we can formulate them

196

only with the same words and concepts. The Christian who does all things "in the Lord" not only fulfills the natural law but also the law of Christ. In areas such as economics and politics Scripture only partially expresses the content of the law of Christ. Recognition of the law of nature here is ipso facto recognition of the law of Christ.

In short understanding in faith the ethical message of Christ entails as its (transcendental) presupposition natural understanding of the lex naturae. Natural insight into the lex naturae necessarily translates itself for the believing Christian into knowledge of the lex Christi. This is the reason moral theology cannot omit natural law from its methodical reflexion. The better a moral theologian understands the law of nature, the better his position to hear and grasp the law of Christ without distortion.

Being grounds ought

How can man by understanding himself in his natural being become aware of a divine law? Catholic natural law doctrine answers that obligation is grounded in being. In grasping what he is, man also grasps what he is to become by his free self-determination. In man every gift is also task. Man's being is a continual free gift of God, man's sole task as person is to freely accept what as God's creature he is.

Scripture makes the same point. Once darkness, Christians are now light in the Lord and should act as children of the light (Eph 5:8-11). Christ's grace is always both gift and command, but first of all gift. In the reflex grounding of moral precepts, moral theology and philosophical ethics ought to have the same formal guiding principle, the interpretation of the demands of our God-given being. Moral theology can be defined as theological anthropology translated from the indicative to the imperative.

Room for change?

Since there are elements of continuity and change in man's being, a distinction must be made between moral norms based on man's unchangeable metaphysical nature and those grounded in man's changing historicity. The questionable restriction of natural law norms to those based on the unchangeable metaphysical nature of man seems to stem from a fear of relativism

197

and an attempt to avoid its dangers by estimating what is historically changeable in man as narrowly as possible.

But the ought's ground in being leaves room for change, since it only states the correlation between them. The extent to which man remains the same through historical change is a problem for metaphysical anthropology, not ethics. Precisely to the extent that man's being changes with time must the applicable ethical norm also change in every case.

Some examples will clarify this concretely. Children owe their parents love, reverence, and obedience until they come of age--then the duty to obey ceases. Put abstractly, because the growing person's being changes, the obligations demanded of him also change. Or what of the NT admonition that wives be subject to their husbands in all things? This obviously presupposes a lack of "age" on the wife's part no longer valid--at least for most of the Western world. Today the model for the relation of husband and wife is rather one of equal partners with no one-sided superiority or subjection. There is no problem with relativism, for the husband/wife relationship has objectively changed and with it the ethical precepts appropriate for them.

How can one tell if traditional moral precepts still contain God's will today? The more general and abstract the moral principles, the more reason there is to think they have a timeless validity. One cannot doubt that Christians of all times have to prove their authentic faith by their love of neighbor. But there is more reason to consider concrete and detailed prescriptions timebound and to re-examine their demands. Since every moral precept is justified by the God-given being of man, here and now its continuing validity must in principle be able to be perceived from that given reality.

Even moral precepts in the NT must be checked since they were directed to Judeans, Corinthians, and Philippians, and in the twentieth century we are simply not the same men they were. The difficulties of a natural law grounding of moral precepts cannot be avoided by recourse to Scripture, since its own ethical message must be interpreted. Interpretation that depends on the movement from is to ought is difficult because of the character of ethical knowledge and proof.

A problem of proof

There are peculiar difficulties in ethical proof. The understanding grounding the ought must penetrate to the essential char-

198

acter of human existence and not remain in the merely empirical or factual area. The latter is precisely the contingent, the non-necessary, and cannot ground the absolute necessity of moral law. For example, the growth of male facial hair cannot ground a prohibition to shave. Man can interpret his being as an ought that concerns him absolutely only because he understands that being as a meaningful absolute value. Since moral values are primary, perceptible only by a kind of intuition, the moral value of truthfulness, for example, cannot be demonstrated "conclusively" like a mathematical proposition. All that can be done is to turn another's attention in the direction where he must look to perceive the value of honesty. Because of their being underived, primary character, ethical precepts can only be exhibited phenomenologically.

Moral theologians and ethicians often do not take trouble to investigate phenomenologically those areas of life which are judged morally. For example, the venial seriousness of lying is based on the meaning of speech, where speech is understood as a medium for communicating thought. But closer analysis shows that speech can also be a means of self-communication and of personal encounter. A falsification of this personal relationship is much more serious than mere false information.

Insight into moral values depends not only on my intellectual clarity and penetration, but on the right attitude of my will and affective life, my early childhood experiences, and the cultural, social, and historical factors of the milieu. To indicate the objective validity of moral norms and values, moralists must incorporate knowledge from modern sociology and psychology--a task hardly begun. Nor does it further moral theology to exclude philosophical reflection on the natural law. All these factors, philosophy included, help achieve a competent moral theology.

God's word in OT and NT with its twofold aspect of proclamation and law, indicative and imperative, has been entrusted to the Church's magisterium whose authority extends to the whole law of God, both lex naturae and lex Christi. How does the magisterium obtain for Catholics certain knowledge of God's will in ethical matters? The point here is not to distinguish the extraordinary magisterium from the Church's ordinary, "authentic" teaching. Rather the point concerns the binding force of the non-infallible decisions of the Church's teaching authority.

Magisterium counts

First of all, the attitude of the magisterium to a given question certainly makes a difference. A given opinion may be explained as erroneous or not yet certain or as dangerous and open to mis-understanding. On some moral questions, the position taken by the magisterium has more or less weight depending on the wording of the teaching. But all authentic teaching has the common feature that it is not strictly excluded from containing some error.

But the abstract possibility of error is not sufficient to justify doubt about the correctness of authentic teaching. The non-in-fallible magisterium also has the special assistance of the Holy Spirit and its decisions bind Catholics in conscience. Doubt about authentic teaching can only be justified on serious grounds shared by a large number of competent Christians regarding the teach-ing in question. In general, one can adopt an opinion that varies from authentic teaching only if he is certain of the magisterium's silent approval, amounting to a practical retreat from the earlier teaching.

One point of this common teaching about the magisterium could be improved--it proceeds in a purely a priori way. Could it not be filled out by some a posteriori considerations? Should not two thousand years of non-infallible decisions be examined for the errors now admitted even by the magisterium itself? Perhaps one could know in a more detailed way to what extent the Holy Spirit preserves authentic teaching from error; one could then give more concrete conditions for knowing when authentic teaching loses its binding force for the faithful.

There is no easy solution to the many problems facing moral theology today. It would be an error to make Catholic natural law teaching responsible for their solution. The most pressing task for moral theology today is the rethinking of the peculiar character of moral knowledge and ethical proof. This can be accomplished only by intensive philosophical work.

Notes begin on page 334.

Natural Law, Theology, and the Church

John J. Reed, S.J.

Whatever is to be thought of our age and the quality of its morals, at least it cannot be said to be uninterested in morality. Paradoxically, it would seem that one of the severest challenges to Christian charity results from the very zeal and sincerity of the various champions engaged in debate upon issues of morality. Both this interest and this activity extend well beyond the ranks of what we might call the professional moralists. Indeed, it has been said that in the matter of morals there are no experts. The moral theologian will find this difficult to accept--in fact, unacceptable; and while he may be suspected of prejudice, he is certainly in a better position to know. But what is more important than the issue of the individual moralist's expertise is the basic concept from which this persuasion follows as a corollary: that morality is a matter of reason, and one man's reason is as good as another's. The reference, of course, is to natural morality, or to what is called natural law. And the precise point in which this question

of authority in morals is extremely important is the relation of
natural morality, or natural law, to the teaching authority of the
Church.

This is not just a possible question. It is a question which has
actually been raised more than once: for instance, in discussions
of conjugal morality in general and of the regulation of fertility
in particular. Considering that much of the argument has been
conducted in terms of natural order, some maintain that the
Church is incompetent, because the object of its teaching authority is not reason but revelation, or at least--since the magisterial organs have actually made declarations on the matter--
that such pronouncements could not be infallible. The purpose of
these pages is to discuss the more general question of principle,
the relation of natural law to theology and to the teaching authority
of the Church.

Natural law and theology

Moral theology is the study of the active participation of man
in the realization of his vocation to be united to God in charity,
through the inhabitation of the Blessed Trinity in this life and the
consummation of beatitude hereafter. More concretely expressed,
moral theology is the study of the Christian life. The actual
destiny of man is, of course, a supernatural one, exceeding the
capacities, the implications, and the exigencies of human nature
considered in itself. As a supernatural end, it is gratuitous, in
the sense that nothing man can naturally do can merit it condignly.
But in the divine plan it is not only to be a gift; it is also to be
earned, in the sense that it postulates a response on the part of
man to the various manifestations of God's intent for him in the
constantly evolving situations of his life. Whereas in our human
experience, therefore, a gift is not earned and what is earned
is not a gift, supernatural beatitude is both a gratuitous inher-
itance and a retribution granted in consideration of the acts which
God Himself enables man to make. . . .

But there can be no question of merit or demerit, reward or
punishment, except in the supposition of freedom, of dominion
over one's conduct, of the capacity to act otherwise. The moral
quality of an act, however, the aspect by reason of which it is
called good or bad, is not to be found in the physical or psychological constituents of the free act, which are identical whether
good or bad is done, whether one gives an alms or commits a
theft. Moral goodness consists rather in the relation of conformity

between the act and some norm, and moral evil in the absence of conformity.

The immediate norm in relation to which the morality of an act is evaluated is the judgment of conscience, on the part of the prospective agent himself, affirming that the act under consideration of being placed here and now is good or evil, better or worse. But conscience does not create the morality of the act. It is rather the function of conscience, in the sense of the total process of moral evaluation, to discover and, in its final judgment, to represent the relation between the prospective act and a criterion outside of and prior to itself. Besides the immediate, subjective, internal norm of conduct, which is conscience, there is the external, objective, remote norm. Insofar as there is question of simple rectitude of conduct, and not of greater or lesser perfection, this external, objective norm is law. And it is with this that we are concerned at the moment. Not that law is the only, the ultimate, or the highest measure of human conduct, but that, considered in its broadest significance, so as to include the whole law of God, it constitutes an order within which human conduct must be contained and from which not even the highest sanctity can prescind.

Hence the Christian life, with which moral theology is concerned, consists in this, that, united to God in charity, man uses his freedom to do the things which he judges pleasing to God, and thus not only avoids displeasing God but deserves to be united more perfectly to Him in grace on earth and in beatitude in heaven. In the dogmatic Constitution on the Church, the Second Vatican Council, writing of the vocation of all to sanctity, stated:

> It is therefore evident to all that all the Christian faithful of every state or degree are called to the plenitude of the Christian life and the perfection of charity; and by their holiness a way of life more conformed to human nature is promoted even within the society of this world. With a view to the achievement of this perfection, let the faithful make use of their capacities according to the measure of Christ's granting, in order that, following in His footsteps, and brought into conformity with His example, obedient to the will of the Father in all things, they may dedicate themselves with their whole souls to the glory of God and the service of the neighbor.

In accordance with the scope of the present study, it is not our intention to consider all the ways in which the will of the Father becomes manifest as a norm of personal conduct--in the precepts of divine positive law, in the counsels of Christian perfection, in the legitimate enactments of ecclesiastical authority, in the special inspirations individually granted by the Holy Spirit--but only in the form of what has long been called the natural law.

Drastically condensed, the process by which the concept of natural law is evolved comprises three steps: perception, reflection, and conclusion. The first step is the perception of an order, in the observance of which creatures realize their potentialities and finality: as the capacity of speech may be used to enlighten, encourage, inspire, or to defame, calumniate, deceive; as the respect for property possession ensures provision for oneself, family, and others, while theft and damnification frustrate these endeavors; as the potentialities of sex are used to bring forth children destined to beatitude and to express the highest human dedication to another, or to indulge in self-gratification to the detriment of one's own personality, another's human dignity, the child's opportunity for proper life; as the equality and brotherhood of men is expressed in the relations of charity and justice, or perverted by the reduction of another to the status of means or of inferior, in slavery, homicide, or racial persecution. The second step is a reflection upon the implication that the Creator, infinitely wise and holy, cannot be indifferent to the observance or nonobservance of this order with a view to the realization of his intentions, but necessarily wills its execution, by an internal necessity flowing from His own perfections and consequent upon His own free election to create. The third step is the conclusion, that this will of God induces in His creatures a necessity--in His free creatures, an obligation--to observe this order. It is this final judgment, this recognition of a moral necessity, that contributes the formal notion of law, the notion of an obligatory norm. As Leo XIII expressed it: "This dictate of human reason cannot have the force of law, except insofar as it is the voice and interpreter of a higher reason, to which our mind and will must be subject."

For the purposes of the present discussion it is extremely important, indeed crucial, to observe the distinction between two elements in this analysis of the concept of natural law: the constitution of the law and the cognition of the law. Natural law is constituted as an obligatory norm by the will of God; it is God-made. It is, or may be, known by man without any special inter-

vention of God; to that extent it may be called man-discovered.
The consequences of the distinction are vast. In the first place,
it is evident that, in the whole context of the Christian life, it is
much more significant intrinsically that this law is God-made
than that it is man-discovered. It is not proper at all to refer to
natural law as the "law" of reason; it has the character of law
precisely and only because it is an order established and willed
by God, not because it is an order perceived by man.

Secondly, from the aspect of cognition, it is evident that the
factor of natural knowledge is not an essential part of the notion
at all. The norms so willed by God may, to some extent, be perceived by a natural process of reasoning, as suggested above, but
they may also be revealed by God in a positive revelation, without
ceasing to contain any of the constituent elements of what we call
natural law, namely, that they be modes of conduct whose propriety
or necessity is inherent in some relationship established by the
Creator and realized in a concrete historical situation, and that
it is the will of the Creator that this relationship be respected
and human conduct regulated in conformity with it. From the fact,
therefore, that the natural law is said to be the object of reason,
it does not follow that it is not the object of revelation. The mode
of cognition is a question of methodology; the constitutive element
of natural law is the divine reason and will. Obviously, therefore,
natural law is not only an object of philosophy; it is an object of
theological inquiry.

Most opposition to natural law is reducible to one or another
of the following attitudes or positions, which may be referred to
as nominal, positivistic, philosophical, and theological.

Many, especially of the legal profession, admit the existence
of a natural morality, an order established and willed by God,
antecedent to and normative for human conduct and human law, but
do not believe that the word "law" should be applied to these norms,
preferring to restrict this term to positive human law. Evidently
this is a problem of terminology only, a nominal opposition; and
the designations "natural morality" or "moral order" are usually
acceptable.

The second position, of legal positivism, exists in varying
forms and degrees. Its basic postulate is that law is constituted
simply and solely by the command of a legislator. It may not be
a good law, but it is law. This may be coupled with a mere
prescission from the moral order, or with a denial of any higher
norm as a point of reference to which positive law must conform.
While there are obvious dangers inherent in either attitude from

the moral theologian's point of view, the theory is less harmful
than it might appear, since the jurists, in formulating legal norms,
do in fact consider man's nature and relationships and the needs
of society, and are really guided, therefore, to a large extent by
what the moralist would call natural law.

Opposition to the traditional concept of natural law comes also
from that form of existentialism which, in its application to the
field of morals, is called situation ethics. In this view it is not
possible to have absolute affirmations of morality based upon fixed
natures and applicable in any situation, but every existing situation
is unique, and the right thing to do must, in each case, be decided
individually. There are, of course, variations in the theory, which
may extend to the denial of any "essential" rules at all, or admit
certain general norms, from which, however, an exception is always possible in any existing situation in response to the call of
God given in, and according to, the exigencies of the case. While
it is not possible here to expound or evaluate the whole question
of natural law versus situation ethics, it may be observed that
a great deal of time and energy has been wasted in deriding the
idea of a changeless order built upon the supposition of immutable
essences. For many decades now, natural-law discourse has been
conducted, in the teachings of the popes at least, and by the moral
theologians, not in terms of absolute, immutable essences or
natures, but in terms of order, finality, and relationships in the
dynamic operations of life, and the problem has been situated in
the determination of the varying applications of a relatively small
number of basic principles in a constantly changing environment,
rather than in the supposition of a complete and detailed compilation
of "laws" already fixed and permanent. The immutability of the
natural law is very relative. Its basic premises are as stable as
the relation upon which they are founded (equality, brotherhood,
finality, etc.); but inasmuch as the historical reality to which they
must be applied is constantly in motion, the immediate conclusions
--what the natural law requires or permits at any particular mo-
ment--are constantly under scrutiny, and the question is always
being asked whether new obligations or freedoms are arising from
a new demand of a new culture, or whether an old obligation or
freedom remains intact because all of its constituent elements are
still present in the contemporary problem. The immutability of
the natural law cannot be asserted or denied without distinction,
and the attempt to do so inevitably entails a misrepresentation
either of the absoluteness of the norms or of the contingency of
the situations.

The fourth source of objection to the "Catholic" concept of natural law, which has been entitled the theological objection, is the doctrine of Protestant theology on the corrupting influence of original sin upon the nature of man and consequently upon his natural ability to know clearly what his nature is and what it postulates. As a result, the Protestant theologian is apt to dis-approve the reliance of the Catholic moralist upon natural law, on the ground that natural reason is not capable of deducing with certainty various doctrines attributed by the latter to natural law. Two points in this position are particularly relevant to our purpose. First, it places the emphasis on that aspect of natural law which, from the theological point of view, is the less significant. Theologically it is less important that natural law is man-discovered than that it is God-made. Secondly, this view introduces the question of the process by which the natural law is actually known by man, and, far from being at variance with Catholic doctrine in the matter, it coincides at least partially with the position of Catholic theology that, even with regard to those truths about God and His eternal will which are not in themselves imperceptible by reason, it is only with the assist-ance of positive revelation that they are made available for all to know, even in the present state of human nature, readily, with certainty, and without adulteration of error.

For the Catholic moralist, therefore, natural law belongs to theology not only by reason of its material object, because it forms part of the pattern by which the Christian conforms his life to the will of God, but also by reason of his method, because he comes to the knowledge of it through the instrumentality of authentic teaching as well as by natural reason.

Hence it is important to distinguish the source of the law from the source of our knowledge of the law. A norm belongs to natural law if it has its origin in the order and demands of nature. This remains true, and therefore it remains natural law, whether one comes to the knowledge of it by natural reason or by the teaching of the Church. Natural law is constituted as such not by the fact that it is naturally known but by the fact that it is founded in nature. Because it is founded in nature, it follows that it will be, more or less, knowable without supernatural assistance; but it does not cease to be natural law when it is known, or known with certainty, through some such assistance.

This is not to imply that one cannot, or does not, know the natural law, even in some of its more remote applications, by reason alone. Indeed one can, and one does. It is rather to assert

207

that one can also derive one's certitude about natural law from
another source, without prejudice to its distinctive attributes as
divine, rather than ecclesiastical, law. But it is also intended
to suggest that we do in fact, perhaps more than we have thought,
derive our certitude in such matters rather from the authority
of the magisterium than from reason. The arguments demonstrate
at least the reasonableness of a particular controverted position,
more or less convincingly, and their validity is confirmed by the
teaching; but it is possible that the factor bridging the gap between
reasonableness and that certitude which does not admit the probability or tenability of the opposite may come from another and
higher source. Such a position does not cut off dialogue with the
non-Catholic theologian or moral philosopher. On the contrary,
it is a position more acceptable to him than the implication that
he fails to see the cogency of the Catholic argument. He is, quite
rightly, not prepared to admit that the Catholic has a reason or
a degree of sincerity which he has not; but he already knows that
the Catholic has a faith which he has not. By the same act of faith
by which the Catholic accepts the Church itself, he accepts its
magisterium as an authoritative guide, not only in dogma but also
in morals, not only in positive but also in natural morality. The
remainder of this study will be concerned with a more detailed
elaboration of this statement.

Natural law and the Church

1) The Church teaches the natural law. While Catholics do not
claim a monopoly of natural law, or of the knowledge of it insofar
as it is knowable by reason, the magisterium of the Church has,
in fact, consistently asserted without distinction that the teaching
of morals as well as of dogma is part of its magisterial office;
it has exercised this authority constantly in passing judgment on
the morality of concrete modes of conduct; it has, in many instances, declared that a certain moral principle was precisely a
precept of natural law, thus not only stating the rule but identifying
the source of the rule; and it has explicitly affirmed its competence
with specific reference to the teaching of natural law both in principle and in concrete application. In more recent times the popes
and bishops have engaged in teaching of this sort even more frequently perhaps than in the past--in pronouncements on political
structure, social order, race relations, the conduct of war,
conjugal morality, medico-moral problems, etc.--and have been
more explicit in referring to their authority and responsibility
precisely in matters of natural law. . . .

2) Given the fact that the Church has this authority of teaching the natural law, the precise mode of its relation to the teaching mission of the Church in general is important indeed, but secondary. For the most part the popes are content to say that it is part of the whole moral order, the way to God, holiness, and sanctification, and hence belongs to its function of directing men on the way of salvation, without describing precisely how this specific function is related to the Church's general mandate of preserving and teaching the deposit of revelation. Systematic theologians, more concerned with the relations between reason and faith, offer varying explanations: that the concept of revelation embraces both natural and supernatural revelation, that the various parts of natural law taught by the Church are contained implicitly in those moral doctrines which have been formally and explicitly revealed, or that matters of natural law come indirectly under the Church's teaching authority because of the necessity of truth in these matters in order properly to safeguard the purity of truth and practice in matters of faith and morals which are revealed.

Be this as it may, evidently the popes consider that they are not merely propounding matters of philosophy or offering counsels of human prudence, but that they are inculcating something which belongs to the total deposit of truth entrusted to them by Christ, and therefore in some way part of the total Christian revelation and within the adequate object of the Church's teaching authority. It is significant, too, that doctrines which are referred to, on the one hand, as the "law of nature" are also called, in the same context, "Christian doctrine." In various references to the fact of revelation and the mandate given the Church, in order that matters not in themselves impervious to reason may be known by all securely, certainly, and without mixture of error, there is no indication that this applies only to a limited area of natural morality. On the contrary, it is explicitly stated that the entire moral law has been entrusted to the Church by Christ--language which strongly implies that it is not separable from "revelation," in the sense in which the teaching of revelation is the mission of the Church. "Both of these--the natural law written in the heart and the truths and precepts of supernatural revelation--Jesus, our Redeemer, gave to His Church as the moral treasure of humanity in order that she might preach them to all creatures, explain them, and hand them on intact and safeguarded from all contamination and error from one generation to another."

The same identification of natural precept and divine communication appears in the following words of Pius XI:

For the governance of mankind God could have prescribed
only the one law of nature which He wrote upon the mind of
man at his creation and thenceforward He could have ruled
the steps of this law under His customary providence. Instead He preferred to give us the Commandments to prepare
us, and in the course of the centuries from the origin of
mankind to the coming and teaching of Christ Jesus He
wished Himself to teach man the duties that rational beings
owe their Creator. . . . Now if God has spoken . . . there
is no one who does not see that it is man's duty to believe
God absolutely in His revelations and to obey Him without
qualification in His Commandments; and precisely that we
may rightly fulfill both duties for the glory of God and our
own salvation, the Only Begotten Son of God founded His
Church upon earth.

3) This does not mean that the natural law, even in its more
detailed applications, cannot be known and demonstrated with
certainty from reason alone, or that the arguments from reason
are not important. We are speaking here of the role of the Church
in general with reference to natural law. Moreover, the Church's
teaching does not dispense with the necessity or diminish the
importance of the arguments from reason adduced by the theologians.
It is a general principle of all the Church's teaching that the promised guidance of the Holy Spirit does not obviate the necessity of
employing human methods. The care with which the popes and
councils have proceeded in issuing definitions is evident in their
acta. The principle is reaffirmed in the Constitution De ecclesia
of Vatican II: "The Roman Pontiff and the bishops, in view of their
office and the importance of the matter, by fitting means diligent-
ly strive to inquire properly into that revelation and to give apt
expression to its contents. . . ."
    In matters of natural morality the process of discussion and
argumentation is evidently part of this human co-operation with
the divine guidance; and in this process not only the hierarchy
and clergy but also the laity have their part, as has been clearly
expressed by the same Council: "Christ, the great Prophet . . .
fulfills His prophetic office not only by means of the hierarchy,
who teach in His name and with His authority, but also by means
of the laity, whom He has constituted His witnesses and endowed
with the spirit of faith and grace of speech to this end, that the
power of the gospel might shine forth in their daily lives, in
family and community." Similarly, Pope John acknowledged the

role of both clergy and laity in the evolving of the Church's teaching on social order. The significance of these preliminary stages
of discussion consists in this, that while the Church possesses the
fulness of truth and does not derive or learn her knowledge from
natural arguments, the process of argumentation does play a
part in explicitating and formulating in human terms the Church's
consciousness of the truth in general and of natural law in particular. The arguments also serve the purpose of showing the conformity of the teaching with natural reason. And, in turn, the
teaching confirms the value of the argumentation.

4) Even when the magisterial instruments of the Church employ arguments in the course of proposing a principle of natural
law, however, the value of the teaching does not depend upon or
come from the native force of the argument, but from the authority itself of the Church to teach, with a corresponding obligation on the part of the faithful to accept its teaching. This
is simply an application to the area of morals of the doctrine,
commonly presented in terms of dogmatic teaching, but universally valid, of the "authentic" magisterium of the Church. It is
not a scientific or philosophic source of knowledge, in which the
authority of the teacher and the security of the doctrine are contingent upon the potency of the arguments and proofs. The Church
bears witness to the truth, in morals as well as in dogma, and
its authority rests upon the mission of Christ and the guidance
of the Holy Spirit rather than upon the internal effectiveness of
the reasons alleged or their ability to convince. It is the conclusions
which are guaranteed, not the premises. As Pius XII explains:

> Therefore, when it is a question of instructions and prop-
> ositions which the properly established Shepherds (that is,
> the Roman Pontiff for the whole Church and the bishops for
> the faithful entrusted to them) publish on matters within the
> natural law, the faithful must not invoke that saying (which
> is wont to be employed with respect to opinions of individuals):
> "the strength of the authority is no more than the strength
> of the arguments." Hence, even though to someone certain
> declarations of the Church may not seem to be proved by
> the arguments put forward, his obligation to obey still
> remains.

5) Moreover, the Church may teach the natural law infallibly.
The scope of the pledge of infallibility is the whole of revelation,
i.e., the whole deposit of truth entrusted by Christ to His Church

211

to be faithfully preserved and communicated without error. This has been stated in the clearest terms in the Constitution De ecclesia of Vatican II: "This infallibility with which the Divine Redeemer willed His Church to be endowed in defining a doctrine of faith and morals extends as far as extends the deposit of divine revelation, which must be religiously guarded and faithfully expounded."

It was indicated above that matters of natural morality are not excluded from this total object by reason of being also, to a degree, naturally knowable, but rather that they have been positively declared to form a part of the teaching mission of the Church precisely as received from Christ. Evidently, as with many matters of dogmatic truth, a particular demand of natural law may be contained only obscurely, implicitly, or virtually in the deposit of revelation. Evidently, too, the judgment of what is so contained and what is, therefore, within the scope of the Church's teaching mission will be made by the same teaching authority. Hence it cannot be asserted antecedently that the natural law, or any part or requisite of it, is outside the scope of the Church's right to teach, or to teach infallibly. On the contrary, in the selections cited above the popes refer explicitly to the entire moral law as within the competence of the Church to teach without error.

As with other exercises of the teaching authority of the Church, the note of infallibility may attach either to solemn definitions on the part of a pope or ecumenical council, or to the teachings of the ordinary magisterium, under the same conditions of constancy and universality as for other forms of doctrine. It is evidently not correct, therefore, to conclude that a principle is not infallibly taught because it has never been the object of a solemn definition. The clear teaching of Vatican I has been reiterated by Vatican II: "Although the individual bishops do not enjoy the prerogative of infallibility, they can nevertheless proclaim Christ's doctrine infallibly. This is so, even when they are dispersed around the world, provided that while maintaining the bond of unity among themselves and with Peter's successor, and while teaching authentically on a matter of faith or morals, they concur in a single viewpoint as the one which must be held conclusively."

6) Besides infallible teachings of the magisterium, however, whether in solemn definition or in constant and universal ordinary teaching, there is that exercise of its authority which, while not infallible, is still authentic and binding. This is perhaps even more important in matters of natural law than in other areas of Catholic doctrine. In this connection it is important to distinguish the notions of infallibility and certainty. In matters of conduct, a

212

doctrine which is not taught with the plenitude of infallibility may still be taught with certainty, in the sense of moral, practical, certitude, so as to exclude any solidly probable opinion to the contrary here and now, i.e., with the effect that at a given time a particular mode of conduct is certainly licit or certainly illicit, without the abstract question of its relation to right order being definitively closed. Infallibility excludes the absolute possibility of error. Certitude, in the sense of moral, or practical, certitude, excludes the prudent, proximate fear of error. While such a teaching does not altogether close the question from a speculative point of view, it does normally preclude the possibility of acting in contradiction of the doctrine, relying on the principle of probabilism. Ultimately the thesis of probabilism does not rest simply upon the point that a doubtful law does not bind. There is no serious contention that it does bind by any force of its own. Probabilism depends upon the justification that while there is still the possibility of a material violation of law, yet one who acts with reliance on a solidly probable opinion is not exposing himself imprudently to this danger--which is not true when one acts on the basis of a mere possibility or a tenuously probable view. But when the authentic magisterium of the Church professedly teaches a particular moral doctrine, it will not be easy to say that one who acts in contradiction of it is not exposing himself imprudently to the danger of violating the moral law. For the assistance of the Holy Spirit is always present to the Vicar of Christ and the other bishops, and in their purposeful pronouncements they will have used more than ordinary human means as well.

There are many statements of the magisterium itself inculcating the fact and the binding effect of the noninfallible exercise of its teaching authority. . . .

The existence of this authentic but not infallible teaching raises the question of discerning, not between infallible and noninfallible pronouncements (for a single declaration is not to be taken as a definition unless it is clearly intended as such), but between such as are "purposeful" (data opera), with the effect of creating the obligation of acceptance, and other statements which might be made in the course of a communication without the intent of professedly teaching the doctrine as Catholic. The Constitution of Vatican II provided very valuable criteria: the nature of the document (as is well known, the popes are accustomed to choose one or another form of presentation--constitution, encyclical, motu proprio, allocution--with a view to the solemnity traditionally associated with them), the frequency of a doctrine's recurrence in papal discourse, and, perhaps the most significant single criterion, the verbal formula employed (ex dicendi ratione). In a medico-moral study of the problem of mutilation and with specific reference to the interpretation of papal pronouncements, Fr. Gerald Kelly proposed three criteria, of which the first was the verbal formula, the other two being the historical context of the declaration and the purpose of the speaker (which, in turn, will be learned partly from the language of the text).

A second problem in this matter is the determination of the precise effect of such an authentic but not infallible teaching. What is generally taught as the effect of such teachings in dogmatic matters would be applicable here, except that the question of actual conduct also arises. That is to say, from a teaching of this sort two consequences follow, one external and absolute, the other internal and conditional. In the external order there results the obligation not to contradict the doctrine in public speech or writing. Concretely, this would prevent taking the position that the contrary opinion is solidly probable and applicable in practice. It would prohibit confessors from giving contrary advice or permitting contradictory conduct on the part of penitents. That would be to set oneself up as a sort of private magisterium, in competition with the magisterium established by Christ. And whatever the limits on one's obligation to accept the judgment of the latter, one is certainly not entitled, either singly or in company with other private theologians, to enter into conflict with it. But this would not exclude all speculative discussion of the question on the part of theologians, supposing a discreet selection of audience and method of discourse, with a view to clarifying the issues and finding the answers to difficulties involved. As was noted above, to say that a question is not "liberae disceptationis inter theologos" does not seem to mean that it cannot be discussed among theologians, but rather that it is not to be approached as something on which either side is of equal standing or could be equally followed.

In the internal order there results per se the obligation of intellectual assent to and acceptance of the teaching. But since, in the supposition, the teaching is not infallible and there remains the possibility of the opposite, there must remain also the absolute possibility that someone, exceptionally qualified in some aspect of the question upon which the conclusion depends, may have grave reason to think that the proposition is not certainly true. In this event the individual, while bound by the teaching in the external order, would not be obliged to yield internal assent. In matters of one's own purely private conduct, indeed, it would seem that he might act according to his own opinion, unless it is clear that the authority teaching intended not only to teach a point of natural law but also, insofar as necessary, to impose a norm of conduct in virtue of its jurisdictional authority. That this may sometimes be the intention is indicated by the references made in papal pronouncements to the "obedience" due teachings of this nature. But it must be emphasized that the exception con- templated here is a rather extraordinary thing, more likely to be verified when questions of fact enter in than in matters of principle. Since generally this sort of teaching will already be Catholic doctrine or a simple application of it, and will not be propounded without careful study and consultation of periti, it will not easily or commonly happen that the ordinary faithful, the ordinary priest, or even the ordinary theologian will be in a position prudently to depart from the sort of authentic teach- ing at issue here.

It is in this way, and for this reason, that an opinion which at one time is not solidly probable because of contrary teach- ing by ecclesiastical authority might become so later, without any prejudice to Catholic principles on the value of the teaching of the Church. After remarking that special study was being made of the morality of certain forms of fertility regulation, Pope Paul VI went on to say: "But meanwhile We say frankly that up to now We do not have sufficient motive to consider out of date, and therefore not binding, the norms given by Pope Pius XII in this regard. Therefore they must be considered valid, at least as long as We do not judge it Our duty to modify them."
. . .

7) The teaching authority of the Church in matters of natural law extends not only to the enunciation of abstract principles but also to their application in the concrete. The Church is not limited to stating that one must be just, or charitable, or chaste, but may teach that a certain concrete social situation is unjust, that a definite impending or existent legislation is immoral, that a specified conjugal practice is illicit. Wherever a moral issue is involved, the Church has the right to point out what the moral obligation of the faithful is in that situation. In this connection Pope John XXIII wrote: "It is clear, however, that when the hierarchy has issued a precept or decision on a point at issue, Catholics are bound to obey their directives. The reason is that the Church has the right and obligation, not merely to guard the purity of ethical and religious principles, but also to intervene

authoritatively when there is question of judging the application of these principles to concrete cases." And Pius X: "Whatever a Christian man may do, even in affairs of this world . . . all his actions, insofar as they are morally good or evil, that is, agree with, or are in opposition to, divine and natural law, are subject to the judgment and authority of the Church." Similarly Pius XII, describing a position which he subsequently disapproves: "Let the Church, [some modern writers] do not hesitate to say, propose her doctrine, pass her laws as norms of our actions. Still, when there is question of practical application to each individual's life, the Church must not interfere; she should let each one of the faithful follow his own conscience and judgment." Needless to say, the Pope was not denying the obligation to follow one's own conscience; he was speaking of the Church's role in the formation of conscience.

In such a case the Church is not constituting an ecclesiastical obligation or exercising its jurisdiction in the field of politics, or sociology, or domestic psychology, or some other area outside the sphere of its competence. It is teaching the moral obligation already existing in that situation. Obviously, the exercise of this authority must be regulated by prudence, and supposes a situation sufficiently clear factually to justify a declaration of this sort; but it is not outside the scope of the magisterial office.

8) The authority of the Church to teach the natural law resides not only in the pope and the college of bishops, whether in council or in the ordinary universal magisterium, for the whole Church, but also, as taught by Vatican II, proportionately, in the individual bishop with respect to the faithful of his territory. "The bishops teaching in communion with the Roman Pontiff are to be respected by all as witnesses to divine and catholic truth; and the faithful have a duty to concur in the judgment which their bishop expresses in the name of Christ on matters of faith and morals, and by an act of religious submission to make it their own." And the Code of Canon Law: "While the bishops, whether teaching individually or gathered in particular councils, are not endowed with infallibility, yet with regard to the faithful entrusted to their care they are truly teachers and masters" (can. 1326).

As with the magisterium in general, this authority of the bishops individually is not limited to the enunciation of abstract principles, but extends also to concrete applications, in matters of social abuses, or legislative excesses, or educational rights, etc., within their territory, whenever a moral issue is involved, under the same conditions of sufficient factual information and prudence

216

in action. (As a matter of fact, our bishops have often taken action of this sort as the occasion required.) And, in general, the same effect results from the teaching of the particular magisterium with respect to its subjects as in the case of the supreme authority with respect to the whole Church, i.e., the obligation of obedience in conduct and, per se, of internal assent, though, from the nature of the matter, the possibility of exception to the latter is some-what less unlikely in this case.

9) The teaching authority of the Church in matters of natural law is exercised not only directly, in pronouncements of the magisterium itself, collectively or separately, but also, in an indirect way, through its influence of supervision and vigilance over the doctrines of the theologians and others in a nonmagisterial capacity. Given the responsibility of the Church for the purity of moral doctrine communicated to the faithful, and the fact that the hierarchy cannot be unaware of the teachings regularly and public-ly circulated in the popular vehicles of instruction and in books and periodicals dedicated to theological and moral discourse, it follows that norms of conduct commonly and constantly enunciated in those sources from which priests and faithful principally derive their moral training come to be attributed to the magisterium it-self, and to be designated and accepted as Catholic doctrine. That a common opinion of moral theologians should come to be regarded as Catholic teaching, therefore, is not due simply to the native ingenuity of the moralists, or to some sort of usurpation by which in the course of time they have pretended to magisterial power; it rests upon two suppositions: that the bishops throughout the world are sensitive of their obligation to inform themselves about the moral doctrine circulated within their territories, espe-cially in the most influential publications professedly propounding moral theology in principle and application, and that they are diligent in executing their responsibility. The law of the Church requires that writings on morals shall not be published without previous examination and the permission of the local ordinary. The imprimatur does not mean that the ordinary necessarily agrees with the opinions of the authors, but it does mean that the work has been judged at least consonant with accepted and ac-ceptable principles of faith and morals. The hierarchy, there-fore, cannot fail to share the responsibility for a doctrine com-monly and consistently taught by the moral writers. "Bishops, for their part, by conferring this faculty [to teach] are not de-prived of the right to teach; they retain the very grave obligation of supervising the doctrine which others propose, in order to

help them, and of seeing to its integrity and security."

10) There is a significant difference between the Church's teaching of the natural law and the Church's making laws of its own. The Church is free to change the latter but not the former. Even if, and to the extent that, a teaching on morality is reformable, it is not reformable at the free choice of the Church, a matter of legislative will, but only if and because the former teaching is perceived to have been imperfect or to be no longer applicable in a changed situation. In one case the Church recognizes a law already in existence in the order of creation willed by God, and the Church simply declares that this is so. In the other case the Church itself constitutes the law, within the scope of its authority and with a view to the salvation and sanctification of souls, as the law of fast and abstinence, or of hearing Mass on Sundays, or of the Eucharistic fast, or of matrimonial form and impediments, or of clerical celibacy, etc. The Church can change the laws which it makes, but not those already constituted by God. It is the failure to appreciate this difference that leads to prophecies that the Church will have to change "its law" on various points which moral theology ascribes to the law of God. And it is for this reason, too, that the more significant thing about the natural law, from the theological point of view, is not that it is man-perceived but that it is God-constituted.

It was with this point that our study began. It was suggested, indeed, that this is the crucial point in the theological approach to natural law. Because it is something established by God in the order of creation, it will be knowable, to a degree, by reason. But it has also been communicated by Christ, along with the total deposit of Christian revelation, to the Church, in order that it may be known by the faithful commonly, readily, and without error. Hence it belongs to the magisterial office of the Church to teach natural law, whether infallibly or in the non-infallible but authentic exercise of teaching, whether by the Roman Pontiff alone or by the bishops in communion with him throughout the world, whether in solemn definition or in the ordinary methods of instruction, whether in the abstract or in concrete application, whether directly in documents emanating from the magisterial organs themselves or indirectly by the implication inherent in its responsibility over the common and constant teaching of the theologians.

Evidently this is an attempt to outline, in rather raw and legalistic language, the naked facts of the Church's authority to teach the natural law--the existence, the extension, the limits of this authority, and the modes of its exercise. Evidently, too, much could be said about the discreet selection of the proper time to speak, about the method of preparation of the instrument of instruction in collaboration with the other members of the episcopal college and with consultation of the lesser clergy and of the laity, and about the terminology in which the teachings might be most effectively and pastorally communicated to the world at large or to some particular flock. What the Church can do, and whether the Church ought to do it, or to do it at this time or in this way, are quite distinct issues. For the most part the present study has considered only the first of these. The reason is that, as a matter of fact, the most important questions which have been raised with regard to the Church and the natural law have not been concerned simply with the timeliness, the method, or the tone of its teaching.*

Notes begin on page 335.

*Editor's note: Since this article was written in 1965, Pope Paul has given the Church his encyclical Human Life, July 25, 1968. Directly or indirectly in this encyclical the natural moral law is referred to twenty-one times, and the doctrine regarding the teaching authority of the Church in matters pertaining to natural law, as developed here by Father Reed, seems to be clearly upheld by Pope Paul VI.

Situation Ethics
and Objective Morality

Louis Dupré

It has been said that the term "situation ethics" or its equivalent "contextualism" has become too large to be meaningful.
In an article in the Harvard Theological Review, James Gustafson
convincingly shows how the term covers moral systems which
significantly differ from each other. He even maintains: "The
debate between context and principles . . . forces an unfair
polarization upon a diversity of opinion that makes it both aca-
demically unjust, and increasingly morally fruitless. Persons
assigned to either pole are there for very different reasons,
and work under the respective umbrellas in very different ways."1
Gustafson is obviously right in asserting that men come to
contextualism from different starting points and that "the place
from which they start sets the pattern for what considerations
are most important in the delineation of Christian ethics."2 It
is equally certain that "moralists of principles" differ consider-
ably from each other. But the assertion that the distinction itself
between situation ethics and ethics of principles has become too

vague to be a fruitful topic of discussion is true only if the meaning of the term "ethics of principles" is extended beyond that of
"objective morality." Such is obviously the case for Gustafson,
who includes under ethics of principles several authors whom
objective moralists would definitely characterize as situationist
(in fact, all the moralists whom he discusses with the exception
of Paul Ramsey). From an "objective" point of view, Gustafson's
distinction is a distinction within situationism.

It is the thesis of the present article that the distinction between objective morality and situation ethics remains relevant
and even necessary to a fruitful discussion. Both objectivists and
situationists complain that the other party misrepresents their
position. This confusion indicates that the distinction between
the two trends of thinking is not clearly defined. To clarify this
distinction situationism must be divided into two entirely different moral approaches.3

One asserts that objective norms can never be absolute. The
other rejects any immanently human standard (subjective or objective) as an absolute criterion of morality. The former approach,
which is primarily philosophical, has both secular and religious
adherents. It is an emphatic assertion of the irreducibly subjective character of human freedom against any moral system which
subjects this freedom to the norms of its own objective expressions.
The latter approach is theologically inspired: its followers are
mainly Protestants who wish to develop a moral theory that is
more consistently in accord with the Christian revelation of sin
and redemption than a morality based upon the natural law.

We will discuss both approaches successively, even though they
cannot always be kept distinct. Those who favor the philosophical
line of thought often introduce theological elements into the argument. Similarly, all "theological" situationists at times borrow
from a philosophy of the subject. Still, the two standpoints are so
basically different that they must be treated separately.

The philosophical approach

A common objection leveled against situation ethics is that it
has no absolute principles. Nothing could be more false. For the
situationist, the human person is an absolute value that cannot
be subordinated to anything else. It is precisely because of its
absolute character that he refuses to subjugate the original, subjective impulse of freedom to principles arising out of the objective expression of this freedom.

The situationist agrees with the objective moralist that human nature is an absolute norm of action. But he basically disagrees on the definition of this nature. For him, the nature of a free being is exactly the opposite of an objective, given datum: it is subjective creativity. Whatever promotes creative freedom is moral; whatever hampers it is immoral. True, this rule provides no ready-made solution for every possible moral problem. But the crucial question in morality is not whether the ethical rule prescribes a universal line of action for each particular situation, but whether it provides man with certain guidance in each situation for bringing his behavior in conformity with his true (primarily subjective) being. And this, the situationist claims, his principles do.

The situationist refuses to accept objective rules of good and evil as absolutely valid because the moral intention cannot be determined exclusively by the objective structure of an act (even if this structure is correctly evaluated). Good and evil belong to the interior realm of freedom before belonging to the objective expressions of freedom. Of course, the situationist is well aware that subjectivity is not pure inwardness; the human subject necessarily expresses itself in objective forms. For that reason, man must also lay down objective rules for conduct. Situation ethics must not be confused with Kantian ethics, in which the morality of an act is determined entirely by the intention, independently of the object as such. Yet, objective rules alone are insufficient to determine morality, since freedom always retains an absolutely unique element of subjectivity which cannot be circumscribed objectively.

The insufficiency of objective norms as absolute criteria of morality was first worked into a moral theory by Søren Kierkegaard. According to the Danish thinker, inwardness is the essence of man as free being. It also is his ultimate end, attainable only in a confrontation with the transcendent Ground of his freedom. In striving toward inwardness, freedom leaves behind all its objective expressions as essentially inadequate. No objective moral standards, then, can properly measure the inward movement of the spirit. Nevertheless, Kierkegaard emphasizes, the moral law is important as an indispensable steppingstone toward the religious stage of life. Only he can transcend the law who has seriously tried to live up to its demands. Even within the religious life the moral law remains important (at least in Kierkegaard's later writings), since it now becomes reincorporated into man's relation to the transcendent: the fulfilment of the law becomes an act of religious love.

I am not sure that situationists today would follow their great precursor on this last point. For them, the creativity of freedom commences forever anew and the objective norms that guided man's behavior in the past can never be more than empirical guidelines, assisting him but not compelling him in the present realization of his freedom. If people think that objective norms are absolute, this is only because until recently man's general state remained relatively stable. Walter Dirks, a Catholic situationist, writes:

> A peasant's son, held by the regulations of his milieu to be a peasant, and growing up in a world penetrated with the duties of his state in life, was far less in a position than his counterpart today not to know what God wanted from him. What God expected from him was that he be-come a good peasant, and that meant doing in his place and time everything that a good peasant had always done; he had only to ask his elders and to do what they all did. The simpler and the more solid are the rules of the social order in which the possibilities of the human being are firmly and clearly articulated, the more is good realized in acceptance and submission.[4]

However, as the human condition has undergone a succession of rapid changes and placed us in entirely new situations, the rules of the past appear to be less universal. Situation ethics brings out the often-neglected element of creativity which should weigh heaviest in any moral theory.

Yet, the objective moralist cannot but wonder whether this isolation of the subjective aspect of freedom from its objective expression must not become self-destructive in the end. As Father Herbert McCabe pointed out in <u>Commonweal,</u>[5] without objective norms the situationist is not able to define, much less to apply, his own criterion of morality, namely, love or respect for the human person. Even to evaluate the "situation" itself, he must recur to objective norms. Who in a conflict situation should have the priority of my love? What is the most moral expression of love, for example, toward someone who seems to need the love of a person whom he or she is unable to marry? To leave such questions to one's creative subjectivity can only result in utter perplexity, or in a self-deceiving rationalization of emo-tional inclinations. Freedom is subjective, but it realizes itself in an objective world.

223

The situationist will retort that the attitude of the objective moralist is not so very different from his own. To certain acts he applies principles which he does not apply to similar acts in different situations. Of what avail are objective, general rules when, in the final analysis, the situation alone determines whether we will apply them or not? Is the objective moralist not deceiving himself in maintaining universal principles?

Here it is the objective moralist's turn to complain that his position is misunderstood. True enough, an identical act can be good in one situation and bad in another. No general precept of veracity binds the prisoner of war interrogated by the enemy about military secrets of his country. But does this mean that no universal precept applies to this case? Not at all, for one and the same universal principle may very well have two opposite applications. In this case the universal precept is not "to speak the truth under any circumstances" but "never to use language in a way which jeopardizes man's life in a community." This precept both obliges man to speak the truth to whoever has a right to it, and forbids him to reveal a truth that could seriously endanger the safety of his legitimate society (even though he would have to mislead those who seek its destruction). In the latter case, speaking the truth would destroy the very value which the precept of veracity is supposed to protect. What we have, then, is a truly universal and objective principle that must be applied in different and sometimes contrary ways depending upon the situation. Yet, it is never the situation itself nor my subjective impulse which ought to determine the course of action. To be moral, a decision must synthesize a <u>universal</u> moral principle with an <u>objective</u> evaluation of the present situation.

The situationist is quite right in pointing out that some concrete precepts exclude the application of others. But the objective moralist rejects his conclusion that <u>therefore</u> no moral principles are universal. The questions to ask are: "Which essential values of human nature are at stake?" and "How can I do justice to <u>all</u> these values without excluding any one of them in the present situation?" In trying to answer the second question, I may discover that a concrete maxim used in similar circumstances to promote a value may in a particular case jeopardize another equally essential value. The only conclusion which follows from such a discovery is that <u>this particular way of pursuing</u> the value is inadequate and should be rejected, for no essential value may be pursued to the exclusion of all others.

Here the situationist will object that it is impossible to do justice to all essential human values involved in a particular situation and therefore one must at times choose one value while deliberately excluding another. However, this statement reveals a pessimism concerning human nature which the objective moralist is unable to share. To settle for the lesser of two evils may seem necessary to the situationist. To the objective moralist it is immoral, because human nature cannot contradict itself to the point where every possible course of action in a particular situation becomes destructive of an essential human value. The whole discussion, then, turns upon two opposite concepts of human nature. Now this opposition may well be caused by different theological positions. But just as often the situationist's stand is simply a reaction against an outdated, static concept of human nature. This concept is seldom explicitly stated, but it becomes painfully evident in the way the moralist handles casuistics. The assumption underlying most casuistic ingenuity is that, <u>since human nature remains always the same</u>, moral science can work out enough "cases" over a period of time to protect all essential human values in all possible situations. The casuist, then, attempts to foresee every eventuality so that even the most concrete precept becomes provided with some sort of absolute universality. Wherever <u>that</u> situation occurs, <u>this</u> solution applies. Of course, the casuist is the first to admit, moral textbooks have to be updated, but this is mainly a matter of addition and subtraction: the new editor's task consists in integrating into the existing system the situations created by recent technological inventions, and in eliminating those situations which have become obsolete.

Many situationists, though feeling the inadequacy of this solution, still unquestioningly accept the premise of a static human nature. They have resigned themselves to the contradiction and see no other way to evade it than by a retreat into the purely subjective.[6] Such an attitude is unsatisfactory from a theoretical viewpoint. Still, it deserves credit for implying at least on a practical level that human nature is not the immutable, given entity which the traditional casuist all too frequently assumes. Freedom excludes the possibility of drawing up a set of <u>definitive</u> concrete moral rules. Man's cultural and moral evolution requires much more from the moralist than a mere adaptation of his long-established solutions to the present state of technological progress. To use one example, the basic question in the current problem of birth control is not whether the newly-invented steroids must be termed "sterilizing" or not, as if that could decide the entire moral issue. The real problem is whether a temporary sterilization (or whatever one calls a deliberate interruption of the ovulatory process) which was considered to be illicit in the past, is still immoral when the total human situation with respect to procreation has become basically different.

The objective moralist is undeniably right in assuming that human nature remains basically identical and, consequently, that its most fundamental principles are absolutely universal. But these principles are to be specified in a number of particular precepts, and if the moral law is the law of a dynamic, self-creating being, most of its particular precepts cannot be fixed once and forever. The distinction between absolutely universal principles and their less universal specifications is not a new invention in objective morality; it was already made by St. Thomas Aquinas in the Summa theologiae:

> We must say that the natural law as to the first common principles is the same for all both as to rectitude and as to knowledge. But as to certain more particular aspects, which are conclusions, as it were, of those common principles, it is the same for all in the majority of cases, both as to rectitude and as to knowledge, and yet in some few cases it may fail both as to rectitude, by reason of certain obstacles . . . and as to knowledge.7

Even more explicit is a seldom-quoted text of De malo:

> The just and the good . . . are formally and everywhere the same, because the principles of right in natural reason do not change. . . . Taken in the material sense, they are not the same everywhere and for all men, and this is so by reason of the mutability of man's nature and the diverse conditions in which men and things find themselves in different environments and times.8

This essential distinction between an absolute and a relative element in the moral law receives hardly more than lip service from many objective moralists. That is precisely the reason why situationists tend to go to the opposite extreme and deny the existence of any universal objective principles. But in doing so, they seem to adopt the thesis of the most rigid natural-law moralists, namely, that any relativization of the concrete moral precepts jeopardizes the universality of all objective moral principles.

This, however, is a false assumption; for the distinction between universal principles and less universal applications of
these principles by no means implies that all concrete moral
precepts allow of exceptions. Some acts are always and under
any circumstances destructive of an essential human value.
An act of adultery, for instance, cannot but violate the universal
precept of justice and is therefore always wrong. The biblical
example of Judith is often cited as a proof to the contrary. But
if Judith's intention was to seduce Holofernes to adultery (which
is not altogether clear from the text), even the most flexible
objective moralist will find no better explanation for her action,
I am afraid, than the primitive character of Judith's (or the
author's) moral consciousness. That the narrator commends
her for her patriotism is quite irrelevant. The books of the
Bible reflect the moral mentality of their authors' time and environment. They reveal the religious meaning of man at a particular stage of his moral development, but by no means do they
indicate that this stage has attained the highest ideal of moral
refinement.

The theological approach

So far we have interpreted situation ethics merely as a reaction against a rationalist and ahistorical moral-law theory.
For Protestant moralists, however, situation ethics is obviously more than that. The basic reason for their disagreement with
natural-law theory is not, as is sometimes said, a misunderstanding of the theory due to the shabby and inaccurate manner
in which it is set forth in some standard texts, but rather a different theological concept of human nature. Any ethical theory
which neglects the difference between man's situation before
and after the Fall must look a priori suspect to the Protestant.
Only in the original state of innocence could human nature
provide an absolute norm of morality. After the Fall this original
nature became an unattainable ideal rather than a realistic moral
norm. The notion of an absolute natural law that continues to rule
in man's present condition is, for the Protestant situationist, an
unsuccessful attempt to maintain identical moral norms despite
drastic changes in man's moral condition. The distinction between invariable, universal principles and the variable precepts
through which these principles are to be applied has, in his
eyes, no other function than to "adapt" the law of man's innocence to a situation in which this law can no longer be fully

227

observed. Rather than camouflage the relativity of any moral law in the fallen state of man by a contrived and ineffective absolute law, the situationist openly admits that since the Fall human nature can no longer be an absolute norm of morality.

The natural-law moralist will undoubtedly reply that this is a misinterpretation of his concept of "relative" precepts. The moral law was already relative before the Fall; the relativity does not result from any concessions to the corruption of human nature, but from the necessity of applying the absolute to a variety of situations.

The answer is correct, and many Protestant situationists would undoubtedly do better to study first the basic meaning of the concepts which they reject. Yet, I fear, a better understanding of the terms will still not convert them to the natural-law position; for the essential question remains whether human nature after the Fall is still able to provide an absolute norm for action. The answer of Reformed theology to this question has been traditionally negative and would, therefore, seem to be irreconcilably opposed to a natural-law morality.

Still, modern theologians engaged in rethinking the historical element of the original sin seem to become increasingly reluctant to found the relativity of all natural law upon historical change of which we know nothing. Perhaps we may therefrom conclude that man's sinfulness no longer provides as strong a basis for rejecting a natural-law theory as it used to do.

More emphasized today is the different way in which Reformed theology conceives of God's relation to man. By its subjective, strictly personal character, this relation eschews the dominion of objective rules. While Catholics usually think of grace as an objective, common state provided through the Church and the sacraments, salvation for most Protestants means a unique and strictly personal call of God in Christ. But if the call is personal, so are the obligations. What God expects from His elect does not necessarily coincide with the immanent laws of human nature. Abraham's sacrifice is there to illustrate this. Any immanent determination of God's relation to man jeopardizes its transcendent character and is an assault on His absolute supremacy. Of course, insofar as the world is a coherent totality, it is intrinsically bound to certain objective rules which God Himself must respect. To break these rules constantly could only lead to chaos and destruction. But there is no reason why the divine election of an individual person must be subjected to similar restrictions.

228

The usual Catholic objection to this attitude is that God must be consistent with Himself. If He has created man in accordance with certain laws, He owes it to Himself to respect these laws. As Josef Fuchs, S.J., puts it: "God's personality and freedom do not exclude but presuppose that his own essence is 'given before' all personal and free volition. It therefore constitutes the 'measure' of everything. God, precisely because He is God, cannot deny or give up His own essence. Likewise, He cannot deny or give up the image of His essence which is man."[9]

But is this objection really responsive to the Protestant position? If God's demands in the order of salvation would constantly be in conflict with the objective requirements of human nature, they would obviously jeopardize His creation. But the Protestant situationist does not hold such a position. He does not even deny the existence of some sort of objective moral law. He merely says that this law is insufficient to express man's personal relationship with God in Christ. Objective moral laws promote man's immanent development. But they must not restrict man's obedience to transcendent divine orders, even if those orders occasionally conflict with these laws. God's commands can no longer be called transcendent if they are entirely subjected to the rule of man's immanent laws. Moreover, the Protestant situationist may turn the tables upon his opponent by pointing out that too much insistence on the necessity of a strict conformity between the transcendent and the objective immanent order could have results which the Catholic would be most reluctant to accept. It would, namely, exclude all miracles as arbitrary interferences of God with the universal rules of His own creation. Finally, references to the image of God such as the one in the above-quoted text are preposterous as long as we have not defined to what extent this image is preserved in man's sinful nature. Can we call objective morality a pure reflection of God's own essence? This question must be settled before the objective moralist can ever hope to convert the situationist to his position.

A third and perhaps even more basic Protestant objection to the natural-law theory is shared by many secular moralists. We mentioned it in the beginning of this article. An objective ethical system cannot do justice to the creative element in morality. Man must seek what is right for him, and this search will never be finished. Right and wrong are not simply given. Even to say that he "discovers" moral values is not sufficient if it implies that values pre-exist to his finding them. Moral values are never simply there; they are created in the moral act itself. What goodness is becomes clear only in good acts. Moral goodness exists only to the extent that people are actually good. Men of heroic virtue, therefore, are much more than examples; they are authentic creators of moral virtue.

If one agrees with this position, the only relevant question with respect to the present discussion is whether man's moral creativity is better preserved in situation ethics than in an objective moral system. Many objective moralists would deny this. The absolute "obedience" to God's Word which some situationists advocate is hardly more creative than the most rigid natural-law theory (e.g., Emil Brunner in Das Gebot und die Ordnungen). Whether it is God's Word that orders me or an "immutable law of nature" makes little difference. Many situationists have broken through the legalism of "nature," only to fall victim to an equally rigid legalism of the Word of God. Their morality still consists in fulfilling obligations that remain extrinsic to personal freedom. What is needed is not another extrinsic source of moral obligation, but a more dynamic concept of human nature. Such a concept can be worked out within an objective moral system as well as in situation ethics.

But that is not all; for the objective moralist will object that in denying the absolutely normative character of all objective rules, the situationist, instead of liberating the creative aspect of freedom, merely ends up with an aimless impulse. It is true enough that no fixed norms can adequately determine the course of human freedom. Since freedom is an inventive and creative forward surge, human nature--that is, what is given originally and what has been acquired through past decisions--can never provide a definitive rule of action. But this does not mean that freedom determines itself in a vacuum. Freedom can exercise itself only within the objectivity of nature. Unless it respects the objective, given part of the self, the creative impulse becomes destructive.

Conclusion

The preceding confrontation between objective morality and situation ethics calls for a theory that combines the subjective-creative with the objective-rational element of freedom. No moral system in the past has done full justice to both these elements. Nor does the concept of natural law, with its heavy hereditary taint of objectivism and rationalism, seem particularly apt to reconcile both views. Nevertheless, some absolute objective and immanent standard appears to be indispensable.

The main problem is whether such a standard would be acceptable to both Protestant and Catholic theologians. Catholics have traditionally maintained an objective moral theory. But usually it was done in such a rigid and inflexible fashion that the dynamic aspect of human nature completely disappeared. In principle, however, Catholic theology does not object to a more dynamic moral theory as long as the notion of an objective moral law is preserved.

Nor would an objective basis of morality conflict with Reformed theology. Few Protestants would deny that human freedom implies some intrinsic norms independent of any revelation. We do not need the gospel to recognize that mass murders in concentration camps basically conflict with the dignity of man. Some may perhaps argue that without Christ's redemption human nature cannot avoid committing such crimes. But everyone will admit that non-Christians are able to recognize these acts as essentially immoral and that they do not indulge in them any more than Christians do. Protestant situationists may object that natural law cannot be a sufficient norm for Christian ethics. We wholeheartedly agree with them: nature can provide only general norms and some negative concrete precepts. But at least one must admit that there is some basic standard of morality which can be known without the aid of the revelation. It is important to stress this at a time when all men must co-operate to prevent certain criminal actions of recent history from ever being repeated.

Nor does the acceptance of man's nature as an absolute moral norm interfere with the strictly personal aspect of his relation to God. This relation is not made less personal by the fact that all men participate in the same incarnated freedom. Objective guidance in the exercise of freedom does not eliminate the ineffable character of the choice. Each man's vocation, therefore, remains unique and incomprehensible to others, even though it shares with others the same objective rules for the preservation of a common nature.

Protestants justifiably refuse to accept every single law that Catholic moralists, at one time or other, have presented as "natural law." In fact, none but the most general (and, I think, negative) precepts can ever be safely said to belong to the moral law of nature. However, the purpose of this discussion is not to discover a set of unchangeable concrete precepts. The position here presented has nothing in common with that of the objective moralist who overlooks the dynamic, personal aspect of human nature and simply attempts to present all rules that were indispensable at one time as eternal laws of God. My point is rather that a dynamic concept of nature and a personal relation to God are not incompatible with absolute moral objectivity. Indeed, without such objectivity man's moral activity is bound to operate in a vacuum. Not even a nominalist philosophy in which God's free decision alone makes good and evil could prevent such a position from being ultimately self-destructive.

Notes begin on page 336.

Capitalism and Ethics

John C. Bennett

The phrase "the Protestant ethic" is familiar in the discussion
of the motives that underlie capitalism as a way of life. The use
of the phrase in this context was stimulated chiefly by Max Weber's
speculation concerning the influence of 17th-century Calvinism,
especially in its Puritan form, on the development of what he
called the spirit of capitalism. There is an enormous literature
about Weber's thesis, much of it critical of his claims for it,
but there is little doubt that aspects of Calvinistic spirituality
help to explain the fact that among middle-class Protestants there
did develop the tendency to emphasize economically productive
work as itself a religiously sanctioned vocation, unlimited production and unlimited profit, and a disciplined life that made
it natural to save and invest rather than to spend.

Protestants were not the first people who have sought financial
gain, but dedicated participation in this rationalized system of
profitable work and saving seems to have been favored by a major
type of Protestantism. There was an economic dynamism here that

was not characteristic of Catholicism and that cannot be taken for granted in any culture. The early religious sources of this dynamism are now generally forgotten, but today among middle-class Protestants something of this ethos persists. One illustration is the tendency of Protestants with this Puritan background to feel guilty, perhaps only slightly guilty, when they are not working. Deep within the Catholic tradition there is the assumption of the superiority of the contemplative life. Is it not possible that the secularization of the contemplative life may be leisure without a sense of guilt?

Discussions of the Protestant ethic as a support for capitalism often refer to Richard Baxter, whose book on moral theology, A Christian Directory, had great influence on 17th-century Puritans. He writes: "It is a sin to desire riches as worldlings and sensualists do, for the provision and maintenance of fleshly lusts and pride; but it is no sin, but a duty, to labour not only for labour's sake, firmly resting in the act done, but for that honest increase and provision, which is the end of our labour; and therefore to choose a gainful calling rather than another, that we may be able to do good, and relieve the poor."

The fact that responsible Protestant teachers could write in this way about the duty to seek "an honest increase and provision" and to choose a more "gainful calling" is a mark of the stereotype of the Protestant ethic. It should be made clear that this was not the ethic of the great reformers, that it was not the ethic of all forms of Protestantism, but it was an ethic that has been strong among forms of Protestantism that have flourished in several northern countries, especially our own.

Great changes have come in capitalism and also great changes have come in the teaching of ethics within Protestantism and it is to the relationship between these two developments that I shall now turn.

Within the past century there have been at least three stages in the corporate ethical thinking of Protestant churches in regard to capitalism. During the first period that extended into the first decade of the 20th century, the Protestant attitude toward capitalism was one of uncritical acceptance. This was along the lines of what I have called the stereotype of the Protestant ethic. The second period involved an increasingly critical attitude toward capitalism and in the 1930's and 1940's there was a tendency to reject capitalism. A third period, in which we are living today, is characterized by a more open attitude toward some of the aspects of capitalism, combined with hope for the development of present-day capitalism under the pressures for social justice in our society. During this third period I think that Protestant thinking and Roman Catholic thinking tend to converge. Though there are some differences of methodology, I am aware of no distinctive Protestant position now that can be contrasted with the economic ethics reflected in the social encyclicals of Pope Pius XI and Pope John XXIII.

The first stage of Protestant teaching within the past century was almost a celebration of capitalism, especially unreformed laissez-faire capitalism. Theologians were uncritical of the productive processes. They opposed all tampering with so-called economic laws that were believed to be God's laws. They had no sympathy with the efforts of labor to organize because this would interfere with the operations of these laws. They often regarded poverty as a sign of sin and wealth a mark of divine favor. Responsible Christian thinkers, who in other areas are still much admired, were often uncritical defenders of a form of capitalism that is now outmoded.

A great change began to come toward the end of the 19th century. There was an increasing tendency to criticize capitalism. During the period between the two World Wars, Protestant ethical thinkers became strongly anticapitalistic. Often they were Christian Socialists. If we take as an example the year 1930, we would find that most of the great names in Protestant theology were opposed to capitalism. This was true of Karl Barth, Emil Brunner, Paul Tillich, Reinhold Niebuhr, Archbishop William Temple and a host of lesser figures. Of the men whom I have named, the most conservative was Emil Brunner, a Swiss reformed theologian who has had great influence in the United States. He wrote, about 1930, in his The Divine Imperative: "[The capitalist system] is that system in which all that we can see to be the meaning of the economic order from the point of view of faith is being denied: in which, therefore, it is made almost impossible for the individual to realize, in any way through his economic activity, the service of God and his neighbor. This system is contrary to the spirit of service; it is debased and irresponsible; indeed we may go further and say: it is irresponsibility developed into a system."

One of the most significant statements that reflect the strong criticisms of capitalism, though it does represent the beginning of the tendency to acknowledge the hopeful side of reformed capitalism, came out of the first Assembly of the World Council of Churches at Amsterdam in 1948. This statement was a part of the report of one of four sections of the Assembly. At the time

235

it received a great deal of publicity and was interpreted as more dogmatically anticapitalist than was the case. It said that the Church should make clear that there are conflicts between Christianity and capitalism, as well as conflicts between Christianity and communism. It recognizes, however, that capitalism varied from country to country and that "often the exploitation of the workers that was characteristic of early capitalism has been corrected in considerable measure by the influence of trade unions, social legislation and responsible management." The statement then emphasized four criticisms of capitalism: "1) It tends to subordinate what should be the primary task of any economy--the meeting of human needs--to the economic advantages of those who have most power over its institutions. 2) It tends to produce serious inequalities. 3) It has developed a practical form of materialism in western nations in spite of their Christian background, for it has placed the greatest emphasis upon success in making money. 4) It has kept the people of capitalist countries subject to a kind of fate that has taken the form of such social catastrophes as mass unemployment."

Would you not regard that list of criticisms as a good check list of the moral weaknesses of capitalism that do call for continuous watching and correction in every period? These criticisms are different from the over-all Marxist criticism that there is an inevitable historical judgment on capitalism exposing its inner contradictions and causing it to be displaced everywhere as a system through revolution.

A more open attitude toward important aspects of capitalism does characterize the present period--what I have called the third period. There are at least three such aspects. The first is the pluralism of capitalism that is made possible by the existence of many centers of initiative and power in contrast to a collectivism that unites and centralizes political and economic power. This pluralism is favorable to many forms of freedom, not only the more obvious forms of economic freedom such as freedom of enterprise, freedom to choose one's vocation and to some extent one's residence and one's job, freedom of consumer's choice, but also freedom of cultural initiative by providing sources of support for educational institutions and mass media that are independent of the state, and political freedom that comes from the existence of social forces that are not controlled by the state, including the power of private business and organized labor.

The second aspect of capitalism that has always been much praised by its long-time defenders but that now is often acknowledged by those who are inclined to be its critics is its creative dynamism. Critics of capitalism have often contended that the profit system as a guide to production and distribution is irrational because, instead of moving directly to meet human needs, it meets these needs as a by-product of the profit-seeking of individuals. The tendency to over-exercise the profit motive has often been regarded as immoral because it may make men more acquisitive than they might be under another system.

There is truth in these criticisms, and I shall suggest some ways of taking account of this truth later. Yet I think that this self-serving and often family-serving motive is a given factor that needs both to be tamed and to be used. I think that our ethical response to it should be both a yes and no, and that under some conditions the yes should come before the no. The energies that capitalism has stimulated because of its use of the profit incentive have led to the great benefits as well as to the many ills of modern industrial society. On balance, this process has surely been constructive. This applies to much more than the profit incentive in the restricted sense that relates it only to the return on equity capital; it applies to the seeking of economic advantage down the line to include all forms of income that stimulate effort and efficiency.

There is much foolishness in what is said in this whole area. Collectivists often deny the creative role of these economic incentives. Defenders of capitalism often speak as though these were the only incentives in the business world, thus insulting themselves. They overlook the other incentives which both supplement and correct the profit motive: the fascination of a game and the building of an empire; the enjoyment of status which, when it involves social approval, can correct raw acquisitiveness and empire building; the love of creating, loyalty to an organization, loyalty to the common good. There is a blend of all of these motives in professionalized management. Today the stress on social responsibility is conspicuous.

I think that the teacher of social ethics should handle this matter of incentives with more discrimination than either dogmatic individualists or dogmatic socialists. There's an element of necessary evil in the use of the more self-regarding economic incentives as even Communist societies are discovering. Even in non-profit institutions there is a subordinate place for economic incentives. This is true of differentials in salary that accompany recognized contributions and enlarged responsibilities. It is also true that nonprofit institutions, even churches, gain by having to win at least partial financial support from contemporaries

instead of coasting indefinitely on endowments. There are problems here when threats to withhold support tempt institutions to
betray their essential purposes, but the best institutions need to
face some equivalent of the moment of truth that the prospect of
either profit or loss creates for private business.

The third aspect of capitalism which deserves acceptance
within limits is the role of the market in guiding economic activity as an index of what is needed--though in the first instance
what is wanted by those who are able to pay for it. The market
provides considerable freedom for the consumer. Again, what
is good is on the edge of much evil and corruption. Insignificant
wants encouraged or even created by advertising may have
priority over real needs. We should not absolutize a want
system and assume that it is always good to produce what is
wanted. And yet, as a rough guide to the direction of economic
activities, the market is preferable to detailed central planning
that seeks to impose what the planners believe to be good on a
nation of consumers. There are self-correcting elements in an
open market that in the long run have their effect in reducing
the effects of overeager and sometimes unscrupulous salesman-
ship. Corrections are needed also by government regulation as
well as by improvement of taste in the society and by a juster
distribution of purchasing power. No economic system can be
free from the defects of the society within which it operates or
can be expected to solve all its problems.

I have said many positive things about the embodiment of
ethical values in the institutions of capitalism. I can do this in
large measure because capitalism has changed so profoundly
within the past half century. The rise of the labor movement
to check the arbitrary power of employers--it often was extremely arbitrary in this country before 1935--has helped to
make capitalism morally tolerable. The social legislation that
has gone far to create a welfare society has corrected many
of the injustices of traditional capitalism and has done much to
save capitalism from itself. Many of you will share my memory
that in this country the social changes that have made capitalism
morally tolerable have come in the teeth of the opposition of
those who dominated our capitalistic institutions. Their suc-
cessors in many cases--I hope in most cases--have come to
accept these changes and would not return to the more ruthless
capitalism of an earlier period. Those who today have the
power within the institutions of capitalism--both corporations
and labor unions--have to satisfy a pervasive sense of justice

in the society as a whole. The recent history of countries in which capitalism is dominant indicates clearly that capitalism is not a self-sufficient system, that it has been changed and will continue to be changed by political decisions.

In what follows, I shall deal with two aspects of this larger ethical frame to which capitalism is subject, first in the United States where we can indicate very precisely some of the limitations of capitalism and, second, in the international sphere where we see capitalism competing with other systems and facing many new problems.

In the United States our actions make it clear that capitalism, as the free enterprise system, is not self-sufficient. So much that needs to be done is not economically profitable for any private person or institution. There are large areas of public need on which capitalism seems unable to focus. Professor Galbraith has helped to illumine the situation by giving currency to the contrast between private wealth and public poverty. This helps us to see what economic targets are missed when the emphasis is only on maximizing the wealth of individuals even though there may be reasonable success in the case of most individuals. The community may still be very poor in schools, in housing, in opportunities for recreation, in many health services, in the failure to combat the pollution of water and air, in the ugliness of so much of the environment that is allowed to deteriorate, and not least in the public transportation, of which so many citizens are daily victims while their excellent private vehicles remain parked near home. This kind of public poverty, which involves real deprivation in fact for citizens in their private capacity, can only be overcome by strong public initiatives, which in various degrees may co-operate with or co-ordinate private initiatives.

Those who stress in theory the moral priority of free enterprise may accept in fact most of the institutional changes that now enable society through government to supplement and co-ordinate and regulate the activities of private agents, but there is a lag in basic thinking when it is assumed that private initiative is, except in the case of national defense and a few other matters, inherently better than public initiative. Why should it not be just as sound for the community as a whole to act for its own welfare as it is for any individuals or private organizations to take initiative for profit?

There is one subject that is on the minds and consciences of all of us: the poverty of our cities, in this case often both public and private poverty, poverty that is dramatized for us by the ghettos in which so many millions of our fellow citizens are imprisoned. These are both a racial and an economic problem. The existence of this poverty side by side with our enormous productivity and prosperity should cause us all to make explicit the fact that capitalism is not self-sufficient. In the 1930's the overwhelming interference with human freedom caused by mass unemployment did a great deal to broaden American thinking about the conditions of freedom. Those who did not learn the lesson then are in many cases learning it now as they see before them the destruction of freedom in our cities today, for which free enterprise alone cannot provide the remedy. The whole society working through government has to take bold initiatives to create the conditions that favor more freedom of choice for the victims of our institutions. One of the things that always has to be learned over again is that comfortable people do not do enough until they are pushed. If the Negro minority did not have votes to threaten our national political parties and if they had not taken to the streets in direct action, middle-class Americans would not be as ready as they are now to face the radical action required by the plight of our cities. When shattering events create anxiety concerning the structure of society, consciences are also stirred and changes fortunately are accepted from a mixture of motives.

I said earlier that Protestant and Catholic economic ethics have converged in recent decades. This is especially true in regard to the relationship between public and private initiatives in economic life. Neither Protestants nor Catholics believe in an all-encompassing state. However, both emphasize the legitimacy, indeed the necessity, of the increasing role of the state in economic life. Both seek to preserve the social and economic pluralism that is favored by the many units of economic decision and initiative which we associate with capitalism. Both give ethical sanction to private property as a source of and protection for personal freedom, though the arguments for private property must be understood as arguments for the widest possible distribution of property.

Pope John's encyclical Mater et Magistra and reports that have come from the Assemblies of the World Council of Churches preserve the same balance on this issue. Pope John speaks of the "tendency to be found in the ever-widening activity which the common good requires that public authorities undertake." This statement is immediately corrected by these words: "The state and agencies of public law should not extend their ownership except where evident and real needs of the common good dictate it."

240

One of the reports that came from the Evanston Assembly of the World Council of Churches in 1954 preserved the same balance by first saying that "while the state is sometimes the enemy of freedom, under many circumstances the state is the only instrument which can make freedom possible for large sectors of the population" and then by warning "against the danger that the union of political and economic power may result in an all-controlling state."

The necessity of supplementation and correction of the effect of capitalism is vividly illustrated by the recommendations of the President's Commission on Technology, Automation and Economic Progress, chaired by Dr. Howard Bowen. This commission's diagnosis of trends was certainly free from extreme or alarmist predictions but some of its recommendations broke the pattern of individualistic social thinking very radically, especially its recommendation that "economic security be guaranteed by a floor under family income" and that "this floor should include both improvements in wage-related benefits and a broader system of income maintenance for those families unable to provide for themselves." (Technology and the American Economy) This recommendation is close to one adopted in February, 1966, by the General Board of the National Council of Churches that "our burgeoning productivity makes possible, and our Judeo-Christian ethic of justice makes mandatory, the development of economic policies and structures under which all people, regardless of employment status, are assured an adequate livelihood." (Statement on "Christian Concern and Responsibility for Economic Life in a Rapidly Changing Technological Society") I am sure that both statements presuppose the idea that such income maintenance must be recognized as a basic right, just as the right of all children to educational opportunity. This can be defended both in the public interest and as a condition for personal freedom and welfare in the case of millions of persons. This seems very remote from the stereotype of the Protestant ethic to which I have referred. Someone may be tempted to quote St. Paul's words: "If any one will not work, let him not eat" (II Thessalonians 3:10). But we should not turn a condemnation of an especially obnoxious group of parasites into a universal law applicable to all economies, at all levels of productivity. Moreover there are other verses in the New Testament including the words in the story of the Last Judgment: "for I was hungry and you gave me no food" (Mt. 25:42).

As we look abroad to other countries, we can see clearly
that capitalism with its most astonishing creativity is not self-
sufficient. The older industrialized countries in which capitalism was dominant have retained many of the elements of
capitalism but these have been transformed to meet the needs
of welfare societies. Their political parties have abandoned
both a dogmatic individualism and a dogmatic socialism. American rightists see in this development a victory for communism,
as they do in the case of similar trends in this country, but they
could not make a greater mistake for these developments have
rendered nations immune to communism. Communism as a
revolutionary movement and a conspiracy thrives on neglected
social problems. Rightists see freedom being lost, for their
model of freedom is the uncontrolled economic behavior of
strong men in a frontier society rather than the maximizing of
opportunities for real freedom of choice on the part of all classes
in an interdependent industrialized society.

It is remarkably ironic that while Karl Marx expected a ripe
capitalism in western Europe to prepare the way for Communist
revolution, communism has in fact developed in nations that
were in large measure pre-industrial and pre-capitalist and has
proved to be a quick and ruthless way of modernizing and in-
dustrializing. The developments in Communist countries have
shown that communism is no monolithic or unchanging system,
that it is more open-ended than we in the Western countries
imagined possible. The irony becomes complete as advanced
and mellower Communist nations begin to develop some of the
characteristics of an open society including a measure of economic pluralism and of reliance on economic incentives. In any
case there have been enough changes in European communism
to blur the conflict between social systems and to soften the
hostilities of the cold war. It is a favorable sign that important
business leadership in this country seeks increased East-West
trade and is becoming open to trade with Communist China.

Denys Munby, an English economist who has given great attention to the relation between economics and ethics, has recently written that "although the industrialized world is divided
between the western and eastern blocs, the old issues of socialism and capitalism are dead." He goes on to say that there are
more similarities between western and eastern Europe than
either side would admit, and as the "East" begins to learn how
to apply traditional economic theory and modern mathematics
to its directed planning, the "West moves in the same direction

from laissez faire to indicative planning and thence to target planning" (Economic Growth in World Perspective, Denys Munby, editor). I can believe that many of you will regard that as a considerable overstatement but it is significant that it appears in the Foreword to a symposium representing the thought of scholars in many countries and written in preparation for a world conference of churchmen that met in Geneva in July, 1966. At that conference, which represented 70 countries, there was a continuous expression and even dramatization of the assumption that today the issues between what Lord Franks some years ago taught us to call "the North" and "the South" are becoming far more significant than those that have divided "the East" and "the West."

In relation to the third world, or the so-called undeveloped or developing nations, we need to recognize that American institutions cannot be exported universally, that economies in many developing nations will have a much greater socialistic ingredient than may be desirable in the United States, that foreign aid should not be used to prevent such socialistic developments. Also, American corporations and labor unions should not support sterile and oppressive oligarchies in nations to the south of us, because they deserve an order which, however unjust, provides some security for business dealings. One major test of American capitalism will be the capacity of its leaders to open the possibility that some nations, whose oligarchies have drifted for generations without doing anything important about the massive poverty of their people, may need to be changed by leftist revolutions. And we may hope that such revolutions will not be followed by more revolutions but by real nation-building and economic development. Fear of communism should not be used to justify the United States in being a counter-revolutionary force in all such explosive situations, especially in view of the fact that we know now that communism is not monolithic and that some Communist nations already show signs of being able to develop into more humane and open societies. We should do what can be done to help any nation that needs radical change to find a constructive alternative to communism, though often this may not be much.

"Capitalism and Ethics." Capitalism as we know it has elements that are ethically desirable even though they may not always be possible. We should be thankful where they now are part of the pattern of dynamic societies that are quite open and are moving toward greater social justice. They should also be part of any objectives that we regard as adequate for other societies. Those who stress them should also recognize that capitalism is not a self-sufficient system and that there must be the most varied combinations of private enterprise, public planning and initiative.

There are universal moral norms by which all systems should be judged. All should serve justice, not a static justice but a continually transforming justice, humaneness and diversity in society. All should serve the freedom of persons, of persons in all roles and not only those who have economic advantages. There is needed a conception of the depth and dignity and transcendence of the person that involves a far more inclusive form of freedom than that associated with the stereotyped and dated Protestant ethic that is often associated with traditional capitalism. Professor Brzezinski, who is one of the chief authorities on the conflict between East and West and who has proved his toughness in regard to immediate political problems, says that the issues of the cold war "are no longer the basic issues facing mankind." He says: "In the second half of the 20th century the developed nations, given new scientific and social developments, will face a real threat to the continued existence of man as a spontaneous, instinctive, rather autonomous and even somewhat mysterious being; the less developed countries, because of overpopulation, economic backwardness and potential political disorder, will be challenged by a fundamental crisis of survival of organized society." (Foreign Affairs, July, 1966)

This position leads me to say that while we should hold fast to universal moral criteria and objectives, not least those that recognize and protect the person as more than an economic being, as a "somewhat mysterious being," we need to be skeptical concerning the absolute claims of institutions and systems. Openness to unimagined institutional developments in the economic sphere and moral discernment concerning what is good for persons are both necessary to prepare us for the future.

Notes begin on page 336.

PART FOUR

Ethics of Revolution, War, and Pacifism

The Right of Revolution Reconsidered

Donald Atwell Zoll

To a society as comparatively well-developed and stable as that of the United States, thinking about "revolutions" is generally either academic or unpleasant or both. Thus, when confronted with "revolutions" (not of the mind or spirit but of the more conventional violent sorts), the society understandably recoils. The fact that the American nation was created by an actual revolution (albeit a somewhat singular one)--a fact which contemporary revolutionaries delight in reminding us--does not change U. S. Society's predictable reaction to the prospect of dismantling itself by violent upheaval and being reconstituted on premises which appear, at the very least, alien and peculiar.

This anti-revolutionary feeling proceeds from three quite different assumptions. The first two of these assumptions are intriguing because they presume some type of objective ethical criteria against which the validity of revolutions can be measured: (1) the revolutionary activity is condemned because the objectives or philosophical values of the revolutionaries are

deemed to be undesirable or their grievances fundamentally unjustified; (2) their basic objectives or bill of complaints are justified, but their methods (force and violence) are either not now
justified or are never justified. The third assumption underlying
opposition to revolutionary ferment is relativistic and is an en-
dorsement of the Realpolitik; (3) the ethical issue does not hinge
upon a justification of the revolution, but the moral question turns
solely on the liberty of individuals and groups to preserve what
they have (power, property, privilege, etc.) in the face of efforts
to deprive them of it by any means.

This range of anti-revolutionary sentiment is exceeded only
by the diversity of revolutionary movements themselves, particularly in their intellectual and ethical characteristics. The historical extremes can be illustrated by two well-known rebellions,
the Nike Insurrection in Byzantium in the sixth century and the
American Revolution. In the former, the attempted overthrow of
the regime of Emperor Justinian, provoking massive loss of life
and property--much of which was the result of the counterrevolutionary restoration of order--began as a quarrel regarding
chariot-racing fans who "politicalized" the factionalism existing
in the Hippodrome. The latter case was a major military confrontation of lengthy duration which had its genesis in what was
essentially a legal dispute and in which the revolutionists were
in many respects more politically conservative than their opponents, since they sought the enforcement of traditional rights
rather than social reform or innovation.

In the first instance, Byzantium, the cause of revolution we
would deem trivial, even if the test of force was critical and the
fate of a huge and powerful autocratic empire hung in the balance
(to be preserved, indeed, only by the unusual military talents of
an "establishment" general). In the second circumstance, the
cause would be described as highly significant (granted a legalistic
orientation) as it touched matters relating to individual liberty,
due process, constitutional limitation of power, and so on. The
result was not only a test of force (like the Byzantine revolt
actively participated in, however, by only a minority of potential
supporters of the contesting factions), but culminated in a decision
of immense historical significance. Thus, revolutions appear to
run the gamut from the irrationality of the Nike Insurrection to
the intellectuality that characterized the revolt of the 13 colonies.

This range in the typology of revolutions raises considerable
doubts as to the efficacy of some efforts to generalize about the
"anatomy" of revolutions. While it may be true that revolutions

247

display some procedural similarities (leadership by elites, popular identifications, emergence of terror, counterrevolutionary retrenchments and the like), the reasons why people choose to revolt appear extremely varied. I would like to suggest six such reasons, drawn from a historical over-view of the revolutionary phenomenon: (1) direct, usually physical, persecution; (2) imagine or implicit persecution; (3) denial of minority concessions (religious, cultural, linguistic) considered imperative; (4) desire to aggrandize property or formal power; (5) enthusiasm for innovation, social turmoil and excitement; (6) attempt to obtain goals considered to be morally superior. To this list might be added an effort to secure legal or constitutional guarantees of individual rights, but the American Revolution appears altogether unique to this category.

This summary of causes of revolutionary activity does not, by itself, imply moral judgment. In an ethical sense, none of the conditions or aspirations constitute a prima facie justification for the use of force and violence. All of these "causes" are philosophically contentious. Physical persecution, for example, can be viewed as a form of divine purpose to which the individual must remain compliant. Imagined or implicit persecution may not be persecution at all. Denial of minority concessions may be justified by the majoritarian principle or the goal of cultural integration. Aggrandizement by force of power and property can be construed as immoral. That some goals are "morally superior" to others may be true, but such claims require specific proof of demonstration. That social innovation and turmoil is preferable to social stasis or gradual modification is equally an arguable contention. Even the defense or guarantee by legal or constitutional process of individual "rights" involves the judgment of relative values, and its merit is not closed to discussion.

The question becomes, if dealt with in ethical terms, is revolution ever morally justifiable? And, if it is, then what criterion of judgment is tenable in appraising revolutionary movements? It is not enough to merely condemn the "Greens" (or the "Blues") in ancient Byzantium for causing the deaths of over 60,000 people for "trivial" reasons and to extoll the virtues of the constitutional and libertarian objectives of the American revolutionists of 1776 who, nonetheless, precipitated a considerable blood-letting themselves.

To begin with, I presume that revolution must mean social violence (so as to distinguish it from its rhetorical usage in phrases like "artistic revolution," etc.). To revolt is to initiate violence. I should also like to consider revolution as a term embracing the employment of social violence against other institutions than the state and its subordinate governmental bodies. In this regard, I think it is necessary to speak of revolutionary activity directed against such social institutions as universities, political parties, and large corporate organizations. Also, I think we ought to specify that "violence" may mean any form of pressure clearly implying the sanction of physical force--thus, blocking traffic, preventing access to buildings, constricting communications, and destroying or immobilizing property are violent acts, although they do not explicitly involve fighting, that is to say, physical combat between people. I believe, also, that threats to employ physical force or conspiracies to employ force constitute violent activities.

To ask the question, "Is revolution ever justifiable," is to ask whether social violence is ever justifiable. Unless one adopts a consistent pacifism (a position not to be summarily dismissed as indefensible), one must deal with the issue of determining under what conditions violence is condonable. If one can agree that individual violence is, under certain circumstances, ethically defensible (e.g., self-defense, protection of family and property), then it is equally obvious that some forms of social violence or collective and organized violence are to be generally accepted--the use of force by the State in war or in its police function is the most elementary illustration. We have been speaking of what might be termed "legal" violence in that the acts alluded to, individual and collective, fall under the aegis of legal activity. Most revolutionary activity, on the other hand, is clearly extra-legal and therefore represents social violence thought to be in conflict with the established concepts of order. This by itself, however, does not permit a general ethical judgment of revolution, since it must be assumed that law is the product of the prevailing political system against which the revolution is in whole or in part directed. The moral efficacy of revolutionary action must rest upon some criterion which, in turn, is implicitly applicable to the law itself. The possibility of a legal system or a jurisprudential code being wholly immoral (or at least without substantial ethical sanction) is not to be dismissed.

If one wishes to argue an ethical relativism with regard to law--say, Austin's "law is the command of the sovereign" or its equivalent--one result would be to render irrelevant any ethical judgment on revolutions. If legal mandate proceeds wholly from

249

a power base, any revolution is justifiable if it is successful. This constitutes a sort of ultimate social instrumentalism, and we are back to Hobbes' peculiar contention that successful rebellions are legal because they demonstrate that the Sovereign was not in fact adequately performing under the social convenant.

If, conversely, law is viewed as resting upon some other claim to recognition than the sheer power to enforce, then one is obliged to show just what this other sanction is. An otherwise despotic and inhumane political regime may operate with a sophisticated scheme of jurisprudence (as was the case with Nazi Germany, among others). There have been a number of explanations put forward to describe what this more comprehensive sanction must be. One is the explication of natural law as a means of both justifying and judging law enacted by human societies. While this may be a persuasive explanation in some respects, it does admittedly hinge upon some rather expansive metaphysical assumptions. However, the Common Law rationale is ultimately no less philosophically contentious; its ethical sanction must finally rest upon some appeal to expedience, habit or a quasi-mystical belief in the continuity of some variety of prudential wisdom. Sir Henry Maine's famous "from status to contract" argument does not really satisfy the ethical requirements of putting law beyond the moral claims to collective disobedience. It may be possible, in my view, to draw a useful distinction between a "system of law" and a "system of order," describing the first as a series of ordinances, however imperfect, that have as their genuine intention the social well-being, as contrasted with a series of commands designed to preserve the existing political arrangement. But this concept has its serious flaws, too, in that it is surely a matter of subjective judgment whether the aim is the general welfare or the protection of the political system, and it is conceivable that lawmakers--consciously acting upon the first premise--might be deluded and would, in truth, operate in terms of the latter. Not all tyrants, individual or collective, are as candidly and rationally egocentric as Machiavelli's hero-rulers, and many must be described as being motivated by high ideals of public and humanitarian service, however pathological might be their pursuit of these ideals.

The position of the legalist in dealing with the moral justification of revolution is made difficult by the problems presented by an ethical defense of legal sanction, but his difficulties are not insurmountable. In the first place, all things being equal, order is preferable to anarchy. This premise does not entail a discrimination between law and order, but, at the same time, it does not

preclude the moral legitimacy of revolution inasmuch as the at-
tackers of the status quo themselves represent a potential system
of order. Second, there exist grounds for some judgmental
evaluation of systems of law, however lacking in precision they
may be. To argue the contrary--that no grounds exist by which
systems of law can be compared as to their general endorse-
ment of humanitarian values and the propagation of the interests
of the commonweal--seems far less tenable and artificial and
arbitrary. A historical account of human institutions reveals
broad standards for the nature of law. No jurisprudence, for
example, primitive or civilized, significantly departs from the
conviction that the settlement of disputes ought to be on some
basis of ex aequo et bono in contrast to the will of the stronger
or the selfish caprice of the magistrate.

The third defense put forth by the legalist is related to the
first: however uncertain may be the ethical claims of law, the
burden of proof of its moral imperfection or duplicity rests
with those who seek to over-turn or disobey it. And this required proof is not secured at the barricades, but by rational
argument, and lacking such argument the presumption must be
that the law stands against the revolutionary opposition, which,
in turn, can be subjected to legal restraint.

If one maintains, then, that the burden of proof falls upon
those who endorse the revolutionary act, the issue of the legitimacy of extra-legal social violence can again be pressed. It
appears to me that most of the historical discussions of the
justification of disobedience and, by implication in some instances, revolt, are not particularly useful in resolving this
question. Permit me to pose three "classical" examples: (1)
revolt is morally permissible if the opportunity to practice
the Christian religion is denied; (2) revolution is legitimate if
it opposes authority which is in violation of natural law; and
(3) revolution is justifiable if authority denies individual "natural
rights." I would contend that these assertions are fundamentally
archaic for quite straight forward reasons. The issue of the
freedom to live the Christian life is hardly a matter in dispute
(save in some Communist states) and is not germane to the type
of pluralistic society which characterizes Western civilization.
The concept of political authority resting on a natural law base
is an attractive one in some respects, but it is doubtful that the
current nation-state (as a sovereign entity) can be judged as to
its moral posture by an appeal to natural law. If neither contending
party, political authority or revolutionaries, presumes to operate

from natural law assumptions, it is somewhat academic to evaluate their respective claims in terms of metaphysical premises as explicit as those to be encountered in the formulation of natural law.

The difficulty with the Lockean "right of revolution" argument is that its seminal presumption--individual natural rights--has not weathered the critical attacks upon it in the nineteenth and twentieth centuries. The collapse of natural rights theory has led, in turn, to the quite divergent assumptions that individual "rights" either trace their genesis to social dispensations or to legal concepts of rights that are not "natural" but are either rational or prescriptive (in the Burkean sense). If one accepts the first, the Benthamite, viewpoint, revolution is either never to be tolerated (as there is no appeal against the majoritarian verdict) or, paradoxically, society is perpetually revolutionary in that there are no moral infringements against securing majority consent by any effective means.

The second stance, identified with idealism, rationalistic or vitalistic, more or less precludes outright the legitimacy of revolution. One suspects that both the Benthamite and Hegelian positions are simplistic in that the Utilitarian ethic is manifestly unsatisfactory and the Hegelian ethic of moral self-realization by unquestioning obedience to the State is equally unpromising as an account of the moral life.

There is another historical justification for revolution that is not quite so apparently inapplicable: revolution is ethically condoned by virtue of the fact that it conforms to the inevitable determinism that underlies historical change. There are two fundamental objections to this hypothesis: (a) the assertion that historical process is deterministic or dialectical in structure is highly questionable; (b) the ethical implication that follows from this premise is that the moral criterion is explained by the conformity of the act to the advancement of the determined historical evolutions.

This contention is demonstrably untenable. The supposition must be that the historical process is valuational (although the express reasons for this are not at all clear in most expositions of dialectical visions of history, Marx's for a case in point); the valuational character of the process must be, therefore, in order to be logically consistent, either self-evident or a matter to be interpreted and expounded by those possessed of unique qualification and insight. That it is not the former seems inescapably evident, so we must presume the latter. But if this is the case, then the moral mandate results from subjective value choices which, in turn, become socially institutionalized. This would not be so disreputable except for the fact that serious disagreement predictably arises regarding the heuristic significances of the dialectical process to the extent that what is deemed "moral" cannot be intrinsically justified, even in terms of the "logic" of the dialectic, but must be defined in terms of judgments made by those capable of exercising the power to coerce. Revolutions, in turn, become "bad" or "good" in accordance with shifting interpretations of the meaning of the dialectic, since no ethical constant can be maintained.

A simple ends-and-means ethic would fit this situation quite adequately if it were not for the fact that this sort of candid relativism is incompatible with the absolutistic injunctions which proceed from the historicistic world-view. The prime difficulty with either a Hegelian or a Marxist ethic developed from a dialectical base is that in abandoning a substantive description of the ethical in favor of a dynamic one, one is confronted with the problem of the superannuation of one's ethic as directly dictated by one's dialectical commitment. To illustrate: Hegel's ethic is conceivable only in terms of the continuation of the State, but it must be admitted that a fuller actualization of the Absolute could entail the metamorphosis of the State into something else. At this point, Hegel must agree that either the ethic changes, no longer having the State as its _raison d'etre,_ or that ethics cease to be, because the Absolute becomes totally realized and, therefore, process ends.

In the case of Marx, one must assume that the final culmination of Communism ends the dialectical process; the ethical aspirations of man are fully met. But the argument that this Communist society, fully developed as he envisions it, represents the end of the process (and a process which he insists can be described in materialistic language), the arrival at stasis, cannot be validated by conceptual historical deduction, but rather by an appeal to a concept of value --what is the ultimate and highest good for society. If one defined the ethical in terms of the advancement of the dialectic, how can one conceive the termination of the dialectic to be based upon the realization of ethical goals? The argument is hopelessly circular. There is nothing which would prevent one from conceiving of the supplanting of Marx's ultimate Communist society by some new convolution of the dialectic, save a subjective value judgment that persuades one that the place has been reached where society has embraced the fullest realization of the good as theoretically formulated. Hence, revolutions are not at all to be judged as "good" because they are dialectically imperative, but because they espouse values thought to be desirable, and we are left with no more concrete formula for the justification of revolution than is provided by an appeal to the presumed superiority of one set of social ideas over another. One could justify a revolution based upon the enhanced social values created by nudity with an equal theoretical coherence to the approval of a revolution designed to bring about the "dictatorship of the proletariat." One is required to weigh on some scale of worth the irresistible moral mandate of nudism or the rule of the working class as against prevailing social arrangements.

These illustrations serve only to make the point that the issue of the ethical justification of revolution is not significantly resolved by a recourse to historical theory. We are forced back once again, in consequence, to the question of what circumstances render collective social violence morally legitimate, more or less unaided by the analysis of the past. There are, as you might guess, three broad alternative answers to the question: (1) it is never legitimate; (2) it is legitimate under certain circumstances; and (3) it is always legitimate as long as groups of people choose to employ it. None of these responses can be summarily rejected, but there are certain preliminary difficulties to be met by arguments (1) and (3). Argument (1) must face up to the fact that there are pertinent examples of human depravity that seem to warrant some collective response. The acquisition of formal authority and its use to commit crimes generally held to be reprehensible by all civilized men would seem to imply the right, even the obligation, of the victims of this public criminality to take steps to bring it to an end.

Argument (3) implies a return to the struggles of the jungle-- the "circulation of elites," augmented by bombs and guns. However, it cannot be denied that, in theory, a case could be made for a culture built on constant violent turmoil. One might advance the hypothesis that no rules ought to exist save naked power, that Hobbes' "state of nature" is to be preferred to Leviathan, if those are the only viable choices. It would seem hard to maintain, on the other hand, that an anarchic disorder and a repressive despotism are the sole alternatives.

We are left, as one might predict, with Argument (2): it is legitimate under certain circumstances. Let us plunge directly into the question by asserting that there are some circumstances in which social violence must be condoned, because such violence is merely a collective extension of violent prerogatives that appear undeniable to the individual. The first of these is clearly self-defense against palpable threats to life emanating from other social groups (unrestrained, for one reason or another, by public authority) or from the State itself, acting without any legal or moral restraints or inhibitions upon its corporeal power. I underscore "palpable threats to life" as contrasted with any vague concept of cultural "genocide." To illustrate: at one time in the nineteenth century it was briefly the deplorable policy of the United States Government to eliminate the "Apache Indian problem" by capturing and transporting these people to an inhospitable island off Florida where it was correctly assumed that they would quickly perish. In this instance, violent means were morally justified, in my view, by these Indians as a means of collective self-defense. On the other hand, I do not reasonably conclude that it is the policy of the government of Mississippi to eliminate the "Negro problem" by the actual extermination of all Negroes resident in that state and, hence, I do not think collective self-defense can justify insurrection in this circumstance, however one might criticize the wisdom or liberality of Mississippi's attitudes on race relations. Needless to add, individual instances of murder and physical abuse by public authorities or private factions must invoke the severest legal penalties and these legal acts do not preclude the right of individual self-defense.

I am inclined to broaden "threats to life" to include torture, as I think torture automatically provokes the right to any violent means to escape it. The issue of whether or not torture is ever morally justifiable does not affect the liberty of the individual to attempt to prevent its commission. Moreover, I think it is undeniable that torture has been employed against distinct groups of persons and I would argue that an extension of individual right is applicable here.

In fact, the "right to revolt" seems an ethical act at any time when public authority (or, again, social groups which are left uncurbed by public authority) commits acts against a collection of persons, small or large, which can be defined as unlawful assaults on the lives and physical persons of those involved. I would quickly wish to define "unlawful" as those acts almost universally held to be crimes against the person (e.g., murder, rape, torture, mutilation, injury) and to specify that these are specific acts against the person, not against either property or prerogative.

A more complex issue is raised by what I shall call unjust detention and restriction of movement. A difficult example of

255

this might be formal confinement on "reservations" or "restricted areas" or the use of discriminatory curfews and pass laws. The question of informal social practices culminating in the existence of "ghettos" can be dealt with if we arrive at some resolution of the more formal forms of actual detention. Detention, even if it is unjust or illegal, is of two types: some forms of detention constitute an assault upon the person (e.g., concentration camps, "schools of political re-education," work camps where individuals are abused and forced to unusual labor and are denied minimal subsistence). Such acts provide an ethical justification for revolt. However, there are other forms of detention which, while they may be unjust, illegal, demeaning, discriminatory, and even psychologically detrimental, do not represent a crime against the person in our original meaning. I do not think that this type of detention, however it is to be regretted, provides a justification for collective violence. The same assertion holds true for restrictions on movement. I am willing to admit that this may seem a harsh conclusion, particularly as I am construing detention of this second type as being, prima facie, both illegal and unjust.

I take this position on the assumption that detention represents a provocation insufficient to justify the employment of collective violence. The criterion that must be over-riding is the maximization of the social good. But this standard does not deprecate the need to guarantee the individual against criminal acts perpetrated against him by the State and by organized groups. Many forms of vigorous action must be undertaken in defense of individual liberties, but however lamentable may be instances of particularized transgressions on individual and group rights, excluding the physical protection of the person, the remedy of revolution is an excessive response that creates in its wake more social misery than it seeks to alleviate. This contention, I wish to repeat, does not condone in any fashion the abrogation of individual or group liberties and it strenuously endorses all means--save revolt--to rectify these criminal abuses. It does seek to argue that the employment of violence is not commensurate with the injury, however it is to be regretted.

One may argue that my position is a tacit acceptance of tyranny, where, if you like, people are detained illegally, their property confiscated and their political activities curtailed (I will extend my reservations about revolt to cover these last two situations presently), all without any legitimate right to revolt. In answering this allegation, I would like to make two points: (1) I am arguing expressly that revolution--collective violence--is morally

unjustifiable in the face of these admitted abuses, not that opposition to their perpetration be discontinued. (2) It is inconceivable to me that a despotism that does not practice terror,
physical persecution and the use of concentration camps and
similar devices, even though it is guilty of illegal detention, confiscation, and abridgement of political action, could long endure
under the active opposition of its citizens. If it did survive, it
could only do so on the basis that its policies were supported,
at least tacitly, by the consensus of its population.

Now, which is to prevail, the authority and the continuity of
the consensus, or, if you will, the preservation of individual and
minority prerogatives? Personally, I would enthusiastically support the latter. But upon what basis do minority or individual rights
depend in any case? If the answer is constitutional or legal guarantee, what in fact has been said is that minority and individual
rights rest upon what the consensus of the society deems right,
just, and moral. If one argues that the denial of minority and
individual rights can result from the usurpation of formal authority by some tyrannical oligarchy, so be it, but it is not plausible
to suppose that this oligarchy can perpetuate its rule denied both
of two conditions: (a) the use of physical persecution against the
citizenry, and (b) support by the social consensus. If we put aside
(a), the elements preserving oligarchic power are the same from
whence minority rights and guarantees emerge, and I fail to see
how revolution in this instance can alter this arrangement without
adopting the same coercive instrumentality represented by (a),
by the replacement of one oligarchy by another, since, by definition, the revolutionaries constitute a minority. And, of course,
in the ensuing struggle for power all manner of damage results.

The treatment of individuals and groups (barring the use of
physical coercion and terror of the type rejected) is a matter
involved with the level of civilization and humanity displayed by
the society at large. It is an inescapable and somber conclusion
of history that revolutions--whatever other merits they might
enjoy--do little by themselves to transfigure these intangible cultural qualities. The three great "classical" revolutions are
cases in point: the American Revolution created a new political
organism, but the virtues of that entity were rooted in the cultural capabilities of the society which spawned it (and the question, even today, of who were the more "civilized" of the two
contesting parties is open to, I trust friendly, dispute); the
French Revolution precipitated an orgy of inhumanity and a
dictatorship, and it is a question whether the attainments of

257

French society could not have been realized by less sanguinary means or that this violent experience did not adversely affect the French national development; the Russian Revolution inaugurated one of history's most notorious despotisms, in many respects far less attractive than Czarist autocracy, and it is a fair inquiry whether Russia today would be more or less civilized if it had not undergone the October Revolution and its totalitarian consequences.

As indicated earlier, the same argument used in regard to detention can be applied to the confiscation of property and to the limitation of political action or the denial of the opportunity for political participation. The justice or injustice--or the desirability or lack of desirability--of these infringements is not at issue, although I am certainly convinced that the security of private property and the freedom of political action and the opportunity for political participation are important social values which deserve defense and legal vigilance. But the commission of an injustice is not without reflection the signal for violent reprisal. Injustice is rarely clear-cut (unless it is an assault upon the person); it is very often a matter of subjective opinion and I am inclined to think that on this basis hardly a citizen in this or any other country would not be willing to enumerate a list of petty injustices which he endures. I, for one, consider it unjust that I should be taxed to provide a livelihood for those who are not victims of misfortune, but who are perennial loafers on the public dole. I admit that the line is difficult to draw between an injustice one suffers short of violent remonstrance and those which reasonably require collective violence, but we must make the effort to discriminate.

If we conclude, then, that the "right of revolution" is restricted to responses to physical persecutions, how are we to judge those other implicit justifications listed earlier? Surely we cannot reasonably suppose that the suffering occasioned by revolutionary activity can be morally justified by imagined or "implicit" persecutions? Are we to kill each other in the streets over slights to ethnic manhood or the freedom to smoke marijuana? Or admission to the local country club or the opportunity to gain revenge against snobbish professors by acquiring the right to hire and fire them? Manifest and irrefutable minor injustices are, alas, the human lot --against which we should all have the liberty to protest--but the nature of our protest must be in proportion to the magnitude of the injustice. A person unfairly or illegally given a parking ticket cannot express his sense of hurt and indignation by blowing up

the police station. Such an act--and the thought that fathered it--
is recklessly irrational, to say the least, but it also constitutes a
serious distortion of ethical viewpoint, because it amplifies the
individual ego out of all proportion to the civic ethic. An affront to
one's opinions and values, while no doubt unappealing, does not
create a moral justification for transgressing against the legitimate
prerogatives of other individuals. That I may look upon a computer
as a dehumanizing instrument is scarcely a valid reason for me to
take an axe to it--unless it is my computer, whereupon it can become the victim of my idiosyncratic whims, I suppose.

The matter of minority concession has been dealt with earlier.
I cannot see, I repeat, how the abridgment of self-conceived minority
imperatives can be defended, morally or pragmatically, by taking
up the sword (or the Molotov Cocktail). Force, in any case, is a
puny tool when employed against religious, cultural, and linguistic
commitments earnestly held. If these values cannot, as a rule, be
exterminated by force, they are rarely preserved by the same
method.

Revolutions can, it is true, be endorsed by a bald espousal of
aggrandisement. So, of course, can any doctrine of conquest. Unless one is convinced by Hobbes' "war of all against all" or Hegel's
strange notion that struggle and war are necessary to the national
health and reflect the verdict of history, this argument doesn't make
much ethical sense.

Since we have already dismissed as spurious the idea that revolutions are desirable because turmoil is preferable to order, we
can move to the last and the most formidable of the revolutionary
claims: that revolutions are ethically justifiable because they allow
or instigate the triumph of superior moral ideals. There are two
principal rejoinders to this argument: (a) if certain ideals are in
fact superior, they ought not to require force of arms to bring
about their acceptance, and (b) there is little evidence, historically,
that previous revolutions have ushered in social conditions whose
moral tone and content were unmistakably superior to those which
they overthrew. The first of these objections is the important one
and appears to me to be a telling rebuttal. The revolutionist's
counter-rejoinder, incidentally, has traditionally been that the
justification for using force to insure the triumph of his "superior"
ideals is made necessary by both the unenlightenment (or stupid-
ity) of the great percentage of men and the slowness of nonviolent
change. These are curious arguments if you examine them. The
first one is almost a paradox. Force is required in lieu of the intellectual capabilities of the masses, yet these self-same persons

of presumed low perception are conceived to be the ultimate rulers
of the society, perfectible into organs of heretofore undeveloped
wisdom. The key, it is alleged, is education of some specialized
ideological verity. But if these persons are that susceptible to
education, why do they not more quickly grasp the superiority of
the revolutionary ideals? Time, it is then argued, does not permit
this depth of education. But the parallel argument for revolutionary
force is that nonviolent change is too slow. The matter boils down
to the fact that the revolutionists want to be running things while
the deliberate processes of education take place and, of course,
to direct this education from a position of coercive authority. The
argument ends up in very different mode from its original postulates.

The justification of revolution does not turn, therefore, upon
some analysis of the relative superiorities of ideas. It is not a
question of selecting what ideas are superior and then saying, in
effect, that these justify launching a revolt against the prevailing
system in order to apply them. That some ideas are better than
others I have no doubt, yet I am not convinced that the superior
idea requires brute force to prove its excellence or, even, that
the desire for its acceptance by others should persuade me to win
acquiescence for it by offering to exterminate the prospective convert as the alternative to his reluctance. I am aware that Charle-
magne brought many souls to accept Christianity by this method,
but I remain unconvinced of its desirability.

I am further unconvinced, as a matter of fact, that most men
ought to die for ideas. Some men should, because they live by
ideas, but most men do not, and I think they are misled when
they are persuaded that this is what they ought or are obliged to
do. There are, for most men, things worth dying for, but they
are not ideas, they are loved ones, homes, country, habits, and
even friends. The great crime of revolutionaries, when all is
said and done, is that they ought to shed their blood and die for
ideas which are, in reality, only the predominate values of the
revolutionists themselves. Non-revolutionary politicians are
often stained with the same guilt. "Go," they say, "and defend
with your lives the principles of democracy or the imperishable
liberties of free men" and so on, ad nauseum. They would display
greater wisdom and infinitely better taste if they simply said:
"Go and defend your homes." [Life, civil, religious liberty, etc.]

It is because most men do not live by ideas but by sentiments
that the plans of revolutionists and their quietistic comrades, the
utopianists, are eventually upset. Most revolutionaries seem to end
up as bitter men (again, like many democratic politicians) declaim-

ing on the perversity and intractability of human nature. They never appear to realize that as a class (much like their natural enemies, the philosophers) they are a <u>rara avis;</u> they are victims of ideas and are, thus, reasonably superfluous, however successful they may be at introducing anger and discord. Philosophers, who serve a better and more modest end, are somewhat akin, although they are too perceptive (or at least most of them are) to be "victims" of ideas and realize instead that they are "servants" of ideas. The philosopher knows his place and, for purely selfish reasons, has no strong wish to desecrate the serenity of his ideational retreat by inducing one and all to take up the life of ideas. But the revolutionary suffers from an evangelical contagion; he is a compulsive seeker after adherents. The etiology of his malady is yet to be fully explored and I leave that enterprise to those better equipped for the task than I, but as we are propelled into what appears starkly to be a revolutionary era in which the more repulsive of human capacities for violence are wedded to the tyranny of the Idea, I would wish that, for once, the revolutionary managers would pause and reflect before they raise the ancient shout and "cry havoc and let slip the dogs of war."

The sum effect of these observations is to radically narrow the ethical justification for revolution. This ought not to be as surprising as it may be. Violence is, after all, an atavistic activity, which is one reason why it ought not to be totally excluded from the civilized society. Yet this very civilized society is understandably wary about the emergence of any atavistic behavior that is too fulsome and widespread. War is a distinct problem in this regard and is, more now than ever, an awesome alternative to other forms of political settlement. Revolution is equally a technique not to be hastily unleashed. Yet the revolutionary fervor in our society has a curiously naive tone, not unlike the attitude towards war a century or more ago. I have seen on my TV screen time and time again the weeping face of a girl, who, as a participant in some episode of social violence, has witnessed for the first time what violence is really like, bloody heads, the flailing of weapons, the snarling desperation of men in combat. Why did she not know, I ask myself? Did she expect revolution to be clean and brave and somehow glorious--like the mood of the troops who marched off from Washington with their picnic lunches to chase away the Rebels at Manassas Creek? Had she never read (even if she had lived a sheltered life) Hemingway's unforgettable description of the increasingly insane killing of the supposedly pro-Franco officials in <u>For Whom the Bell Tolls</u>? Her face (a

collection of faces) haunts me; it is the visage of an almost un-
believable innocence. It has been said that war is for the generals,
they ply their trade while other men suffer and die. The same
holds good for the professional revolutionary in our contemporary
society. Those who rush into the streets upon his command are
most apt to pay the price--not only in broken heads, but in terms
of the fact that they may be unsustained by the hypnosis of fanaticism.

Revolution is a desperate social act, provoked, in an ethical
sense, only by the most fundamental justifications. No university
ever existed, by illustration, whose wickedness was so oppressive as to require insurrection as a remedy. Social violence
will elicit a response. It is extraordinary that those who initiate
violence are shocked and stunned by the fact that they are met
with comparable or superior force. Because it is fashionable to
adopt revolutionary methods to support comparatively trivial
causes, it cannot be supposed that the counter-force arrayed
against those methods will be commensurate with the triviality
of the cause rather than the threat of the revolutionary force.
Yet that seems to be the strange presumption made by those who
provoke violent confrontations. They proceed on the dangerous
supposition that society will be more charitable than they, and
this is true to a point. Beyond that point is counter-violence and
even retribution. What makes terror a dubious political instrumentality is that it invariably induces a counter-terror. We are
on the verge of triggering this sort of reciprocal force and the
hope that remains, perhaps a faint one, is that underneath the
layers of moralistic language there may lurk a genuine ethical
concern which will put the "right of revolution" back in its
proper perspective.

Notes begin on page 338.

The Theology of Revolution

Richard A. McCormick, S.J.

The March 27, 1968 issue of Le monde carried the conclusions
of a conference on "Christianity and Revolution" held at Paris. It
reads as follows:

> The situation of violence which reigns in the world be-
> cause of the domination and misuse of the capitalistic sys-
> tem in all its forms, the impossibility of resolving the
> contradictions inherent in this system . . . by means of
> gradual reform, constitute the objectively necessary con-
> ditions of revolution. But the subjective conditions of revolu-
> tion depend on the will of the men collectively committed
> to promote it. Revolution appears to us, therefore, as the
> only way possible and it supposes a radical change of polit-
> ical and economic structures. But there will not be a struc-
> tural revolution without a cultural revolution. We are per-
> fectly aware of the fact that this revolution implies a ques-
> tioning of Christianity in its forms of thought, of expres-

sion, and of action. We are convinced that our commitment ought to identify itself with the struggle of the classes
and of the oppressed masses to achieve their liberation,
in France and elsewhere. The revolutionary struggle ties
itself closely to the prospect of the construction of the
kingdom of God without identifying itself with this kingdom. We acknowledge the right of every Christian as well
as of every man to participate in this revolutionary process,
including armed struggle. We express, as a community,
our support for the believers who, because of their commitment, are put aside by their local church and feel
themselves alone in the faith.[1]

This paragraph draws on and summarizes rather well much
of what is being said about revolution in theological literature.
This literature rather commonly presents an analysis of sociopolitical structures, a theological interpretation, and draws
conclusions on these bases. Revolution is going to occur with
or without the Church. It was perhaps this realization which led
Harvey Cox to state that "we are trying to live in a period of
revolution without a theology of revolution. The development of
such a theology should be the first item on the theological agenda
today."[2] However, Bishop Marcos McGrath (Santiago de Veraguas,
Panama) has stated that "we already have a theology of revolution
thanks to the encyclical Populorum progressio of Pope Paul, but
what we need is a theology of violence which makes precise that
which is legitimate and that which is not."[3] The difference in
these two statements probably lies in the understanding of the
word "theology." By theology I suspect that Cox would mean the
broad underlying perspectives of a social ethic which support the
more practical statements of Populorum progressio.
Be that as it may, the first thing to be said about revolution is
that the meaning of the word is ambiguous. G. Zananiri[4] lists four
general senses the term can have: violent insurrection unleashed
before having exhausted the possibilities of dialogue; violent insurrection justified as a response to violence and out of desperation; pacific action undertaken to accelerate urgently-needed
reforms; pacific action undertaken progressively over a period
of time more or less determined (evolution). Thus the term
can refer to everything from a simple military Putsch with or
without bloodshed to radical socioeconomic changes within constitutionally established processes. This ambiguity is never
totally overcome in some of the literature, but increasingly

the term is understood in a sense close to that stated by the
seventeen bishops of the Third World in their excellent statement: "a break with some system that no longer ensures the
common good, and the establishment of a new order more likely
to bring it about."[5]

What is the nature of this break? Gustavo Pérez-Ramírez,
approaching revolution from the sociological point of view, concludes that there are several components which distinguish a
true revolution from a simple coup d'état and other forms of
aimless subversion.[6] For example, he insists that in a true
revolution it is the relationships of man to man and classes to
classes that are primarily affected. The relationship of men to
things is secondary. Thus the true revolution has as its aim
that "man should be the agent of, and take part as a subject in
the achievement of his own advancement." The most important
element of revolution, however, is ideology understood as a
complex of norms and values. Therefore revolution, when described in structural terms, is "the transition from one given
social system, morally authentic but with now obsolete values,
to a new order in which the new system of social control is
authenticated by values and norms formerly considered a source
of dissolution." This understanding of revolution as involving a
"complex of norms and values" relates it immediately to theology.

The emphasis in recent theological literature has centered on
two points: the relation of Christianity to revolution; the relation
of Christianity to revolutionary violence. Here we can present
only a sample of the articles touching on these two points.[7]

Relation of Christianity to Revolution

A good introduction to the study of the theology of revolution
would be Paul J. Weber's excellent summary.[8] Weber highlights
the premises and emphases of current theological writing in this
area. For instance, the starting point of the Christian's approach
to the total social fact of underdevelopment is a view of history.
"Just-revolution" theologians reject a static view of history
(creation is a finished work to be preserved) and build from the
premise that history has a direction and that God is working in
history. The biblical message shows us that this direction is
toward greater justice, love, freedom. In working out this direction, God encounters human intransigence, especially as found
in social structures which are oppressive and unjust and ultimate-

ly constitute a form of violence. It is this basic view of history which provides the substructure of the theology of revolution.

A specific example of this view of history would be a recent article by Johannes B. Metz.[9] Complaining of the privacy and individualism of transcendental, existential, and personalist theology, Metz calls for a "political theology."[10] Its primary task would be to reassess the relationship between eschatological faith and social life. "The eschatological promises of the biblical tradition--freedom, peace, justice, reconciliation--cannot be reduced to a private matter. They constantly force themselves into the sense of social responsibility." These promises are never simply identified with any given social situation, but we move toward them in social situations. Thus the eschatological promises render every social situation provisional and they necessarily render Christian attitudes toward social situations critical. That is, because of its orientation toward the eschatological promises, faith develops a constantly fresh critical attitude toward its social environment. Metz sees the liberating function of the Church's criticism exercised in three ways: the defense of the individual, criticism of totalitarianism, and love as the principle of revolution. He argues that love must be interpreted in its social dimension and be made operative. "This means that it must be understood as the unconditional commitment to justice, freedom and peace for others." Understood in this way, love implies a criticism of mere force, but it may at times command revolutionary force.

Heinz-Dietrich Wendland (West Germany) argues that the gospel contains a revolutionary element.[11] He then seeks the connection between the revolutionary element in the Bible and revolution in history. This connection involves both an affinity and a distinction. As for the affinity, the Bible is at one with historical revolution in its eschatology. The coming of the kingdom confronts the Christian with the principle societas semper reformanda. This reformation is not precisely a Christian revolution, because the Christian's task is to humanize the secular orders. Or, in Richard Shaull's words, "as a political form of change, revolution represents the cutting edge of humanization."[12] The biblical revolution is distinct from historical revolution, because no historical revolution "opens the door to the reign of freedom, which at the same time offers the inexhaustible satisfaction of all human needs." Ultimately, therefore, Wendland understands the revolutionary element in the Bible as one with only indirect social repercussions. That is, the rule of God operates through the quiet and unarmed force of loving action and the service of Christian groups scattered throughout the world.

Princeton's Richard Shaull is one of the more prominent pro-
ponents of the theology of revolution in this country.[13] Shaull accepts the fact that God is at work in human history. And more
specifically he states, with Dietrich von Oppen, that the revolutionary impact of Jesus is that all institutions lose their sacral
character. They are merely functional and exist to serve men.
If this attitude permeates a culture, then institutions will appear
which are open, flexible, and subject to constant criticism.
Creation of these institutions is the very context of human liberation; for they allow for the discovery of selfhood and nourish a
new will to shape the future. It is this discovery of selfhood and
this new will to shape the future which are at the heart of the Negro
revolution, the student uprisings, and the social unrest in the Third
World. Because this is true, "then we should feel ourselves closely identified with this struggle and the achievement of this goal
should be our central concern as Christians at this time." However, these movements have met with tremendous efforts on the
part of those in power to preserve the status quo.

Shaull admits that one cannot prove the action of God in history.
But to make the wage of faith is to bet that the symbols and stories
which make up biblical tradition have the power to make transparent
to us the deeper meaning of historical processes. Now the basic
Christian symbols are death and resurrection. Personally, we
move to maturity as we allow the old to collapse and the new to
rise. This means that for the Christian birth is the fruit of death.
We must understand not only personal but also social history in
the light of these symbols. The collapsing of the old to allow the
new to be born is a thought-structure connatural to the Christian.
It is an outlook which suggests to him that he view social structures as functional and provisional, subordinate to the birth of the
kingdom and human liberation. It is precisely as Christians that
we are free of the self-imposed limitations of American liberalism
(American liberals are for liberation of the depressed "as long
as they do not upset too much the present system or run the risks
of violence") and capable of shattering the systems of thought which
give security but inhibit human liberation.

Some of these same emphases are present in the fine study of
Rolland F. Smith, S.J.[14] Smith describes a historical Christianity
as one which finds God revealing Himself in the events of history
which are continually giving way to new events. The Christian
distinguishes carefully the revelatory event from the Revealer,
and is therefore continually ready to criticize and transcend
particular revelatory events. Upon this notion of history Smith

builds a distinction between revolution and rebellion. Revolution idealizes an event, whether past or future; it fixates forms and tends to absolutize them, whether these be political, economic, or religious. Rebellion, on the other hand, continually calls these forms into question. Following Camus, Smith sees the rebel as affirming a value in the present structures at the very time he is questioning and toppling them. The rebel, therefore, both criticizes the present and participates in it. Smith understands the new theology of hope with its stress on man's position between promise and fulfilment (Moltmann, Metz) as an attempt to set forth a historical Christianity and therefore a theology of rebellion.

These are but a few examples of the more speculative writings on the relationship of Christianity to revolution.[15] We may summarize by citing two sentences from the remarkable statement of the bishops of the Third World: "As soon as a system ceases to ensure the common good to the profit of some party involved, the Church must not merely condemn such injustice, but dissociate herself from the system of privilege, ready to collaborate with another that is better adapted to the needs of the time, and more just." Later the document asserts: "Christians and their pastors should know how to recognize the hand of the Almighty in those events that from time to time put down the mighty from their thrones and raise up the humble, send away the rich empty-handed, and fill the hungry with good things."[16] The first statement acknowledges the subordinate and provisional character of social structures. The second recognizes the action of God in the transformation of the structures. Such statements are straight out of the developing theology of revolution, and therefore tell us what it is at root all about: a search in the biblical message and symbols for a deeper understanding of man as a sociopolitical being. It is easy to agree with George Celestin[17] that these speculations are incomplete and sometimes simplistic. But even if there are loose ends, these beginnings are promising and exciting.

The Relation of Christianity to Revolutionary Violence

If Christian love involves an unconditioned commitment to justice, freedom, and peace for others, what concrete forms may this love take as it moves into the area of political and social structures? Vatican II stated: "Where public authority oversteps its competence and oppresses the people, these people should nevertheless obey to the extent that the objective common good demands. Still it is lawful for them to defend their own rights

268

and those of their fellow citizens against any abuse of this authority, provided that in so doing they observe the limits imposed by natural law and the gospel."[18] What are these limits? Can violence be justified as a means toward urgently needed social change?

This is not an easy question to answer. First of all, the term "violence" covers a broad spectrum of actions and human experiences, as Ivan Illich has pointed out.[19] For instance, violence against property and things is different from violence against persons. Generalizations ignore these marked differences at their own risk. Secondly, in the circumstances under discussion the problem of force confronts the Christian in a relatively new form. We are no longer dealing with the open aggression of one sovereign state against another (war), but rather with the concealed, legally protected, complex violence endemic in oppressive social structures. Violent response to such systemic injustice raises new questions, both tactical and moral. For instance, does violence inevitably beget violence and turn out to be self-defeating-- hence disproportionate in a moral sense? To what extent is violent response to sclerotic social structures compatible with love of the oppressor? On the other hand, does nonviolence in the face of injustice actually end up supporting the unjust status quo? Is G. Thibon right when he concludes that systematic refusal of violence can lead straight to the reign of absolute violence?[20] Or does the use of violence absolutize the social structure one proposes to introduce and thus compromise the transcendence of eschatological faith? These are only some of the knotty questions this discussion raises.

Many of the responses to these questions have merely stated a rather general position on force without analyzing it at length or attempting to apply it. A few examples of this type of statement will suffice here. Dom Jorge (the Bishop of Santo Andres, Brazil) said on television that "armed revolution by the people is justified when oppression rules and famine wages obtain."[21] Similarly Mons. Fragoso (Bishop of Crateus, Brazil) asserted that "at times violence is the only possible way of liberating man from an established, permanent and grievous violence. We have to recognize that the mature conscience of the citizens has the right to opt for violence."[22] At the World Conference on Church and Society (Geneva, 1966) most of the delegates from South Africa and Latin America approved the use of force at times. Delegates from the more industrialized countries were more reserved.[23] Ultimately the Conference urged Christians not to resort to force, even in the most unfavorable circumstances. But it added that a question could arise "whether the violence which sheds blood in planned revolutions may not be a lesser evil than the violence which, though bloodless, condemns whole populations to perennial despair."

Johannes Metz believes that Christian love "may in certain circumstances command something like revolutionary force. Where a social status quo is so full of injustice that it might equal that created by a revolutionary movement, then a revolution . . . cannot be ruled out in the name of love."[24] Richard Shaull is on record with the statement that "there may be some situations in which only the threat or use of violence can set the process of change in motion."[25] Paul Verghese is convinced that Christians certainly cannot completely oppose the counterviolence of protest if this means allowing systemic violence to continue and be disposed of at a pace chosen by the oppressor.[26] The Theological Commission of the Christian Peace Conference allowed in its report for the use of force as ultima ratio. Their reason: existing social relationships represent a structure of power which uses force in the most varied, even if concealed forms, to maintain the status quo.[27] These are all guarded statements, and frankly they do not help a great deal, but they do manifest a drift of thought.

Several essays I have recently[28] encountered contain a longer reflection on Christianity and revolutionary violence. Bishop McGrath first states the problem as it is often formulated:

> Where the few are established in power and this power is systematically used to augment their own interests and block efforts at improving the situation of the majority who are in need, then, these Christians say, violence is already present. To strike out against this violence requires no further ethical argument. It is merely self-defense.[29]

In commenting on this, Bishop McGrath makes several points. First, counterviolence can be against the system or against the persons enforcing the system. Generally it is against the persons. But it is precisely the system that needs to be changed. Furthermore, what will violence achieve? Certainly it will "throw the scoundrels out," but unless deliberately provoked revolution has clear goals and the means to reach them, it very easily represents another form of paternalism. It refuses to face the long uphill struggle the masses face before they can be brought to be the authors of their own improvement. McGrath also wonders whether Christians involved in violent revolution can maintain their values in whatever actions they initiate. Christians soon find themselves associated with those for whom terrorism and indiscriminate killing are a hobby. Add to this the fact that prolonged violence crushes the basic human and Christian values of life and respect for others. Adverting to the loss of mutual confidence in the people of Vietnam, Bishop McGrath asks: "How long will it take to rebuild the inner humanity of a people thus destroyed?" Finally McGrath rejects vehemently any generalization about the existence in Latin America of institutional violence of the kind justifying counterviolence.

Juan Luis Segundo, S.J., argues that to face realistically the question of violence in Latin America one has to demythologize certain notions and images.[30] First, it is true that the violence of the masses should be conceived of as a response to yet another existing violence under the guise of a legal regime. But things are not that easy. "Latin American social reality is not that of the jungle where violence is natural, nor is it that of developed countries where politics is concerned with the welfare of the people." Therefore the first problem with violence in South America is its very introduction. Life has to become so unbearable that the masses have nothing to lose. Then the right climate for revolution is created. But revolutionaries must take responsibility for creating this climate, since truly monstrous governments (e.g., Batista's in Cuba) are wisely avoided by those in power. There is a moral dilemma here.

Secondly, Segundo asserts that the real violence exercised by the unjust established order justifies in principle a violent response as self-defense. Yet how far can one carry this principle? That is, the general validity of the idea of self-defense does not tell us what means can be employed in self-defense. For example, certainly one threatened at gunpoint may draw in self-defense and fire on his aggressor. But could an individual, knowing his aggressor to be quicker on the draw, hide in the bushes and attack him from behind? Further, realizing his inability to take the aggressor by surprise in any way, could the innocent person kill one of his own friends and lay the responsibility on the enemy and get at him in this way? Segundo insists--and rightly--that Christ's message must guide not only causes but the means used.

Almeri Bezerra de Melo, a Brazilian priest, disagrees.[31] In an otherwise extremely interesting essay he grants that it is not difficult to demonstrate that the message of the Gospels is a message of peace and love, not of war and violence. But the Gospels also carry a message of liberation. "When we are considering the liberation of entire peoples, currently subjected to every kind of slavery, the end to be attained must take precedence over the means employed, and in the case under consideration these are revolutionary violence, armed insurrection." With the facile stroke of an ipse dixit, de Melo has adopted a principle which cuts him adrift from a long and cherished tradition. Not all traditions are wise, of course. But some of them are. And it is the peculiar danger of desperation to blur the distinction and render it ultimately irrelevant.

One of the great "revolutionary texts" constantly appealed to is that of Pope Paul VI in Populorum progressio. There the Pontiff had referred to situations where whole populations are the victims of injustice. In such situations "recourse to violence, as a means to right these wrongs to human dignity, is a grave temptation." He then added:

> We know, however, that a revolutionary uprising--save where there is manifest, long-standing tyranny which would do great damage to fundamental personal rights and dangerous harm to the common good of the country-- produces new injustices, throws more elements out of balance, and brings on new disasters. A real evil should not be fought against at the cost of even greater misery.[32]

The underscored phrase above is frequently cited as a good description of what is the case in several Latin American countries. Hence Paul VI was being cited as a champion of violent revolution. Recently the Pope has returned to the subject to straighten the records. In his general audience of March 27, 1968, in a speech commemorating the first anniversary of the publication of Populorum progressio, Pope Paul stated:

> Thus, so it seemed to some . . . that when We denounced in the name of God the very grave needs in which so much of humanity suffers, We had opened the way to the so-called theology of revolution and of violence. Such an error is far from our thought and language. Revolution is altogether different from the positive, courageous, and energetic activity necessary in many instances to establish structures of social and economic progress.[33]

Civiltà cattolica jumped on the phrase "tentazione della violenza" as an opportunity to point out that what is characteristic about contemporary thought on violence is its theorization. Violence has

272

always existed, but now we are theorizing it into a value.[34] Hence it is no longer contrasted with the evangelical spirit, but regarded as a consequence of it. In this sense the Christian is increasingly experiencing violence as a temptation, something presenting itself under the appearances of good. The editors of Civiltà rightly squirmed at this and warned against the temptation to extend the tolerability of violence beyond instances of evident and prolonged tyranny.

This inadequate roundup of opinion will indicate at least one thing: we are dealing here with one of the most exciting aspects of contemporary Christian thought. It is obvious that Christians are beginning to come alive to social responsibility. The tone is often militant, even at times somewhat unrestrained and uncritical. But beneath it all something wonderful is happening. To face this situation with complete casuistry of licits and illicits would be tantamount to substituting a kind of Western moral imperialism for the existing financial imperialism. On the other hand, to rule out moral reflection as irrelevant is to play the deadly game of spiritual suicide. If a Christian dare not absolutize law and order at the expense of justice, neither can he allow efficacity of means to be the supreme criterion; for this would only prepare the rationale for tomorrow's totalitarianism. The Christian absolutizes only the eschatological promises; and it is in light of these that he must formulate his basic ethical questions about violence.

As a person cast between promise and fulfilment, the basic posture of the Christian would seem to be that of "involved transcendence," as Paul Verghese puts it. His witness is "to be basically in sympathy with the protest yet not be drawn into the maelstrom of hatred and destruction that counterviolence generates."[35] The Christian will not absolutely disown the cross of violence, but only the hatred so often its twin. A good practical summary of the moral judgments involved in preserving his "involved transcendence" is supplied by Bishop McGrath:

> Each Christian must form his own conscience, but with an accurate knowledge of the situation he is in and a clear grasp of the principles and the dangers involved. He should look well, very well, before leaping. There must be real justification--as to the end, as to the means, as to a program and as to the likelihood of success, not only of the overthrow of a regime but of the program to follow.

Let him remember that our greatest commandment is to love our neighbor. Even if violence may be chosen, we may not hate.[36]

Notes begin on page 339.

Christianity and Modern War

Paul R. Ramsey

How are we to think Christianly about politics and about the
political use of violence in war? A Christian, I believe, must always have two things in mind, one positive and the other negative.
He will think politically in the light of Christ, and he will think
politically in the light of the revealing shadow thrown by Christ
over this our fallen human existence.

This darkness does not envelop that light. Neither does the
light diminish, it rather throws the shadows. So it will be to
the end of time when Christ comes to ask not whether there is any
peace or even any just peace, but whether there is any faith in
the earth.

"Christian realism"

First, to accent the negative. Taking into account the shadows
cast by the light of Christ simply means "Christian realism" in
politics. It means that there is no man, and certainly no collec-

tivity, in which Cain exists no longer. This realism need not be expressed in terms of these Christian dogmatic certainties. Much the same political outlook can be stated in other terms. This, Max Kohnstam of Holland did in his address to the 1966 Geneva Conference on Church and Society. Christians need to learn, he said, in dealing with international relations, the lesson we have already learned about domestic society, namely that "love passes not directly from man to man, but through structures." There are no solutions in international relations but to look inside the existing structures for cracks where a change must take place. And meantime, it may be inferred, no one can discharge the political leaders of a nation, in the structurally-defective nation-state system, from their responsibility for initiatives or actions that sometimes may oblige them to resort to armed force.

The important point Kohnstam made was that structures serve to protect against the unpredictabilities of other collectives, not especially or not only against their evilness (against Cain). The nation-state is surrounded by arbitrariness on all sides; the other is always a stranger and a potential enemy where there are no dependable structures through which identification may pass. The present international system has in it such defects that only the preparation, threat or the actual use of force can safeguard against the other collective's unpredictability.

Structures considered

This seems an important point to stress for Christians in the United States, for the sake of the maturity and understanding we need to have in all that we think and say about the responsibilities of public office. It cannot simply be said that the "cold war" is over and that there are now opportunities for reconciliation. To say only that would be to identify Christian political ethics with the American ethos which in war makes all-out war, and after every war, hot or cold, makes all-out peace. The question rather is whether there are cracks where a change in international structures can be initiated and take root, over which reconciliation may pass. It is not that the State and Defense Departments prepare always for the worse, when they should have a better picture of the world. It is rather that public officials must prepare for the unpredictabilities, and this means they have to attend to the capabilities of other dynamic collectives, not their hypothetical intentions. E.g., no president can or should risk national security, even though he

may and should seek to make national interests coincide with the
wider interests of others, and he, too, needs to look inside the
structures to see where new structures may be possible along
which identification can pass.

Is "just war" theory passé?

The nation-state system is in a state of war. That had better
not be denied in the course of saying that even a state of war is
not without moral limits governing it, or in the course of charting
the direction in which that system may be changed. It is often said
these days that the "just war" theory is passé, no longer applicable.
If this is the case, then truly mankind is left in dereliction. For
jus ad bellum in the form of jus contra bellum provides the moral
force behind every effort to make love pass, not from man to man,
but through more adequate structures identifying the national common good with the world common good. And jus in bello states the
tests of a responsible statecraft in the meanwhile--likely a long
meanwhile.

It is Christian realism or any other realistic theory of statecraft that has been most lacking in our discussions of Vietnam.
One has to go elsewhere than to a Christian view of politics even
to understand the animus, the exacerbation, the petulance infecting
our public debate and protests over this war. The explanation is
to be found in the utopian notion that it is bound to be the case
that the government must be doing something wrong if there has
to be, or if there has to continue to be, a political use of violence.
The explanation is to be found in the conviction that it is always
possible to negotiate so that negotiation will never fail, and yet
attain a just peace, or one that will barely hold together. Then,
of course, if our political leaders do not know this it must be
because they have not listened to the right people. The underlying
premise of modern man's political expectations (however disguised
this may be by expertise in "area studies") is that there can be
"at the same time the free expression of the individual [nation]
. . . and absolute social cohesion"--which was J. L. Tolman's
definition of all utopianism in politics. The explanation of the
petulance of the protests lies in the optimistic denial that there
can be such a thing as an arbitrament of arms, a denial that conflicts can arise among men and nations that are so unbridgeable
that they defy ratio and drive nations to the ultima ratio of war.

277

Positive accented

Secondly, to accent the positive. The justifiedness of possible
Christian participation in war can be shown because this might well
be a requirement of charity--of the light of Christ penetrating
man's political existence. It was a work of charity, we would all
agree, for the Good Samaritan to give help at some personal cost
to the man who fell among thieves on the road to Jericho and who
beat him and left him for dead. What do you imagine Jesus would
have had the Samaritan do if in the story he had come upon the
scene when the robbers had just begun their attack and while they
were still at their fell work? Would it not then be a work of charity
to resort to the only available and effective means of preventing
or punishing the attack and resisting the injustice? Is not anyone
obliged to do this if he can?

Thus do we come to the first fork in the road for Christian conscience. Some at this point will take the path of pacifism, focusing
their attention in Christian love upon the enemy. Others at this
point will justify participation in war, focusing their attention in
Christian love upon the victims of the hostile force that is abroad
in the world.

One thing seems to me for sure: Jesus would not have told a
parable about a band of Good Samaritans who, confronted by this
choice between the robbers and their intended victim, "went limp"
on the Jericho road in the belief that "nonviolent resistance" is
qualitatively always more righteous than the use of armed force.
The infinite qualitative difference is between resistance and non-
resisting, sacrificial love. If then out of this self-same Christian
love and responsibility one makes the decision that resistance is
the necessary and most loving thing to do for all concerned, if
one judges that not to resist is to have complicity in the evil he
will fail to prevent, then the choice between violent and nonviolent
means is a question of economy in the effective force to use. The
judgment must be one of over-all effectiveness, untrammelled by
any prior or absolute decision that nonviolent direct action may be
moral while violent direct action cannot be.

A Christian who has taken the nonpacifist road must thereafter
be concerned with the morality of war, and not mix this up with
the morality contra bellum on which his pacifist brother relies.

He will, first, know something about the intention, direction
and thrust of an act of war if this is ever justifiable. The objective of combat is the incapacitation of a combatant from doing
what he is doing because he is this particular combatant in this

278

particular war; it is not the killing of a man because he is this particular man. The latter and only the latter would be murder. From the proper direction of just action in war upon the combatant and not upon the man flows the prohibition of the killing of soldiers who have been captured or who by surrender have taken themselves out of the war and incapacitated themselves from continuing it. The robbers are not to be killed when effective robbery is no longer in them, since it was the robber and not the man who had to be stopped.

From this also flows the cardinal principle governing just conduct in war, namely, the moral immunity of noncombatants from deliberate, direct attack. In this principle of discrimination there are two ingredients: One is the prohibition of "deliberate, direct attack." This is the immutable, unchanging ingredient in the definition of justice in war. You have only to get to know the meaning of this in contrast to "aiming indiscriminately." The second ingredient is the meaning of "noncombatancy." This is relativistic and varying in application. "Noncombatancy" is a function of how the nations or the forces are organized for war, and of military technology.

Labels unjustified

What would be quite inexcusable is for anyone, who does not take responsibility for the agonizing decision to withdraw rather largely from the political life of his nation in the present, very imperfect international system, to continue to berate his government with an indiscriminate requirement that acts of war be discriminating in an abstract sense which the definition of "legitimate" targets, "collateral damage" and justice in the "just conduct" of war never meant, and never could mean. The doctrine of justice in war is not a legalistic device for disqualifying, one by one, all wars in this age of insurgency. Instead, the meaning of noncombatancy is always a function of the current organization of nations and forces for war. The doctrine of justice in war is an explanation to statesmen of how within tolerable moral limits they should undertake, if need be, to defend and preserve such politically embodied justice as there is in the world.

For the rest, decisions in regard to the political use of violence are governed by political prudence. This is to say, whether a particular war should be fought, or whether it should be fought at a higher level of violence for hopefully a shorter time or be de-escalated and fought for a longer time, and many another question one must ask in justifying a particular political option rather than another, depend on one's count of the costs and the benefits, upon weighing greater and lesser evils in the consequences. In technical language, this is called the principle of proportion, which requires that the good achievable or the evil prevented be greater than the values destroyed or the destruction involved in any resort to arms.

The principle of proportion, or prudence, can be violated by acts of omission as well as commission, while the principle of discrimination in war can be violated only by acts of commission. These are the main limits which the Christian who engages in politics knows to govern the political use of violent means. Then no one should fling around the word "immoral" with any other meaning when he is debating these questions, or when he criticizes the Administration's course of action.

Balance in judgments

On the matter of weighing the greater and the lesser evil, one can only mean to say that the present policy is prudentially wrong--which may be disastrous enough!--not that it is inherently "immoral." If current policy or his own proposal, either one, were the correct course for a charitable political prudence to take, it would hardly be inherently wrong to do it. On the matter of discrimination in acts of war, if one is going to use this assertedly "medieval" notion, he should use it correctly, and he should be able to recognize a medieval fortress when he sees one buried underground in Vietnam-- beneath villages.

When Pope Paul VI made the suggestion that the Vietnam conflict be taken to the U.N., this was spoken almost as a prayer. "Who knows," he asked, "if finally an arbitration of the United Nations, confided to neutral nations, might tomorrow--we would like to hope even today--resolve this terrible question. Let us pray to God for this." He also carefully noted that "judgment of political questions" was outside his competence as a religious leader--or that of a Christian as such; and he distinguished his long record of appeals for peace from "pacifism, which ignores relative rights and duties in the conflict in question."

In other words, it is for political prudence, and for men (both citizens and magistrates) in the political sector to decide (without imagining any conclusion on this can be derived from their religious faith) whether an opportune moment has arrived when

it will be useful to hold meetings for negotiation, to take it to
the U.N., or such-like questions.

Advice for the Christian

At this point let me say that Christians should endorse completely something that Rabbi Arthur Hertsberg of Kansas City
wrote: "It is easy enough to defend priests and rabbis and sometimes even columnists and editors, in their right to hold opinions,
rooted in their spiritual convictions, about the problems of the
day. There is in such a defense a rekindling of our high dedication to freedom. Nonetheless, it is particularly important for
political and theological liberals to remember that there is at
least one other dimension to the situation. The relevance of religion in the modern world cannot mean that there is a direct and
clear mandate from God either to get into South Vietnam further
or to get out entirely or to recognize Red China tomorrow morning."

This means that the engine of religion or morality cannot be
placed behind any person's prudential political diagnosis, or
behind the opposite opinions about Vietnam. It is only with this
reservation made entirely clear that a Christian, speaking as
such, should allow himself to enter upon a discussion of concrete,
specific options. A governmental or a nongovernmental analysis
may be mistaken; neither can be direct implications of Christian
faith and ethics.

However, Christians and the churches can very definitely say
something about the meaning of discrimination in acts of war.
This the Vatican Council did in its central declaration. "Any act
of war aimed indiscriminately at the destruction of entire cities
or of extensive areas along with their population is a crime
against God and man himself. It merits unequivocal and unhesi-
tating condemnation" (Pastoral Constitution on the Church in the
Modern World no. 80).

But then, a Christian today will have to be vigilant in telling
what this means intrinsically, and in actual practice. He will
have to do some sound and discriminating thinking. One does not
justify terror tactics and attacks on civilians on the grounds
that these acts are selective. Not even with the additional finding
that the insurgents win the allegiance of people by many other
appeals or also by a program of national liberation. The fact
that insurgency resorts to terror, when it does, only minimally
or only upon selected people does not qualify it as a discrimi-

nating resort to force. Decisions as to the inherent evil of an act of war or revolution cannot be settled by the body count. There is not a prudent number of villagers, schoolteachers or petty local officials and their families that it would be right to disembowel in the village square to dissuade others from allegiance to the existing social processes and institutions, all to the good end of destroying the social fabric of a traditional society and taking over and reforming the country.

What is guerrilla warfare?

Guerrilla war by its main design strikes the civil population (albeit selectively and as rarely as need be) in order to subvert, while striking as few legitimate military targets as possible. This is an inherently immoral plan of war or of revolution, and one that cannot be rendered morally tolerable by reference to the social reforms by which insurgency mainly proposes to succeed.

Without invoking the domino theory, it is a fact of life that the nuclear stalemate has made the world safe for insurgency warfare. This is modern war. The question facing the world for decades to come is whether it is possible to oppose these revolutionary wars successfully without joining them in direct attacks upon the very people a government may be trying to protect while social progress is secured with liberty. Is counterinsurgency, like insurgency, bound to be warfare over people as a means of getting at the other's forces?

Discrimination

If the guerrilla chooses to fight between, behind and over peasants, women and children, is it he or the counterguerrilla who has enlarged the legitimate target and enlarged it so as to bring unavoidable death and destruction upon a large number of innocent people? Since it is the shape of insurgency warfare that defines the contours of the legitimate combatant destruction and the unavoidably associated civil damage, it then may (so far as the principle of discrimination is concerned) be just to inflict evil in order to oppose it, subject only to the limitation that this be the proportionately lesser evil. To draw any other conclusion would be like, at the nuclear level, granting an enemy immunity from attack because he had the shrewdness to locate his missile bases in the heart of his cities. It is rather he who has deliberately enlarged the extent of foreknowable but collateral civil destruction in the attempt to gain a privileged sanctuary through a military posture that brought more of his own population into range. The design of insurgency does this to the people of a society it assaults. The onus of the wickedness of placing multitudes of peasants within range cannot be shifted from insurgency to counterinsurgency.

The principle of discrimination governing the proper conduct of war has no other meaning than this. Some call this a "medieval" notion. One should then be able to recognize a medieval fortress when he sees or hears of one buried under villages in South Vietnam. No Christian or moralist has a right to demand that statesmen or commanders fail to take account of these facts in their policies and plans. This is to suggest, all too briefly, that the main design of the counterinsurgency mounted in Vietnam need not be and likely is not an inherently evil or morally intolerable use of armed force--not in any meaning that the distinction between discriminate and indiscriminate conduct on war ever had or should have.

This is not to deny that peripheral to the "central war" against the insurgents there may be taking place many intrinsically wrong actions in this confused and bloody war. There are those who say that if any of the acts of war violate the canons of justice in war, or if justice is violated by frequent actions that, however, do not or need not fall within the main thrust or design of the war, it is still on the whole unjust and no Christian should support or participate in it. This position is far more to be honored than the indiscriminate use of the principle of discrimination that is current today. Still, to uphold it seems to me to uphold a legalist-pacifist version of the just war doctrine, as if the purpose of this teaching was to bring peace by discrediting, one by one, all wars. Instead, the just war doctrine is intended to indicate to political decision makers how, within tolerable moral limits, they are to defend and preserve politically embodied justice in the present world.

Political prudence

Determining the greater and lesser evil in accord with the principle of proportion and the application of the principle of discrimination in the face of some new organization of military forces calls for an exercise of political prudence on the part of magistrates and citizens alike. In the particulars of this no

Christian can fault the conscience of another. It may be the case that the conflict in South Vietnam has long since been destructive of more values than there is hope of gaining. If this seems to be the case so far as the Vietnamese alone are concerned, one must not forget that there are more values and securities and freedoms to be reckoned in any judgment concerning the proportionally lesser evil. Tragically, or in God's inscrutable providence, neither villagers nor nations are impervious to one another in our fated and fateful togetherness. Again in the particular decision concerning the greater or lesser evil in the whole of Southeast Asia, no Christian can fault the conscience of another. Then in this no Christian can fault the possible correctness of the conscientious estimations made by his government when he states with all urgency his disagreement with it.

Outcomes are uncertain

Finally, although there must be some international arrangement for peace in Southeast Asia, the point to be made here is simply that such an arrangement has not been possible since the decision was made at a meeting of the communist party leaders in North Vietnam to aid and abet the insurgency in the South, and that a tolerably peaceful and just arrangement still eludes attainment. This is what the fighting is all about. If and when the day comes on which negotiations are opened that stand a chance of attaining the internationally guaranteed neutralization and protection of the peoples of Southeast Asia, no Christian in the United States should suppose that now at last his government has made peace--a just peace--by peaceful means alone, while before we were doing wrong by fighting. Instead, the present use of armed force, no less than somebody's mediation of the conflict, will both have served to make such an arrangement possible.

We Christians should, of course, be the first to acknowledge that such a fragile historical outcome is not in one sense worth a single Vietnamese or American life, nor is a life to be exchanged for the values of an entire, more durable worldly civilization that also passes away in the course of time. We have it on the highest authority that the whole world is not worth a single human soul. But to bring this judgment directly into politics would be to compare incommensurables. It would be to weigh temporal accomplishments against a human life which is a sacredness in the temporal and in the political order. This would be to refuse to accept what Paul Tillich called the ambiguity of all finite sacrifice. Such, however,

284

is not the only assessment to be made of the lives sacrificed and taken in political encounters in this world in which political purposes and the use of force are joined by a tie not lightly broken, nor likely to be broken.

Notes begin on page 342.

Pacifism and Ethics

Frans van Raalten

Uneasiness over the spread of new weaponry and the intensification of military power is growing steadily. The possibility
of nuclear war and even annihilation is turning people toward
pacifism; and even when they ultimately reject it, the rejection
is made with an increasingly bad conscience.

Although ethicians rejoice over this growing interest, what
types of weapons are currently unpopular is ethically irrelevant.
The distinction between a limited and a more unlimited realization of a goal is no criterion by which to judge a goal's ethical
correctness. Total war and limited war are only quantitatively,
not qualitatively, different. At most, nuclear weaponry has a
didactic effect and thus can serve to emphasize the significance
of the gospel message.

The motives behind pacifism and the questions they raise are
ethically important. The basic motivation seems to be fear for
the survival of the human race. This leads to several questions.
Will an aggressor in confrontation with nonviolent opposition

abandon his aggression? If this is doubtful, how great a sacrifice
will pacifism demand of its adherents? And if this cannot be
answered, can one say that pacifism at least guarantees the
survival of the adversary and thus of mankind at the cost of its
own adherents? In this case, can pacifism support itself as an
ethical value higher than military power when pacifism--exactly
as military power--demands the risk of its own life?

Other motives are the high economic cost of the arms race,
the humanistic worthlessness of the military effort, and the pedagogical reflection that military influence during the sensitive
age at which military duty is fulfilled is harmful for many young
men. The proliferation of such motives tends to confuse the ethical
discussion.

Probability of values

First of all the utilitarian values of pacifism are at best only
probable. Slaps on the cheek can be blocked effectively; and one
wonders whether pacifism is not proposing an ethical utopia in
the face of a morally indifferent nature where war has played not
only a destructive but a constructive role. Is pacifism ignoring
the deepseated aggressive and defensive drives of human nature?

Economically the abolition of the armaments industry would
be disastrous. And even on a general ethical level, it can be
shown that military efforts help pacify instinctive human needs.

So on a natural level there is simply no firm foundation for a
pacifist ethic. Every existing being strives to further its own
existence, and one can ethically decide that what furthers human
life is morally good and what destroys it is morally evil. On the
natural level pacifism is but one among many valid choices. The
choice of the pacifist will perhaps seem more noble to us because
it is more in harmony with man as a spiritual person; but people
do opt strongly, even emotionally, for the more universal, natural dependence on power. As a result, dialog between pacifists
and their opponents breaks down quickly.

Approach to just war

The just war approach has been an attempt at compromise
between universal, natural thinking and evangelical or Christian
thinking. But this has not worked. The church, on the basis of
its own ethic (viz. defend truth or justice), can be obliged to
operations and service which do not harmonize with its inten-

287

tions and purposes. Everyone, indeed, has arguments for his supposedly just waging of war. As a result the most horrible means
are held to be, if not holy, at least allowable. In this way church
ethics can be used for nearly every political and military purpose.
In this the church itself is guilty because it has engaged in a
compromise between the evangelical or Christian and the natural,
universal, or political demands. Therefore traditional ethics and
its consequences are highly unsatisfactory, and we must try to
get out of this dead end. But one cannot free himself as long as
he remains loyal to traditional ethics.

Pacifism in general can be based on the different arguments
noted above, but pacifism as a decision of faith is distinguished
by its grounding in the revelation of God in Christ. It does not
appeal to what is timely, i.e., the historical situation, but to
the eternal in the temporal, i.e., to Christ as an historical,
divine person.

Divine history completes itself in the relationship between God
and man as a sinner. In this history reconciliation takes place.
Christ sacrificed himself for our sins. We cannot isolate this
core fact just within dogmatic and liturgical bounds and give it
reality only in the believer's interior faith. The core fact of
Christ's sacrifice ought to be decisive for the Christian's whole
existence because it was decisive for Christ himself.

Christ loved life

In Gethsemane Christ battled to bring his will into harmony
with his Father's. His willingness to sacrifice his life was preceded by an awful struggle which indicates his bond of love for
life itself. Christ was not the cowardly despiser of life who
welcomed death as a salvation from everything earthly. Even
less was he the elevated stoic who could dispassionately ignore
death. Christ gave his life to effect reconciliation as a witness
to the kingdom of God. Gethsemane signified for Christ an overcoming of self. He is the Lord of creation, but his sacrifice
does not mean that his love for creation disappears. God's love
for the created becomes twofold in Christ. It is not only the
immediate love of creator for creature, but also the love of
conciliator for sinner. The latter can demand suspension of the
former. Therefore we speak of sacrifice, of a deed through
which one gives up something dear for the sake of a higher goal,
of a love-motivated decision to serve others. Christ did not love
his life until the end. He spent it as an expiatory sacrifice.

Therefore he became a martyr to God in the original meaning of the word: witness.

If the sacrificial character of the life of Christ is at the center of the kerygma, it must also be central to our ethical considerations. This means that pacifism must be a choice of faith, a choice of following Christ not by simple imitation of his life style, but by the personal shaping of the Good News to the concrete living of our times. The pacifist must consider the nonviolence of his life as a value higher than preserving his life.

Nor will the pacifist have illusions about the direct conversion effects of his existential witness. If he does hope for conversions, he cannot expect successes which will at the same time be to his own advantage. In this way the cross of Christ assumes an ethical reality which the pacifist joyfully embraces, for he knows that his sacrifice means a religious victory.

Jean Lassierre in his book War and the Gospel asks, "Should one say that the anti-militarist thesis risks conducting the church to the cross?" And he answers, "Without doubt! But this leads equally to glory. But today the church with its falsified gospel is deprived of both cross and glory! . . ."

War's demand

There are, however, a number of practical questions that necessarily follow from Christian pacifism. First, the situation of martyrdom has an ethical alternative. One can recant his opinion, whereas war does not allow this alternative. War requires one to kill or be killed. If the choice is between burdening the conscience of a man who might kill us and the killing of that man, is not the inequality of the choice obvious? What nonpacifist would not prefer a possible burdening of his conscience to being killed?

But has the pacifist, by going to death in nonviolent witness to faith, the right to make his neighbor defenseless? Is this not claiming an authority that does not belong to him? Here we have a collision of ethical responsibility and religious duty of faith. The choice of the pacifist is never without tragedy. Either he chooses the ethical (protection, defense, and the use of power) and loses his religious dimension, or he chooses the religious side and loses his ethical solidarity with the rest of men. Thus if we consider pacifism from a religious point of view, that is, as a category of the kerygma, we find ourselves in the sphere of a subjective absolute which cannot be relativized by any rational, emotional, practical, or ethical consideration.

Roland Bainton correctly distinguishes a Christian pacifism of renunciation and a secular pacifism of prudence. The secular pacifism involves a strategy for survival. Christian pacifism is not a strategy but a witness to the following of Christ. In the same way we can distinguish between a moral or humanistic pacifism, which considers that the undefined spiritual worth of a man prohibits all wars, and a Christian pacifism, which has a transcendental foundation. In short, for the religious content of Christian pacifism, ethical categories are inadequate.

The behavior of Christ was beyond ethics because he required his disciples to sacrifice their lives. Here again we face the question whether nonviolence has the right to endanger the lives of others and make sacrifices of them by failing to defend them. This question is also valid for secular and humanistic pacifism as well as for militarism. Personal decisions in any of these ethical stances can endanger the lives of others and even mean the unwilling sacrifice of lives. In this situation, the pacifist and nonpacifist have the same responsibility.

Christian pacifism

This responsibility is less difficult for the Christian pacifist insofar as he finds in his faith in Christ authorization for his behavior. His faith frees him from the ethical dilemma; for if the content of Christian pacifism is truly religious, it is not supported by natural ethical values of any kind. Christian pacifism follows solely from the believer's relationship to Christ. Universal ethical values cannot be brought into harmony with this religious content. Therefore solidarity with the overwhelming majority of one's own countrymen for the defense and protection of one's people and the possibility of one's own self-preservation are all subordinated to the religious concern of pacifism.

At the same time this does not mean that the Christian morally withdraws from the state and allows the question of war to be a concern which the state freely and independently decides. This would imply two standards of morality, one for the state and one for the individual pacifists. There is no separate morality for the state. Rather there is a collision between a majority- and a minority-morality within the state.

The beliefs of the pacifist minority equally and legitimately belong to the whole state. Insofar as these beliefs are represented

by worthy and loyal citizens, they ought not be rejected as dis-
loyal to the state. There must be a dialog between the majority
and minority political moralities. The majority must consider
the argument of the pacifist minority on its merits and resist
the temptation to consider its own views unquestionably correct.
The need for justification arises either through deficiency in
fulfilling the law or through problems consequent upon this fulfilment. If either side merely assumes its own justification,
any attempt to arrive at a more Christian and possibly more
fulfilling attitude becomes paralyzed.

Another question is whether pacifism is not really sub-
ethical since it seemingly avoids ethical action and behaves
passively where high ethical engagement or responsibility is
demanded. Pacifism preaches passivity where deeds are demanded; it preaches nonviolence where the highest danger must
be confronted. Therefore does not the pacifist choose an easy
exit when he withdraws himself from all military action? Is he
not on a sub-ethical plateau?

The question can only be answered by stating that the pacifist
needs an entirely different energy than that demanded of a soldier.
This energy is the divine power which proceeds from Christ's
reconciliation. To put on the armor of God (Eph. 6) demands
action which in power and intensity goes beyond all natural
activity. Pacifism is not passivity but the highest interior activity, which finds a practical outlet in nonviolent resistance.

It is true that the religious uniqueness of Christian pacifism
could lead to an ethical isolationism detrimental to its witness
value. Christian pacifists must dialog with other pacifists and
even nonpacifists over the practical implications of their stance
--the historical, economic, psychological, political, and legal
implications. Moreover, to avoid falling prey to legalism and
fanaticism or becoming simply another isolated sect within
Christendom, pacifists must openly and honestly consider even
nonpacifist motives and premises.

Qualifying situations

Finally, the pacifist must consider whether or not there can
ever be situations which demand the use of force. Two cases
come to mind: tyrannicide and police power. Can tyrannicide
become so unavoidable from an ethical viewpoint that even the
pacifist decision of faith must retreat or modify itself into the
decision to kill out of Christian responsibility? Here we simply

face the mystery of deepest personal decision which is responsible to God alone, and which, therefore, no one can judge. But on the other hand, the Christian's aim to convert his enemy is thwarted by killing him.

Police power has always caused a problem for pacifists. But police, who arbitrate between crime and ordered society, and the U.N. peacekeeping force, which stands between fighting peoples, are entirely different from the anxiety-provoking deterrents of the modern powers of war. Their goal is protection and peace; they attain it not primarily through killing but through arrest and pacification. An absolute pacifistic "NO" to this kind of police action is a legalism which logically but irrationally rejects the best attainable at the moment.

Notes begin on page 343.

The Future of U.S.-Soviet Relations: Convergence or Confrontation?

Joseph Schiebel

I Soviet Foreign Policy

Those who do not heed the lessons to be learned from the past history of Soviet foreign policy and of Soviet-American relations are doomed to learn them the hard way. This fact may be entirely satisfactory to those who, by philosophy or temperament, are disposed to deal pragmatically with the problems posed by the Soviet Union, but the cost of this approach and the high risk contained in it suggest that we would do well to draw on some of the achievements of Western man in analysis and reasoning which permit us to be more rational, critical, and prudent.

The Soviet system of power is as clear an example as we have of an enterprise operated by people who act consistently with their beliefs--and who act consistently and systematically because their beliefs are consistent and systematic. Throughout its history, the Soviet Union has conducted its affairs on the basis of firmly held and well-structured assumptions and

293

concepts, which have permitted a maximum of resourcefulness and flexibility in practical decision-making. This flexibility is readily apparent in the continuous and often startling changes and elaborations that have characterized the political behavior of the Soviet regime--behavior which, it should be stated at the outset, has led many observers of Soviet affairs to infer that Soviet foreign policy is arbitrarily formulated and executed more or less in response to the international situation at any given moment in time.

Notwithstanding this kind of mistaken analysis, it is essential to bear in mind that the assumptions and concepts which under-gird Soviet foreign policy have traditionally been, and continue to be, remarkably evident in Soviet foreign policy decision-making. These assumptions and concepts have been internally consistent both ideologically and metaphysically and have been neither ignored nor compromised during the first five decades of Soviet rule.

Unless--or at any rate, until--the Soviet leadership ceases to act politically in conformity with its established ideological vision and conceptual political framework, or changes substantially its ideological and operational principles, these will also provide the basic premises with which Soviet international political behavior must be consistent in the future. When employed as one of the constant factors in trying to predict Soviet behavior, an awareness and understanding of them is one of the essential ingredients of successful analysis.

Not only have the basic and currently unrepudiated concepts and principles of Soviet foreign policy been consistent since their earliest formulations, which makes an understanding of the history of that policy relevant to its current analysis and to the anticipation of its future, but Soviet foreign policy has also been, throughout, dynamic and outgoing, not to mention aggressive. This fact has crucially affected the dynamics of international relations because the Soviets have taken initiatives and created realities which have necessitated responses by the other powers.

Fundamentally, Soviet foreign policy has been unlike that of most non-Communist states whose interest in international politics is basically regulatory, mainly concerned with relations among states and with stabilizing those relations. It has, rather, been concerned not with preserving the existing order, but with transforming it--on three levels. The first level of this transformation of the international order was to make room in it for the Soviet Union as a state of conventional form but unconventional purpose, to defend it and to secure acceptance for it. The second level comprises the struggle for strategic power in the world. On the third level, Soviet foreign policy is concerned with the fulfillment of the visionary rationale of the Soviet system, the transformation of not only the world state system, but of the very structure and nature of the social order, from its pluralism of evolved forms to the so-called socialist form--that is, toward the ideal of the totally rational, perfectly managed society.

Historical materialism, which expresses pseudo-scientifically but sincerely the Communist understanding of the world social revolution, not only states that Communism exists because the irrational old order is doomed to be replaced by the new order-- whose only legitimate master is the "proletarian vanguard,"-- but makes the pursuit of that vision the sole reason and condition for being a Communist. All this is meant to suggest that it was the Soviet Union which exercised the bulk of the initiative in its relations with other states and societies in the past, that not only political realities but also a fundamental ideological commitment made the Soviet dynamic and aggressive initiatives expectable and necessary, and that any analysis of Soviet foreign policy is likely to be sound only when it is assumed that nations or groups of nations, in their relations with the Soviet Union, over the long run do not act, but react to Soviet initiatives, subtle though some of these may be.

This view of Soviet foreign policy as the systematic imple- mentation of a firmly held, long-range vision and as an ag- gressive contributor to the dynamics of international relations is, of course, only one of several interpretive frameworks. It will be necessary to make a case for this interpretation, and to present it along with a critical discussion of other existing approaches. This having been done, it will be possible to identify the main features of both the theory and practice of Soviet foreign policy over the past fifty years. Finally, a correlation of what the Soviet leadership has done, and is now doing in its foreign enterprises, to its stated primary goals and concepts will allow of some careful surmises of what may be expected of it in the near future, and of what place the United States occupies in the Soviet scheme of a transforming world order.

Since our academies have so far withstood the assaults of those
who wish to whip them into goose-stepping conformity with the
social revolution, and the essential institution of controversy has
thus been preserved, differing interpretations are not only expectable but also creative. But the savage competition of ideas
bordering on academic civil war has deeper roots. Consuming
passions and ambitions are involved in the elaboration of interpretations because they are often meant to serve as operational
doctrines for official policies and because they inescapably must
engage both our understanding of the world and our hopes for it.

It is fair to say that the bulk of scholarly production on Soviet
foreign policy expressly denies that there is any significant consistency in Soviet political behavior, either in time or with
ideology, or that there is a fundamental aggressiveness in Soviet
policy, or that it has provided the major initiatives in international
political relations.

Challenging the contention that Soviet foreign policy can be
understood by taking seriously the ideological beliefs of the
Soviet leadership are the cynics--those who, professing to live
and act according to no beliefs and principles of their own, find
it impossible to accept that anyone else does. The cynics see in
the Soviet leadership an essentially good-natured group of problem-
solvers, reasonable and intelligent though fallible men who pragmatically do the best they can in maintaining the Soviet position
in international relations from one day to the next, with no more
than a normal attachment to the past and to ideology, and with no
more concern for the future than is absolutely necessary. One
can start with the New York Times in looking for such views.

Whether or not human behavior in fact consists of only conditioned reflexes or whether ideas are a basic prerequisite for
action are questions which are too ambitious in this context. They
are, at any rate, irrelevant, since neither the Marxists nor the
authentic pragmatists (i.e., those who have thought about prag-
matism) claim ideas to be superfluous or of secondary importance.
To project onto the Soviet leadership an indifference to ideology
which one mistakenly attributes to oneself is an error. This
projection may very well be the basis for rejecting the notion of
fidelity to ideology among the Soviet leaders, since the pose as
a non-ideological problem-solver has become very fashionable
in American and European politics of late. It is no more than
a pose. Even our own leading politically ambitious "problem-

solver, " Senator Charles Percy, once organized the compilation of "Goals for America."

James Burnham, as long ago as the Eisenhower administration, identified the earnest, decent, competent men who could grasp every problem except that of Communism as something more than another conventional nation-state. It is, indeed, astonishing that intellectuals have been able to attribute enormous ideological obsessions to Germans, Catholics, Arabs, Ku Klux Klanners, Rhodesians, Gaullists and to almost everyone else except to the Soviet leadership. If the test of any proposition is to be found in practice, those who maintain that the Communists are not only pragmatic but also intelligent ought to consider the possibility that the Soviet leadership crushed Czechoslovak reform, imprisoned intellectuals, and produced cliché-ridden propaganda, among other things, not because these are the least offensive and most effective ways to win friends and influence people, but because Communist ideas and beliefs are at stake, not their political prosperity.

Another school of thought appears to believe that the kind of ideological and political single-mindedness and toughness which makes a foreign policy both consistent and aggressive can appear only in a monolithic system. One meets them at cocktail parties, among other places, terminating even the most carefully hedged warnings against certain Soviet objectives with the grand phrase that "of course everyone knows that the Soviet Union is no longer a monolith," expecting thereby to have proven beyond the shadow of a doubt that it is sheer insanity to consider the Soviet Union as anything other than peaceful and progressive, or to think about her at all. One might argue that what is said at cocktail parties is irrelevant, but then there is more than a presumption of evidence that a considerable amount of diplomacy is conducted through this institution, and a good deal of foreign policy is formulated there.

To say that the Soviet system is no longer monolithic, whatever is meant by that, is neither startling nor original. It never has been monolithic; if anything, the intraparty and intramovement struggles are better managed now than they were in the past. Perhaps Trotsky, the Purges, and the dissolution of the Comintern have been forgotten. Nor does the break-up of a monolith turn political wolves into sheep. The Hitler-Mussolini-Tojo axis was nonmonolithic but was able to create considerable damage nevertheless. National Socialism became most bestial and war most total after one axis partner broke away and the relationship with the other had become virtually meaningless and after the empire began to fall apart from the inside. The maintenance of the established pattern of Soviet foreign policy requires a very high concentration of command functions in the Soviet Union and within the Communist state system, but disintegrative events and processes have so far not limited Soviet behavior or objectives, though they obviously affect Soviet capacity.

More credible is the position of those who maintain that Soviet foreign policy was, indeed, at one time nothing less than systematic aggression, but that the character of the leadership and the institutional nature of the system have changed, that the ideological obsessions and the revolutionary élan have disappeared as the Soviet Union has moved from revolution to restoration and has become a status quo power which has taken its proper place in the world community of conventional states. Thus, the interests of the Soviet Union in its early years are no longer her interests today, or so it is said, and even though claims and ideologies have not been jettisoned, reasonable men in the Soviet Union are bound to see that their interests are served best when the interests of the world community are served, or so it is hoped. This view appears to be taken for granted by the establishment, i.e., the Democratic (and probably the Republican) administration, their ideological mentors, and the mass of newspaper writers and readers. Official documents, expert opinion, scholarly studies, newspaper comment, and political rhetoric make it clear that a large part of the public and of the policy-making establishment is convinced that profound changes have occurred in Soviet thought and practice (which ought not to be denied), and that these changes have led to the unilateral cancellation of the Cold War by the Soviet Union (which ought to be questioned). One prominent newspaper, in fact, termed the invasion of Czechoslovakia a Soviet declaration of Cold War II, implying that Cold War I had ended sometime before. From this view emerges the conclusion, fuelled by fear of nuclear war, that a period of cooperation and détente between the United States and the Soviet Union has become possible, a period which will result in a mutual interrelatedness and in a political stabilization of world politics (the Teheran-Yalta-Potsdam vision of Big Power peacekeeping appears at long last in view), assuring a general peace.

Detente and cooperation are, of course, highly desirable. The question is how one goes about achieving both, and what conditions and terms of such a reconciliation and mutual moderation of goals and power will have to be accepted. The attempt has already been made in the Soviet-American partition of the world at the end of World War II, and in an explicit commitment at Teheran, Yalta, Potsdam, and elsewhere to cooperate in the maintenance of world peace, guaranteed by (choose one:) two, three, four, five big powers. That attempt has failed. The Soviet Union has, since 1945, projected her power far beyond her "assigned" sphere of influence, particularly into the third world, and has promoted international conflict rather than reducing it.

More important, since those facts could be explained as neces-sary actions in international balance-of-power politics, there has been no change whatsoever in the basic Soviet theoretical state-ments which describe any state of cooperation and détente as necessarily temporary. Peaceful coexistence loses its meaning, according to every relevant Soviet statement, when the achieve-ment of a preponderance of Soviet power and a shift of the nuclear balance favorable to the Soviet Union make it possible to proceed with the "unfinished business of the revolution"--the social trans-formation of the world and the elimination of inferior, i.e., non-Communist, social systems. If a preponderance of power is achieved by the Soviet Union sometime in the future, those Com-munists who wield that power will not be compelled and, there-fore, not inclined to discuss any terms of détente (no more than the Germans were asked in 1945 under what terms they would be willing to normalize their relationship with the rest of the world).

Until the Soviet leadership conclusively, in theory and practice, makes a presently temporary commitment to détente and co-existence permanent, it would be well to discuss and scrutinize the terms severely to avoid another disappointment when a program of international cooperation once again turns out to have promoted Soviet power rather than world peace. No one, at any rate, here or in the Soviet Union, really knows whether certain temporary Soviet commitments to international cooperation, nonviolent com-petition, and the maintenance of the status quo will in fact become permanent. It is simply too early to tell whether the presently cooperative aspects of Soviet policy will ultimately turn from a tactical and strategic expedient into a permanent posture. While such a transformation must be hoped for and promoted, premature and careless initiatives toward détente and cooperation ought not to be permitted to provide a sanctuary for Soviet strategic growth and encouragement for renewed aggression.

It is also too early to tell whether, as is often claimed, the Soviet leadership has abandoned its original revolutionary posture, whether the Soviet Union can now be characterized as a conventional

nation-state, and whether Soviet international behavior is, therefore, no longer irrational, aggressive, and inscrutable, but
rational, cooperative, and predictable.

For historical reasons--the Soviet Union does occupy somewhat
the same territory and confronts somewhat the same powers as
did the Russian Empire--and for ideological reasons, Soviet
theory holds that in the time between the assumption of power by
the Communist party and the consolidation of domestic and world-
wide control, Socialism must have a fatherland and conventional
political institutions must be maintained. There is more than a
surface resemblance between much of Soviet political behavior
and, on the one hand, traditional tsarist patterns and, on the
other, the international political behavior of other nation states.
Here again, it is a question of whether the Soviet Union will
ultimately abandon political practices temporarily taken over
from the old order which it was otherwise determined to re-
pudiate and annihilate, or whether these patterns will significantly alter Soviet political behavior against original goals. It is also
a question of whether the fact that the Soviet Union is forced by
the realities of power and international environment, as is ideologically acknowledged, to behave according to established patterns of international relations for as long as it does not enjoy
a preponderance of power over all other nations will in time
produce permanent changes in the goals and methods of Soviet
foreign policy.

The Soviet leadership has clearly stated that during this phase
(the length of which cannot be predicted) of forced coexistence
and competition with conventional nation states, the Soviet Union
is required to behave in some essential respects like such states.
It has stated just as clearly that it intends, during that phase,
to continue to pursue its advantage until a sufficiency of power
permits the liquidation of this stage and the establishment of an
ideological world hegemony and a world-wide social transformation. The ultimate outcome can only be ascertained and verified
by historians, and they can do so only when this historical episode
has come to a close.

The political and academic analysts of Soviet foreign policy
who appear to have been most influential are those who share the
basic belief that the Soviet Union pursues power in the conventional
sense, and that this power is pursued and maintained by means
of rational politics. They insist that the study of Machiavelli, the
correlation of Soviet behavior with that of other nations, and the
observation of that behavior will yield a correct understanding,

while ideological statements are irrelevant and their evaluation misleading.

The Soviet leadership, in short, is said to have limited or abandoned proclaimed Communist objectives, to have accepted the principle of a multi-centered world political structure, and to have adopted a disposition towards cooperation because these are reasonable.

Aside from reiterating the view that the permanent character of these postures cannot now be established, it is necessary to state that the concrete evidence for this analysis is not conclusive and frequently contrary. Since empirical and immanent analysis is therefore problematical at best, while statements of policy and theory are unambiguous, it would appear to be wise for the purpose of scholarly investigation and essential for the purpose of policy determination to rely primarily on the latter as indicators of Soviet objectives and guides to analyzing and predicting Soviet international behavior.

While many of those who question the relevance of ideological and conceptual commitments to the formation of Soviet foreign policy concede that Soviet behavior can in fact be characterized as having been aggressive and dynamic, there are others who reject that premise as well. Prominent among them are people with affinities either for the convergence school of thought or for the theory of the capitalist encirclement of the Soviet Union. Basic to the convergence view is the assumption that developmental laws or changing realities are inexorably moving the Soviet Union away from those patterns of politics which require of her leadership an aggressive, expansionist posture and are making a defensive, cooperative attitude not only worthwhile but indeed inevitable. While it is necessary to point out that the convergence theory is completed by insisting that the United States inexorably moves in the opposite direction until all contradictions (and, therefore, if Marx is correct, tensions) between them disappear in the resulting institutional homogenization, one does the theory no favor by doing so. One can, for instance, inquire why two social systems should develop in exactly opposite directions (one toward pluralism, the other toward centralism) for exactly the same reason: increasing industrial complexity. One could also wonder why the United States should move to converge at all because, if the movement of Soviet society in the American direction will render the Soviets more cooperative, then presumably an American drift in the Soviet direction will render the United States less cooperative and more aggressive. Since the prospects for any kind of significant convergence are, at any rate, exceedingly dim, and since the history of mankind is replete with many fearful wars between states which appear institutionally to have been highly compatible (or "converged"), we need do little more with the theory than to state its existence.

Another view is that advanced in a sizable body of literature, both Communist and revisionist, which has its roots in the assumption that the Soviet Union has, from its inception, been surrounded by enemies bent on its destruction and that any Soviet diplomatic or military action which exceeded purely domestic aims has been preventive or defensive in nature. This, like the view that the United States has never sought to force her influence on any outside state or society, is essentially a metaphysical proposition which is believed not because it has been proven to be true but because it stills ideological thirsts, however pretentious the scholarly apparatus of the supporting arguments may be. One does not dispute statements of faith; one either accepts or rejects them. Since even those Soviet statements which characterize the first fifty years of Soviet foreign policy as an attempt to break out of the capitalist encirclement are advanced within the context of arguments that the successful defense of the Soviet Union must necessarily be followed by Communist expansion, there is no reason whatsoever for accepting this interpretation.

III Ideological and Institutional Mainsprings

It is one thing to insist that Communist theory provides a broader and more meaningful basis for analyzing Soviet foreign policy than the observation of political behavior alone. It is another to define and describe that theory. Our concern must be with ideology as the metaphysical basis for all political action and with the operational aspects of Communist theory, that is, those propositions which directly determine and delimit concrete goals and action.

It appears unreasonable to assume that the Soviet leaders, alone among all men who have ever held political power, plan their political roles solely as the servants of the Soviet state and the promoters of universal tranquility and prosperity or that, in the Machiavellian sense, they exercise that power because it is there and someone has to do it. Power is sought and held either for the sake of that power and the psychological appetites its possession creates or fills or for the sake of a non-immanent vision of a more or less perfect, more or less universal social order. Usually it is both vision and power which provide the drive and basic incentive.

While it is necessary to say that the sweep of the vision and the claim for power can be satisfied only by the so-called world revolution, it is also, alas, necessary to insist that the Communist world revolution is very much more sophisticated and real a matter than the notions of bomb-throwing anarchists. Trotskyite rabble-rousers, sinister spies, shoe-pounding missile-wavers, and martial conquerors maliciously or naively associated with that term. The Soviet leadership pursues power for the sake of a vision of a perfect universal social order in which it believes. It is in this respect that ideology is important. The Soviet leaders believe themselves to be acting not by preference, but according to the ineluctable process of history, a proposition which has not changed in any respect from Marx's earliest writings to the most recent official Soviet formulations. They believe themselves to be in possession of the scientifically verified laws of history according to which the entire old order (i.e., non-Communist world) is doomed and deserves to be doomed because it is not rational and therefore has prevented mankind from achieving full happiness. Man will be perfectly happy, they believe, in a rationally and scientifically regulated social and political environment which satisfies all his material and physiological wants (or at least needs), and from which the element of competition and tension has been removed. The means for achieving this millenium, Communists believe, have been placed in their hands, and with it they claim to have been charged with the duty to bring this utopia into being, regardless of human or other cost. From this certainty that they are the saviors of mankind, they derive their militancy and their stubborn pursuit of world revolutionary goals in almost every corner of the globe --even at this point in time, when it would be clearly to their advantage to abandon them and to consolidate the enormous gains they have made in the past fifty years.

This was Lenin's vision. All Soviet leaders since 1924 have claimed to be Leninists--and we may take them at their word. Virtually all analysts agree that Lenin took his ideology seriously, applied it creatively and flexibly to changing conditions without changing its basic tenets, pursued Soviet power for the sake of the utopian vision, and left to the Soviet leadership a legacy and trust which has to this day not been repudiated, not even in China.

As a social and political system, the Soviet Union represents a unique type. If the word is to be left with any meaning at all, the Soviet state is most decidedly not a socialist state, whatever may be meant by that in Sweden, Yugoslavia, Great Britain, or in the Great Society. It is also far from being either a conventional, multi-centered nation-state or a modern totalitarian manifestation of dictatorship. It combines, instead, three major historical trends in the organization of political power which give it an inner cohesiveness, a concentration of power and resources, and an outer toughness never before achieved by any state. Its base is the structure of an Asiatic despotism, that is, a political system in which a single ruler, with the assistance of a ruling bureaucracy, dominates a society which is politically, socially, and economically atomized. This society does not have the institutions through which it can effectively limit the power of the state. Added to this are techniques of dictatorship developed in Western Europe partly from enlightened absolutism and modern forms of dictatorship. Finally, the motivating element behind this system of power is a messianic ideology which makes a total claim on the allegiance of man.

There are undoubted signs of disintegration evident within the Soviet Union, and the Soviet leadership faces domestic crises of enormous magnitude. But the anticipation of an imminent collapse of the Soviet system, or its even less likely transformation into an open, cooperative society must be tempered by the realization that systems of total power far weaker than the Soviet Union have withstood challenges far more serious than those confronting the Soviet leaders at the present time. Experience indicates that internal opposition to a centralized state can be successful only if the system is also assaulted from without. There exists no significant outside threat to the Soviet system today; those who are disposed to challenge the Soviet Union are unable to do so effectively, viz., Czechoslovakia or perhaps Communist China. And the policies of the leading non-Communist powers, including the United States, are based on the assumption that the interest of world stability is best served by promoting the stability of the Soviet system.

Because of these policies, which may be defended on other grounds, the Western powers are, as they have been on several previous occasions, providing crucial support to the Soviet leadership in maintaining the integrity of its system. They may, ironically, be preventing those changes from taking place which convergence and evolution theorists have noted or predicted. To be

fair, a body of unilateralist opinion, private and official, has
advanced the theory that in time the Soviet leadership will have
to, or want to, respond positively to such generous concern for
its own welfare and for unilateral stability. These unilateral-
ists propose that Western initiatives will be predictably responded to by a rational Soviet leadership, that exchanges of
signals will reveal to each side what the other expects of it and
is prepared to accept, and that out of a period of signal-com-
munication there will emerge a modus of mutual cooperation.

The signal-calling, which has been in progress since 1961,
has revealed some truths, among them some highly unexpected
ones. The outlook, particularly since 1965, has become dimmer
rather than brighter for Soviet-American cooperation as indicated
by Soviet responses and actions. The Soviet Union has dramati-
cally increased, not reduced, its role in Vietnam, has been hell-
bent on the development of sophisticated arms systems while
talking of nuclear controls and limitations, has penetrated, not
left, important strategic areas such as the Middle East, and
has crushed institutional and artistic liberalization and reform
at home and in the satellites. While our signal-callers have
prophesied an end to Stalinist aggression and oppression, the
Soviet leaders have restored not only the memory of Stalin but
much of his outlook and statecraft as well.

The Stalinist period has been mistakenly identified as shaped
by Stalin's personality rather than Communist theory and structure. It will be equally misleading to interpret the new Soviet
course or mood as the expression of the personalities of this or
that faction. Soviet theory embodies long-range planning and
objectives, and Soviet operational doctrines and institutional realities strongly bind and influence succeeding generations of
leaders. Style and tactics may reflect personality and factional
politics. Concepts and objectives reflect Soviet ideology and
institutions.

IV Fundamental Strategic Concepts of Soviet Foreign Policy

"The fundamental thing . . . is the rule which we have not
only mastered theoretically, but have also applied practically,
and which will, until socialism finally triumphs all over the
world, remain a fundamental rule with us, namely, that we
must take advantage of the antagonisms and contradictions
between two capitalisms, two systems of capitalist states, inciting one against the other. As long as we have not conquered

305

the whole world, as long as, from the economic and military standpoint, we are weaker than the capitalist world, we must adhere to the rule that we must know how to take advantage of the antagonisms and contradictions existing among the imperialists."[1] Here, in the remainder of this speech, given in September, 1920, Lenin bares what have been the two major premises of Soviet foreign policy since 1920. The first is the assumption that, for a considerable period of time, the socialist powers will be weaker than the non-Communist states, and will, therefore, in order to defend the revolution and to create opportunities to advance it, have to operate within the existing international order. The second is the assumption that during this "third stage," as Stalin called it, a strategy of promoting and inciting major international conflicts among non-Communist states must divert the energies and efforts of non-Communist states and peoples to serve Soviet ends. I would call this the jiu-jitsu style of foreign policy: the technique of turning political energies of non-Communist states against themselves. This makes diplomacy, propaganda, and political manipulation the primary means of securing and advancing Communist power.

Reliance on theoretical statements here does not constitute citatology, or the custom of finding an explanation for Soviet behavior in this or that obscure quotation from Communist scriptures. Not all Communist statements are of equal weight, nor do they refer to matters of equal magnitude. The Leninist concepts referred to here, which have been constantly reiterated ever since his time by other Communist leaders, established principal goals for a major period of Soviet policy. Every significant concrete initiative in the past fifty years has reflected them, which alone would indicate that they should be taken seriously. Disregarding these concepts, Soviet policy may be interpreted in many different ways. With them, the task of evaluating Soviet behavior becomes not only more manageable, but the likelihood that our analysis reflects actual immanent goals, rather than imputed motivation, becomes very much greater.

Observing both theory and practice, and departing from Lenin's 1920 formulations, these have been the major sets and levels of contradictions around which the operational basis of Soviet foreign policy has been constructed.

1. An actual and potential conflict between the United States and Japan over strategic mastery of the West Pacific and East and Southeast Asia was identified early. While there is no justification for arguing that Soviet policy is solely responsible

306

for the U.S.--Japanese war, though it had been called for by the
Communists, more thorough investigations of the pre-war Soviet
apparatus in Japan and the work of Communist and pro-Communist
elements in the Japanese government and army (and in other
states) may well yield indications that, along with known Soviet
political activities, the diversion (and even development) of
Japanese initiatives toward the United States and China and away
from Siberia and the Soviet Union was influenced by them. The
Moscow-initiated Communist-Nationalist united front of 1937 in
China did engage Japan in China, the Soviet-Japanese Neutrality
Pact of April, 1941, did leave the latter free to prepare for her
confrontation with the United States, and the Japanese occupation
of large areas of East and Southeast Asia did provide the Communists with the opportunity to establish Communist party hegemony over the various national-liberation movements which laid
the basis for the successful as well as unsuccessful post-war
takeover attempts. Soviet interest throughout was both defensive
and expansionist. With the exception of the hoped-for major
tensions between Great Britain and the United States, Soviet
expectations materialized to a great degree. If it goes too far to
credit Soviet diplomacy with responsibility for conflicts which
might have come about without it, it nevertheless did play a role
at crucial junctures in maximizing, rather than minimizing conflict when the Soviet Union had an opportunity to do the latter.

    2. Stalin had characterized Germany as the "mine under
Europe." This phrase reflects the earlier Leninist and present
Communist conviction that the latent conflicts between Germany
and the major Western powers, and among the latter over Germany, have the greatest potential for intra-Capitalist wars from
which the Soviet Union can gain, and for the prevention of that
general solidarity among the major non-Communist powers which
would be disadvantageous to the interests of the Soviet Union and
the Communist movement. Lenin and Stalin foresaw a magnif-
icent opportunity to exacerbate deep hostilities between "van-
quished" and "semi-colonial" Germany and the victorious and
domineering Western powers into a general world conflagration,
preferably with the Soviet Union as an uninvolved bystander. The
main results of this posture were expected to be the prevention
of an anti- or non-Communist alliance against the Soviet Union,
the greatest possible perpetuation of European political, social,
and economic instability, a general European war providing the
Soviet Union with a variety of opportunities for political and ter-
ritorial expansion, a weakening of the Western powers to reduce

their ability to resist Communist advances into dependent and semi-dependent non-Western areas (decolonization) and a preoccupation with Germany as the major problem of world diplomacy to divert attention from the problems and challenges posed by the Soviet leadership. All these expectations were fulfilled to a remarkable degree. While the Japanese policy has had to be downgraded after World War II for a number of reasons, Germany remains today the principal focus of the Soviet strategy of maintaining, to its advantage, a divisive world-wide concern with that country.

The Soviet Germany policy could not have been more consistently applied in the past fifty years. It began with Soviet support for German revisionist anti-Versailles interests and the secret rearmament of Germany in the Soviet Union after World War I. It was reflected in the Communist efforts to undermine the Weimar Republic. This policy also explains the crucial assistance provided by the German Communist Party to the National Socialists in their struggle against the republic and German social democracy from 1928 to 1933. It was behind the Soviet efforts in the formation of an anti-German alliance in the nineteen-thirties. It reached its peak in the Soviet-German non-aggression pact and partition of Poland which permitted the commencement of the tragic chain of events leading to World War II from which the Soviet Union, despite her own destructive and unanticipated involvement, emerged as a major world power.[2] After an initial post-war attempt to mobilize hoped-for German resistance to integration with the Atlantic powers, the Soviet Union returned, with the Twentieth Party Congress of 1956, to a persistent policy of promoting, through diplomacy and propaganda, anti-German postures among her potential and actual partners, with the goal of perpetuating Germany's position as an object of big-power competition and of undermining her role as a productive partner in a general rapprochement and integration. Concrete gains are expected from external tensions over Germany and from internal disintegration and radicalization, both of which are actively being promoted.

3. While the strategy of dividing the principal non-Communist powers has been primarily defensive and only occasionally expansionist, a strategy was devised for expanding into the strategically weak area of the so-called third world of underdeveloped, backward, or neutral nations while the main powers were being limited, co-opted, or paralyzed. Lenin drew on the experience of the Russian October revolution which, as organized by him,

308

had placed a small Communist elite at the head of a general anti-autocratic movement of liberation with the mass support of the peasantry whose adherence had been gained by offering them a fraudulent land reform program. The road to Paris was said to lead through Peking, a formulation which expresses the Communist judgment that the prospects for major revolutionary gains are for the time being greater in the so-called colonial countries than in the capitalist societies which had unexpectedly withstood the revolutionary tide which had emerged in 1918, and that the establishment of Communist control over colonial areas--on which the Western powers were believed to depend for economic survival--would weaken those powers in preparation for a later direct confrontation.

The class struggle was now redefined as including antagonisms between oppressor nations and all the peoples, including the national bourgeoisie (the class enemy of tomorrow), of the colonial countries, and the presence of a mass revolutionary force was seen in the peasantry whose land-hunger was noted. The strategy of the Communist movement now had become the organization and control of movements of national liberation which were, when they had succeeded, to be converted into Communist regimes. As particularly exemplified by Comintern efforts in China, the expectation in the 1920's was that a Communist-infiltrated national movement would achieve independence and power, whereupon a coup would convert the new regime into a Communist dictatorship, with those having ridden the tiger ending up inside. In the 1930's, Communist movements frantically attached themselves to nationalist movements and regimes to remain viable, and to influence national policies as much as possible to contribute to the polarization of the world that was desired, namely the emergence of opposing blocs of "fascist-militarist" and "democratic-imperialist" states. In the 1940's, Moscow-led Communist parties "became" anti-fascist resistance movements and "leaders" in the struggle for national liberation from fascist and militarist oppression, a strategy which resulted not only in a great number of outstanding recruits and much good will, but in the political and military base essential to the post-war efforts to establish Communist regimes wherever conditions permitted them. During that time also, "agrarian reform" became an important strategic factor through which was won not only great support among the masses, but from Western intellectuals, propagandists, and governments as well. In the 1950's, the third-world strategy was attached to the so-called process of decolonization, and non-

Communist nationalist regimes were enlisted in a general posture of neutralism which, while it was not particularly helpful to Communist expansion, was immensely harmful to the strategic position and moral prestige of the West. The offensive to form Communist-led national-liberation movements and to convert extreme nationalist regimes through Communist coups was resumed in the late 1950's and continues into the 1960's. While hitherto there has been a cannon-fodder approach to such movements and regimes, with the Soviet Union providing little concrete assistance, or pretending not to, the 1970's quite likely will see an increase in both the militancy of national-liberation wars and movements, and in direct strategic Soviet support for them. The anticipated result will be a far-reaching Soviet hegemony over a substantial portion of the world's territory and population which, together with major advances in Soviet strategic military power and a disintegration of the cohesiveness, power, and will of the non-Communist nations, will decisively tip the balance in favor of the Soviet Union and permit it to proceed with the next two points on the original Leninist agenda, the mobilization of another round of intracapitalist confrontations, and the final showdown between the "two camps."

4. Lenin and Stalin had identified the latent tensions between the United States and her democratic allies as the fourth major set of contradictions which would weaken the non-Communist world and provide expansionist opportunities for Soviet power. Clearly documentable applications of this strategy of driving wedges between them can be found consistently since the 1920's, and its intensification, and success, in the past few years are so evident as to scarcely require mention. The thrust of the bulk of Communist propaganda, Communist-led opposition movements, and bona fide dissident expression has been that the United States is morally and strategically unfit for leadership of the non-Communist world. The aim has been to create a crisis of confidence between the United States and other states and peoples leading to the isolation of the United States as a world power. Opposition to the Vietnam War, to the American strategic and developmental presence in various parts of the world, the denigration of American culture, exposure of American racial and social problems have centered around the point that the United States must not be emulated, followed, cooperated with, or respected. Ironically, American inability or unwillingness to provide decisive assistance or leadership has also been used in propaganda intended to convey the message to some nations that dependence on an unreliable super-power is unwise. There is a multitude of ways, some sim-

ple and others very subtle, to promote discord and distrust among
non-Communist nations, and the Soviet leadership has missed few
opportunities to seek to alienate the United States from the rest
of the world.

V Prospects for Soviet Foreign Policy and Soviet-American Relations

The fifth major set of contradictions identified by Lenin in 1920
was the struggle for strategic power between the United States and
the Soviet Union, in which the issue over which social system
prevailed would be finally decided. Available evidence would indicate that it is premature to assume the Soviet Union to now be
determined to avoid such a clash. At the same time, the existence
of nuclear and other horror weapons has made a direct confrontation improbable and the experience with Communist China has
indicated the strong likelihood that Communism, once established
world-wide, will promptly break up and disintegrate. I believe that
the Soviet leadership has adjusted to these realities by aiming now
at absolute strategic hegemony over the world, but not a political
and military conquest or occupation.

Highly effective systems of rule over large foreign areas have
been maintained in the past through select and largely remote
controls rather than by a physical mass presence. One such
historic "occupation by strategic controls" was experienced by
the Russians in the Mongol period; the most recent example of
a state which achieved virtual world hegemony through a highly
limited apparatus of strategic, military, economic, and cultural
controls was 19th-century Great Britain. I see strong indications
that the new Soviet style of world politics is going to resemble
more and more the old British style of empire-building. The
Soviet leaders have been slow to push for the establishment of
bona fide Communist regimes in various areas of the world,
creating instead a whole series of dependent relationships as if
aware that hegemony is, in the long run, more effectively maintained by control than by occupation. A whole array of military
and particularly naval developments and the imminent succession
by the Soviet Union to strategic bases (especially those which
would permit the Soviet Union almost total domination over the
Near and Middle East) vacated by Great Britain point to a preoccupation with techniques of empire by strategic control. The
emergence of the Soviet Union as a substantive provider of de-

velopmental aid (with strategic strings attached to much of it),
as a marketer of major competitive goods (oil, advanced air-
planes, etc.) and as a factor in the international money market
indicate a growing capacity in this medium of political controls.
Finally, and there is no British corollary here, while various
arms limitation agreements were sought under the assumption
that both the capacity and the willingness to develop further major
weapons had levelled off here and in the Soviet Union, it is no
longer denied even by the Department of Defense that the Soviet
Union has made major developmental and production advances in
strategic military capacity.

The long-range aims seem, for the moment, to be reasonably
evident. The Soviet Union will pursue, in every way possible,
strategic, political, economic, psychological, and every other
advantage in order to achieve a monopoly or such a preponderance
of power over all other nations that, without a world-wide occupation, which would be self-destructive, and without a direct
confrontation with the United States, which would be even more
so, an ideological and political hegemony, a Pax Sovietica, can
be established in the shadow of whatever social transformational
goals remain to be accomplished.

To compare this concept of empire to the British example is
not, of course, meant to obscure the fact that enormous differences existed between pluralistic, democratic England and the
single-centered, despotic Soviet system, and that the result of
British rule was often (as Marx, for one, acknowledged) progress
and the export of democratic institutions and ideals, while no
such gains will accrue to the beneficiaries of the new Soviet
imperialism.

The German strategy, the national-liberation strategy, and
the strategy of isolating the United States as a world-power will
dominate operational aspects of Soviet foreign policy in the fore-
seeable future.

After nearly a century of incessant anti-German propaganda
in the West, and after the Hitler period, Communists have no
difficulty in finding responses to propaganda aimed at persuading
people, for perfectly good reasons of their own, to undermine
German-Allied cooperation in the interest, unknown to them, of
the Soviet Union. But there is more to it than propaganda. It has
been suggested that the Soviet occupation of Czechoslovakia in
August, 1968, amounted to a major Soviet strategic troop deployment in preparation for an attack on West Germany. If American guarantees for the defense of Germany were to wither and if

312

political disintegration within Germany were to render the constitutional government impotent, such an invasion would not only
be possible, but likely. Soviet leaders, at any rate, have said
so. While I do not believe the German option to have the highest
Soviet priority, I do believe it to be active, because it is reasonably possible. There are political candidates in the United States
who a) could be elected and b) would reduce the American commitment in Germany. And Communist agitational work in West
Germany has become so effective and organized that the Bonn
Republic may well go the way of the Weimar Republic, which was
undermined by smaller groups of political and ideological degenerates and wreckers than are today assembled in West Germany
--which, if anything, is more permissive of such things than the
old republic.

Wars and movements of national liberation will intensify and
promise to be particularly rewarding to the Soviet leaders in
Africa and the Middle East. There, they can be supported far
more directly and effectively than in Vietnam, the slogan "No
more Vietnam's, especially in Africa" will paralyze American
response for a long period, and if initial national-liberation wars
are directed against regimes which the United States is presently
pledged to isolate and eliminate, such as Rhodesia and Angola,
the Communists can also have their forces supported by the United
States.

There has been a concentration of attention on developments
and events within the Soviet Union which point to the making of
a serious internal crisis of control. Communism is popular only
where it is either unknown or misunderstood, and the Soviet
people are no doubt fed up with the system at a time when the
disparity between Soviet life and the outside world becomes not
only greater but also better known to them. To conclude, however, that a dramatic crisis, which at any rate is limited to a
challenge by men and women with convictions and ideals (which
leaves out the cynics and managers who may complain but who
have neither the guts for nor the interest in revolt at the peril of
their status), can only lead to a deliberate loosening up of control
and more cooperative international behavior is to overlook the
abundant power and potential for domestic repression and foreign
expansion.

The Soviet system of today is, indeed, not the crude and
blundering revolutionary and expansionist enterprise of yesterday. Its apparatus for analysing and appraising social and
political conditions around the world is highly sensitive and

sophisticated. Soviet foreign policy is opportunistic in the best sense of the word. Equipped with overall analytic concepts and strategic goals, every discontent, every conflict, every manifestation of unintegrated power is evaluated and creatively exploited. The Soviet leadership, in addition to its troubles, also has a good many things in the world today favoring it, not the least of these being the fact that no Soviet initiative has been and will be resisted when it is not recognized or understood. The Soviet leaders are not omnipotent supermen. They owe their successes to the fact that they were able to so organize and arrange their advances that there would be no enemies.

Notes begin on page 344.

NOTES TO PIET SMULDERS, S.J.
Teilhard and the Future of Faith*

Smulders, Piet, S.J., is professor of dogmatic theology and
patrology at the Catholic School of Theology, Amsterdam University. Father Smulders has written extensively on the Council
of Trent, the doctrine of the Trinity, and the documents and
theological problems of the Second Vatican Council. His books
and articles on Teilhard de Chardin have received wide acclaim
from scholars throughout the world.

1 Teilhard de Chardin, La vision du passé, Oeuvres III (Paris:
Seuil, 1955), 265. Translation: The Vision of the Past (New York:
Harper and Row, 1966).
2 "Le Coeur de la matière" (unpublished essay 1950); see P.
Smulders, The Design of Teilhard de Chardin (Westminster,
Md.: The Newman Press, 1967), 302 f.
3 Le milieu divin., Oeuvres IV (Paris: Seuil, 1957), 94 f.
Translation: The Divine Milieu (New York: Harper and Row,
1960).
4 P. Smulders, The Design of Teilhard de Chardin (Westminster, Md.: The Newman Press, 1967), 231-232.
5 St. Thomas, De Potentia, q. 3, a. 10, ad 4.
6 Teilhard de Chardin, Le groupe zoologique humain, Oeuvres
VIII (Paris: Seuil, 1965), 9. Translation: Man's Place in Nature
(New York: Harper and Row, 1966).
7 Ibid., 137.
8 L'avenir de l'homme, Oeuvres V (Paris: Seuil, 1957), 307.
Translation: The Future of Man (New York: Harper and Row,
1966).
9 "Comment je crois," (unpublished essay 1934); see P.
Smulders, The Design of Teilhard de Chardin, 120.
10 Teilhard de Chardin, Science et Christ, Oeuvres IX (Paris:
Grasset, 1956), 162. Translation: Science and Christ (New York:
Harper and Row, 1968).
11 "Comment je Vois," (unpublished essay 1948); see P.
Smulders, The Design . . ., 239 f.
12 Science et Christ, 141 f.
13 L'avenir de l'homme, 264 f; see P. Smulders, The Design
. . ., 109.

*Reprinted with permission of Theology Digest, Vol. 17 (Win-
ter 1969), 326-337.

315

14 P. Smulders, The Design . . . , 119.

15 Teilhard de Chardin, "Reflexions sur le bonheur," Cahiers II (Paris: Seuil, 1960), 69.

16 The Divine Milieu. Translation (Harper and Row, 1966), 238.

17 Teilhard de Chardin, The Phenomenon of Man. Revised translation (Harper and Row, 1966), 238.

18 Ibid., 308, n. 2.

19 Gaudium et spes, art. 39.

20 Teilhard de Chardin, L'avenir de l'homme, 267-268; see P. Smulders, The Design . . . , 116.

21 See his notes on the development of dogma in the book by B. de Solages, Teilhard de Chardin, témoignage et étude sur le développement de sa pensée, Toulouse, 1967, 347-350.

22 Teilhard de Chardin, "Note pour servir à l'évangélisation des temps nouveaux (1919)," Ecrits du temps de la guerre (1916-1919), (Paris: Grasset, 1965).

23 Letter of April 15, 1953, see P. Smulders, The Design . . . , 118.

24 Letter of July 22, 1916, see translation, The Making of a Mind (New York: Harper and Row, 1965), 114.

25 Compare the words of Teilhard a few months before his death: "I am going to Him who is coming;" see P. Smulders, The Design . . . , 8.

26 Teilhard de Chardin, Science et Christ, Oeuvres IX (Paris: Seuil, 1965), 166.

NOTES TO NORBERT M. WILDIERS, O.F.M. Cap.
The New Christian of Teilhard de Chardin*

Wildiers, Norbert Max, O.F.M. Cap., professor of theology
in seminaries and theologates in Belgium and Holland. He has
been general editor of the works of Teilhard de Chardin. His book
An Introduction to Teilhard de Chardin has been translated and
published in nine languages.

1 The Divine Milieu (New York: Harper and Row, 1960), p. 43.
2 Ibid.
3 Herman Nohl, Hegels theologische Jugendschriften (Tübingen,
1907), p. 224.
4 Ernest Renan, L'avenir de la science (Paris: Calmann-Lévy,
1890), Préface, p. xv.
5 M. Merleau-Ponty, Sens et Non-Sens (Paris: Nagel, 1963,
4th ed.), p. 307.
6 Claude Cuénot, Pierre Teilhard de Chardin (Paris: Plon,
1958), p. 19.
7 The Divine Milieu, p. 62.
8 Ecrits du temps de la guerre (Paris: Grasset, 1965), p. 5.
9 "Somewhere, there must be a standpoint from which Christ
and earth can be so situated in relation to one another that it is
impossible for me to possess the one without embracing the other,
to be in communion with the one without being absorbed into the
other, to be absolutely Christian without being desperately human"
(ibid., p. 46).
10 The Divine Milieu, p. 71.
11 "Hérédité sociale et éducation," in Etudes, t. 245, 1949,
p. 92.
12 In ipso condita sunt universa . . . (Col. 1:16-17).
13 Cf. Eph. 1:10; see L. Cerfaux, Le Christ dans la théologie
de saint Paul (Paris: Ed. du Cerf, 1951), pp. 318 ff.
14 L'énergie humaine (Oeuvres, t. VI) (Paris: Le Seuil, 1962),
p. 192.
15 The Divine Milieu, p. 62.

*Reprinted with permission of the author and Thought, Ford-
ham University Quarterly, Vol. 43 (Winter 1968), 523-538.

NOTES TO ROBERT L. FARICY, S.J.
Individual, Societal, and Cosmic Dimensions of Salvation *

Faricy, Robert L., S.J., professor of theology at the Catholic University, an internationally recognized student of Teilhard de Chardin's works. His articles on Teilhard have appeared in many journals, and his widely read book Teilhard de Chardin's Theology of the Christian World includes some valuable and interesting insights into the mind of Teilhard as these are set forth in his letters and writings.

1 See the writings of P. Teilhard de Chardin, especially The Future of Man (New York, 1964), pp. 52-57.
2 This is the exegesis of H. Schlier, "The Pauline Body-Concept," in The Church: Readings in Theology, ed. at Canisianum-Innsbruck (New York, 1963), pp. 44-58.
3 I am following S. Lyonnet, "The Redemption of the Universe," in The Church (n. 3 above), pp. 136-56.
4 P. Teilhard de Chardin, Science and Christ (New York, 1969), p. 122.
5 P. Teilhard de Chardin, Writings in Time of War (New York, 1968), p. 213.
6 P. Teilhard de Chardin, The Future of Man (New York, 1964), p. 224.
7 Ibid., p. 237.

*Reprinted with permission of the author and Theological Studies, Vol. 30 (September 1969), 460-472.

NOTES TO ENRICO CANTORE, S.J.
Scientific Humanism and the University*

Cantore, Enrico, S.J., is currently engaged in research at
Heythrop College, Oxford University, England. He holds doctoral
degrees in both physics and philosophy, and has written numerous articles. At present he is working on a book to be published
shortly, Atomic Order: An Introduction to the Philosophy of
Microphysics.

1 See for instance Science is a Sacred Cow by A. Standen
(New York: Dutton, 1950). This witty satire is the work of a
chemist and editor of the Encyclopedia of Chemical Technology.
2 See for instance F. A. Hayek, The Counter-Revolution of
Science: Studies in the Abuse of Reason (New York: Free Press
of Glencoe, 1955). Also F. W. Matson, The Broken Image: Man,
Science and Society (New York: Braziller, 1964).
3 E. Husserl, Die Krisis der europäischen Wissenschaften
und die transzendentale Phänomenologie: Eine Einleitung in die
phänomenologische Philosophie (Haag: Nijhoff, 1954), p. 70.
Cf. also pp. 26-32 and footnotes on pp. 300f.
4 Cf. Husserl, op. cit., p. 52.
5 One great opponent of science as an allegedly dehumanizing factor was Goethe. See for instance E. M. Wilkinson and
L. A. Willoughby, Goethe: Poet and Thinker (New York: Barnes
and Noble, 1962), p. 145. Cf. also Heisenberg's lecture to the
Goethe Congress (Weimar, 1967).
6 A classical example concerns the X-rays. Strange effects
had been noticed before; Goodspeed of Philadelphia went so far
as to make an X-ray photograph on February 22, 1890. Yet the
real discovery was only to be made by Röntgen (December 1895).
Concerning the meaninglessness of mere factual information see
O. Glasser, W. C. Röntgen (Springfield, Ill.: Thomas, 1958),
pp. 84f.
7 L. de Broglie, Physics and Microphysics, trans. M. David-
son (New York: Grosset and Dunlap, The Universal Library,
1966), p. 208.
8 Victor F. Weisskopf has aptly spoken of the "quantum ladder."
See his Knowledge and Wonder: The Natural World as Man Knows It
(Garden City, N.Y.: Doubleday, 1962), pp. 127-51.

*Reprinted with permission of the author and Thought, Fordham
University Quarterly, Vol. 43 (Autumn 1968), 409-428.

9 <u>Dialogue concerning the Two Chief World Systems</u>, quoted by L. Geymonat (trans. S. Drake), <u>Galileo Galilei</u> (New York: McGraw-Hill, 1965), p. 130.

10 Significantly, M. Polanyi entitles his philosophical assessment of science <u>Personal Knowledge</u> (Chicago University Press, 1958, 1962). See also his <u>The Study of Man</u> (Chicago University Press, 1963).

11 <u>Physikalische Zeitschrift</u> 17 (1916), p. 101; English translation by G. Holton, in <u>American Journal of Physics</u> 29 (1961), p. 806.

12 A. Einstein in C. Seelig, ed., <u>Ideas and Opinions of Albert Einstein</u>, trans. by S. Bargmann (New York: Crown, 1954), p. 292. For Einstein the objective orderliness of material reality was an absolutely central problem. See his <u>Lettres à Maurice Solovine</u> (Paris: Gauthier-Villars, 1956), p. 114.

13 Newman's ideal of university education remains relevant. See <u>The Idea of a University</u> (Garden City, N.Y.: Doubleday, Image Books, 1959), p. 451; also "Knowledge viewed in relation to learning," <u>ibid.</u>, pp. 148-69.

14 M. Scheler, quoted by M. Buber, <u>Between Man and Man</u>, trans. R. G. Smith (London: Collins-Fontana Books, 1961), p. 220.

15 "The new Philosophy calls all in doubt. . . . This all in peeces, all cohaerence gone . . .," John Donne (1611), quoted by A. Koyré, <u>From the Closed World to the Infinite Universe</u> (New York: Harper Torchbook, 1958), p. 29.

16 "Qu'est-ce qu'un homme dans l'infini?", "Le silence éternel de ces espaces infinis m'effraie."--Pascal, <u>Pensées</u>, texte établi par J. Chevalier, Nos. 84 and 91. See also J. Kepler, <u>De Stella Nova</u>, quoted by Koyré, <u>op. cit.</u>, p. 61.

17 "But the real man, man who faces a being that is not human, and is time and again overpowered by it as by an inhuman fate, yet dares to know this being and this fact, is not unproblematic: rather, he is the beginning of all problematic."--Buber, <u>Between Man and Man</u>, p. 181.

18 Buber, <u>op. cit.</u>, p. 195.

19 Buber, <u>op. cit.</u>, p. 155.

20 Very significant help to the philosophical understanding of basic concepts is offered by genetical epistemology. See especially J. Piaget, <u>Introduction à l'Epistémologie Génétique</u> (Paris: Presses Universitaires de France, 1950).

NOTES TO ANTON C. PEGIS
"Who Reads Aquinas?"*

Pegis, Anton C., professor of the history of philosophy at the
Institute of Medieval Studies, University of Toronto, he was edi-
torial director of the Catholic textbook division for Doubleday
and Company, Inc., 1954-1961. Dr. Pegis has contributed numerous
articles to philosophical journals and also to the more popular type
periodical. His best known books are Basic Writings of St. Thomas
Aquinas, Wisdom of Catholicism, St. Thomas and the Problem
of the Soul, St. Thomas and the Greeks (Marquette University
Aquinas lecture [1939]), St. Thomas and Philosophy (Marquette
University Aquinas lecture [1964]), Christian Philosophy and
Intellectual Freedom, Middle Ages and Philosophy. Dr. Pegis
is also visiting professor of philosophy at Marquette University.

*Reprinted with permission of the author and Thought,
Fordham University Quarterly, Vol. 42 (December 1967), 488-
504.

NOTES TO WILLIAM OLIVER MARTIN
The Institutional Effects of Anti-Philosophy *

Martin, William Oliver, presently professor and chairman of the department of philosophy at the University of Rhode Island, the author of numerous articles on philosophy, and the following books, Order and Integration of Knowledge and Metaphysics and Ideology. The last title named was the 1959 Aquinas Lecture, Marquette University. Dr. Martin is an associate editor of the new periodical, Triumph.

1 William P. Alston and George Nakhnikian, eds. Readings in Twentieth Century Philosophy (London: Collier-Macmillan Ltd., 1963), p. 421. All page numbers above refer to this book. All italics are those of Carnap.

2 The fact that Carnap later "broadened" his theory to include semantics as well as logical syntax is irrelevant to any point we are making. Also, the fact that over the years some of the members of the circle have changed their minds in some respects is not relevant to the main point. Their minds have not changed enough. On this matter I would refer to an article by Herbert Feigl, "Logical Positivism after Thirty-five Years," Philosophy Today, VIII (Winter 1964), 228 +.

3 Alston and Nakhnikian, op. cit.

4 General Education in a Free Society. Report of the Harvard Committee (Cambridge, Mass.: Harvard Univ. Press, 1945. Reprinted 1962).

5 Time, 88 (January 7, 1966), 24-25.

6 Lewis S. Feuer (formerly professor of philosophy and social science at the University of California, Berkeley, and now professor of sociology at the University of Toronto) insists that "academic philosophy" is dead. Cf. his "American Philosophy Is Dead," New York Times Magazine, April 24, 1966, 30 + . His analysis of the reasons is worthy of serious consideration. However, his solution is highly questionable, for he would turn over the philosophical enterprise to non-philosophers. Furthermore, he does not consider a more rational alternative, namely, to perfect academic philosophy. This alternative is being pursued; a notable example would be the philosophy department at Fordham University.

*Reprinted with permission of the author and The Intercollegiate Review, Vol. 4 (March-April 1967), 153-160.

NOTES TO MAURICE BLONDEL
Philosophy Fulfilled in Christianity*

Blondel, Maurice, was one of the leading philosopher-theo-
logians of the present century. This scholarly French intellectual, at his death in 1949, left unfinished the second of his great
trilogies, La philosophie et l'esprit chrétien. These works discuss the nature of human intelligence and knowledge, God as the
source and cause of being, the nature of the Church and the act
of faith. Two of his books are in English, Letter on Apologetics,
History of Dogma, and in collaboration with Rierre, Teilhard
de Chardin: A Study.

*Reprinted with permission from Theology Digest, Vol. 11
(Spring 1963), 27-32. Originally published in Exigences Philosoph-
iques du Christianisme as "L'unité catholique" (Paris: Presses
Universitaires de France, 1950), 97-111.

NOTES TO HENRI DE LUBAC, S.J.
The Church in Crisis*

De Lubac, Henri, S.J., is professor emeritus of the Institut
Catholique in Lyon, France. He is a member of the Papal Commission for Non-Believers and Non-Christians and the International
Theological Commission. A revised French version of this lecture
appears in Nouvelle Revue Théologique 91 (1969), 580-596.

1 Commission of studies on violence, November 25, 1968.
2 "Art represented the world as disintegrated by the 'bomb'
before the bomb was invented, just as Picasso and Kafka described
concentrationalized society before it became a reality." Oliver
Clement: "A propos de la beauté: crises et promesses, " Axes 1
(1969), 12.
3 Erik Weil, Philosophie politique (Paris: Vrin, 1956), 94-95.
"Society, by its very principle, requires that an individual's individuality disappear. Yet society makes this demand on individuality, knowing that it is only from this very same individuality that
it can hope to obtain it. [But] individuality remains indomitable
because society forces it to sacrifice itself and thereby cements
it in a situation of conflict. . . ."
4 "Violence et langage, " La Violence (Recherches et débats)
(Paris: Desclée De Brouwer, 1969), 83-84.
5 Ibid., 92. These lines were written one year prior to the
events of May-June 1968 in France. Jacques Pirenne writes much
along the same lines in Les grands courants de la civilization
universelle, II, 313: "Without so much as giving it a second thought,
the West has suffered profoundly from the rupture with the centuries-
old culture of the East. In losing touch with its fantasy, its humanity, it began to tend towards that iron materialism which, orientated
more and more to the realization of a direct, tangible utility would,
it is true, attain an uncontested mastery of the world in just a few
centuries, but at the price of a 'realism' which would one day hand
it over to the most terrible of crises that humanity has ever known,
and in the course of the crisis it would throw itself into a merciless
work of self-destruction because it had lost the meaning of real
values." Quoted by Th. Strotmann, "Karl Barth et l'Orient chrétien, "
Irenikon, 42 (1969), 42.

*Reprinted with permission of Theology Digest, Vol. 17 (Winter
1969), 312-325.

6 I made an initial analysis of this situation in my work, L'Eternel Féminin, étude sur un texte du Père Teilhard de Chardin (Paris: Aubier, 1968), part 2, chapters 1 and 2.

7 Yves Congar, Au milieu des orages (Paris: Editions du Cerf, 1969), 57.

8 "Institutions et charismes," La Théologie du renouveau (Actes du congrès théologique de Toronto, September 1967). (Paris: Editions du Cerf, 1968), I, 319; and "Thoughts on Theology after Vatican II," The Dublin Review (1968), 106-113.

9 Ninth University Sermon, December 2, 1832, no. 25.

10 "And with Saul's sin, Saul's portion awaits his followers-- distraction, aberration; the hiding of God's countenance; im- becility, rashness, and changeableness in their counsels; judicial blindness, fear of the multitude (i.e. of the opinion of the multi- tude); alienation from good men and faithful friends; subserviency to their worst foes, the kings of Amalek and the wizards of Endor. . . . Such is ever the righteous doom of those who trust their own wills more than God's word." Newman, Ibid.

"Newman, a highly strung spirit, was suffering inward agony from the assault of Liberalism on his beloved Anglican Church": John C. Thirlwall, "John Henry Newman: His Poetry and Conver- sion," The Dublin Review (1968), 83.

11 See Marguerite Lena, "Dimensions de l'intelligence," Axes 3 (1969), 13-21: "We are assisting at a specialization of intelli- gence in the problems of the means and at a vast confusion of reflection on the ends. The extraordinary success of technology and the equally evident failure of man to reach agreement on a political plane are perceptible signs. . . . We have at our dis- position an incomparable network of means of communications, and yet the communications come to nothing. . . ."

12 Georges Crespy, "Une théologie pour demain," La Vie protestante, April 19, 1968.

13 Yves Congar, Au milieu des orages, 8: "It is not in the conciliar work that certain disputes find their inspiration, at times in direct contradiction with the Council--disputes which materialize and which at times aim at pulling down and at creating confusion."

14 Karl Barth, Credo, 226. I have shortened the text slightly. Barth more than once put Catholics on guard against the temp- tation of falling into the same errors committed in the past by Protestant thought.

15 Yves Congar, op. cit., 86: "Today there is a certain way of appealing to and conceiving of the idea of the people of God which

is not entirely correct. Today the faithful frequently claim the
freedom of decision or take an initiative, saying: 'We are the
people of God,' as if the expression had the political meaning of
'people' as opposed to governments; as if the phrase designated
a mere totality or undifferentiated mass and not a structured
community. . . ." Along these same lines the democracy of today is set in opposition to the paternalism of yesterday, where
the word paternalism is used with reference to all real exercise
of spiritual authority.

16 I have treated several of these points in my partial com-
mentaries on the three major conciliar constitutions: La Révéla-
tion divine (a commentary on the preface and first chapter),
(Paris: Editions du Cerf, 1968), I; Paradoxe et mystère de l'
Eglise (Paris: Aubier, 1967); Athéisme et sens de l'homme,
(une requête de Gaudium et spes) (Paris: Editions du Cerf, in
the collection "Foi vivante," 1968).

17 Pierre Henri-Simon was not criticizing in an unfounded way
when he wrote of "those theologians in the vanguard who express
their opinions in the 'in' newspapers so as to offer incense to
idols." Choisir, Geneva, April 1969, 29. See 2 Tm, 2:17-18.

18 See the first chapter of the Constitution Dei verbum.
Franz Mussner, "Evangile et centre de l'Evangile," Le Message
de Jésus et l'interpretation moderne (Paris: Editions du Cerf,
1969).

19 More than one very concrete experience strengthens my
firm belief that many today who become discouraged or who seem
to run the risk of the worst possible disorders, do so out of
ignorance, or fear, or their desire to conform, though their
fidelity remains intact.

20 See Dom Christopher Butler's intervention at the second
session of the Council (1963).

21 See Hans Urs von Balthasar, "Chi non ama il Signora, sia
anathema," Osservatore Romano, April 5, 1969, 3.

22 Rom 8:38-39.

23 See Henri de Lubac, L'Eternel Féminin, followed by Teilhard et Notre temps, part 2, chapter 4, especially 296-297
(Paris: Aubier, 1968).

24 Hans Urs von Balthasar, "La Gloire et la croix," Theologie
(Paris: Aubier, 1965), 397-398: "A separation . . . between the
Jesus of Old Testament prophecy, who would be in the background
of the Synoptics, and a Jesus divinized in the writings of St. Paul
and St. John, has never been able to be properly established. The
texts do not permit such a separation, unless they are philologically

massacred to such an extent that the overall spiritual figure, which is clear and transparent in the hypothesis of identification, degenerates into an enigma full of contradictions. . . . If the calm straightness of the road which leads Jesus to his destruction were a subsequent construction of the disciples, they would have possessed a religious genius so superhuman as to have far outdistanced that of their model. . . ."

25 Heinz Schürmann, "L'Herméneutique de la prédication de Jésus," Le Message de Jésus et l'interprétation moderne, 149. See Christopher Butler, The Idea of the Church (Baltimore: Helicon, 1962), 205: "It is not very likely that the collective consciousness created the Jesus of the New Testament . . .; it is far more likely that this very collective consciousness has not succeeded, in handing down the facts, in doing justice to his grandeur and the full radiance of his thought."

26 See Antoine Delzant, "La science, mythe de la philosophie," Axes 2 (1969).

27 Rom 1:31 RSV--"heartless" (astorgoi).

28 See Henri de Lubac, Images de l'abbé Monchanin (Paris: Aubier, 1967).

29 Jean Ladrière, "Pour une conception organique de l'Université," Nouvelle revue théologique (1968), 163. Also Paul Toinet, Promotion de la foi (Paris: Beauchesne, 1969), especially chapter 6: "Actualité de Jésus."

30 La Joie de croire (Paris: Editions du Seuil, 1968), 7. See p. 8: "As the result of a certain number of things which have occurred over these past months, I had a great desire to go to Rome. Rome, for me, is a sort of sacrament of Christ and the church. I was anxious to make this step in the fulness of faith; spend a day at St. Peter's and do nothing but pray there. I arrived at 8:45 a.m. on May 6. . . . I went directly to St. Peter's. I left two or three times to eat or do other errands in the neighborhood. Otherwise I stayed there where it seemed to me to be the best place for prayer: the altar of the pope and the tomb of St. Peter. I took the train back that evening at 10:10 p.m."

31 See Yves Congar, op. cit., 65ff: "Authority, Initiative, Coresponsibility," as well as 115-120: "The Church, My Maternal Home."

32 See Bishop Christopher Butler, loc. cit., 106-107.

NOTES TO JOHN COURTNEY MURRAY, S.J.
Freedom, Authority, Community*

Murray, John Courtney, S.J., until his sudden death in 1967, was an internationally recognized theologian and political philosopher. Since 1936 he had taught all areas of theology and philosophy at the Jesuit theologate, Woodstock, visiting professor at a number of Ivy League universities, editor of Theological Studies, the Jesuit theological quarterly, a peritus at Vatican II, one of the authors of the Declaration on Religious Freedom of Vatican II, author of innumerable articles in periodicals and learned journals, and of three widely known books, We Hold These Truths, Problem of God, and Yesterday and Today.

*Reprinted with permission of America, National Catholic Weekly, Vol. 115 (December 3, 1966), 734-739.

NOTES TO CARDINAL JEAN DANIELOU, S.J.
What Good Is Institutional Christianity? *

Danielou, Jean, S.J., is professor of the History of Primitive
Christianity at the Institut Catholique in Paris and editor of the
Jesuit journal, Etudes. Father Danielou is truly an example of a
prolific writer, and his many articles and books have become
widely known around the world in both French and foreign lan-
guage translations. Some of his best known books in English are
Holy Pagans and the Old Testament, The Dead Sea Scrolls and
Primitive Christianity, The Bible and the Liturgy, Christ in Us,
God and the Ways of Knowing, Theology of Jewish Christianity,
Scandal of Truth, and Prayer as a Political Problem. In 1969
Danielou became a Cardinal of the Catholic Church, and is now
in Rome doing theological research and writing as well as serving
on a number of the committees in the Congregations of the Curia.

*Reprinted from the June/July 1967 Critic, Copyright 1967,
by the Thomas More Association, Chicago, Illinois.

NOTES TO KLAUS RIESENHUBER, S.J.
Rahner's "Anonymous Christian"*

Riesenhuber, Klaus, S.J., is presently assistant professor of philosophy at the Jesuit seminary Berchmanskolleg, Pullach near Munich. His writings deal with the research he is doing on the metaphysical psychology of St. Thomas Aquinas, and they have been contributed to numerous journals in Germany and other nations of Europe.

*Reprinted with permission from Theology Digest, Vol. 13 (Autumn 1965), 163-171. Originally published in Zeitschrift für katholische Theologie, 86 (1964), 286-303.

NOTES TO JOHN A. ROHR, S.J., AND DAVID LUECKE
The Church's Proper Task and Competence*

Rohr, John A., S.J., is completing his doctoral studies in political science at the University of Chicago. His articles have appeared in many journals of political science and periodicals for a more general group of readers. The article in this book, "The Church's Proper Task and Competence," was written in collaboration with Pastor David Luecke of St. Louis.

Luecke, David, is a Lutheran minister from St. Louis finishing his doctoral studies in business administration at Washington University. He has collaborated with John A. Rohr, a young Jesuit doing doctoral work at the University of Chicago, to write "The Church's Proper Task and Competence," that appears in this volume.

* Reprinted with permission of the authors and America, National Catholic Weekly, Vol. 119 (November 16, 1968), 480-487.

NOTES ON JOHN J. HARMON
Toward a Theology of the City Church *

Harmon, John J., is an Episcopalian priest, formerly rector
of a parish in Roxbury, Massachusetts, presently an associate
director of Packard Manse, an ecumenical center in Stoughton
and Roxbury, Massachusetts, which is deeply concerned with the
renewal of both Church and society. The article we have selected
for our use in this book was given as a lecture at the 1964 con-
vention of the National Catholic Conference for Social Action
(NCCSA). Other important articles by Father Harmon will be
found in Cross Currents, America, Catholic Mind, Commonweal, etc.

*Reprinted with permission of the author and Cross Currents,
Vol. 14 (Fall 1964), 401-415.

NOTES ON PAUL M. HARRISON
Religious Pluralism and Social Welfare *

Harrison, Paul M., is professor of sociology in the department of religious studies at Pennsylvania State University. Dr. Harrison is a frequent contributor to periodicals and journals on the subject of the sociology of religion, ethical aspects of social problems, and is the present director of the United Church of Christ study of theological education. He has written Authority and Power in the Free Church Tradition.

* Reprinted with permission of the author and Theology Today, Vol. 24 (April 1967), 15-26.

Used with permission of the copyright holder, "The Institute for Religious and Social Studies of the Jewish Theological Seminary of America," and to be included in the printed symposium containing the Institute Series on "Pluralism: Its Costs and Benefits for Religion."

NOTES TO BRUNO SCHÜLLER, S.J.
Can Moral Theology Ignore Natural Law?*

Schüller, Bruno, S.J., is professor of moral theology at the Jesuit theologate at Frankfurt, Germany, and author of numerous articles. His two books that have been published deal with the subject of Protestant theology and the foundation of human rights, and the theological and philosophical foundation of civil law.

* Reprinted with permission of Theology Digest, Vol. 15 (Summer 1967), 94-99. Originally published in Lebendiges Zeugnis, Vol. 1 (1965), 1-25.

NOTES TO JOHN J. REED, S.J.
Natural Law, Theology, and the Church *

Reed, John J., S.J., was professor for many years at the
Jesuit theologate at Woodstock, Maryland, where he has taught
all branches of both philosophy and theology. A number of his
articles have appeared in periodicals and journals of theology.
His special field of research is that of the relationship between
philosophy and theology, the natural moral law and the magisterium
of the Catholic Church.

* Reprinted with permission of the author and Theological
Studies, Vol. 26 (March 1965), 40-64. The original article,
fully documented and footnoted, is in that issue.

NOTES ON LOUIS DUPRÉ
Situation Ethics and Objective Morality *

Dupré, Louis, is professor of philosophy at Georgetown University. His articles on philosophical subjects have appeared in numerous periodicals and journals, and his books include Kierkegaard as Theologian, Contraception and Catholics: A New Appraisal, and Philosophical Foundations of Marxism.

1 James F. Gustafson, "Context versus Principles: A Misplaced Debate in Christian Ethics," Harvard Theological Review 58 (1965) 192.

2 Ibid., p. 185.

3 This is not meant to deny further distinctions within situationism, but only to limit the discussion to what is absolutely essential from an objective point of view.

4 Walter Dirks, "How Can I Know What God Wants of Me?" Cross Currents 5 (winter, 1954) 81.

5 Herbert McCabe, "The Validity of Absolutes," Commonweal 83 (1965-66) 436.

6 Let it be noted that the position described here is primarily a Catholic one. The Protestant situationist deduces his conclusions mostly from theological premises which we will discuss later.

7 Sum. theol. 1-2, q. 94, a. 4.

8 De malo 2, 4, ad 13 (italics added).

9 Josef Fuchs, Natural Law (New York, 1965) p. 129.

* Reprinted with permission of the author and Theological Studies, Vol. 28 (June 1967), 245-257.

NOTES TO JOHN C. BENNETT
Capitalism and Ethics*

Bennett, John C., president of Union Theological Seminary since
1964, is a member of numerous religious and civic associations and
societies and an official non-Catholic observer at Vatican II. Dr.
Bennett is a frequent contributor to many journals of theology, political
and social philosophy, and among his many books we merely list a few:
Social Salvation, Christian Ethics and Social Policy, Christianity and
Communism, The Christian as Citizen, Christians and the State,
Foreign Policy in Christian Perspective. He is co-editor of Christianity
and Crisis, and editor of the following books: Nuclear Weapons and the
Conflict of Conscience, Christian Social Ethics in a Changing World.

*Reprinted with permission of the author and Catholic Mind, Vol.
65 (May 1967), 42-52.

NOTES TO DONALD ATWELL ZOLL
The Right of Revolution Reconsidered*

Zoll, Donald Atwell, associate professor of philosophy and political science at the University of Saskatchewan, is the author of numerous articles and of three books--Reason and Rebellion, The Twentieth Century Mind, and Ethics and Hierarchy: An Inquiry into the Roots of Justice.

*Reprinted with permission of the author and The Intercollegiate Review, Vol. 5 (Spring 1969), 167-176.

NOTES TO RICHARD A. McCORMICK, S.J.
The Theology of Revolution*

McCormick, Richard A., S.J., is professor of moral theology at the Jesuit theologates in the Chicago Province of the Jesuit Order. He has regularly contributed articles to both learned journals of theology and to popular periodicals on all of the areas of moral theology and related sciences. His annual contribution to Theological Studies, summarizing the most pertinent articles that had appeared during the previous six months in numerous journals, is a work of great importance and value to both professionals in this field and to the interested student of moral values and problems of contemporary secular city. It is from the January-June 1968 "Notes on Moral Theology" that we have reprinted the section on "The Theology of Revolution" in our present volume.

1 Cited in "La tentazione della violenza," Civiltà cattolica 119 (1968) 313-17, at 314.
2 Harvey Cox, The Secular City (New York: Macmillan, 1965) p. 107.
3 Cf. José de Broucker, "Has the Church Opted for Revolution?" New Blackfriars 49 (1968) 540-43, at 543.
4 Gaston Zananiri, "L'Eglise et la révolution en Amérique latin," Ami du clergé, Vol. 78 (1968), 187-192, at 187.
5 Cf. "Gospel and Revolution," New Blackfriars 49 (1967) 140-48, at 141. The document is also available in Catholic Mind 66 (1968) 37-46.
6 Gustavo Pérez-Ramírez, "The Church and the Social Revolution in Latin America," in Faith and the World of Politics (= Concilium 36; New York: Paulist Press, 1968) pp. 124-35.
7 The literature used in this summary contains a rather full bibliography.
8 Paul J. Weber, S.J., "A Theology of Revolution?" Catholic World 207 (1968) 220-23. For a different perspective, cf. Georges Morel, "Réflexions sur l'idée de révolution," Etudes, May, 1968, pp. 681-700.
9 Johannes B. Metz, "The Church's Social Function in the Light of a 'Political Theology,'" Concilium 36 (n. 6 above) 2-18.

*Reprinted with permission of the author and Theological Studies, Vol. 29 (December 1968), 686-697.

10 This is also the emphasis of T. Westow, who states that "politics are the very heart of concern with the brother"; cf. "Violence and Brotherhood: A Case of 'trahison des clercs,'" New Blackfriars 49 (1968) 229-32.

11 As in J. M. Lochman, "Ecumenical Theology of Revolution," Scottish Journal of Theology 21 (1968) 170-86. This article reports on the relevance of theology to revolution, discussions held at the World Conference on Church and Society (Geneva, 1966).

12 Ibid., p. 172.

13 Richard Shaull, "A Theological Perspective on Human Liberation," Ido-c, no. 68, April 28, 1968. Cf. also "Theology and the Transformation of Society," Theology Today 25 (1968) 23-36.

14 Rolland F. Smith, S.J., "A Theology of Rebellion," Theology Today 25 (1968) 10-22.

15 For outlines of an ethic built on hope, cf. V. Eller, "The Ethic of Promise," Christian Century 85 (1968) 963-65.

16 As in Catholic Mind 66 (1968) 40.

17 George Celestin, "A Christian Looks at Revolution," Listening 3 (1968) 137-44.

18 The Documents of Vatican II, ed. Walter M. Abbott, S.J. (New York: Association, 1966) pp. 284-85, emphasis added.

19 Ivan Illich, "Violence: A Mirror for Americans," America 118 (1968) 568-70, at 570.

20 G. Thibon, in La Violence (Paris: Desclée de Brouwer, 1967) p. 121.

21 As cited in de Broucker, art. cit., p. 542.

22 Cf. Almeri Bezerra de Melo, "Revolution and Violence," Ido-c, no. 68, July 14, 1968, p. 11.

23 Cf. Lochman, art. cit., p. 177.

24 Metz, art. cit., p. 14.

25 As in Lochman, art. cit., p. 176.

26 Paul Verghese, "The Christian and the Revolutionary," Theology Today 25 (1968) 141-44.

27 In "The Just Revolution," Cross Currents 18 (1968) 67-76, at 69.

28 For an earlier study, cf. Karl Rahner, "The Theology of Power," Theological Investigations 4 (Baltimore: Helicon, 1966) 391-409.

29 Marcos McGrath, "Development for Peace," America 118 (1968) 562-67.

30 Juan Luis Segundo, S.J., "Christianity and Violence in Latin America," Christianity and Crisis 28 (1968) 31-34.

31 Cf. de Melo, art. cit.

32 AAS 59 (1967) 257-99, at 272, emphasis added.

33 AAS 60 (1968) 258. Earlier Pope Paul, speaking of Latin America, had said in his message to the College of Cardinals at the end of 1967: "We invite the entire world to resist the temptation to violence in order to seek wisely and in a Christian way a dynamic and constructive peace, a source of development and civil progress" (AAS 60 [1968] 31). Similarly to the participants at the Conference of Teheran he once again rejected violence as a means to redress economic misery and ideological oppression (AAS 60 [1968] 285). In his August (1968) visit to Latin America the Pope reiterated his rejection of violent reform.

34 Civilità cattolica 119 (1968) 313-17.

35 Verghese, art. cit., p. 143.

36 McGrath, art. cit., p. 567.

NOTES TO PAUL R. RAMSEY
Christianity and Modern War*

Ramsey, Paul R., Harrington Spear Paine professor of religion at Yale University since 1957, a frequent contributor to
the professional periodicals and journals on subjects dealing
with the ethical and moral dimension of contemporary social,
economic and political problems, the author of Basic Christian
Ethics, War and the Christian Conscience, Nine Modern Moralists,
Deeds and Rules in Christian Ethics, War and Political Ethics, Who
Speaks for the Church?, Lively and the Just, and editor of the following books, Freedom of the Will, Religion, Faith and Reason:
The Theology of H. Richard Niebuhr.

*Reprinted with permission of the author and Dialog, Vol. 6 (1967)
18-29. In summary form, as it appears here, it was reprinted in
Theology Digest, Vol. 16 (Spring 1968), 47-53.

NOTES TO FRANS VAN RAALTEN
Pacifism and Ethics*

Raalten, Frans van, who received his doctorate in divinity
from the University of Amsterdam, at present is teaching theology
and philosophy in Holland. His book Shame and Existence, published in 1965, is closely related to, and based on, the writings
of Søren Kierkegaard.

*Reprinted with permission of Theology Digest, Vol. 17 (Sum-
mer 1969), 156-159. Originally published in Zeitschrift für evan-
gelische Ethik, Vol. 12 (1968), 22-36.

NOTES TO JOSEPH SCHIEBEL
The Future of U.S.-Soviet Relations: Convergence or Confrontation?*

Schiebel, Joseph, director of the Russian area studies program and assistant professor of history at Georgetown University, has served as research associate of the Russian and Chinese history project at the University of Washington (1962-1964), and as senior assistant of the East European Institute at the University of Fribourg (Switzerland, 1964-1965). Dr. Schiebel is a former Earhart Fellow, and has published many articles in Studies in Soviet Thought and other journals.

1 Lenin, V.I., Selected Works (New York, International Publishers, 1943) vol. VIII, pp. 279-280. Cf. also Lenin, Collected Works, vol. 31 (Moscow, 1966), pp. 448-450 and Stalin, J., Works, vol. 6 (Moscow, 1954), pp. 98-110, 267-295.

2 In anticipation of one objection, let it be understood that, whatever may be said to minimize Soviet culpability in the origin of World War II, the Soviet Union did not have to support Hitler's ambitions at this point by signing the pact. And whatever may have been said about this matter in the Soviet Union subsequently, the Soviet leadership clearly stated its interest in a revisionist, i.e., anti-Western Germany, and a general capitalist war before 1939.

*Reprinted with permission of the author and The Intercollegiate Review, Vol. 5 (Winter 1968-1969), 101-113.

INDEX

Aquinas, St. Thomas
  as medieval theologian, 65
  as philosopher, 61-65
  Cajetan and John of St. Thomas,
    66
  decline of interest in, 60, 65
  divine pre-motion doctrine in,
    93
  in Catholic colleges, 60
  natural law in, 226
  types of Thomism, 63 ff.
Aristotle
  and St. Thomas Aquinas, 66
  distinctions of, 60
  in thirteenth-century univer-
    sities, 71
  interest in, 61
Augustine, St.
  City of God, 71
  interest in, 61
Authority. See Church, Ethics,
  Law

Bainton, Roland
  Christian vs. secular paci-
    fism, 290
Baxter, Richard
  and "Protestant ethic," 234
Bennett, John
  social work, 185
Bergson, Henri
  as philosopher, 67, 72
  religion: open and closed,
    132
Bernard, St.
  God in man's actions, 93
Bonaventure, St.
  greater interest today, 61
Bonhoeffer, Dietrich
  his ideas abused, 106
  spirit of Christ and revo-
    lution, 162
Bowen, Howard
  guaranteed annual income
    and, 241

Brzezinski, Zbigniew K.
  programs for less developed na-
    tions, 244
Bultmann, Rudolf
  teachings misused, 106
Butler, Bishop Christopher
  and church authority, 104

Capitalism. See Economics, Eth-
    ics, Protestantism
Carnap, Rudolf
  "Viennese Circle" philosophers
    and, 81
Christianity
  and history, 3, 22, 28, 102, 132,
    192
  "anonymous" Christians and,
    142 ff.
  as fruitful for man, 10, 20, 119,
    156
  capitalism and, 233 ff.
  Communism and, 293 ff.
  community in, 119 ff., 276
  conservatism and, 15, 19, 165,
    181, 265
  conversion to, 34-42, 102, 112
  cosmic dimensions of, 2 ff., 31,
    34 ff.
  freedom of man and, 119, 125,
    128, 136, 147
  "Good News" of, 91, 156
  Gospel as dynamic, 2, 16, 20,
    27, 265
  in Middle Ages, 21
  institutional aspects of, 131 ff.,
    155 ff.
  just and unjust criticism of,
    105 ff.
  love and, 12, 34, 112, 120, 128,
    136, 147, 167, 189, 266, 276
  meaning of convergence and,
    10-12, 29

  natural moral law in, 192 ff.,
    201 ff.
  open to future, 10, 15, 265
  pacifism and, 286 ff.
  philosophy fulfilled in, 89 ff.,
    194
  revelation and church au-
    thority, 202 ff.
  revolution, war, and, 246 ff.,
    264 ff., 275 ff., 286 ff.
  social work of, 180-87
  Teilhard de Chardin and, 19-
    32, 33-42
  See also Church, Ethics,
    Law
Church
  alien to life, 23, 131 ff., 165 ff.
  attacked today, 103, 131 ff.
  capitalism and, 234 ff.
  conversion to, 34 ff., 136
  economic substructures and,
    139
  freedom and authority in,
    118 ff., 198, 208
  in crisis, 100 ff., 167 ff.
  membership in, 142 ff.
  natural law and, 192 ff.,
    201 ff.
  racial problems and, 164 ff.
  will of Christ and, 131 ff.
  See also Christianity, Ethics,
    Law, Teilhard de Chardin
Churchill, Winston
  as student of history, 7
Communism
  and world peace, 293 ff.
  "capitalist encirclement"
    and, 301-02
  coexistence with, 300
  cold war of, 298
  its nature, 80, 242
  socialism and, 300
  Teheran, Yalta, Potsdam,

and, 299
See also Revolution, Soviet Union,
War
Comte, Auguste
opposition to religion, 23
philosophy of, 44
Copernicus
modern man and, 56
sublime intellect of, 48
Councils
Bishop Butler and, 104
Church's authority in Vatican II,
118, 123, 212
human progress in Vatican II,
15, 120
infallibility doctrine in, 212
political authority and Vatican II,
268
Vatican II and faith, 2, 107, 118
war doctrine of Vatican II, 281
World Council of Churches, 235,
240
Cox, Harvey
revolution-theology and, 264

Dalton
existence of atoms and, 46
de Melo, Almeri Bezerra
war and violence in Gospels, 271
Dirks, Walter
situation ethics, 223

Economics
built-in defects of systems of,
236 ff.
capitalism and, 233 ff.
moral law and, 197
profit motive in, 237
See also Ethics, Law, Protestantism

Education
Aquinas' doctrine in, 60 ff.
meaning of liberal, 76
philosophy in, 76-88
Einstein, Albert
as a reflective scientist, 51
comprehensibility of world
and, 51-52
electro-dynamics and, 46
Ethics
capitalism and, 233 ff.
natural law and, 201 ff.
profit motive and, 237
situation, 220 ff.
war, pacifism, revolution,
and, 246 ff., 264 ff., 276 ff.,
286 ff., 293 ff.
See also Economics, Law,
Protestantism, Revolution,
War
Euclid
geometric system of, 56
Evolution
awakening of human con-
sciousness in, 7 ff.
complexification and, 4
orderliness of, 47 ff.
Teilhard de Chardin and,
4 ff.

Faith
"anonymous" Christians and,
145 ff.
Christian faith and history,
3, 30
human society dependent on,
115
law of Christ and, 196
meaning of, 2
supernatural nature of,
195 ff.

347

Fénelon
philosophy leads to revelation, 96
Fragoso, Bishop R.
revolution and violence and, 269
French Revolution
as revolt against God, 119
as turning point in modern history,
8, 30
Fuchs, Josef
man's nature and moral law, 229

Galbraith, John Kenneth
private wealth and public poverty,
239
Galileo
earth motions and, 46, 49
on intellect of Copernicus, 48
Gilson, Etienne
and Thomism, 67 ff.
Grace
existential nature of man and,
143 ff.
moral law and, 193 ff., 202 ff.
Greeks
and history, 3
utopian ideas of, 7
Gustafson, James
meaning of "situation ethics"
and, 220

Harnack, R.
institutional religion and, 132
Harvard University
nature of philosophy and, 84 ff.
Hegel, G. W. F.
morality of revolution and, 252,
253, 259
opposition to institutional religion,
23
Heidegger, Martin
as existentialist philosopher, 67,
72

Hertsberg, Rabbi Arthur
on war in Vietnam, 281
History
Christian faith and, 3 ff.
makes sense, 3 ff.
man makes, 3 ff.
war, revolution, and, 246 ff.,
293 ff.
Hobbes, Thomas
rebellions and, 250
"state of nature" and, 254
"war of all against all"
and, 259
Humanism
culture, science, and, 43 ff.
scientific, 43 ff.
Huxley, Julian
on the origin of man, 25

Illich, Ivan
theology of violence, 269

Jewish people
and Torah, 193 ff.
messianic hope and, 90
moral obligation according
to, 193 ff.
John XXIII, Pope
authority of Church and, 215
looked to future, 32
Pacem in terris doctrine,
32, 162
revolutionary spirit of
Christianity and, 162
social doctrine of, 235, 240
"socialization" and, 121
Jorge, Bishop
and revolution today, 269

Kant, Immanuel
  and science of Newton, 72
  as philosopher, 67
  situation ethics and, 222
Kennedy, John F.
  student of history, 7
Kepler
  as scientific astronomer, 46,
    49
Kierkegaard, Søren
  moral doctrine of, 222
King, Martin Luther
  Christianity and revolution and,
    162
Kohnstam, Max
  love and social structures, 276

Lassierre, Jean
  anti-militarism of, 289
Law
  development in natural, 192 ff.
  how "being" grounds moral law,
    197
  law and order needs justice,
    273
  natural moral, 181, 187, 192 ff.,
    202, 250
  nature of natural law, 202,
    222 ff.
  "ought" as moral law obligation,
    197, 204
  revelation and natural law, 205
  theology and natural law, 202 ff.
  See also Ethics, Revolution,
    War
Leibnitz, G. W.
  how God's causality functions,
    93
Lenin, V. I.
  Communism and, 303
Leo XIII, Pope
  authority and freedom in Church,
    119

Locke, John
  right of revolution, 252

McCabe, Herbert
  and situation ethics, 223
McGrath, Bishop Marcos
  theology of violence, 264,
    270, 273

Machiavelli, N.
  hero-rulers of, 250
Malebranche
  God's causality and, 93
Maritain, Jacques
  desacralization of civili-
    zation, 135
Marxism
  and Christianity, 23
  and revolution, 253
  future of history according
    to, 8
  influence on social sciences,
    8
  socialism, Communism, and,
    242
Merleau-Ponty, Maurice
  opposition to Church, 23
Metz, Johannes B.
  history and revolution, 266,
    270
Morality. See Christianity,
  Church, Ethics, Law,
  Revolution, War
Munby, Denys
  economics and ethics, 242
Murray, John Courtney
  truths that we hold, 188

Nature
  and grace, 142 ff.

man's nature and grace, 145 ff.
natural law, 181, 187, 192 ff.,
222 ff.
supernature, 145 ff.
Newman, John Cardinal
criticizes opposition to church
authority, 104
Newton, Isaac
law of gravity and, 47
scientific syntheses of, 47
success of his physics, 56
Niebuhr, Reinhold
justice and community, 186

Pacifism. See Christianity, Ethics,
Revolution, War
Paul VI, Pope
and freedom of Church, 119
dialogue of salvation, 126
ethics of war, 280
science and religion not opposed,
135
theology of revolution and, 264,
272
Philosophy
concrete and personal, 67
effects of anti-, 76 ff.
natural moral law and, 202 ff.,
221
opinion vs. truth in, 77, 78
"teachers" of, 79-81, 188
Thomism as a system, 60 ff.
"Viennese Circle" system, 45,
81
Pius IX, Pope
"Syllabus of Errors," 30
Pius XI, Pope
natural law and Church, 210
social doctrine of, 235
Pius XII, Pope
natural law and church authority,
211, 216

Plato
and Heraclitus, 73
death of Socrates and, 73
nature of man's origin and, 25
Thomism and, 67
Plotinus
meaning of existence ac-
cording to, 90
Progressives
and conservatives, 15, 30
and criticism of present,
15
Protestantism
capitalism and, 233 ff.
conservatism in, 182 ff.
liberalism in, 181 ff.
natural moral law and,
207, 221
original sin and, 207
racial problems and, 168
situation ethics and, 227 ff.
social work in, 180 ff.
subjective and objective
morality and, 221

Racism
Church and, 164 ff.
Rahner, Karl
and act of faith, 196
Ramsey, Paul
and situation ethics, 221
Reformation, Protestant.
See Ethics, Law, Prot-
estantism, Revolution,
War
Renan, Ernest
and Christianity, 23
Revolution
de Melo, 271
Hegelian and Benthamite
positions and, 252
Illich and, 269

Locke and, 252, 259
McGrath on, 264, 270, 273
Metz and, 266
right of, 246 ff.
Segundo and, 271
Smith and, 267
theology of, 263 ff.
Thibon on, 269
Third World bishops and, 268
three classical revolutions, 257
Zananiri on, 264
Ricoeur, Paul
on absurdity of existence, 102

Salvation
and redemption, 6
and secularism, 109
grace and, 7, 33 ff.
history of, 5
love of Christ and, 112
of cosmos, 33-42
Sciences
and philosophy, 81 ff.
and universities, 43 ff., 54,
76 ff.
creativity and, 48
do not give all truth, 57
humanism and, 43 ff.
theology and, 43 ff., 45, 53
Segundo, Juan Luis
violence and revolution in Latin
America, 271
Shaull, Richard
on revolution, 266, 267
Smith, Rolland F.
history and revolution, 267
Society
and man, 33 ff.
structures and, 267
See also Christianity, Church,
Economics, Ethics, Law,
Revolution, War

Soviet Union
China and, 309
convergence school and, 301
foreign policy of, 295 ff.
ideological nature of actions,
293
"intellectual liberals" and,
296 ff.
Lenin and, 306
Stalinism and, 305
totalitarianism and, 304
vis-à-vis U.S.A., 295
war with, 293 ff.
West Germany and, 312
world hegemony and, 311
Spinoza
God's causality and, 93
unique substance that is God,
95
Stringfellow, William
on obligation of churches
toward the poor, 172

Teilhard de Chardin
and evolution of cosmos, 1 ff.,
24
Divine Milieu of, 19
love of Christ, 113
meaning of faith and, 2, 113
modern nonbelievers and,
19-22, 135
prophet of the future, 1 ff.,
17, 100
scientist and priest, 2,
16, 24
societal evolution, 1 ff.
temporal mission of, 25,
135
vocation to religious life,
24
Theology. See Christianity,
Church, Ethics, Law,
Sciences

Thibon, G.
  injustices beget violence, 269
Thomism. See Aquinas, St. Thomas;
  Church; Ethics; Law; Philosophy
Tillich, Paul
  ambiguity of finite sacrifice, 284
  new type of religious man and,
    135

Utopias
  and history, 7
  See also Lenin, V. I.; Marxism;
    Soviet Union; Teilhard de
    Chardin

Vatican II. See Councils
Verghese, Paul
  on "involved transcendence,"
    273
Viennese Circle. See Carnap,
  Paul; Philosophy

War
  Christianity and modern, 275 ff.
  ethics of, 275 ff.
  in Vietnam, 161, 281
  "just war" theory, 277
  pacifism and, 286 ff.
  revolution and, 264-67
  Soviet Union and, 293 ff.
  total and limited, 286
  violence and, 249
Weber, Max
  on capitalism, 233
Weber, Paul
  on theology of revolution, 265
Weil, Erik
  boredom of life today, 101 ff.
Wendland, Heinz-Dietrich
  Gospel and revolution, 266

Zananiri, G.
  meaning of revolution, 264